PERSPECTIVES ON THE
SECURITY OF SINGAPORE

The First 50 Years

World Scientific Series on Singapore's 50 Years of Nation-Building

---

Published

50 Years of Social Issues in Singapore
  edited by David Chan (Singapore Management University, Singapore)

Our Lives to Live: Putting a Woman's Face to Change in Singapore
  edited by Kanwaljit Soin and Margaret Thomas

50 Years of Singapore–Europe Relations: Celebrating Singapore's Connections
  with Europe
  edited by Yeo Lay Hwee (EU Centre, Singapore) and
  Barnard Turner (National University of Singapore, Singapore)

Perspectives on the Security of Singapore: The First 50 Years
  edited by Barry Desker and Ang Cheng Guan (S. Rajaratnam School of International
  Studies, Nanyang Technological University, Singapore)

50 Years of Singapore and the United Nations
  edited by Tommy Koh (Ambassador-at-Large, Singapore),
  Chang Li Lin (Prime Minister's Office, Singapore) and
  Joanna Koh (Institute of Policy Studies, Singapore)

Forthcoming

Food, Foodways and Foodscapes: Culture, Community and Consumption in
Post-Colonial Singapore
  edited by Lily Kong and Vineeta Sinha (National University of Singapore, Singapore)

Singapore's Health Care System: What 50 Years Have Achieved
  edited by Lee Chien Earn (Changi General Hospital, Singapore) and
  K. Satku (National University Health System, Singapore)

50 Years of Chinese Community in Singapore
  edited by Pang Cheng Lian (Former Singapore's Ambassador to Switzerland
  and Italy)

50 Years of Engineering in Singapore
  edited by Cham Tao Soon (Emeritus President, Nanyang Technological University,
  Singapore)

50 Years of Environment: Singapore's Journey Towards Environmental Sustainability
  edited by Tan Yong Soon (Former Permanent Secretary of the Ministry of the
  Environment and Water Resources, Singapore & Former Permanent Secretary in
  the National Climate Change Secretariat in the Prime Minister's Office, Singapore)

(Continued at end of book)

World Scientific Series on
Singapore's 50 Years of Nation-Building

PERSPECTIVES ON THE
SECURITY OF SINGAPORE

The First 50 Years

Editors

Barry Desker
Ang Cheng Guan

S. Rajaratnam School of International Studies,
Nanyang Technological University, Singapore

World Scientific

ICP Imperial College Press

Published by

World Scientific Publishing Co. Pte. Ltd.

5 Toh Tuck Link, Singapore 596224

USA office: 27 Warren Street, Suite 401-402, Hackensack, NJ 07601

UK office: 57 Shelton Street, Covent Garden, London WC2H 9HE

Library of Congress Cataloging-in-Publication Data
Perspectives on the security of Singapore : the first 50 years / [edited by] Barry Desker (S. Rajaratnam School of International Studies, Nanyang Technological University), Ang Cheng Guan (S. Rajaratnam School of International Studies, Nanyang Technological University).
    pages cm -- (World Scientific Series on Singapore's 50 Years of Nation-Building)
  Includes bibliographical references.
  ISBN 978-9814689328 (hardcover : alk. paper) -- ISBN 978-9814689335 (pbk. : alk. paper)
  1. National security--Singapore. I. Desker, Barry, editor. II. Ang, Cheng Guan, editor. III. Ang, Cheng Guan. Singapore's conception of security Container of (work).
  HV6433.S55P47 2015
  355'.03305957--dc23

                          2015023688

British Library Cataloguing-in-Publication Data
A catalogue record for this book is available from the British Library.

In house editor: Rajni Gamage

Typeset by Stallion Press
Email: enquiries@stallionpress.com

Printed in Singapore

Contents

About the Contributors   ix

Introduction   xvii

Part 1   1

Chapter 1   Singapore's Conception of Security   3
                 Ang Cheng Guan

Chapter 2   National Security and Singapore: An Assessment   21
                 Norman Vasu and Bernard Loo

Chapter 3   Deliquescent Security Threats: Singapore
                 in the Era of Hyper-Globalisation   45
                 Alan Chong

Chapter 4   Singapore and Global Governance:
                 Free-Rider or Responsible Stakeholder?   65
                 Tan See Seng

Chapter 5   The Challenge of Strategic Intelligence
                 for the Singapore Armed Forces   87
                 Kwa Chong Guan

Chapter 6   Desecuritisation and after Desecuritisation:
                 The Water Issue in Singapore–Malaysia Relations   103
                 S. R. Joey Long

Chapter 7   Singapore's Security in the Context
                 of Singapore–Malaysia–Indonesia Relations   121
                 Bilveer Singh

Chapter 8   Singapore's Relations with Malaysia and Indonesia   135
Theophilus Kwek and Joseph Chinyong Liow

Chapter 9   International Missions of the Singapore Armed Forces:
How Far Would You Go?   153
Katie Tan and Ong Weichong

Chapter 10   Why the FPDA Still Matters to Singapore   173
Ralf Emmers

Chapter 11   Singapore in ASEAN's Quest toward
a Security Community   189
Mely Caballero-Anthony

Chapter 12   Singapore and the Great Powers   207
Khong Yuen Foong

Chapter 13   The Changing Terrorist Threat Landscape in Singapore   229
Rohan Gunaratna

Chapter 14   Managing Religious Diversity in Singapore:
Context and Challenges   253
*Mohammad Alami Musa
and Mohamed Imran Mohamed Taib*

Part 2

Personal Reminiscences   277

Chapter 15   Safeguarding Singapore's Security:
Defence and Diplomacy   279
S. R. Nathan

Chapter 16   Organising for National Security — The Singapore
Experience   285
Peter Ho

Chapter 17   Pragmatic Adaptation, Not Grand Strategy,
Shaped Singapore Foreign Policy   295
Bilahari Kausikan

Chapter 18   Dr Goh Keng Swee and the Building
of Singapore's Defence Industrial Capability:
A First-Person Account of the Early Challenges
in Building the Republic's Defence Industry   309
Philip Yeo

Conclusion   Strategic Certainties Facing Singapore in 2065   317
Barry Desker

About the Contributors

Alan Chong is an Associate Professor at the S. Rajaratnam School of International Studies (RSIS), Nanyang Technological University (NTU). He has published widely on the notion of soft power and the role of ideas in constructing the international relations of Singapore and Asia. His publications have appeared in *International Relations of the Asia-Pacific*; *The Pacific Review*; *The Review of International Studies*; *Alternatives: Global, Local, Political*; *Armed Forces and Society*; *Journal of Strategic Studies*; and the *Cambridge Review of International Affairs*. He is also the author of *Foreign Policy in Global Information Space: Actualizing Soft Power* (UK: Palgrave Macmillan, 2007). His interest in soft power has also led to inquiry into the sociological and philosophical foundations of international communication. In the latter area, he is currently working on a manuscript titled *The International Politics of Communication: Representing Community in a Globalizing World*. In tandem, he has also developed research interests in information warfare stemming from his seasonal teaching duties at the Goh Keng Swee Command and Staff College in Singapore. Alan Chong has frequently been interviewed in the Asian media and consulted in think tank networks in the region.

Ang Cheng Guan is Head, Graduate Studies at the S. Rajaratnam School of International Studies (RSIS), Nanyang Technological University (NTU). He is the author of *Vietnamese Communist Relations with China and the Second Indo–China Conflict, 1956–1962* (Jefferson: MacFarland, 1997; reprinted in paperback, 2012); *The Vietnam War from the Other Side: The Vietnamese Communists' Perspective* (London: RoutledgeCurzon, 2002; paperback, 2006); its sequel, *Ending the Vietnam War: The Vietnamese Communists' Perspective* (London: RoutledgeCurzon, 2004; paperback, 2006); *Southeast Asia and the Vietnam War* (London: Routledge, 2010, hardback, paperback and e-book); *Lee Kuan Yew's Strategic Thought* (London: Routledge, 2013, hardback, paperback and e-book); and *Singapore, ASEAN and the Cambodia Conflict, 1979–1991* (Singapore: NUS Press, 2013). He is currently working on two book projects: *Southeast Asia and the Cold War, 1945–1991: An International History* and its sequel, *Southeast Asia and the Post-Cold War: The First Thirty Years.*

Barry Desker is Distinguished Fellow and Bakrie Professor of Southeast Asia Policy at the S. Rajaratnam School of International Studies (RSIS), Nanyang Technological University (NTU), Singapore. He is a Member of the Presidential Council for Minority Rights, Singapore and a Member of the Board of Directors of the Lee Kuan Yew Exchange Fellowship. He was CEO of the Singapore Trade Development Board (TDB) (1994–2000) and was Singapore's Ambassador to Indonesia (1986–1993). He was the founding Dean of RSIS (2007–2014) and was Director, Institute of Defence and Strategic Studies (IDSS) (2000–2014). A President's Scholar, he was educated at the University of Singapore, University of London and Cornell University. He was awarded an Honorary Doctorate by Warwick University in 2012 and by the University of Exeter in 2013.

Bernard Loo is Associate Professor and Coordinator of the Master of Science in Strategic Studies degree programme at the S. Rajaratnam School of International Studies (RSIS), Nanyang Technological University (NTU). His research interests include defence policy, war studies, strategic theory, conventional military strategies, strategic challenges of small and medium powers, and problems and prospects of military transformation. His edited volume, *Military Transformation and Operations* (London: Routledge, 2009), was translated into complex Chinese for the Taiwan market. He is a regular commentator on defence matters in a number of regional newspapers.

Bilahari Kausikan retired in June 2013 and is currently Ambassador-at-Large and Policy Adviser in the Ministry of Foreign Affairs (MFA). From 2001 to May 2013, Bilahari Kausikan was the Second Permanent Secretary and Permanent Secretary of MFA. He has previously served in a variety of appointments including as Director for Southeast Asia, Director for East Asia and the Pacific, and as Deputy Secretary for Southeast Asia. He had also served as the Permanent Representative to the United Nations in New York and as Ambassador to the Russian Federation. Bilahari Kausikan has been awarded the Public Administration Medal (Gold) and the Pingat Jasa Gemilng (Meritorious Service Medal) by the government of Singapore. He has also been awarded the "Order of Bernardo O'Higgins" with the rank of "Gran Cruz" by the President of the Republic of Chile and the Oman Civil Merit Order by the Sultan of

Oman. He was educated at Raffles Institution, the University of Singapore and Columbia University in New York.

Bilveer Singh teaches at the Department of Political Science at the National University of Singapore (NUS) and is also an Adjunct Senior Fellow at the Centre of Excellence for National Security (CENS), S. Rajaratnam School of International Studies (RSIS), Nanyang Technological University (NTU). He is also President of the Political Science Association, Singapore. Formerly Deputy Head of the Department of Political Science and Acting Head of CENS, he specialises in regional security issues including great powers in Southeast Asia, the challenge of radicalisation, violent extremism and terrorism in Southeast Asia, and the defence and foreign policy of Indonesia and Singapore. The courses he teaches include: Government and Politics of Singapore; Singapore's Foreign Policy; and International Politics of Southeast Asia. He recent books include: *Politics and Governance in Singapore: An Introduction*, Second Edition (Singapore: McGraw-Hill Asia, 2012); *Myanmar's Rohingyas: Challenges Confronting a Persecuted Minority* and *Implications for National and Regional Security* (Indonesia: Gadjah Mada University Press, 2013); and *Quest for Political Power: Communist Subversion and Militancy in Singapore* (Singapore: Marshall Cavendish, 2015).

Joseph Chinyong Liow is Professor of Comparative and International Politics and Dean at the S. Rajaratnam School of International Studies (RSIS), Nanyang Technological University (NTU). He is concurrently Lee Kuan Yew Chair in Southeast Asia Studies at the Brookings Institution, Washington, DC. Joseph Chinyong Liow is the author of *Dictionary of the Modern Poiltics of Southeast Asia*, Fourth Edition (London: Routedge, 2014).

Katie Tan is a Senior Research Analyst at the S. Rajaratnam School of International Studies (RSIS), Nanyang Technological University (NTU). She is attached to the Military Studies Programme at the school's constituent unit, the Institute of Defence and Strategic Studies (IDSS). She had served as a Military Engineering Officer (MEO) in the Singapore Armed Forces from 2001 to 2014, and continues to serve in the capacity of an NS-Volunteer as a Staff Officer in Joint Staff.

Khong Yuen Foong is Professor of International Relations in the Department of Politics and International Relations, and Professorial Fellow, Nuffield College, Oxford University. He has taught at the Department of Government, Harvard

University, and the S. Rajaratnam School of International Studies (RSIS), Nanyang Technological University (NTU), where he also served as a Senior Research Adviser. Recent publications include "The American Tributary System," *The Chinese Journal of International Politics* (2013) and "The United States' Response to China's Rise," *International Security* (2013/2014). He is currently working on two book projects — *International Politics: The Rules of the Game* and *The American Tributary System.*

Kwa Chong Guan works on the intersections of history, security studies and international relations of Southeast Asia. As an Honorary Adjunct Associate Professor and Visiting Fellow at the Archaeological Unit of the Nalanda-Sriwijaya Centre at the Institute of Southeast Asian Studies (ISEAS), Kwa is interested in the long cycles and emerging deep history of Southeast Asia's past. As Senior Fellow at the S. Rajaratnam School of International Studies (RSIS), Nanyang Technological University (NTU), he works on a range of regional security issues with a focus on the implicit narratives underlying our framing of regional security issues. Kwa Chong Guan was called up for National Service after graduating from the old University of Singapore in Philosophy and History, and continued to serve as a reservist officer in various command and staff appointment for the next 20 years.

Mely Caballero-Anthony is Associate Professor and Head of the Centre for Non-Traditional Security (NTS) Studies at the S. Rajaratnam School of International Studies (RSIS), Nanyang Technological University (NTU). Until May 2012, she served as Director of External Relations at the ASEAN Secretariat. She also currently serves in the UN Secretary-General's Advisory Board on Disarmament Matters and Security and is a member of the World Economic Forum (WEF) Global Agenda Council on Conflict Prevention. Mely Caballero-Anthony's research interests include regionalism and regional security in the Asia-Pacific, multilateral security cooperation, politics and international relations in ASEAN, conflict prevention and management, as well as human security. She was the principal investigator of the MacArthur Asia Security Initiative (ASI) project of Internal Security Challenges in Asia and Cross-Border Implications. She has published extensively in peer-reviewed journals on a broad range of security issues in the Asia-Pacific.

Mohamed Imran Mohamed Taib is an Associate Research Fellow at the Studies in Inter-Religious Relations in Plural Societies (SRP) programme at the S. Rajaratnam School of International Studies (RSIS), Nanyang Technological University (NTU). His current research focuses on resources within the religious traditions for interreligious dialogue, discourse and relations.

Mohammad Alami Musa is Head of Studies in the Inter-Religious Relations in Plural Societies (SRP) Programme at the S. Rajaratnam School of International Studies (RSIS), Nanyang Technological University (NTU). He is concurrently the non-executive President of MUIS Council (Islamic Religious Council of Singapore), Singapore's non-resident Ambassador to the People's Democratic Republic of Algeria, and Singapore's Honorary Business Representative for Middle East and North Africa. He is a leading figure in the promotion of positive interreligious relations in Singapore and the region.

Norman Vasu is Senior Fellow and Deputy Head of the Centre of Excellence for National Security (CENS) at the S. Rajaratnam School of International Studies (RSIS), Nanyang Technological University (NTU). His research interests include ethnic relations, conceptions and practice of multiculturalism, narratives of governance, immigration and national security. His most recent publications are two co-edited volumes *Nations, National Narratives and Communities in the Asia Pacific* (London: Routledge, 2014) and *Immigration in Singapore* (Netherlands: Amsterdam University Press, 2015).

Ong Weichong is an Assistant Professor at the S. Rajaratnam School of International Studies (RSIS), Nanyang Technological University (NTU). He is attached to the Military Studies Programme at the school's constituent unit, the Institute of Defence and Strategic Studies (IDSS) where he is coordinator of the Asia Pacific Programme for Senior Military Officers (APPSMO). He is also Course Director of the Campaign and War Studies (CWS) and Operations Other Than War (OOTW) modules at the Goh Keng Swee Command and Staff College (GKS CSC), Singapore. He has also taught at the advanced school and officer cadet school levels at the SAFTI Military Institute, Singapore. In National Service, Ong Weichong is a Functional Specialist Support Staff Officer (Army) with the Singapore Armed Forces. In addition, he was an Affiliated Researcher with the Department of Leadership and Management, Swedish National Defence College and a Guest Professor at the Ecole Navale, France.

Peter Ho is the Senior Adviser to the Centre for Strategic Futures (CSF) and a Senior Fellow in the Civil Service College (CSC). He is also the Chairman of the Urban Redevelopment Authority (URA) of Singapore. When he retired in 2010 after 34 years of public service, he was Head, Civil Service, concurrent with his other appointments of Permanent Secretary (Foreign Affairs), Permanent Secretary (National Security and Intelligence Coordination) and Permanent Secretary (Special Duties) in the Prime Minister's Office (PMO). Before that, he was Permanent Secretary (Defence). He was also the founding Chairman of the Maritime and Port Authority (MPA) of Singapore.

Philip Yeo is Chairman of SPRING Singapore, a government development agency responsible for enterprise development (since April 2007); Chairman of Economic Development Innovations Singapore Pte Ltd (EDIS) focusing on developing and managing integrated cities and providing industrial development advise to overseas governments; a Member of the United Nations Committee of Experts on Public Administration (2010–2013); a Member of the World Health Organization Expert Working Group on Research & Development Financing (January 2009–January 2010); and Special Adviser for Economic Development in the Office of the Prime Minister of the Government of Singapore (April 2007–August 2011). Philip Yeo's previous appointments were: Chairman of the Agency for Science, Technology and Research (February 2001–March 2007); Senior Adviser for Science and Technology in the Ministry of Trade and Industry of Singapore (April 2007–September 2008); Chairman of the Economic Development Board (EDB) (January 1986–January 2001); Founder Chairman of the National Computer Board (1981–1987); and Permanent Secretary in the Ministry of Defence for Defence Research, Technology and Logistics (September 1979–December 1985).

Ralf Emmers is Associate Dean and Associate Professor at the S. Rajaratnam School of International Studies (RSIS), Nanyang Technological University (NTU). He completed his MSc and PhD under the supervision of the late Professor Michael Leifer in the International Relations Department of the London School of Economics and Political Science (LSE). His research interests cover security studies and international relations theory, maritime security, international institutions in the Asia-Pacific, and the security and international politics of Southeast Asia. Ralf Emmers is the author or editor of 11 books and has published numerous articles in peer-reviewed journals. He is the Co-Series Editor of the Warwick Studies in Globalisation (Routledge Book Series) and an Editorial Board member of *The Pacific Review*.

Rohan Gunaratna is Professor of Security Studies at the S. Rajaratnam School of International Studies (RSIS), Nanyang Technology University (NTU), and Head of the International Centre for Political Violence and Terrorism Research (ICPVTR), Singapore. He received his Masters from the University of Notre Dame in the US where he was Hesburgh Scholar and his Doctorate from the University of St Andrews in the UK where he was British Chevening Scholar.

A former Senior Fellow at the Combating Terrorism Centre at the United States Military Academy at West Point and at the Fletcher School of Law and Diplomacy, Rohan Gunaratna was invited to testify on the structure of the Al-Qaeda before the 9/11 Commission. The author of 15 books including *Inside Al-Qaeda: Global Network of Terror* (New York: University of Columbia Press, 2002), Rohan Gunaratna interviewed terrorists and insurgents in Afghanistan, Pakistan, Iraq, Yemen, Libya, Saudi Arabia and other conflict zones. For advancing international security cooperation, Rohan Gunaratna received the Major General Ralph H. Van Deman Award in June 2014.

S. R. Joey Long is Associate Professor of History at the National University of Singapore (NUS). He was formerly Director of the History Program at the School of Humanities and Social Sciences, Nanyang Technological University (NTU). His published work specialises on the Cold War in Southeast Asia, US foreign relations, Asia-Pacific security, and Singapore's history and security. He is the author of *Safe for Decolonization: The Eisenhower Administration, Britain, and Singapore* (Ohio: Kent State University Press, 2011), and his articles have been published in *Contemporary Southeast Asia, Diplomatic History, European Journal of International Relations, Journal of Southeast Asian Studies, Rethinking History, South East Asia Research* and a number of edited volumes. Fellowships and awards he has received include a Fulbright Grant and the Lawrence Gelfand-Armin Rappaport Fellowship from the Society for Historians of American Foreign Relations.

S. R. Nathan is Singapore's longest-serving President, having held office from 1999 to 2011. Before he became Head of State, S. R. Nathan had a long and distinguished career in the public service. He held several key appointments at crucial moments in Singapore's history, serving in leadership roles in areas from defence to foreign affairs. He was the First Permanent Secretary in the Ministry of Foreign Affairs (MFA) from 1979 until 1982. He then became Executive Chairman of Singapore Press Holdings (SPH). He was also High Commissioner to Malaysia in 1985 and Ambassador to the United States in 1990. He was also the founding Director of the Institute of Defence and Strategic Studies (IDSS — the predecessor of the S. Rajaratnam School of International Studies or RSIS) before he became President.

Tan See Seng is Deputy Director of the Institute of Defence and Strategic Studies (IDSS), founding Head of the Centre for Multilateralism Studies (CMS), and Associate Professor at the S. Rajaratnam School of International Studies (RSIS),

Nanyang Technological University (NTU). His most recent publications include "Mailed Fists and Velvet Gloves: The Relevance of Smart Power to Singapore's Evolving Defence and Foreign Policy" (forthcoming, 2015, in the *Journal of Strategic Studies*); *Multilateral Asian Security Architecture: Non-ASEAN Stakeholders* (London: Routledge, forthcoming, 2015); and *The Making of the Asia Pacific: Knowledge Brokers and the Politics of Representation* (Netherlands: Amsterdam University Press, 2013).

Theophilus Kwek is a student of History and Politics at Oxford University, where he serves as Vice-President of the Oxford Students' Oxfam Group, an Editor of the *Journal of Politics and Constitutional Studies*, and previously Publications Director of the think tank OxPolicy. Beyond an interest in international relations, he is also a photographer and poet.

Introduction

This collection of essays is specially prepared to mark the 50th anniversary of Singapore's independence. The unifying theme is "Singapore's Security" in its broadest sense and dimension. Written by scholars and associates of the S. Rajaratnam School of International Studies (RSIS), the book explores security issues and concerns of the nation-state over the last 50 years with a closing chapter that looks into the future. The book showcases the range of expertise in the School which at its inception as the then-Institute of Defence and Strategic Studies (IDSS) in July 1996 was funded by the Ministry of Defence with the aim of developing proficiency in understanding the evolving conception of security and its implications for Singapore in the post-Cold War world. IDSS has, since January 2007, evolved into the S. Rajaratnam School of International Studies but remains an integral component of the School. The School is named after Singapore's first Foreign Minister, Mr S. Rajaratnam, and appropriately so, given that foreign policy and defence are very much two sides of the same coin.

The book is divided into two parts; the first which forms the bulk of the content, comprises 14 chapters covering all aspects of "security" both conventional and non-traditional. The first chapter by Ang Cheng Guan describes and contextualises Singapore's conception of security as articulated by its political leadership from 1965 to the present distilled from the most significant speeches, parliamentary debates and writings on security matters of the last 50 years. They reveal that the political leadership's understanding of the concept of security has been comprehensive and not confined to physical or territorial security and the use of force, although in Singapore's formative years, that was understandably the immediate concern.

Continuing the theme on conceptualising Singapore's "security", Norman Vasu and Bernard Loo discuss how the Singaporean government secured the nation-state and the "good life" for its people. They argue that the Singaporean government has been remarkably successful at protecting two key national security concerns of the city-state as identified since independence: (1) the protection of Singaporean sovereignty; and (2) the maintenance of public order. However, due to the expanding threat horizon and the complexity of ever-evolving threats, for continued success, the process of securitisation in Singapore — that is, who is permitted to frame a threat and who decides what the best response is — may have to alter with time.

Next, Alan Chong scrutinises the SARS crisis of 2003, the politicisation of the entry of foreign talent into Singapore, the radicalisation of certain segments of the Muslim citizenry by terrorist propaganda and the Little India riot of 2013. These are instances of what may be best analysed as "deliquescent insecurities" of an open economy operating alongside a nationalistic society. These threats to the well-being of the Singaporean nation-state are metaphorically "liquid" in the sense that they are the direct consequence of opening to the world economy, while the government continues to adhere to the idea of an essentialist Singaporean identity that ought to be politically sanitised for globalisation, or vice versa. A tendentious clash of identities therefore manifests as a whole new security frontier that eludes effective management.

Analysing the links between governance and Singapore's security, Tan See Seng notes that the city-state's recent international behaviour suggests its growing awareness of the importance of being a responsible stakeholder as well as its commensurate willingness to assume responsibilities in global governance. In that respect, this chapter examines Singapore's contributions in four areas, namely, its leadership of the Global Governance Group (3G) vis-à-vis the G20, its role in the (failed) Small Five (S5) in championing the "responsibility not to veto" idea, its participation in international disaster relief and peacekeeping, and the roles of its leaders and diplomats as Chairpersons of key international committees and conferences at the United Nations and/or the International Monetary Fund. This is followed by Kwa Chong Guan's careful deliberations on the importance of strategic intelligence to Singapore's security. Very broadly, he discusses examples of intelligence failures and international crises, and points out the lessons policy-makers and Singapore can learn from them.

The next three chapters look at Singapore's relationship with its near neighbours. S. R. Joey Long looks at the securitisation and desecuritisation of water and its effect on Singapore–Malaysia ties. He argues that Singapore's endeavour to loosen its dependence on Malaysian for water has been successful. It holds to the position that the water issue in Malaysia–Singapore relations should no longer be perceived as a hard security matter, requiring the use of military force to ensure that the water from Malaysia, as contracted, continues to flow

to Singapore. Bilveer Singh notes that the dominant driver of Singapore's security is its geopolitical location between Malaysia and Indonesia. Singapore's
security, both internal and external, he argues, is mainly underpinned by its
relations with Malaysia and Indonesia, which in turn, shapes Singapore's
approach to the external powers, creating a complex security architecture that
has thus far helped to guarantee Singapore's sovereignty and territorial integrity. Theophilus Kwek and Joseph Chinyong Liow explore Singapore's relations with Malaysia and Indonesia through the administrations of three
Prime Ministers, whose approaches to Singapore's immediate neighbours
reflect a continuity of outlook tempered with strategic and personal adaptation. While the key influences through five decades of their leadership were,
undoubtedly, the three states' underlying bilateral complexities coupled with
momentous changes in Southeast Asia's broader security context, each
Premier also brought a sense of his own style and convictions to the role,
which lent Singapore's foreign policy under each administration a flavour
distinctive to its time.

The next two chapters focus on the military. Katie Tan and Ong Weichong
look deep into the Singapore Armed Forces' role in overseas deployment —
particularly that of Operations Other Than War (OOTW). Their essay explores
the extent the SAF would go in future international missions, and the size,
scope, frequency, duration and distance of such operations. Significantly, they
ask the question of whether future international missions would be a significant departure from those of present day deployments. The chapter also takes
stock of the SAF's contributions to international missions since its first foray in
1970 and explores its prospects for further development and change. Looking
at security more regionally and through multilateral institutions, Ralf Emmers
argues that the Five Power Defence Arrangements (FPDA) remains important
for the city-state for three main reasons, namely: its confidence-building role
in bilateral relations between Singapore and Malaysia; its existence as a channel
for direct relations with three external parties (Australia, the United Kingdom
and New Zealand) and for indirect relations with the United States (US); and
finally, its contribution to Singapore's regional defence diplomacy. This chapter
also briefly describes the historical and institutional evolution of the FPDA,
before delving into an elaboration on each of the three reasons outlined in the
argument.

Examining ASEAN, Mely Caballero-Anthony argues that Singapore's
engagement with ASEAN in advancing regional political and security cooperation is closely intertwined with its own historical narrative of a post-colonial
state that went through a difficult period of separation from Malaysia to now

become one of its leading members. Singapore's transformation as one of the most advanced economies and politically stable states in Asia is critical to advancing political and security cooperation in ASEAN. Now that ASEAN has become an established regional grouping that claims centrality in Asia's regional security architecture, Singapore's role in moving ASEAN's vision of becoming a political and security community becomes even more salient given what Singapore has to offer in terms of ideas and leadership in maintaining regional peace and security and deepening regional cooperation.

Khong Yuen Foong looks at Singapore's relationships with the US and China. He argues that Singapore has already chosen the US — soon after the British withdrawal from East of Suez. He further suggests that that choice has served Singapore well. Finally, he argues that the dilemma Singapore faces after 50 years of a very successful foreign policy (vis-à-vis the great powers) is whether to stick with the US or gravitate toward China, given the shifting power distribution in Asia. Singapore's actions in recent years suggest that it continues to strongly favour the US when it comes to military security; on the economic and political-diplomatic fronts however, it appears to be more even-handed in engaging the US and China.

Moving onto terrorist threats, Rohan Gunaratna underlines the threat of terrorism and its precursor, ideological extremism, to Singapore. With increased globalisation, securing Singapore from transnational and indigenous threats is a growing national security challenge. Both the Singapore government and its inhabitants — citizens and residents — are at increasing risk from terrorism and ideological extremism. Through sustained efforts, the Singapore government seeks to mitigate the threat of an attack from overseas and from radicalisation of a vulnerable segment of its citizens. Having understood the changing nature of the threat, Singapore has invested in a spectrum of counter-measures from international security cooperation and collaborations to building a strategic partnership with community leaders and organisations.

Finally, with regard to religious harmony, Mohammad Alami Musa and Mohamed Imran Mohamed Taib note that Singapore has achieved a high degree of social cohesion since its independence 50 years ago and that the existence of religious peace over such a long period can be attributed to the contributing role of religious leaders and community institutions, effective custodial role of the state, strong legal framework, and strict enforcement of policies. Along with principles of secularism and freedom of religion, the management of diversity in Singapore has largely been a success. Their essay traces the development of religious harmony in Singapore and highlights the changing context and challenges that led to specific policy responses. It discusses the role of religion as a partner in nation-building in the early years, the challenges posed by religious resurgence from the 1980s, the globalising phase of the 1990s that accelerated new forms of diversity, and the post-9/11 landscape with heightened global conflicts and security issues. The chapter concludes that governance of religious diversity is an indispensable part of the Singapore Story.

Part 2 of the book consists of personal recollections of four key officials who have played an immense leadership role in managing Singapore's security over the last 50 years, namely, Mr S. R. Nathan, Mr Peter Ho, Mr Bilahari Kausikan and Mr Philip Yeo. RSIS is very proud of their association with the School. Indeed, Mr S. R. Nathan was the founding Director of IDSS.

Having considered the past and the current, this edited volume appropriately ends with an essay by Barry Desker that looks over the horizon at the security concerns of Singapore in another 50 years, after 100 years of independence. Barry Desker observes that when discussing the possibility of changes, the tendency is to think in terms of incremental shifts. He proposes that we should think of the possibility of paradigm shifts instead. Despite spending a huge proportion of its resources on building a credible defence capability, through astute diplomacy, creating a modicum of balance of power in the region, Singapore's security has been assured, a formula that is likely to be continued in the coming years.

Part 1

Chapter 1

Singapore's Conception of Security

Ang Cheng Guan

> But some things are not negotiable. My survival and how I design my security is not negotiable. This is something fundamental. We may be small but we are sovereign, and we decide how we ensure our own security — Lee Kuan Yew.[1]

> This is a purely physical security … There are other aspects of security which are equally pertinent in the long run: your economic viability, the capacity of your political structure to withstand pressures of a social, cultural or whatever nature. It is a multi-coloured question — Lee Kuan Yew.[2]

This chapter attempts to describe and contextualise Singapore's conception of security as articulated by its political leadership from 1965 to the present based on a number of key speeches, parliamentary debates and writings over the last 50 years which, in the view of this author, are worth revisiting and remembering. It shows that Singapore's security as conceived by its political leaders has been consistent throughout the last 50 years. From very early on, their understanding of the concept of security has been comprehensive and not narrowly conceived as just physical or territorial security and the use of force, although in Singapore's formative years, that was the immediate concern.

Singapore's national security practice has historically been directed by a small elite group. For the last 50 years, the general public, by and large, has not questioned the assumptions held by their elected leaders and decision-makers. Space does not permit me here to indulge in a lengthy discussion of the ever-broadening definition of "security" which has been a subject of much debate, particularly since the end of the Cold War,[3] except to highlight two points both borrowed from Muthiah Alagappah. The first is that security continues to rank highly on national agendas worldwide and in most countries, enormous amounts of resources continue to be devoted to defence.[4] Singapore is no exception. And, second, security is "situational" or "context-sensitive".[5] In the case of Singapore, its history, location and size are important determinants.

The Foundation Years

The 50th anniversary of Singapore's independence is a fitting occasion to revisit and reflect on this very important subject. And there is no more appropriate place to begin this than the Yang Di-Pertuan Negara's opening speech at the first session of the first parliament of independent Singapore on 8 December 1965 when he said that "our survival as a people, distinct and separate from our neighbours in South-East Asia depends upon our patience and resolution in dealing with physically bigger and hence difficult neighbours and upon our perseverance in seeking long-term solutions to the problems of finding a new balance of forces in this part of the world …".[6] Scholars have often described that the conception of security during the Cold War years was "state-centric and political-military-power oriented" and focused principally on the use of "force".[7] In the case of Singapore, this was not completely true as the Yang Di-Pertuan Negara went on in his speech to state that "the best guarantee of our future as a distinct and separate people" in the region "is the creation of a tolerant multi-racial society" and warned against both "communalists" and "communists". They are not unconnected. The communists were assessed to be the "more potent of the two groups as they were supported by external sponsors" and "play on communal heart strings, if only more skilfully and cynically".[8] There was particular concern about the intentions of Indonesia and Malaysia, which is not surprising given that Confrontation hostilities only ceased on 11 August 1966 with the signing of the Bangkok Accord; and Singapore and Malaysia separated just a few months ago due to irreconcilable differences. Thus, Singapore "must anticipate and prepare for all contingency".[9]

Finally, the Yang Di-Pertuan Negara spoke of the "two new responsibilities" Singapore had to now shoulder as an independent Republic — Defence and Foreign Affairs — "two closely inter-related subjects" which were closely related to the country's survival. Foreign policy choices determine defence commitments which in turn limit the range of options of Singapore's foreign policy. Singapore's security depended upon having the minimum number of unfriendly countries and the maximum number of friendly ones "for no other reason than that we wish to be as independent of foreign defence assistance as possible". Singapore had to "accept British bases for some time to come" because it was then unable to defend itself. The creation of a "hard, well-trained, if small, regular army supported by a large people's volunteer force" would form a significant item in Singapore's annual budget. As the Minister of Defence Goh Keng Swee pointed out during the second reading of the Singapore Army Bill on 23 December 1965, the army is meant to defend

Singapore and its people against external aggression. However, at present "we are unable to do this task ourselves" and "it is no use pretending that without the British military forces in Singapore today, the island cannot be easily over-run within a matter of hours by any neighbouring country within a radius of 1,000 miles, if any of these countries care to do so". But Singapore cannot always depend on Britain. As early as December 1965, Goh was already laying plans for an eventual British withdrawal. In his words:

> British military protection today had made quite a number of our citizens complacent about the need to conduct our own defence preparations. These people assume that this protection will be permanent. I regard it as the height of folly to plan our future on this assumption. And if there is any basis on which we, as an independent country can plan our future, it will be on the opposite assumption, that is, the removal of the British military presence at some time in the future. Nobody — neither we nor the British — can say when this will be. It may be 5, 10 or 15 years — maybe longer, maybe shorter. Whatever the time may be, it will be useless then to think of building up our defence forces. The time to do so is now ...[10]

In his speech, the Minister of Foreign Affair S. Rajaratnam also addressed the issue of the security of Singapore and the British bases. Prime Minister Lee Kuan Yew had in August 1965 said that he would not allow the British bases to be used as "jumping points for aggression, not even aggression of Indonesia". The bases were to protect the two million Singaporeans and nine million Malaysians.[11] S. Rajaratnam reiterated that the bases were "not for any aggressive or imperialistic purposes but for the defence of Singapore and Singapore's national interests" as the new nation's capacity to defend itself against external threats was limited. Singapore would of course build its own defence forces "to the fullest extent" it is capable of but "we are interested in the defence of Singapore in the context of a major conflict in regard to major and more powerful neighbours. We are in no position to build or finance an army capable of defending Singapore in a conflict of this kind. Even big powers with far greater resources of money, men and material plan their defence on the basis of friends and allies," he explained.[12]

As it happened, due to fiscal pressures, the British announced in 1967 that it planned to withdraw from East of Suez, which it eventually did from Singapore (and Malaysia) in 1971. When National Service (NS) was introduced in 1967, it was based on the assumption that the British military presence would remain in Singapore till at least 1975. The rate of military build-up was thus paced accordingly. But when the British in early 1968 announced they were speeding up their withdrawal to be completed by the end of 1971, the build-up had to be accelerated. Today, the capability of the SAF is well-recognised. Looking back to the 1960s, Lee Kuan Yew recalled that "such an outcome was far from my thoughts in April 1966 when I flew to London hoping for assurance from Prime Minister Harold Wilson that British forces would remain in Singapore for some years".[13] Lee described the years from independence to the British withdrawal in 1971 as "the most difficult years" and that only when the main units of the British forces had left and Singapore did not suffer severe unemployment did he feel a lesser sense of vulnerability.[14]

On the subject of Foreign Affairs, S. Rajaratnam gave the following guidance to insure Singapore's security: (1) in the hard world of international realities, there are bound to be degrees of friendship between countries and those closest to us will naturally be those whose foreign policy principles and deeds coincide with our national interests and our basic aspirations. There may be differences and disagreements on occasions on specific issues, but so long as the fundamentals of their foreign policy and their deeds coincide with Singapore's, then they should remain close friends and allies. Singapore should not allow "temporary irritations and minor disagreements" to affect its foreign relations; (2) in international politics, it is not wise to formulate policies on the basis of permanent enemies; (3) it is necessary for Singapore to adhere to a policy of non-alignment "because to be aligned to any big country would eventually have meant the loss of our freedom of action even in domestic fields, because foreign policies are in fact an extension of domestic policies into the international field". Non-alignment, however, did not mean indifference "to the real issues of peace and war" or "even feigning blindness as to what is right and wrong". On the contrary, a non-alignment policy gives Singapore greater freedom of manoeuvrability on specific international issues based on its national interests. An aligned position, on the other hand, would automatically oblige Singapore to adopt the stand of the major ally; and (4) the pursuit of national interests is not absolute as national independences need to be balanced against the reality of interdependence between nations. There will arise occasions when Singapore may have to make some sacrifice of our interests for the long-term interests of the nation. This echoed what Lee Kuan Yew said on the 100th day of Singapore's independence, that "a foreign policy must be designed to bring the surest guarantee of Singapore's survival and our prosperity", in short, "trade and industry" is as important as "defence and security".[15]

Unlike the Foreign Minister, the fullest and most detailed exposition on the defence of Singapore by the Minister of Defence was not delivered in December 1965 but on 13 March 1967 at the reading of the National Service

(Amendment) Bill. This speech deserves recounting. Goh began by making the point that in thinking of the elements that should be taken into consideration in framing a meaningful defence policy for Singapore, one needed to begin from first principles, that is, "why bother about defending Singapore at all?". He was not facetious in asking this question because there was the view held by "laymen as well as experts" that Singapore was "quite indefensible" and that if there were to be a sustained major attack on the island-state, the likelihood was that Singapore could not hold out without external assistance. As such, it would be useless to expend resources on defence that could be better spent somewhere else. Goh thought otherwise. In his words, "the conclusion drawn from their premise must be that Singapore should revert to a colony or a satellite of whoever wishes to afford it protection. If you are in a completely vulnerable position, anyone disposed to do so can hold you to ransom and life for you will then become very tiresome". He argued that while Singapore could not achieve "complete invulnerability", the fact was that even the larger countries, other than the two nuclear superpowers, were indefensible from a nuclear attack. But that did not stop them from spending enormous sums of money in defence. Small states, if poorly managed, are likely "to be a great source of trouble in the world". They could lead to civil war and disorder, which in turn could tempt larger states to intervene, as in the case of South Vietnam. This scenario is especially relevant for a small state strategically situated like Singapore; thus the need to maintain "adequate defence forces". Goh then went on to make the point that "the real security which we want can be found, not by our unaided efforts alone, but in an alliance with others". Thus, he proposed that Singapore should work towards an establishment of some kind of regional defence arrangement, possibly within a larger international framework.

Lee Kuan Yew put this somewhat more colourfully when he said "I am going to defend myself to best of my ability. And since the best of my ability is not equal to the best of other chaps' abilities, I am going to get whatever help from whoever I can get, to make as good as their abilities and better. And if it is better than the abilities of those who intend to involve me in such a military entanglement, then I will have peace".[16]

There is another dimension to Singapore's defence effort, that is, its role in "nation-building" — which harks back to the Yang Di-Pertuan Negara's remarks regarding "communalists" and "the creation of a tolerant multi-racial society" mentioned above. According to Goh, "nothing creates loyalty and national consciousness more speedily and more thoroughly than participation in defence and membership of the armed forces … The nation-building aspect of defence will be more significant if the participation is spread over all strata of society …".[17]

Indeed, despite what Lee said about defence and economics being equally important,[18] the view of the political leadership in the early years was that defence had a slight edge over economic growth, as Lim Kim San (who had taken over the Minister of Defence portfolio from Goh) pointed out in 1968 that "without this defence build-up, there may come a time when all the economic growth in the world will not stand us in good stead, because we would be captured and it would be too late to regret that we should have given priority to our defence build-up first".[19] It is never a straightforward choice. Lee qualified his premise that "defence and security is indivisible from trade and industry" by adding that it "will have to be left over for some time until the meaning percolates through".[20] Years later, he would describe the nexus as two sides of the same question as "you cannot have a strong defence unless you have a strong finance. And you cannot have strong defence and strong finance unless you have a strong, unified, well-educated and increasingly cohesive society. They are all part of one whole".[21] The promotion of trade was therefore a key objective of Singapore's security (foreign and defence) policy.[22]

The importance of defence was a recurring theme of many of Goh's speeches. Goh Keng Swee has been acknowledged as "the policy architect of Singapore's national defence".[23] He felt the need to constantly explain to Singaporeans why the government spent so much on defence and he used every opportunity to expound on this subject in order to convince Singaporeans that military duty was not "an unpleasant imposition" but "a positive and real contribution to the security of Singapore". For example, he used the occasion of the commissioning ceremony of the 10th batch of Infantry Officer Cadets in July 1972 to engage the sceptics and reiterate the importance of NS. On the question why Singapore could not "avoid these expenditures of effort and money" and "declare ourselves neutral like Switzerland and Sweden", his reply was that both countries were able to stay peaceful and independent precisely "by arming themselves to the teeth". Singapore was in fact learning from the experience of those two Nordic countries — "If history has one lesson to teach us, it is that we can hope to live in peace if we maintain strong defences ... Until a new international order is created whereby small nation states can have an assurance that their territory and independence will be respected, there is no other choice than the example of Switzerland and Sweden".[24] Having said that, Goh was also careful that Singapore did not "give the impression that she is arming herself to the teeth, unnecessarily so, beyond what is legitimate defence and in this way start an arms race" in the region.[25]

Goh Keng Swee was of the view that the security agencies should regularly revisit their *raison d'être* to ensure their relevance because security threats change with time. In Goh's analysis, in the Cold War period, the "clearest threat" was that "arising from communist insurgencies in the region and communist subversion within each country". Since the fall of Saigon and the end of the Vietnam War in 1975, this threat had ceased to be "a distant or academic one". For Singapore, the communist threat was not a military one, and as such, the counter-measures did not lie in the military field. The first defence against communist subversion is "economic", a point that Lee Kuan Yew also emphasised — "Economic development is the most effective inoculation against subversion and revolution."[26] The second line of defence, according to Goh is "police intelligence". The armed forces provide the third and last line of defence.[27]

Malaysia and Indonesia

It is common knowledge that Malaysia and Indonesia have been and continue to be Singapore's principal security concerns. As Ganesan (1998) observed, even though much of the trauma of the post-independence period has been overcome, there is still "the structural condition arising from Singapore's geographical proximity to its immediate neighbours ... the huge disparity between its endowments and theirs". Thus, Singapore's primary security concern is "firmly anchored in the Malay Archipelago".[28] As Lee Kuan Yew said, "your best friends are never your immediate neighbours", a point he reiterated on a number of occasions.[29] Malaysia and Indonesia were mentioned in the Yang Di-Pertuan Negara's opening speech of Singapore's first parliament mentioned above. The Foreign Minister also specifically addressed Singapore–Malaysia relations in his speech. What is relevant for this paper is his observation "based not so much on the constitutional fact as the reality" that the survival and well-being of Malaysia is essential to Singapore's survival and vice versa. But he cautioned against conflating the survival of the two countries with the survival of the governments and political parties. Lee made a similar point when he said that "defence and security is closely interwoven between Singapore and Malaysia" and this premise should not in any way be upset.[30] While it is true that Singapore's neighbours are its chief security concern, one should be careful not to over-exaggerate this fear. What Goh Keng Swee said in 1971 is most instructive and is worth repeating here. According to Goh, many people were inclined to draw similarities between Singapore and Israel, and indeed there were some points of resemblance, such as standard of living and the level of technology as compared to Singapore's neighbours. But it would be "dangerous to read too much into the similarities" between the two countries. There were at least four fundamental differences which are: (1) while Singapore's neighbours might dislike and envy Singapore, they "do not hate" Singapore in the way the Arabs hate Israel; (2) the superpowers were not competing like in the Middle East with the Russians supporting the Arab cause and the Americans supporting Israel; and (3) the Singapore economy, unlike Israel, is extremely vulnerable to economic blockade. The imposition of a naval blockade would be considered by Singapore as sufficient *casus belli*; and (4) unlike Israel which was established as a Jewish state, Singapore is multiracial despite its Chinese majority population. Every attempt to turn Singapore into another "China" is strenuously resisted. In Goh's prognosis, he did not think that there was "any realistic danger of war" between Singapore and her neighbours unless a "madcap regime" was established in either or both countries. But since Singapore cannot be certain that this would not happen, "it is necessary for us to continue to develop our military strength".[31]

The Security of Small States

Lee Kuan Yew's lifelong preoccupation was the security of Singapore, thus explaining his interest in how small states can survive in the international political arena. He has expounded on this subject on various occasions in his long political career. According to Lee, "a small country must seek a maximum number of friends, while maintaining the freedom to be itself as a sovereign and independent nation". Both aspects are equally important and interrelated.[32] Given that small countries cannot change the balance of bargaining or the tussle between the interests of a big developed party and a small underdeveloped party, how can a small state such as Singapore ensure that it does not get pushed around by bigger countries? Small countries can try to gather more weight by combining together, for example, the non-aligned nations. While that was possible during the Cold War, when the smaller countries could play off the Soviet bloc against America and the West, that strategy is not applicable anymore now that the United States (US) is the sole superpower. So, in Lee's words, "quite simply, Singapore takes the position that we are price-takers; we are not price-makers. Our strategy simply is to make ourselves relevant to all the countries that matter to us".[33] Being small is to be vulnerable to predators but as long as there is balance in the triangular US–Japan–China relationship, ensuring international order and giving the region the advantage to grow and prosper, Singapore has the international space to extend its economy globally.[34] Singapore needs to have good relations with both the US and China. Lee acknowledged that "sometimes, it's not easy resolving this dilemma".[35]

In 2008, he reminded his audience of a Chinese saying — "Big fish eat small fish and small fish eat shrimp" (which harks back to his 1966 speech entitled "Big and Small Fishes in Asian Waters").[36] He described Singapore and Dubai as "shrimps". Elaborating, he said that small cities will always be vulnerable to global events, "which today have a much bigger impact due to the highly interconnected globalised environment". Small states are usually weak and vulnerable, "not masters of their own destiny", and perform no irreplaceable functions in the international system "because if they do not exist, the world will carry on as before". He cited Athens, Sparta and Venice as examples of city-states which "all ended up being absorbed into the bigger land mass of Greece or Italy". Hence, small states have to "better organised, alert and nimble to counter or evade threats and seize opportunities", which is what Singapore has done and continues to do.[37]

What is most significant for Singapore in the long term is whether it can survive in a multipolar world which Lee believed would come about regardless of the American wish to remain the sole superpower. It might take 50 to 60 years but definitely by the end of the century, the world will be multipolar — the US, China, Europe — "maybe not a military power but definitely an economic power and a separate power in foreign policy", and perhaps India, Brazil and a few others. [38] Delivering the S. Rajaratnam Lecture in 2009, he told the audience that "friendship in international relations is not a function of goodwill or personal affection. We must make ourselves relevant so that other countries have an interest in our continued survival and prosperity as a sovereign and independent nation". Singapore cannot take its relevance for granted because "small countries perform no vital or irreplaceable functions in the international system". In the case of Singapore, unlike her neighbours with more land, labour and natural resources and thus investment potential, Singapore "is of no intrinsic interest to any developed country".[39] The conception of security as articulated by the first generation of leadership has been passed down to the second and subsequent generation of leaders. One of the earliest expositions of the security of Singapore was by the current Prime Minister Lee Hsien Loong in 1984 when he was Political Secretary (Defence).

Aptly entitled "Security Options for Small States", then-Brigadier General Lee made the following key points in his speech: (1) international relations resemble the law of the jungle and "in the international jungle, justice and righteousness are concepts which are edifying, resonant, but inoperative. The game is survival, and the stakes are life and death"; (2) small countries have "disabilities" which "appear overwhelming" — economically, they cannot be self-sufficient; militarily, they are usually outnumbered, and often lack strategic depth, "their front will also be their rear"; and politically, they have relatively more difficulty sustaining a high quality leadership over time given a much smaller talent pool. In sum, small countries face a serious danger of "gambler's ruin" — a mathematical problem which is "to calculate how long a gambler with a fixed initial capital can last at a casino before going bankrupt, and what the chances are that he will bust the bank instead". Ruin is more often than not the end result; and (3) there is, however, hope. Like small animals in the real jungle, small countries can survive and thrive in the "international jungle". The critical question is how? According to the younger Lee, the price for survival is "eternal vigilance" but vigilance is not enough. There are four sets of strategies that small states should apply to assure their security — "development" which he defined as "the strengthening of the nation internally, by building up a stable and cohesive society, establishing social bonds, encouraging economic growth, and strengthening political institutions", "diplomacy" which is "the totality of a state's relations with other states in the international system", and "deterrence" and "defence" which are required because "diplomacy is no substitute for strength" and "to believe that peaceful diplomatic means can replace immoral military ones is to pursue a chimera". A credible deterrence must be based on a viable defence. These strategies "are not mutually exclusive, and the way to survive is to apply as many of them as possible".[40]

Total Defence

1984 was the year in which the concept of "Total Defence" was introduced. It was a natural progression from 1967 when NS was inaugurated and the Singapore Armed Forces (SAF) was formed. It took a number of years before Singaporeans internalised NS as a way of life, after which the government began to focus on the next logical area — the role of reservists. As the then-Defence Minister Goh Chok Tong explained: "[H]aving spent many years to educate the general public concerning military defence … it is now time to cover the other potential weak spots in Singapore's security. Hence, the mass effort on civil defence starting last year [1983], and greater efforts to educate the public on total defence. Otherwise we … can be caught unawares and Singapore can go down without an aggressor even having to mount a military campaign against Singapore because we are not prepared even psychologically, socially, and in the fields of economics and civil defence."[41] Total Defence has since become a "key component in Singapore's defence strategy" as in the words of Teo Chee Hean (Minister of Defence, 2003–2011), "we need more than the military for a strong defence and "every Singaporean has a part to play to make us more resilient and strengthen the country's ability to protect itself from threats, whatever form they may take, and to overcome them".[42]

The New Millennium

The end of the Cold War and the new millennium has not altered the assumptions underlying the conception of Singapore's security. In 2010, then-Senior Minister Professor S. Jayakumar (Minister of Foreign Affairs, 1994–2004) reminded his audience that "whether then the '70s, now, or the future, some things will never change". The fact that Singapore is a very small city-state is a fundamental geopolitical reality that frames its foreign policy.[43] As Teo Chee Hean said, "at the time of our independence, there were large global forces in motion: decolonisation and the clash between great powers. Like huge tectonic plates, the geo-strategic environment of the world is on the move again. As it was during the Cold War, Southeast Asia lays along the fault lines of these global shifts". Teo identified "Deterrence", "Diplomacy", "Total Defence" and "Technology" as the four key elements of Singapore's defence strategy.[44] Although "Total Defence" was introduced in 1984, long before the 11 September 2001 terrorist attacks on the US and the advent of transnational terrorism, the importance of "community resilience" is all the more critical in today's security environment.[45]

This is perhaps a good place to briefly focus on the role of technology in Singapore's security. The technological transformation of the SAF from the second generation to the third generation beginning in 2004 has been much publicised. The Third Generation (3G) SAF is expected to be a "modernised networked force, capable of carrying out a wider spectrum of operations".[46] Given the speed at which technology improves, it is not unreasonable to envisage a 4G SAF in the foreseeable future. What is important to note for the purpose of this paper is that the focus on technology goes back to the very early years of the formation of the SAF. Goh Keng Swee's guidance from way back in 1971 was that Singapore should at all costs avoid "a rifleman's war", and particularly so against countries which can better bear the attrition of manpower; Goh drew the example of the failure of the US army in Vietnam despite its overwhelming firepower, mobility and weapons. Thus, from the early years of Singapore's military build-up, a lot of thinking has been devoted to the issue of developing of an effective army, air force and navy.[47] This is not an easy task that can be achieved in a short period because even the operation (and maintenance) of basic weapon systems requires training (education), albeit much less sophisticated ones. There is also the limitation of finance, as a country may not be able to afford what it wants, and the more sophisticated the weaponry, the more expensive it is. All this harks back to Lee Kuan Yew's point about the intrinsic link between defence and economics mentioned earlier. Finally, Singapore has to ensure that its defence preparation does not inadvertently create an arms race with our neighbours which would only undermine rather than enhance its security. The recent establishment of the Cyber Security Agency under the Prime Minister's Office "to coordinate public and private sector efforts to protect national systems" is another example of the technology dimension of defence and security.[48]

Apart from technology, there is also the place of "international law". As then-Senior Minister Professor S. Jayakumar who had served in several portfolios including Law, Foreign Affairs and National Security explained, "for a small country, observance of international law is critical to safeguarding our sovereignty, independence and other interests ... Small states cannot survive and thrive in a world in which interaction among states is governed by relative power and not by law".[49] The reality is that small states can only survive in the "interstices created by the major powers". As such, Singapore has an interest in the rule of both international law and institutions.[50] On this, Singapore's position has remained constant. In the recent case of Russia's annexation of Crimea, the Singapore Foreign Ministry declared that "Singapore opposes the annexation of any country or territory as it contravenes international law. Singapore also objects to any unprovoked invasion of a sovereign country under any pretext".[51] The Russian annexation thus sets a "bad precedent".[52] This was the same attitude Singapore adopted with regard to the Vietnamese invasion of Kampuchea in December 1978.[53]

Conclusion

From the above, it can be seen that Singapore's security as conceived by the political leaders has been most consistent, holistic and also forward-looking.[54] Given that the ruling party has been in power since 1965, this is not surprising although not necessarily inevitable. After all, threats do change with time.[55] The recent cyber-attack on Sony is an example — as Lev Grossman put it "the mere act of moving information across the line from private to public can turn that information into a weapon that can inflict all kinds of damage ...".[56] Although not much has been said by the leadership about this form of electronic warfare, one would assume that the defence against cyber-attack would fall under the area of "Technology", one of the four key elements of Singapore's defence strategy. More importantly, in my view, is the enduring geopolitical reality of Singapore which ultimately frames any consideration of Singapore's security. There have been pockets of criticism from opposition leaders and academics although on the whole, the general public has so far been quite unquestioning and appears to be willing to defer to the political leaders on security and foreign policy matters.

For example, in a March 1984 parliament session, there was an exchange between the opposition Member of Parliament (Anson) J.B. Jeyaretnam and Goh Chok Tong in parliament on March 1984 over the high level of defence expenditure.[57] There was also scepticism raised regarding Singapore's acquisition of the E-2C planes. Essentially, the critics, and in this case Jeyaretnam, were of the view that there was "a lack of consultation with the taxpayers" on security matters, particularly defence acquisitions. Goh Chok Tong's response was that the critics "take a snapshot of Singapore when the sun is out and ask, 'Where is the rain? Who says it is going to rain. I do not see any dark clouds' … and that to name an enemy is to make an enemy out of him". There is also the view that national security has been conflated with regime security or maintenance. As Carl Trocki noted, "anything that threatened the power of the PAP government was usually interpreted as a threat to national security".[58] The government's recent handling of Tan Pin Pin's documentary film which featured Singapore's political exiles by giving it a "Not Allowed for All Ratings" classification in the name of "national security" left some of its strongest supporters nonplussed and further provides fuel to the critics' fire.[59] In a recent essay by Thum Ping Tjin, he argued that "the myth of Singapore being exceptionally vulnerable to external threat is also deeply flawed".[60] As Singaporeans have been enjoying a state of peace for almost 50 years, it gets harder for them to see the purpose of spending so much time, energy and resources on defence. The government will need to do more than just repeating the same refrain and should encourage younger Singaporeans to take a greater interest in the country's diplomatic history and the making of its foreign and defence policies. As Moises Naim and Joseph Nye reminded us "even when a conventional military is not deployed in active conflict, its deterrence role remains important" and military power "still structures expectations and shapes political calculations".[61]

Notes

[1] Transcript of a television interview with the Prime Minister, Mr Lee Kuan Yew, by three foreign press correspondents, Mr Creighton Burns of the *Melbourne Age*, Mr Nihal Singh of the *Statesman of India*, and Mr Dennis Bloodworth of the *London Observer*, 28 July 1966, lky/1966/lky0728.doc; Transcript of a press conference of the Prime Minister, Mr Lee Kuan Yew, to a group of foreign correspondents, 11 December 1965, lky\1965\lky1211b.doc. Retrieved 4 May 2015, from http://stars.nhb.gov.sg/stars/public.

[2] Transcript of a press conference given by then-Prime Minister, Mr Lee Kuan Yew, Hydrebad House, New Delhi, 3 September 1966, lky/1966/lky0903C.doc. Retrieved 4 May 2015, from http://www.nas.gov.sg/archivesonline/search.

[3] See for example, Muthiah Alagappa (ed.), *Asian Security Practice: Material and Ideational Influences* (Stanford: Stanford University Press, 1998); Steven Hoadley and Jurgen Ruland (eds.), *Asian Security Reassessed* (Singapore: Institute of Southeast Asian Studies, 2006).

[4] See for example, Alagappa (ed.) (1998), *op. cit.*, p. 11.

[5] *Ibid.*, pp. 692–693.

[6] All quotes by the Yang Di-Pertuan Negara, Defence and Foreign Ministers are from the "Parliamentary Debates of Singapore Official Report" volume 24. All quotations/ citations from the Singapore Parliament Reports in this paper can be accessed from http://www.parliament.gov.sg/publications-singapore-parliament-reports.

[7] Hoadley and Ruland (eds.) (2006), *op. cit.*, p. 10; Alagappa (ed.) (1998), *op. cit.*, pp. 11–12.

[8] Yang Di-Pertuan Negara's Speech, Part 1 of First Session of the Legislative Assembly (to be called the First Parliament), 8 December 1965, Singapore Parliamentary Reports (Hansard).

[9] *Ibid.*

[10] Speech by the Minister of Defence (Dr Goh Keng Swee), Singapore Army Bill, 23 December 1965, Singapore Parliament Reports (Hansard).

[11] See transcript of an interview by foreign correspondents with then-Prime Minister of Singapore, Mr Lee Kuan Yew, 30 August 1965, lky\1965\lky0830.doc. Retrieved 4 May 2015, from http://www.nas.gov.sg/archivesonline/search.

[12] Speech by the Minister of Foreign Affairs (S. Rajaratnam), 16 December 1965 and the Yang Di-Pertuan Negara's Speech: Debate on the Address, 17 December 1965, Singapore Parliament Reports (Hansard).

[13] See Lee Kuan Yew, *From Third World to First: The Singapore Story: 1965–2000* (Singapore: Singapore Press Holdings, 2000), p. 46, see also Chapters 2 and 3; Ang Cheng Guan, "Malaysia, Singapore and the Road the Five Power Defence Arrangements (FPDA), July 1970–November 1971," *War & Society*, 30(3), October 2011, pp. 207–225.

[14] Lee (2000), *op. cit.*, p. 763.

[15] Transcript of an interview with the Prime Minister by Jackie Sam of the Straits Times Press and Wu Shih of *Sin Chew Jit Poh*, 16 November 1965, lky\1965\lky1116a.doc. Retrieved 4 May 2015, from http://www.nas.gov.sg/archivesonline/search.

[16] Transcript of a press conference given by the Prime Minister, Mr Lee Kuan Yew, Hydrebad House, New Delhi, 3 September 1966, *op. cit.*

[17] Speech by the Minister of Defence (Dr Goh Keng Swee), National Service (Amendment) Bill, 13 March 1967, Singapore Parliament Reports (Hansard).

[18] Transcript of a press conference the Prime Minister, Mr Lee Kuan Yew, gave to a group of foreign correspondents, 11 December 1965, *op. cit.*

[19] The Minister of Defence (Mr Lim Kim San), "Estimates of Expenditure for Financial Year, 1st January 1969 to 31st March 1970," 18 December 1968, Singapore Parliament Reports (Hansard).

[20] Transcript of a press conference the Prime Minister, Mr Lee Kuan Yew, gave to a group of foreign correspondents, 11 December 1965, *op. cit.*

[21] Lee (2011), *op. cit.*, p. 32.

[22] See Ang Cheng Guan, *Lee Kuan Yew's Strategic Thought* (London: Routledge, 2013), p. 65.

[23] See Bernard Loo, "Goh Keng Swee and the Emergence of a Modern SAF: The Rearing of a Poisonous Shrimp," in Emrys Chew and Chong Guan Kwa (eds.), *Goh Keng Swee: A Legacy of Public Service* (Singapore: World Scientific, 2012), Chapter 5.

[24] Speech by Dr Goh Keng Swee, Minister of Defence, at the Commissioning Ceremony of the 10th Batch of Infantry Officer Cadets, SAFTI, at the Istana, 19 July 1972.

[25] The Deputy Prime Minister and Minister of Defence (Dr Goh Keng Swee), Budget, Ministry of Defence, 14 March 1978, Singapore Parliament Reports (Hansard).

[26] Speech by Prime Minister Mr Lee Kuan Yew at the dinner in honour of the Prime Minister of Japan, Mr Zenko Suzuki and Mrs Sachi Suzuki, Istana, 13 January 1981, lky/1981/lky0113.doc. Retrieved 4 May 2015, from http://www.nas.gov.sg/archivesonline/search.

[27] Text of speech by the Deputy Prime Minister and Minister of Defence, Dr Goh Keng Swee, at the Commissioning Ceremony of three RSN Ships at Pulau Brani Naval Base, 27 February 1977.

[28] See chapter by N. Ganesan in Alagappa (ed.) (1998), *op. cit.*, p. 591.

[29] See Ang (2013), *op. cit.*, p. 21, footnote 63.

[30] Transcript of a press conference the Prime Minister, Mr Lee Kuan Yew, gave to a group of foreign correspondents, 11 December 1965, *op. cit.*

[31] Closing Address by Dr Goh Keng Swee, Minister of Defence, at the 3rd SCSC course, 19 November 1971. Compare this with Lee (2011), *op. cit.*, pp. 322–323.

[32] Lee Kuan Yew, *The Fundamentals of Singapore's Foreign Policy: Then & Now*, S. Rajaratnam Lecture 2009 (Singapore: MFA Diplomatic Academy, 2009), p. 5.

[33] "Political, Economic Reforms 'Need Not Go Hand in Hand'," *The Straits Times*, 17 August 2004.

[34] "Tales from a 50-Year Journey," *Today*, 22 November 2004, p. 2.

[35] "Culturally Chinese, Politically Singaporean," *The Straits Times*, 23 July 2005.

[36] See transcript of a talk given by the Prime Minister, Mr Lee Kuan Yew, on the subject "Big and Small Fishes in Asian Waters" at a meeting of the University of Singapore Democratic Socialist Club at the University campus, 15 June 1966, lky/1966/lky0422. Retrieved 4 May 2015, from http://www.nas.gov.sg/archivesonline/search.

[37] "Sovereign Wealth Funds 'Useful for Small States'," *The Straits Times*, 3 March 2008, p. 4; "Survival of 'Shrimps' in the Ocean," *The Straits Times*, 4 March 2008, p. 22.

[38] "Changing Face of Political Leadership, through MM's Eyes," *The Straits Times*, 2 April 2005, p. S14.

[39] Lee (2009), *op. cit.*, pp. 5, 7.

[40] "Security Options for Small States," speech by Political Secretary (Defence), Brigadier-General Lee Hsien Loong, Singapore Institute of International Affairs, 16 October 1984. For full text, see *The Straits Times*, 6 November 1984, p. 20.

[41] The Minister of Defence and Second Minister for Health (Mr Goh Chok Tong), Main and Development Estimates of Singapore for the Financial Year 1st April, 16 March 1984, Singapore Parliament Reports (Hansard).

[42] "Strategies for a Small State in Turbulent World," excerpt from a speech by Defence Minister Teo Chee Hean to the Singapore Press Club, 21 April 2005 — *The Straits Times Interactive*, 23 April 2005. Retrieved 21 May 2015, from http://www.cs.cmu.edu/-dgovinda/st/saf.html.

[43] S. Jayakumar, *Reflections on Diplomacy of a Small State* (Singapore: MFA Diplomatic Academy, 2010).

[44] "Strategies for a Small State in Turbulent World," 21 April 2005, *op. cit.*

[45] See for example, "Speech by Minister for Defence Teo Chee Hean at the Launch of the Total Defence Campaign 2006." Retrieved 4 May 2015, from http://www.mindef.gov.sg/imindef/press_room/official_releases/nr/2006/feb/11feb06_nr/11feb06_speech.html#.VNAwZ00cQdU.

[46] See for example, "3G Soldier Has Whole SAF in His Backpack," *The Straits Times*, 1 July 2009, p. 19.

[47] Closing Address by Dr Goh Keng Swee, Minister of Defence, at the 3rd SCSC course, 19 November 1971.

[48] "New Agency to Direct S'pore's Cyber Defence," *The Straits Times*, 28 January 2015.

[49] Jayakumar (2010), *op. cit.*

[50] Bilahari Kausikan, "Small State's Big Challenge to Stay Vital," *The Straits Times*, 2 September 2005.

[51] MFA Spokesman's Comments in response to media queries on the Russian parliament's ratification of a treaty joining Crimea to Russia on 21 March 2014, Ministry of Foreign Affairs, Singapore, 21 March 2014. Retrieved 4 May 2015, from http://www.mfa.gov.sg/content/mfa/media_centre/press_room/pr/2014/201403/press_20130321.html.

[52] "A Less Hospitable World without US Engagement: PM," *The Straits Times*, 2 July 2014. Retrieved 21 May 2015, from http://heresthenews.blogspot.sg/2014/07/a-less-hospitable-world-without-us.html.

[53] See Ang Cheng Guan, *Singapore, ASEAN and the Cambodian Conflict 1978–1991* (Singapore: NUS Press, 2013).

[54] See "SAF Must Remain Strong, Credible Force: Tharman," *Today*, 21 July 2014. Retrieved 21 May 2015, from http://www.todayonline.com/singapore/saf-must-remain-strong-credible-force-tharman. MFA Press Release: Transcript of speech by Emeritus Senior Minister Goh Chok Tong at the S. Rajaratnam Lecture on Friday, 17 October 2014 at 3.00 pm at The St. Regis Singapore.

[55] See "DPM Teo Warns of Increased Terror Threat to S'pore," *The Straits Times*, 9 October 2014. Retrieved 21 May 2015, from http://ifonlysingaporeans.blogspot.sg/2014/parliament-highlights-7-oct-2014.html. See also, Moises Naim, *The End of Power* (New York: Basic Books, 2013), Chapter 6.

[56] "What Sony's Hackers Know: In Cyberwar, Information Is a Weapon — and Our Culture Is the Battlefield," *TIME*, 22 December 2014. Retrieved 21 May 2015, from http://time.com/3643784/what-sonys-hackers-know/.

[57] Main and Development Estimates of Singapore for Financial Year 1st April, 16 March 1984, Singapore Parliament Reports (Hansard).

[58] Carl A. Trocki, *Singapore: Wealth, Power and the Culture of Control* (London: Routledge, 2006), pp. 128–129.

[59] "No Public Screening of Film on Political Exiles: MDA," *The Straits Times*, 11 September 2014. Retrieved 21 May 2015, from http://ifonlysingaporeans.blogspot.sg/2014/09/no-public-screening-of-film-on.html; "Many Singapore Stories, One Resilient Nation," *The Sunday Times*, 3 August 2014. Retrieved 21 May 2015, from http://www.straitstimes.com/the-big-story/asia-report/opinion/story/many-singapore-stories-one-resilient-nation-20140803.

[60] See Thum Ping Tjin, "The Old Normal Is the New Normal," in Donald Low and Sudhir Thomas Vadaketh (eds.), *Hard Choices: Challenging the Singapore Consensus* (Singapore: NUS Press, 2014), Chapter 11.

[61] Moises Naim, *The End of Power* (New York: Basic Books, 2013), p. 125. The quote by Joseph Nye is cited by Moises Naim.

Chapter 2

National Security and Singapore: An Assessment

Norman Vasu and Bernard Loo

Introduction

National security has traditionally been thought of in terms of the employment of military power to protect the territorial integrity of the state in order to safeguard the lives of a nation's people. Thus, national security is, according to such a traditional conception, the necessary foundation for the good life of its citizens to be realised. Consequently, stemming from this, the military was viewed to be the primary instrument of national security, and, if non-military instruments of national security existed, the latter was clearly secondary to the former.

The relationship between the military and non-military instruments of national security may have now altered and securing the nation appears significantly more complex than it used to. While the number of interstate wars has declined since the end of the Cold War, the porosity of territorial boundaries with rapid globalisation[1] has ensured that the cohesion and survival of nation-states remain vulnerable. Recent events such as the Asian Financial Crisis in 1997, Severe Acute Respiratory Syndrome (SARS) and, most notably, 9/11 have been instructional — traditional security concerns such as an invasion by a foreign country need not be the only manner through which the security of a state can be threatened. Moreover, these novel security concerns clearly illustrate that security threats are constantly evolving and no amount of planning can completely eradicate the element of strategic surprise. Without the luxury of 20/20 hindsight, 9/11 and SARS remained off the radar of most governments until after the fact.

In other words, issues falling under the rubric of national security — the things to be secured — have not only increased in number but the threats have also become more unpredictable. In the light of this, the job of securing the nation is made even more challenging due to the finite resources at a state's disposal. Full protection is an impossible task as every possible target cannot be secured fully. For instance, to protect every building in a country from a terror attack would overstretch the finite resources of the state — hence, an attempt to protect every building would be to protect every building poorly. This problem of finite national security resources is compounded by the difficulty in knowing beforehand what the threats are, where it emanates from and how it will manifest itself. Even the technological wizardry of pervasive, multi-dimensional, and redundant reconnaissance and surveillance systems cannot confer upon the national security apparatus omniscience.[2]

Against this backdrop of an expanded threat horizon and a state's limited ability to mitigate all of them, this chapter assesses the measures implemented by the Singaporean government in order to secure the nation-state and the good life for its people. The chapter argues the Singaporean government has been remarkably successful at protecting two key national security concerns of the city-state as identified since independence: (1) the protection of Singaporean sovereignty and (2) the maintenance of public order. However, due to the expanding threat horizon and the complexity of ever-evolving threats, for continued success, the *process of securitisation* in Singapore — that is, who is permitted to frame a threat and who decides what the best response is — may have to alter over time.

The chapter is broadly divided into three sections. In Section One, an overview of the concepts underpinning the conventional division of roles and responsibility of governments and citizens, as well as the strategic culture influencing the process of securitisation in formulating and enacting national security, is discussed. It shows while there may be an implicit social compact founded upon a common strategic culture between the government and the governed — where the roles and responsibilities vis-à-vis national security is clearly defined — this distinct division of roles may be untenable due to an altering international context and widening threat spectrum. The second section both locates and assesses the case of Singapore within this framework. In its analysis, the process of identifying and mitigating issues pertaining to national security in Singapore is revealed. Securitisation in Singapore is marked by three salient factors: (1) the process of identifying threats and responding to them is state-centric and elite-driven; (2) the process is cloaked in secrecy; and (3) the process is conducted with the tacit act of faith among the people not to challenge the sanctioned paradigm in exchange for protection against the identified threats. The section concludes that this process of securitisation has largely been a success thus far. Finally, by discussing two possible threats to Singapore's national security, Section Three will illustrate why securitisation in Singapore, though successful thus far, may have to alter in response to future challenges.

Understanding National Security

Finding theoretical underpinnings in, perhaps most famously, Thomas Hobbes' *Leviathan*, it is conventionally understood that the state is committed to protect its citizens from external and internal security threats. Following Hobbes, fearing the unrelenting merciless competition found within the state of nature where there is no central governing authority, life is "solitary, poor, nasty, brutish and short" and "every man is enemy to every man". In order to transform this state of affairs, members of a society enter a social compact where they relinquish their right to defend themselves to a Leviathan tasked with doing so for them.[3] More succinctly, security is devolved to a higher authority for order and stability to prevail. The implications of this for the process of securitisation — defined in this chapter as the power to frame national security threats and decide on the best response to mitigate them — and national security is as follows: the state is seen to be empowered with the ability to articulate threats to the nation's collective security and execute the means necessary to obtain this end — often with the acquiescence of the people.[4]

This process of securitisation is akin to what some strategists refer to as strategic culture.[5] Strategic culture, as a concept, may be understood as:

> An integrated system of symbols (i.e., argumentation structures, languages, analogies, metaphors, etc.) that acts to establish pervasive and long-lasting grand strategic preferences by formulating concepts of the role and efficacy of military force in interstate political affairs, and by clothing these conceptions with such an aura of factuality that the strategic choices seem uniquely realistic and efficacious.[6]

Specifically, for the purposes of this chapter, however, it is the so-called second generation of strategic culture theory that is more pertinent. Second generation theory argues strategic culture may be nothing more than the creation of images and myths serving to legitimise the strategic choices of political elites.[7]

A key element then to the process of securitisation and what is considered national security is how political elites use images and symbols to both make sense of their strategic environment as well as to generate an identity and self-image of the state.[8] It first begins with the way policy-makers perceive the complex strategic environment in which their state exists,[9] and how they then make sense of why specific events occur.[10] Strategic cultural images and symbols provide a focus that helps policy-makers prioritise and make sense of the overwhelming amount of information coming from the strategic environment.[11] Policy-makers are constrained by their ability and willingness to devote limited time and attention to all incoming information; more often than not, information dissonant with prior expectations, dominant symbols and images tend to be ignored or filtered. In so doing, the strategic cultural lens through which policy-makers perceive and make sense of their operating environment may be the cause of misperceptions and strategic miscalculations. For example, misperception and miscalculation may unconsciously influence policy-makers into believing there are preparations for war by a putative adversary when none exist.

Why is this elite manipulation so important? One answer lies in the importance of political mobilisation for the attainment of these national interests. Another answer lies in the relationship between identity and threat. Strategic culture not only provides the conceptual lens through which policy-makers can perceive the strategic environment, it also allows policy-makers to identify the putative adversaries and assess the immediacy of the threat. There is any number of state and non-state actors in a given state's strategic environment. Which of these actors comes to be identified as the putative adversary is as much a result of rational analysis of "objective" conditions as it is of cultural perspectives. By filtering the vast amount of information from the strategic environment, these symbols and images create the basis for understanding the specific roles and policy actions commensurate with this national self-image. By telling policy-makers what their state is like, strategic culture influences and shapes the sorts of interests and objectives these policy-makers will pursue.[12] Expressed differently, strategic culture informs the process of securitisation — the culture determines what is considered a threat *and* the "proper" response to the threat. Strategic culture helps policy-makers identify the national security interests of the state, and provides the tools with which policy-makers can define and understand the situation they are in, interpret adversarial motives, and suggest approaches by which such challenges to state interests can be dealt with.[13] Finally, however, the legitimacy of elites becomes a function of the preservation or realisation of that conception of national security.[14]

However, while elite manipulation of images and symbols is central to the strategic culture of a state, it does not mean that strategic cultures can change from situation to situation. This resistance to change stems from strategic cultural images acquiring a life of their own once these images are employed for political mobilisation. The process of internalisation of these strategic cultural images and symbols does not occur solely at the mass level; elites are also affected by this process of socialisation such that the political legitimacy of these elites comes to be tied to the specific conception of national security they created to begin with.[15]

Hence, the historical foundations of strategic culture play a large role in the development of a particular culture. The elite manipulation of strategic culture does not occur in a vacuum; it necessarily occurs in a historical foundation — it is part of a wider process of socialisation that is informed by historical events, and must therefore correlate with some form of historically-derived inferential logic.[16] The images and symbols elites use to mobilise popular support for any given objective must draw from and correlate with widely-held societal belief systems; otherwise, such attempts at political mobilisation will likely fail. The process of national self-identification discussed earlier and the related process of identifying the putative adversary cannot be divorced from the historical context. States do not become hostile to one another because of negative stereotypes; those negative stereotypes are the result of a particular interpretation of historically-driven inferences.[17]

Besides the manner in which national security is conceived and the way strategic culture impacts upon the process of securitisation, the Herculean responsibility of ensuring national security has oftentimes earned the security sector of governments — even among the staunchest democracies — the privilege of blanket secrecy.[18] Following from this, it has become customary for deliberations and the framing of national security threats and strategies to operate away from the prying eyes of the public to enable the professionals to work. By tackling the gamut of challenges to the nation's sovereignty and public order in this manner, the state assumes the two weighty burdens of constant monitoring as well as ceaseless mitigating of security threats.

To complicate matters for security agencies tasked with this role, in today's context, non-traditional threats — defined as non-military threats to the security of nations, such as transnational terrorism, environmental degradation and pandemics — are beginning to feature prominently in security agendas worldwide. These issues are becoming increasing difficult to secure with increased globalisation and greater movement of people, goods and services across borders. Unlike traditional threats which are by and large identifiable, non-traditional security threats such as diseases are often not only faceless but also almost impossible to prevent from permeating the territorial boundaries of the state as their ubiquitous perpetrators make them unfeasible to nip in the bud. To complicate matters, unlike in a conventional battlefield where trained military personnel are at the forefront of an enemy attack, the first casualties of an amorphous non-traditional security threat are civilians. In addition, the majority of these citizens have limited access to the black box of their country's securitisation process.

In this respect, the ability of a society to survive any unanticipated national disasters will be shaped by their response to the incident. This response in turn is determined by their understanding of their role in national security which is in turn informed by society's shared strategic culture. On this note, the next section will examine the strategic culture and the current approach to securitisation in Singapore.

Singapore's National Security: Drivers and Passengers of Change

Since independence in 1965 to 9/11, while identifiable threats to Singapore's national security have been dynamic and continually varying, it is clear Singapore's national security strategy remains primarily driven by the two conventional security concerns of protecting Singapore's sovereignty as well as maintaining public order.

The historical foundation of Singapore's strategic culture and, following from this, the process of securitisation in Singapore begins with Singapore's exit from Malaysia in 1965. This exit, so the predominant official historical narrative goes, left Singapore in the unenviable position of being a small state having to contend with the external threat of being sandwiched between larger and possibly hostile neighbours while also facing the internal threat of volatile intercommunal relations prone to sporadic racial and religious violence. Perhaps it is of little surprise that this historical foundation impacted upon the ruling People's Action Party's (PAP) policies vis-à-vis national security. This ubiquitous official historical narrative — known as the "Singapore Story" — has gestated an ideology of survival premised upon Singapore's supposed vulnerability. As such, the urgency of building an armed force to protect Singapore's fragile sovereign status and a police force to maintain law and order topped the pressing concerns of the government. To this end, the Ministry of Interior and Defence (MID) was established in November 1965 to strengthen the country's external and internal defence with control of both the Singapore Armed Forces (SAF) and police force.

By the 1970s and 1980s, Singapore's national security strategy then saw a shift in emphasis towards external defence. The division of the MID into the Ministry of Defence (MINDEF) and the Ministry of Home Affairs (MHA) reflected the acknowledgement of the evolving roles in the internal and external security agencies of Singapore with time.[19]

There are two key reasons for the shift in emphasis towards external defence. Firstly, this was partially due to the assessment that the two internal security threats of communism and communalism had largely been contained by the 1980s as Singapore's economic success undermined their appeal. Moreover, the Internal Security Department (ISD) and severe anti-subversion legislation had also been effective in keeping domestic social and political threats in check.[20] Secondly, while the threats to internal security had diminished over time, this was not the case with Singapore's external defence. The historical lessons of both the Japanese invasion and the tumultuous years in Malaysia imprinted upon the psyche of the old guard the need to secure Singapore's borders at all cost. The Japanese invasion, in particular, remains a crucial element in the National Education syllabus of Singapore schools, and arguably provides the justification for the continuing belief in the absolute necessity of National Service (NS) in defence policy. The haunting fear held by Singaporean leaders that there still existed leaders in Malaysia holding the belief that Singapore should not have been permitted to leave but instead "clobbered" into submission were the faggots that fuelled the historical mistrust between the two countries.[21] While Indonesia was viewed as the lesser of the two security threats from its neighbours especially with the end of the *Konfrontasi*, there were sporadic comments from leaders of the vast archipelago that reinforced the view of Singapore's leaders of the necessity for constant vigilance. One such comment was made by then-President Habibie to then-Second Minister for Defence Teo Chee Hean that "Singapore lies inside [Indonesia]".[22] As a result of the desire to deter external powers from harbouring thoughts of violating Singapore's territorial integrity, the city-state has invested considerably in strengthening its armed forces.[23] Undeterred by constraints such as its lack of strategic depth and manpower, the leaders developed the SAF from scratch to what it is at present — perhaps the most modern, well-equipped and technically proficient armed forces in maritime Southeast Asia.

Hence, it may be argued that before 9/11, Singapore's national security strategy at the point of independence focused on both domestic and international threats. In the 1980s, the national security strategy evolved to focus largely on building strong external defensive capabilities. These external defensive capabilities were "tasked with meeting clear military challenges from state-based threats" and "geared towards fighting a conventional war".[24]

However, since 9/11 and the rise of transnational terrorism worldwide, terrorism has reinvigorated the domestic dimension to national security as it is considered a key threat to public order. In the literature produced by Singapore's National Security Coordination Centre, terrorism is described as "the most serious security threat" Singapore faces "in the immediate future".[25] Unlike Singapore's past incidents of terrorism such as the McDonald House bombing in 1965, the Laju incident in 1974, and the SQ 117 hijacking in 1991 which were "isolated and episodic" and "not at all representative of the transnational terrorism facing us today",[26] the current threat transcends borders, has global

reach, is rooted in ideology, employs sophisticated methods to achieve catastrophic outcomes[27] and is likely to pose a "serious and prolonged threat to
Singapore's national security", requiring Singaporeans to "learn to live with the
real prospect that a terrorist attack could occur in this country".[28] The uncovering of the foiled local Jemaah Islamiyah (JI) plot in 2002 reinforced the existential nature of the threat to Singapore. Consequently, to turn Singapore into a
"hard target", more resources have been allocated to the ISD to better equip
them in the fight against terror, with more resources to be made available
"whenever needed".[29]

Hence, all in all, the shift in the identification of security threats aside,
Singapore's national security strategy remains firmly rooted in the historical
foundation of its genesis. Rupture from Malaysia coupled with periodic communal tension was a strong narrative upon which a strategic culture concerned
with both external and internal threats to the state emerged.

The National Security of Singapore: Roles and Responsibility of the State

With this strategic culture in place, the division of roles and responsibilities for
securing the city-state of Singapore by and large conforms to the conventional
model of securitisation whereby the government sets the security agenda
and appropriates the role each segment of society should play. In the case of
Singapore, three salient factors underline the process of identifying and mitigating issues pertaining to national security: (1) the process of identifying threats
and responding to them is elite-driven; (2) the process is shrouded in secrecy;
and (3) the process is conducted with the tacit act of Hobbesian faith among
the people not to challenge the sanctioned paradigm in exchange for protection
against the identified threats.

Elite-driven process

The elite-driven nature of the process of securitisation in Singapore is not
merely due to the fact that the government remains the only credible agency
with the legitimacy and resources to assume this responsibility. For Singapore,
the process is elite-driven as a result of one important situational factor — the
political dominance of the PAP. With scant opposition members in parliament
and the government bureaucracy effectively under PAP rule, the ruling party is
afforded the opportunity to frame and implement policies across all aspects of
government unchallenged.[30] Moreover, policy-making in the area of defence in
particular has been relatively opaque and dominated by key political leaders,

especially in its formative years, such as Goh Keng Swee and Lee Kuan Yew.[31] For example, in order to impress the lingering communist threat upon the SAF, Goh Keng Swee introduced a course on Marxism-Leninism for selected SAF officers in order to enhance their understanding of communism and combat the threat effectively. The first course began in 1977 and was conducted by Goh, senior civil servants and university lecturers. This course was extended in the following year to senior officers in the Singapore Civil Service and statutory boards.[32]

The elite-driven nature of the securitisation process in Singapore is further supplemented when the little resistance to the government's efforts to gain the compliance of the masses with regard to its defence policies is considered. Aside from the Barisan Sosialis' efforts at galvanising public support to oppose the implementation of NS in the 1960s which by the 1976 general elections had become a non-issue, the rationale behind the state's defence policies have seldom come under public scrutiny.[33] Except for the immediate two years following independence during which social services (Education and Health) topped the expenditure list of Singapore's national budget,[34] the security sector (Defence, Home Affairs and Civil Defence) have received the highest appropriation.[35] Underlying the Republic's uncompromising take on securing its borders from external attacks was its unabated investment in its defence during the Asian Financial Crisis of the late 1990s when its regional neighbours were adhering to a more austere budget. This was justified by the government on the grounds that Singapore had to see through its defence commitments even in times of financial belt-tightening to avoid paying the price of being caught off guard in future.[36] Moreover, with transnational terrorism dominating the security agenda, even though terrorism "[u]ltimately … does not threaten Singapore's very existence as an independent, sovereign nation",[37] that does not necessarily mean the role of the SAF in protecting Singapore from external threats reduces in significance. On the contrary, while "[o]ur defence policy [of diplomacy and deterrence] has served us well" and should remain the "fundamental tenets" of our defence policy in the 21st century, there is a need to "define our security in wider terms to include not only traditional security challenges but also new ones that may arise to threaten our interests in the globalised era".[38] Consequently, the SAF will have to "develop a broader range of capabilities and prepare itself to work with others to tackle some of these challenges".[39] While, according to the Stockholm International Peace Research Institute, the defence budget has exceeded 5% of the GDP only three times since 1988, in response to a question raised in parliament on whether the defence budget was sufficient, then-Minister of Defence Teo Chee Hean, replied that even though the ministry had been provided with what it asked for, "I will not hesitate to ask for more if I feel that I need it and I have confidence that I will be able to persuade my colleagues in Ministry of Finance to provide it for me if I do because there is strong commitment for defence in this country and strong support in this house".[40]

Secrecy in national security

As for the process of securitisation being conducted under a veil of secrecy in Singapore, the sensitive nature of matters pertaining to national security — especially with regard to operational secrecy — reinforces the argument that secrecy is of utmost importance. This is encapsulated in a comment by Chandra Das when he was Chairman of the Parliamentary Committee on Defence and Foreign Affairs in 1987. Das maintained his committee would rely on "quiet diplomacy" in their role of scrutinising policies on defence and foreign affairs as "[these affairs] are such that certain issues can be raised in Parliament, certain issues cannot...".[41] This need for secrecy was further driven home in 1989 when a constitutional amendment was passed to prohibit judicial review of the substantive grounds of detention under the Internal Security Act (ISA) and anti-subversion laws.[42] In effect, the constitutional amendment ensured, in cases constituting a threat to national security, judicial review is confined to the decision-making process rather than the merits of the decision itself.[43] This was illustrated in the threat assessment of MHA with regard to the threat posed by the Jehovah's Witnesses in the case of Colin Chan versus Public Prosecutor. During the case, the presiding Chief Justice opined that "it was not for this court to substitute its views for the Minister's as to whether the Jehovah's Witnesses constituted a threat to national security", and that "[f]rom the evidence adduced, it appeared that the Minister was of the view that the continued existence of a group which preached as one its principal beliefs that military service was forbidden was contrary to public peace, welfare and good order".[44]

Moreover, the issue of security goes beyond the amount of information that is available to the public as the withholding of information even between security agencies themselves appears to be inherent to the job. In addressing the need for information sharing among security agencies in the wake of 9/11, the then-Minister for Home Affairs, Wong Kan Seng, acknowledged such a practice may nonetheless seem "counter-intuitive to intelligence officers as compartmentalization is used to prevent the leakage of sensitive information".[45] In addition, not all detentions under the ISA are made public in the name of national security. When answering a parliamentary question pertaining to specifics of those detained under the ISA between 1999 and 2007, while addressing the questions, the Minister for Home Affairs added that "[a] few of the cases have not been publicized. This is because publicity can compromise on-going operations, or seriously harm national interests".[46]

From the discussion above, it is clear that the framing and definition of national security threats in Singapore fall within the exclusive purview of the state's security agencies and are conducted in great secrecy, often with the tacit endorsement of the masses. In order for the state to carry out its function of protecting its citizens effectively, it appears public participation should be kept to the minimum.

Tacit support and faith of the people

There exists a paucity of studies on public opinions of Singapore's external defence policies. Indeed, this may not merely be due to apathy but the clear drawing of "out of bound" (OB) markers by the government with regard to public discussion on matters pertaining to national security. For example, in the recommendations proposed by the Subject Committees to the Singapore 21 Committee, one recommendation was that

> [i]t is important to establish the out-of-bounds (OB) markers so that civic participation does not adversely affect national security and social stability. *The OB markers should be limited to racial and religious issues which affect social harmony, as well as issues which threaten national security* (emphasis added).[47]

As such, public responses to certain incidences have to be relied upon to provide a glimpse of views from the ground. A debate in the forum section of *The Straits Times* seems to suggest that the privileged status of the security sector resonates with a segment of the population. It began with a letter calling for the "old sacred cow" of defence spending to be reviewed.[48] By highlighting the disparity between the expenditure for defence vis-à-vis the social sector, the writer was of the view that "[j]ust a small percentage in savings from spending on defence/security could substantially fund social and financial-help programmes without having to raise the Goods and Services Tax rate".[49] Acknowledging the "critical importance of a strong defence force", the writer was keen to stress that "what is needed is to objectively strike a balance between the dollars spent on hardware, etc., which are subject to regular scrapping due to depreciation and obsolescence and have not seen real battle, and the dollars needed for the welfare and betterment of the people".[50] The letter provoked a string of responses from members of the public defending the status quo — illustrating how many members of the public have also enmeshed with the dominant strategic culture. These responses served to reassure the Defence Minister who was "gratified to read the recent series of forum page letters to *The Straits Times* on defence spending [which] showed that many Singaporeans understand the need for a strong defence".[51] It is possible to infer from the view — "Singaporeans understand the need for a strong defence" — that many Singaporeans agree that the threats described to them are genuine.

Furthermore, not only was the essence of the letter appealing for more funding and attention to be paid to addressing the social welfare of the people to "mitigate worsening income disparity and prevent the emergence of an economic underclass in the face of global competition"[52] missed by all the rejoinders, an assumption made was that *any* reduction of defence spending will inevitably severely compromise Singapore's Armed Forces' ability to carry out its duty to protect ("military capability, once sacrificed as a result of funding cuts, can take on an inordinate amount of time to restore"), leading to the demise of the nation's sovereignty in the hands of external powers ("[Singapore's] tiny size makes it a tempting target and only a strong SAF keeps potential aggressors in check").[53] It is notable that these arguments mirror very closely the siege mentality of the Old Guard.

Hence, as long as perceptions of threats to the nation writ large exist and are articulated by the traditional security agencies, these threats are generally accepted by the people as genuine owing to the acquiescence of the public towards traditional security concerns.

Thus far, the analysis has illustrated that the framing of Singapore's national security strategies over the years has generally been: (1) an elite-driven process; (2) the process is characterised by secrecy; and (3) the process is conducted with the tacit act of faith among the people. While the roles and responsibilities of the state are clear, what then is expected of the citizens with regard to the national security framework?

The National Security of Singapore: Roles and Responsibility of the Citizen

Based on government initiatives over the years, it may be held that the role of the masses regarding national security is to galvanise government policies and respond in an appropriate manner as determined by the state during a crisis.

For example, the rationale and concept of Total Defence, spearheaded by MINDEF, illustrates this point clearly. Implemented in 1984, Total Defence —

> provides the framework for a comprehensive and integrated response to deal with all kinds of threats and challenges. Whether it is a security threat such as global terrorism, or a national crisis like SARS, Total Defence brings together all relevant government agencies, private sector organisations and all Singaporeans in a total effort to deal with threats and challenges to Singapore's continued survival and success … To help Singaporeans understand how they can be involved, Total Defence is divided into five aspects — Military Defence, Civil Defence, Economic Defence, Social Defence and Psychological Defence. When we take National Service seriously, volunteer in civil defence exercises, help to keeping the economy going, build strong ties with one another regardless of race and religion, and stay committed to defend the country, we are doing something in every sector of our society to strengthen Singapore's resilience as a nation.[54]

In this sense, the identified roles each individual can play — taking NS seriously, volunteering in civil defence exercises, keeping the economy going, building strong ties with one another regardless of race and religion, staying committed to defending Singapore — all pertain to actions to be taken in order to secure Singapore's sovereignty from external threats and public order — especially in terms of communal relations. To ensure that Singaporeans were clear on their role within the Total Defence framework, the government embarked on a nationwide media campaign. A Total Defence Committee was also formed to look at government policies from a Total Defence viewpoint and individual ministries were given responsibility for the various components of the concept.[55] Moreover, public opinion surveys on the public's attitude towards Total Defence in 1985 and 1986 indicated a high proportion of respondents (85% and 88% respectively) agreeing that every Singaporean had a role to play in Total Defence.[56]

The command and control paradigm evident in the dissemination of the public's roles and responsibilities demonstrated by the concept of Total Defence is also consistent in the current national security framework to combat terrorism contained in the National Security Coordination Secretariat's publication *1826 Days: A Diary of Resolve*. The "shared responsibility" to confront terrorism is based on networks that "prevent, protect and respond".[57] In accord with the customary division of responsibility vis-à-vis national security, the current national security framework does divide the domestic and international dimension to national security into two parts:

MINDEF which "develops and directs policies, plans and allocates resources to defend Singapore against external attacks" and MHA which "looks after security within Singapore's borders". [58] However, in recognition that "a strict demarcation of the responsibilities for internal and external security would leave gaps in the defence of Singapore against transnational terrorists", the new national security framework does stress the importance of a "whole-of-government" approach that "brings together all ministries and agencies to deal with this challenge".[59] At the "highest level" is the Security Policy Review Committee (SPRC) which "meets regularly" to study Singapore's "critical national security goals, analyse the changing threats and decide how to tackle them".[60] Next, the National Security Coordinating Committee (NSCComm) "supports and executes SPRC decision", "guides projects to enhance our security" and "oversees other multi-agency working groups and commit-tees".[61] Following on, the National Security Coordination Secretariat (NSCS) at the Prime Minister's Office — comprising of the National Security Coordination Centre (NSCC) and the Joint Counter Terrorism Centre (JCTC) — "supports" SPRC, NSCComm and ICC.[62] The "three vital roles" performed by the NSCC to "keep Singapore secure in the long term" are national security planning, policy coordination and anticipating strategic threats.[63] As a strategic analysis unit, JCTC "studies our level of preparedness in areas such as maritime terrorism and chemical, biological and radiological terrorist threats" and "maps out the consequences should an attack in that domain takes place".[64] Hence, it is evident that the securitisation process — the framing of threats and the appropriation of the necessary means to miti-gate them — is exclusively within the purview of the government.

In addition, the division of responsibility on the ground between govern-ment agencies and the civilians is also clear. At the forefront, the Home Team and the SAF lead the other government agencies in protecting Singapore's critical infrastructure and external borders.[65] To support their work, another "no less vital effort" after the lead security agencies and all other government agencies is the public. The new national security framework calls "all Singaporeans — family, friends, neigbours, colleagues, regardless of race, language or religion, to stand together for each other" to "stand together" in face of the challenges ahead "with the same resolve as we have done so far" by proceeding "[f]rom knowing the threat to knowing how to act in a crisis".[66] Hence, Singaporeans from all walks of life are encouraged to participate in initiatives designed to manage community relations in a crisis such as the Community Engagement Programme (CEP) and various civil defence exercises.[67]

Following from this clear demarcation of responsibilities between government agencies and the public, it appears that the "shared responsibility" to "prevent, protect and respond" in *1826 Days* (2006) can generally be appropriated as such: the government's duty is to "prevent" and "protect" while the civilian population's is to "respond".

Assessing Singapore's National Security

To reiterate, this chapter is an assessment of the Singaporean government's management of Singapore's national security. Thus far, the chapter has shown that the strategic culture of Singapore is framed by a narrative of vulnerability that manifests as the determined protection of both national sovereignty and the maintenance of public order. Furthermore, this culture has led to a process of securitisation marked by three salient factors. They are: (1) the process of identifying threats and responding to them is state-centric and elite-driven; (2) the process is shrouded in secrecy; and (3) the process is conducted with the tacit act of faith among the people not to challenge the sanctioned paradigm in exchange for protection against the identified threats.

Since independence, the national security framework has been tested by various issues. High profile national security issues pertaining to both the twin concerns of national sovereignty and the maintenance of public order include the Marxist conspiracy in 1987, the Asian Financial Crisis of 1997, the outbreak of SARS in 2003, and, of course, the arrests of Singaporean JI terrorists seeking to strike targets in Singapore, as well as the recent arrests of "self-radicalised" Muslim Singaporeans. With regard to the government's management of national security, testimony of success lies in the fact that the yardstick employed to indicate ultimate failure — that is, an assault on Singaporean sovereignty or widespread public disorder — has not transpired. Singapore has managed to weather these crises swiftly without any long-term effects.

However, past performance may not be a good barometer to measure future success. It is arguable that the framework may not be able to be sustained owing to a possible growing disconnect among the public with regard to the process of securitisation. This disconnect lies with the manner in which matters of national security are considered and enacted upon — that is, the very securitisation process in Singapore. As discussed, the process by which threats are identified and responses decided upon has continually been elite-driven, shrouded in secrecy and enacted with the tacit faith of the masses. In this process of securitisation, the masses only enter the process well after threats are identified and responses put in place — they are educated and instructed to respond in an appropriate manner as determined by the state during a crisis.

What significance does this situation have for Singapore's national security in the near future? Based on the preceding analysis, the following section presents two scenarios for Singapore in 2030 with implications for national security. The first scenario discusses implications for Singaporean national security if indeed a crisis that is planned for occurs. The second discusses the implications for Singaporean national security if a crisis occurs that does not correspond to the government's current playbook of possible threats. Such a crisis would be marked by not only by its unconventionality and uncommonness but it would also be as surprising and have as intense an impact as SARS and 9/11. The occurrence of such a surprising crisis is ironically to be expected.[68] After all, it is impossible for any government to be able to foresee, plan and prepare for all possible threats. For ease in discussion and due to the impossibility of articulation, this crisis will be referred to as Crisis X.

Scenario One

This scenario is essentially a reflection of the future painted by the state and its manifestation vindicates the securitisation process in Singapore. This scenario, of course, does not have to be a terrorist attack. It could be, for example, a pandemic or any other possible scenario the national security model has prepared for.

In this scenario, the fragile overarching Singaporean identity carefully constructed after 65 years of nation-building buckles under the pressure of the long-suppressed primordial instincts of the people. As a result and according to script, there are outbreaks of post-event communal violence. Faced with sporadic outbreaks of violence and public disorder, some Singaporeans flee the country and investors indicate that they may consider pulling out of the country if security and order are not promptly restored. This scenario is not cast in complete gloom though. Over time, thanks to pre-crisis government-sponsored initiatives such as the Inter-Racial Confidence Circles (IRCCs) and the Community Engagement Programme, calm and order is eventually restored. Moreover, the government is assessed by the public to have conducted itself to the best of its abilities pre- and post-crisis — in effect, the catch-all term *du jour* "resilience" can finally be confidently employed to capture how Singapore weathered the storm and came out the better for it. Having eventually overcome a national crisis together, the social fabric of Singapore is strengthened as bonds of trust are reinforced among Singaporeans from all walks of life.

Scenario Two

In this scenario, the unthinkable occurs — the Rumsfeldian "unknown unknown" of Crisis X. Crisis X severally tests the social bonds of the Singaporean public and perhaps even results in sporadic episodes of violence. In addition, similar to Scenario One, Crisis X also prompts some Singaporeans to leave the country while investors also indicate that they may consider pulling out of the country if security and order are not promptly restored.

Of greater significance, Scenario Two of Crisis X results in a severe erosion of trust between the government and the people as the government is viewed to have failed to bear its responsibilities within the social compact. This disappointment is aggravated by the tacit division of roles of the security com-pact — the masses having trusted the government to ensure their security.[69] This feeling of disappointment and the disintegration of trust is further exacer-bated because the Singapore public had never been let down in matters of national security before. As a result, the government's ability, in the long run, to protect the people from security threats is persistently questioned by the people given the compromising of the myth of invincibility. Furthermore, besides the ability of the government to protect its people being called into question, another significant result of this scenario is that the loss of trust results in a more cynical populace predisposed towards contesting future measures enacted by the government in the interest of national security.

Conclusion

From these two scenarios, it is possible to see that though the occurrence of Scenario One would be unfortunate and trying, it admittedly would not be the worse-case scenario. As a result of the finite resources of the state and the ever evolving nature of threats appearing over a foggy horizon, the state cannot and should not be expected to prevent and avert all exigencies. Instead, what can fairly be expected of a state is for contingencies, if and when such crises occurs, to be put in place and for responses to be competently executed when tested. Also, with the current planning and preparation invested by the Singaporean government into national security, it is possible to have great confidence that Singapore as a nation should be able to absorb the shock of a crisis and bounce back to normality fairly rapidly in the eventuality of a planned crisis occurring.

In view of the fact that Scenario One is not the worse-case scenario, it is the unknown unknown of Crisis X that would have to be prepared for in planning Singapore's national security for the future. Preparation for Crisis X — that is, putting in place a plan — cannot be done by the very indefinite nature of the crisis. Thus, preparation has to focus on the process of securitisation itself. As the analysis of this chapter has shown, attributable to the elite-driven, secretive and devolved nature of securitisation in Singapore, the public is only brought into the process of national security downstream at the stage when an emergency occurs. This disengagement of the public, where security is communicated rather than dialogued with the people, may then result in the erosion of trust occurring when an unthinkable crisis occurs — responsibility for security is seen to ultimately fall within the sole purview of the government.

In order to prepare for this eventuality, the public may have to be partially brought into the black box of national security. The benefits of bringing the people into the process of securitisation are threefold. Firstly, by drawing the people in further up the process, they can gain a better appreciation, or, to employ the parlance of management consultants, gain or achieve "buy-in" into what is being done for them, why it is being done and also be convinced that everything that can be done is being done. Secondly, security agencies too will profit from an expansion of the number of people involved in the securitisation process. Since globalisation continually churns out new challenges and threats, it would be sensible to utilise the "views from the ground" in order to pick up weak signals of impending but yet overlooked threats and concerns with repercussions for national security. At the very least, the process of fresh views challenging old orthodoxies while not overturning them will serve as an exercise in refreshment of what may have become stale, unquestioned dogma. Thirdly, and perhaps most importantly, the drawing in of the people at a much earlier stage of the securitisation process may strengthen the social compact. Instead of treating national security in a service provider/consumer relationship, national security can then be better understood by all as something everyone has a stake in. Additionally, the public will also better understand the limitations of government and have a more nuanced appreciation of national security.

This call for greater inclusion of the public into the process of securitisation will possibly meet greatest resistance from security agencies owing to the need for operational secrecy. Although admittedly important, operational secrecy should not and does not have to override greater inclusion upstream in the process. In his analysis of the impact of excessive secrecy in undermining the capacity of governments to perform their mission of enhancing national security, Alasdair Roberts argues that contrary to conventional wisdom, a move towards openness in the security sector may actually improve the capacity of societies to preserve security by (1) promoting better policy decisions; (2) improving agency coordination; and (3) fighting bureaucratic inertia.[70] However, Roberts does not argue against the abolition of secrecy in the security sector per se. Instead, he proposes that the bar for withholding information in the name of "national security" should be set high. He proposes two "critical elements' to be observed by the security sector in decisions to withhold information. Firstly, he argues that the standards for withholding security information should be rigorous as a law that requires "a mere apprehension of possible harm is likely to be abused".[71] Hence the onus should be on officials to substantiate that the disclosure of information would pose a serious security threat to public scrutiny. Secondly, he contends that decisions to withhold information on security grounds should be subject to effective review by an independent office for three pertinent reasons. These are: (1) it serves to encourage officials to make their initial decisions about disclosure more carefully; (2) it keeps in check the temptation of agencies to use national security as a pretext for avoiding embarrassment or accountability for misconduct; and (3) the process of independent review encourages public discussion about where the line should be drawn between secrecy and openness.[72]

Ultimately, illustrative of the amount of effort put in by Singaporean national security agencies, it is heartening that an assessment of the management of national security in Singapore has not revealed a fatal flaw that will cause sleepless, uneasy nights. Instead, the analysis here has shown that the Singaporean government has indeed done a sterling job at identifying and responding to threats to national security since the point of independence. However, if Singapore is to meet the threats of the future successfully, security should not be left solely in the hands of the dedicated few. The process of securitisation should become more open to include the participation of the many in order for the burden of responsibility to be shared by all.*

Notes

[1] Globalisation here is understood as a process marked by its velocity, intensity and extentsity. This process has lead to the expansion of national security concerns as states now have to contend with border porosity as faster and cheaper movement (velocity) increases the speed of flow of, for example, ideas, people, material goods and diseases; this interaction is occurring at significantly deeper and more intense levels than ever

---

* A version of this chapter has appeared in Norman Vasu and Bernard Loo, "National Security and Singapore: An Assessment," in Terence Chong (ed.), *Management of Success: Singapore Revisited* (Singapore: Institute of Southeast Asian Studies, 2010). The chapter has been updated for this contribution.

before (intensity) through, for example, a more integrated world economy as well as the creation of an international labour market; and finally, the reach of this interaction is wider than it has ever been (extensity). Hence, if one considers diseases, the process of globalisation now threatens interconnected states as its spread is fast, it has multiple ways of reaching large segments of society and no state is fully insulated from its spread. D. Held, A. McGrew, D. Goldblatt and J. Perranton, *Global Transformations: Politics, Economics and Culture* (London: Polity Press, 1999).

[2] For example, see Kumar Ramakrishna, Norman Vasu and Tom Quiggin, "Iconic Soft Targets: Public Housing Estates, Terrorism and Social Resilience," *IDSS Commentaries* (Singapore: Institute of Defence and Strategic Studies, 2006).

[3] Thomas Hobbes, *Leviathan* (London: Penguin Books, 1985), p. 186.

[4] S. Neil MacFarlane and Yuen Foong Khong, *Human Security and the UN: A Critical History* (Indiana: Indiana University Press, 2006), p. 6.

[5] For instance, see Desmond Ball, *Strategic Culture in the Asia-Pacific Region (with Some Implications for Regional Security Cooperation)* (Canberra: SDSC, 1993); Ken Booth, *Strategy and Ethnocentrism* (London: Croom Helm, 1979); Ken Booth and Russell Trood (eds.), *Strategic Cultures in the Asia-Pacific Region* (New York: St. Martin's Press, 1999); Colin S. Gray, *Nuclear Strategy and National Style* (London and Lanham: Hamilton Press, 1986); Carl G. Jacobsen (ed.), *Strategic Power: USA/USSR* (Basingstoke and London: MacMillan, 1990), pp. 10–49; Carnes Lord, "American Strategic Culture," *Comparative Strategy*, 5(3), Spring 1995, pp. 269–93; Alan Macmillan, *Strategic Culture and British Grand Strategy 1945-1952*, PhD Thesis, University of Wales, Aberystwyth, 1996; and David T. Twining, "Soviet Strategic Culture — The Missing Dimension," *Intelligence and National Security*, 4(1), January 1989, pp. 169–87.

[6] Alastair Iain Johnston, *Cultural Realism: Strategic Culture and Grand Strategy in Chinese History* (Princeton, NJ: Princeton University Press, 1995), pp. 35–36.

[7] For instance, see Lowell Dittmer, "Political Culture and Political Symbolism," *World Politics*, 29(4), 1977, pp. 552–83; Bradley S. Klein, "Hegemony and Strategic Culture: American Power Projection and Alliance Defence Politics," *Review of International Studies*, 14(2), 1988, pp. 133–48; Robin Luckham, "Armament Culture," *Alternatives*, 10(1), 1984, pp. 1–44; Reginald C. Stuart, *War and American Thought: From the Revolution to the Monroe Doctrine* (Ohio: Ohio University Press, 1982).

[8] Valerie M. Hudson (ed.), *Culture and Foreign Policy* (Boulder & London: Westview, 1997), p. 101; Peter J. Katzenstein (ed.), *The Culture of National Security: Norms and Identity in World Politics* (New York: Columbia University Press, 1996), pp. 54–65; Charles A. Kupchan,. *The Vulnerability of Empire* (Ithaca and London: Cornell University Press, 1994), pp. 5–22.

[9] Eric Herring, *Danger of Opportunity: Explaining International Crises Outcomes* (Manchester and New York: Manchester University Press, 1995); Yaacov Y. I. Vertzberger, *The World in Their Minds: Information Processing, Cognition, and Perception in Foreign Policy Decisionmaking* (Stanford: Stanford University Press, 1990), pp. 50–144.

[10] Yuen Foong Khong, *Analogies at War: Korea, Munich, Dien Bien Phu, and the Vietnam Decisions of 1965* (Oxford and Princeton: Princeton University Press, 1992); Jack L. Snyder,

The Ideology of the Offensive: Military Decision-Making and the Disasters of 1914 (Ithaca and London: Cornell University Press, 1984).

[11] Kupchan (1994), *op. cit.*, p. 41; Vertzberger (1990), *op. cit.*, pp. 50–144.

[12] Hudson (1997), *op. cit.*, pp. 1–26, 174.

[13] *Ibid.*, p. 7.

[14] Kupchan (1994), *op. cit.*, p. 22.

[15] *Ibid.*, pp. 22–23.

[16] Daniel Johan Goldhagen, *Hitler's Willing Executioners: Ordinary Germans and the Holocaust* (London: Abacus, 1996), pp. 28–34; Kupchan (1994), *op. cit.*, p. 41; Twining (1989), *op. cit.*, p. 177.

[17] Asher Arian, *Security Threatened: Surveying Israeli Opinion on Peace and War* (Tel Aviv: Tel Aviv University, 1995), pp. 24–25.

[18] Alasdiar Roberts, "Transparency in the Security Sector," in Ann Florini (ed.), *The Right to Know* (New York: Coumbia University Press, 2007), p. 311.

[19] Tim Huxley, *Defending the Lion City: The Armed Forces of Singapore* (Singapore: Talisman Publishing, 2004), p. 16.

[20] Jon S. T. Quah, "Meeting the Twin Threats of Communism and Communalism: The Singapore Response," in Chandran Jeshurun (ed.), *Governments and Rebellions in Southeast Asia* (Singapore: Institute of Southeast Asian Studies, 1985), p. 210; Huxley (2004), *op. cit.*, pp. 14–16.

[21] Lee Kuan Yew, *From Third World to First: The Singapore Story* (Singapore: Times Edition, 2000), p. 22.

[22] Bernard Loo, "Explaining Changes in Singapore's Military Doctrines: Material and Ideational Perspectives," in Amitav Acharya and Lee Lai To (eds.), *Asia in the New Millenium* (Singapore: Marshall Cavendish Academic, 2004), p. 365.

[23] Singapore has a cap to defence spending of 6% of GDP. Through the 1990s onwards, spending on defence has continually matched or exceeded the military expenditure of its much larger Southeast Asian neighbours. For more on Singapore's defence spending, refer to Huxley (2004), *op. cit.*, pp. 27–30.

[24] National Security Coordination Centre (Singapore), *The Fight against Terror: Singapore's National Security Strategy* (Singapore: Atlas Associates Pte Ltd 2004), p. 27.

[25] Goh Chok Tong, "Forward," in Felix Soh, *Phoenix: The Story of the Home Team* (Singapore: Times Edition, 2003).

[26] *The Fight against Terror* (2004), *op. cit.*, pp. 19–20.

[27] *Ibid.*, p. 27.

[28] *Ibid.*, p. 7.

[29] Alfred Siew, "Fighting Terrorism: ISD to Get More Money and Men," *The Straits Times*, 10 April 2007, p. 25.

[30] Ho Khai Leong, *Shared Responsibility, Unshared Power* (Singapore: Eastern University Press, 2003).

[31] For a discussion on the defence policy-making process, refer to the chapter "Command and Control" in Huxley (2004), *op. cit.*, pp. 73–92.

[32] Quah (1985), *op. cit.*, p. 207.

[33] Chin Kin Wah, "Threat Perception and Defence Spending in a City-State," in Chin Kin Wah (ed.), *Defence Spending in Southeast Asia* (Singapore: Institute of Southeast Asian Studies, 1987), p. 203.

[34] *Ibid.*, p. 205.

[35] Ho (2003), *op. cit.*, p. 233.

[36] Chin Kin Wah and Leo Suryadinata (eds.), *Michael Leifer, Selected Works from Southeast Asia* (Singapore: Institute of Southeast Asian Studies, 2005), p. 550.

[37] *The Fight against Terror* (2004), *op. cit.*, p. 59.

[38] *Defending Singapore in the 21st Century* (Singapore: Ministry of Defence, 2007), p. 13. Retrieved 28 December 2014, from http://www.mindef.gov.sg/dam/publications/eBooks/More_eBooks/ds21.pdf.

[39] *Ibid.*

[40] Speech by Mr Teo Chee Hean, Minister for Defence, at Committee of Supply Debate on Defence Budget, 5 March 2007. Retrieved 29 May 2015, from http://www.mindef.gov.sg/imindef/press_room/official_releases/nr/2007/mar/05mar07_nr.html#.VWfKaUYvyjw.

[41] Quoted in Chin (1987), *op. cit.*, pp. 203–204.

[42] Ho (2003), *op. cit.*, pp. 306–307.

[43] Thio Li-Ann, "The Secular Trumps the Sacred: Constitutional Issues Arising from Colin Chan v Public Prosecutor," *Singapore Law Review*, 16(1), 1995, pp. 83–84.

[44] *Ibid.*

[45] Speech by Mr Wong Kan Seng, Deputy Prime Minister and Minister for Home Affairs at the ISD Intelligence Promotion Ceremony on 9 April 2007. Retrieved 16 December 2014, from http://www.mha.gov.sg/news_details.aspx?nid=NTA2-bGv3a7NWYz8%3d.

[46] Written answer to parliamentary question on (1) how many persons are currently detained under the ISA; (2) how many persons were detained under the ISA for each of the years between the period of 1999 to 2007; and (3) what was the nature of the threat to internal security posed by those detained since 1999. Retrieved 14 December 2014, from http://www.mha.gov.sg/news_details.aspx?nid=NTA4-2cM6XVSEep8%3d.

[47] "Summary of the Deliberations of the Subject Committees to the Singapore 21 Committee." Retrieved 27 February 2008, from http://www.singapore21.org.sg/menu_subcom.html.

[48] Quek Soo Beng, "Examine the Old Sacred Cow of Defence Spending," *The Straits Times*, 27 January 2007, p. 67.

[49] *Ibid.*

[50] *Ibid.*

[51] Speech by Mr Teo Chee Hean, Minister for Defence, at Committee of Supply Debate on Defence Budget, 5 March 2007, *op. cit.*

[52] Beng (2007), *op. cit.*

53 The extracts were cited by the Defence Minister in his speech. Lu Junwen, "Arms Unused? Money Well-Spent on Deterrence," *The Straits Times*, 12 February 2007, p. 28; Xiao Fuchun, "Hefty Spending on Defence Justified," *The Straits Times*, 30 January 2007, p. 31.

54 From the Total Defence website. Retrieved 6 December 2014, from http://www. totaldefence.sg/imindef/mindef_websites/topics/totaldefence/about_td.html.

55 Lee Boon Hiok, "Leadership and Security in Singapore: The Prevailing Paradigm," in Mohammed Ayoob and Chai-anan Samudavanija (eds.), *Leadership Perceptions and National Security* (Singapore: Institute of Southeast Asian Studies, 1989), p. 173.

56 Survey findings quoted in *ibid*.

57 National Security Coordination Secretariat (Singapore), *1826 Days: A Diary of Resolve: Securing Singapore since 9/11* (Singapore: SNP Reference, 2006), p. 12.

58 *Ibid.*, p. 56.

59 *Ibid.*

60 *Ibid.*

61 *Ibid.*

62 *Ibid.*, p. 58; The Intelligence Coordinating Committee (ICC) "analyses developments in terrorism-related issues and trends, and provides strategic direction to the Joint Counter Terrorism Centre (JCTC)". *Ibid.*, p. 57.

63 *Ibid.*, p. 58.

64 *Ibid.*

65 *Ibid.*, p. 8. Details of the various measures to harden Singapore's key infrastructure is covered in the section on "Securing Singapore," pp. 18–53.

66 *Ibid.*, pp. 8–9.

67 *Ibid.*, pp. 72–85.

68 These predictably unpredictable events are sometimes referred to as "wild cards". For more on wild cards, see for example, Joanna Ng and Hoo Tiang Boon, "A Brief Look at the 'Wild' Side," *Cognito*, 2008, S. Rajaratnam School of International Studies, Singapore.

69 An interesting insight into the disappointment that would be felt if the public are let down during Crisis X may be found in the public reaction to the escape of JI leader Mas Selamat Kastari from a maximum security prison in Singapore on 27 February 2008. *The Straits Times* online edition captured the disappointment well with an article summarising the public's reaction to the escape titled "Escape of JI leader: How Can This Happen in S'pore?". With quotes from the public such as "How can we feel safe anymore?", "Please, Home Affairs Minister, say something or more importantly, DO something!" and "The whole Singapore is waiting for an answer", these reactions may offer some idea of how the public would react if a major unforeseen crisis occurs. Retrieved 28 February 2014, from http://www.straitstimes.com/Latest%2BNews/ Singapore/STIStory_211368.html.

70 Roberts (2007), *op. cit.*, pp. 309–336.

71 *Ibid.*, p. 327.

72 *Ibid.*

Chapter 3

Deliquescent Security Threats: Singapore in the Era of Hyper-Globalisation

Alan Chong

Singapore's security paradigm in the 2000s is an experiment in progress. Pre-existing doctrines expressed as extensions of deterrence or of locking down homeland security are increasingly anachronistic, even if the government of Singapore maintains that they are not irrelevant. Instead, this chapter proposes that Singapore has entered the phase of deliquescent security. What is to be protected and the source of the threat are both mobile and existential, even embedded in the design of taken-for-granted flows of labour, tourism, trade, finance and information. The object and referent of security under globalising conditions are therefore liquid; they dissolve, or exist in a latent state, until ignited by a confluence of flows that challenge the very essence of a Singaporean national identity. This is what I label the deliquescent security paradigm. Incidentally, it can only come into existence following the cumulative effects of conventional external security and domestic security against revolutionary subversion. Conventional external security presupposes a visible and deterrable enemy, armed with tanks, aircraft and a recognisable army threatening to cross one's borders with impunity. If the enemy attacks one's territory with non-uniformed "volunteers" and *agents provocateur* hidden in legitimate political parties and other social organisations, then deterrence fails to address the root of the threat. As Richard Clutterbuck put it in one of the earliest studies of Singapore's domestic security contextualised during the Cold War, the threat was revolution from within. It was a Leninist stratagem: "an attempt to gain control of student and labour organisations and of a leading political party…; the process being assisted by strikes, student demonstrations and riots."[1] Clutterbuck also correctly appraised Singapore's mostly urban context for domestic security: "City people live from week to week, relying for next week's food on work, wages and a continuing system of wholesale and retail distribution; they also fear the failure of public services, such as water, sewerage, electric power and transport; they therefore have a vested interest in law and order; faced by chaos and a choice between two claimants to power, they will rally to the one which gives them most confidence of a return to normal life — as the Bolsheviks did in Petrograd in 1917."[2] The point about urban destabilisation is relevant to this chapter in the sense that by 1965, given the successive waves of urbanisation of the transient population fostered by British colonialism, the nascent Singaporean population has gradually evolved the desire for a multifaceted security that transcends the mere protection of borders. Even during the Cold War, as Clutterbuck pointedly suggests, there was already a yearning for system security, supply security, occupational security and governmental legitimacy. The communists were a viable rival to the People's Action Party (PAP) government insofar as they were promising the mostly urban population stability in their lives and a secure identity in living in a modernising city-state.

Colonial Transitions

Before the chapter gets to sketch and analyse the present outlines of deliquescent security, a revisiting of the colonial impact in securitising Singapore is relevant in fully appreciating the cumulative arrival of the deliquescent security para-digm. In the many accounts of the founding of Singapore, the story is told by mainstream historians that "after its destruction in the fourteenth century the old settlement [of Singapura] became so much waste land, a site for the huts of Proto-Malayan sea-gypsies … In the eighteenth century, the *batin* seems to have regarded himself as a local noble of the Riau Court; in the nineteenth century, he did not follow the fortunes of Sultan Husain and the *Temenggong*, played no part in the cession of the island to Sir Stamford Raffles and disappeared from local politics in Singapore. But his vassals, the sea-gypsies, constituted themselves into a sort of *imperium in imperio* under the British and referred their petty disputes for settlement to their own headman and (as a final authority) to the head of the family of Sultan Husain…".[3] In an indigenous account of the joint actions of Thomas Stamford Raffles (founder) and Colonel William Farquhar (the First Resident) in governing the early settlement, Munshi Abdullah, a Malay intellectual and translator for the British, noted that the immediate effect of the British delivering security was to generate a climate of law and order within the distinct jurisdiction of British expectations. The following lengthy quotation is therefore needful for its illustration of how this depiction of the circumstances necessitating a policing authority over unruly local circumstances has continued to haunt Singapore's conceptualisations of security:

> All the inhabitants were dismayed by frequent incidents, houses catching fire, robberies taking place in the high noon, people getting stabbed. When morning came people would be found stabbed and wounded to death. The *Temeng-gong's* men, the Sultan's men and the foreigners of all races went about fully armed; some of them robbed people in broad daylight, some broke into houses and stole people's property, for they were afraid of nothing. *For the settlement was not yet on a sure footing, the number of white men was not yet large, Indian troops had not come out and there were only four or five policemen.* Every day it was the *Temenggong's* men who started brawls, for their attitude towards the Malacca men was like that of tigers towards goats. The Malacca men were unarmed, knew nothing of dagger tactics, and had never seen bloodshed. In any kind of clash between the Malacca-born, whether Chinese, Malays, or Indians, and the *Temeggong's* men Colonel Farquhar always took the side of the former for he realized that their nature made them shy of fighting with weapons, but that when it came to using fists none of the other races could stand up to them. The two sides were always at loggerheads, and on many occasions violent quarrels flared up between them, not individual combats but free-for-all fights, when a man of one side harboured a grievance against a man of the other. *If they had not all been afraid of Colonel Farquhar they would have gone on killing each other every day without stopping* (emphasis added).[4]

One immediate impression that can be derived from this long quote is that a strong neutral arbiter was needed to overawe everyone and keep the peace. All of the locals were partisan towards one another, living as some political theorists would put it, in a Hobbesian state of nature. Secondly, racial harmony was not a given in this hastily acquired trading settlement. Thirdly, as I have highlighted in italics, the White Man, representing the arrival of Anglo-modernity and scientific superiority was the one who ultimately deterred criminal behaviour by acting as the civilising outsider. What has this snapshot got to do with Singapore's security in the 21st century? Security in Singapore evolved as an act of modernisation through territoriality and legal intermediation represented by the British colonial proto-state. The plural "Chinese, Malays, or Indians, and the Temeggong's men" had coexisted without the organising structure of an arbitrating state that could be erected on the ground of impartiality to sit in judgment on the rights and wrongs of interpersonal, intracommunity and interethnic disputes. This excerpt also legitimised the coming of the White coloniser as a superior model of civilisation in very uncritical terms. It also implied that until the external intervener arrived on the scene, modern law and order did not exist on the island. Of course, as I have argued elsewhere, a reading of precolonial texts from the Malay World suggests that justice in a borderless, fluid population environment was obtained through the practice of enlightened rulers and unwritten social customs.[5] Modern law and order, however, necessitated a written body of law and a Weberian, impersonal statehood.

As Kay Gillis' work on colonial power and the roles of the nascent Singaporean civil society from the mid-1800s to the 1940s has showed, Britain's governors and high officials hewed closely to a strictly territorial frame of jurisdiction that allowed some degree of lobbying by associations of merchants, ethnic groups, revolutionary movements and cultural associations.[6] But this early British experience has retrospectively also shed light on the governance of Singapore's security under globalising conditions. If we understand globalisation as both the process of, and agency in, the social and political awareness of the perforation of geographical boundaries in labour, information, transportation, finance, trade and pathogenic contagion, then the arrival of the non-native British colonial rulers was an incipient form of globalisation upon Singapore's shores.[7] As outsiders, the British introduced the earliest strands of an impersonal, legal regime based on the letter. It was a subtle imposition in the name of securing a trading spot for the erstwhile British East India Company. Raffles and Farquhar were its agents, and the advent of modern Singapore inherited their modern designs for a territorial and constitutional state that would arbitrate amongst ethnic and social diversity.

Complex Globalisation-Induced Pressures Produce Insecurity

The comprehension of Singapore's entry into the era of deliquescent security ought therefore to begin with the introduction of complex social relations since the British arrival in 1819 and continues to add diversity through the flows of foreign talent, disease, information and trade into Singapore in the 2000s. The net result of these successive waves of globalisation is what geographers of globalisation label "a *pot pourri* of stories".[8] The "world coming to Singapore" is no longer abstract like exotic travellers' tales, they are real and play out in Singaporean neighbourhoods. Foreign accents, fashions and attitudes take root amidst the local landscape and test Singaporeans' tolerance and openness to embracing these new dimensions. In these ways, Singaporeans' sense of security is no longer strictly territorial in terms of the colonial inheritance. It is nonetheless also an insecurity that derives from how lifestyles and attitudes often challenge, even militate against, pre-existing territorial arrangements. Above all, Singaporeans have yet to accept that globalisation's mobility dimension is not always consistent with a nationalistically-inspired territoriality. Sociologist Zygmunt Bauman has warned that the human consequences of modernity-as-globalisation has stratified society into the categories of voluntary travellers, or cosmopolitans by choice, and the involuntary travellers who are compelled to migrate on leaky overcrowded fishing boats, stowaways on freighters and trains, and those who are systematically driven to seek greener economic pastures abroad by dire misgovernment at home.[9] Therefore, the well-heeled tourist, exchange student, hedge fund investor, corporate investor, Chief Executive Officer, industry professional and retired senior living off a substantial pension are the bigger beneficiaries of globalisation while the menial construction worker, factory hand or domestic helper from Indonesia, the Philippines, South Asia, Africa and Latin America seeks to join the labour flows of a global economy because of economic desperation. These macro-drivers of globalisation impact Singaporean administrative territoriality immediately in terms of ramping up pressures on living space, common social spaces, administrative culture shocks, social expectations, welfare provisions, the human rights climate in general and competition for jobs.[10] Moreover, other scholars of globalisation point to the availability to Singaporeans of alternative lifestyle choices, alternative geographies of imagining community outside of a state-constructed "Singaporeanness", and the alteration of loyalties in consonance with amended social landscapes of work and leisure. One can, in the Singaporean context, contrast the Singaporean who lives in a fashionable condominium in Singapore and commutes regularly to Bangkok, London, Shanghai and Sydney for work, and another who works in the manufacturing sector locally who perceives his workplace as an unlevelled playing ground where Filipinos, South Asians and "China Chinese" workers have replaced most of his junior and middle-management colleagues. In both cases, the Singaporean is constantly worried about how his "rice bowl" is no longer guaranteed by the orthodox formula of "hard work, long hours, compliance and thrift". Instead, transnational ethnic kinship networks and "cheaper, faster" employees transform Singaporean employability. In these ways, new dimensions of security emerge.

The Singaporean is least likely to worry about a military invasion from a Southeast Asian neighbour. He or she is more worried about social, economic and cognitive dissonance in a once familiar homeland where the ruling PAP continues to foster official campaigns of demonstrating pride in a "Singaporean heartbeat" in songs, parades and media productions. The "enemy" is invisible and modular: it could be the liberal open door economic policy that accelerates economic growth measured by GDP and GNP; it could be the "speed" of globalising everything in organisational cultures, learning and seizing opportunities in the global economy; it could be the fear of violence arising from a fundamentalist religious revival emanating from another continent; or it could be a hangover of the neocolonial reverence for the "White Man's superiority" in business, management and science. Political scientist James Rosenau has of course labelled these fears as "turbulence" along the domestic–foreign frontier when borders are no longer effectively policed when national governments make it an article of good policy to open borders wide for the beneficial effects of global flows.[11]

At this point it is relevant to briefly quote Gayatri Spivak on the postcolonial dangers of riding the gravy train of globalisation while being blind to its potential exploitation:

> [I]n countries which are recognized as Third World countries, there is a great deal of oppression, class oppression, sex oppression, going on in terms of the collusion between comprador capitalists and that very white world. The international division of labour does not operate in terms of good whites, bad whites, and blacks. A simple chromatism [i.e., a stark, black-and-white perspective] obliges you to be blind to this particular issue because once again it is present in excess. I was trying to show how our lives, even as we produce this chromatist discourse of anti-racism, are being constructed by that international division of labour, and its latest manifestations were in fact the responsibility of class-differentiated non-white people in the Third World, using the indigenous structures of patriarchy and the established structures of capitalism.[12]

This quote must be contextualised as relevant to Singapore insofar as this country made the leap from Third World to First in one generation and yet retains vestiges of its original starting point. Additionally, Singapore's developmental policies have been astoundingly successful due perhaps in large part to the overriding need to be hospitable to "globalisation as Westernisation" to a fault. Borrowing from the preceding insights and critiques of globalisation theory, it is therefore necessary to unpack deliquescent security in Singapore's context in terms of social stratification; the imposition of cultures from abroad; the forcible sanitisation of globalisation; and the risks of global interconnectedness. The illustrative cases to be briefly scrutinised in this chapter include the SARS crisis of 2003, the politicisation of the entry of foreign talent into Singapore, the self-radicalisation of certain segments of the Muslim citizenry by terrorist propaganda, and the Little India riot of 2013. Once again, the treatment of these illustrations can only be brief since my main purpose is to articulate the idea of a deliquescent security frontier in and around Singapore. These cases were also chosen on the basis that they were also quintessential deliquescent security threats facing Singapore in the 21st century.

The SARS Crisis of 2003

As an open economy regularly ranked by various economic intelligence agencies among the top five most globalised states in the world, Singapore was naturally vulnerable to pathogenic contagion. Interestingly, Singapore's indices of globalisation often included measures of foreign tourist traffic and labour entry, as well as the number of cities and ports with which it was connected by scheduled air and sea transport. The Severe Acute Respiratory Syndrome (SARS) was a contagion that was made into a global pandemic by the forces of globalisation: human travellers, mass air travel, droplet infection and transmission by physical contact, and seemingly most transmissible in high density population centres. Singapore's own patient zero, Esther Mok, was on holiday in Hong Kong when she was infected by a doctor from Guangdong province staying in the same hotel. The symptoms included prolonged fever, coughing, breathing difficulties, lung infections and extreme lethargy. These symptoms too were common to a number of known and curable common maladies such as the common flu and pneumonia, but unlike the latter two, SARS had no known cure. It was worse that scientists had insufficiently studied it and had to learn about its mode of transmission as the outbreak intensified. It was alarming that Ms Mok directly infected 22 people upon returning to Singapore. Consequently, a grand total of 238 people were infected through secondary infections. Although the majority were cured by normal anti-flu drugs, some 33 died, including Ms Mok's parents, uncle and pastor.[13]

The immediate impact was obviously interpersonal in terms of social stratification, then it was economic in threatening global flows of labour and tourists to Singapore. Just as importantly, the Singapore model of governance through strict law and order practices came under intense media scrutiny. Singapore's environmental safety image would have come under dire threat if personal hygiene practices were proven to be a significant source of infection. Social stratification manifested in the fear that paralysed human contact amongst Singaporeans. Self-protection meant keeping a safe distance from people in the streets and workplaces exhibiting flu-like symptoms, and worse, keeping well away from healthcare workers. If necessary, most Singaporeans worked from home or minimised activities in common spaces. Food handling, area cleaning and other hygiene came under intense scrutiny in a campaign designed to "sanitise" the country and its economy to assure both

Singaporeans, tourists and investors that the country was "fighting SARS" as if it were "total war". Government ministers launched sub-themed campaigns such as "SARS-free corridors", "temperature checked badges", "Singapore OK" and even an anti-SARS rap song to get Singaporeans to cooperate with the national effort.[14] Premier Goh Chok Tong ordered his cabinet to get various economic promotion agencies, such as the Economic Development Board, to brief key foreign MNC officials and the Chambers of Commerce on anti-SARS measures in the country. More controversially, the authorities implemented the "tough love" approach of Home Quarantine Orders served on both actual and suspected SARS patients in unoccupied housing board flats and even at a trade union operated holiday resort. To top it all, Premier Goh's team persuaded ASEAN states, China and Hong Kong to meet in Thailand to agree to economic assurance measures to keep their economies open for business, especially with regard to keeping airlines operating, shipping ports open, and tourists and investors travelling. In this regard, the Singapore government willingly co-opted an idea hatched by local and foreign scientists to deploy hospital grade thermal scanners at land, sea and air ports of entry to screen travellers showing symptoms of fever — a key characteristic of SARS. Meanwhile, Singapore's entire biomedical community and industry were voluntarily cooperating to develop a SARS test kit and mapping the virus prior to finding an antidote. In the meantime, it helped that systematically administered conventional anti-flu drugs coupled with a patient's highly variable built-in resistance were reducing fatalities to under 20% of those confirmed to have been infected.

Therefore, SARS, the globalisation-assisted disease was reduced to a matter of filtering out "bad global flows" and treated medically. What is relevant for our analysis of deliquescent security is the fact that SARS proved to be a threat that pervaded Singaporean society without direct evidence of border violations and that it called attention to structural factors of human security, such as the validation of personal human hygiene and public communication efforts to clarify the nature of the rapidly spreading fears. Finally, SARS was also a plague upon the global economy of air travel, mass tourism and economic interdependence. Singapore's government had to immediately initiate an international regime to assure its partner economies of its probity in tackling an unknown disease and to put in place detection measures to sanitise the "bad global flow" of the SARS coronavirus. Most importantly, the Western centres of economic and social intelligence abroad had to be assured of Singapore's economic viability under extreme medical crisis. The World Health Organization, the German Chancellor, and the American Chamber of Commerce recognised

Singapore's "whole of government and society" approach as being faster and more thorough than any other member of the international community.[15]

The Politicisation of the Entry of Foreign Talent into Singapore

On another front, population policy in the era of extreme globalisation has reached unprecedented levels of politicisation in Singapore, and therefore has constituted a new flank for defining national security. The official explanation is derived scientifically in a threefold manner. Firstly, an ageing population and the reduction in the total fertility rate will shrink the workforce significantly from 2020 onwards. Secondly, the reduction in the numbers of Singaporean citizens and permanent residents could threaten national cohesion and well-being as knock-on effects. Thirdly, the Singapore government anticipates significant volatility in employment and painful occupational adjustments given the current pace of technological change and globalisation.[16] The government's solution, as echoed by an aligned think tank, reads as follows: adopt a balanced inflow of migrants to plug gaps in Singapore's manpower needs without jeopardising national cohesion; strengthen manpower, education and industrial policy to prepare Singaporeans to adapt to a volatile global economy constantly demanding skill revolutions and reinventing industries; and enhance safety nets for the aged and economically vulnerable amidst high volatility.[17]

This demand and supply rationality has proven to be profoundly upsetting to the ground realities of Singaporean society. Insecurities have arisen with regard to social stratification. The Singaporean university graduate is vastly more nimble in both working with, and competing with, immigrant talent than the semi-skilled and polytechnic-trained. Moreover, the initially liberal admission of semi-skilled and highly-skilled foreign talent had altered the incentives for hiring Singaporeans in the labour market at home. Aside from the desire by Singaporean workers to command higher salaries in order to keep pace with inflation and attain the nationalistically-inspired "Singaporean middle class dream" of a condominium, car, cash, country club membership, career and bringing up children, Singaporean workers have been perceived by a number of private sector employers to be unwilling to build up the necessary social skills to operate in a multinational work environment and to improve their linguistic capabilities to operate across a number of Asian economies. On the other hand, a number of foreign workers from both developed and developing states have shown a willingness to accept lower salaries vis-à-vis Singaporeans in exchange for longer-term job security. Moreover, kinship networks amongst certain Asian nationalities have operated to bias recruitment of employees from within their closed circles to the exclusion of comparably skilled Singaporeans.

These issues were heavily politicised during the general and presidential elections that took place in 2011. This prompted a PAP Member of Parliament, who was also a director in the government-linked National Trades Union Congress, to argue the need for labour means testing so as to rein in employers who were not giving Singaporean workers fair consideration in hiring. The Member of Parliament expressed the insecurity in this way: "anecdotal evidence suggests that the problem is particularly acute for mature PMEs (professionals, managers and executives) above 40 years. These are the ones who have the most difficulty finding work when they are displaced."[18] A Fair Consideration Framework was legislated by parliament as a result. The work permit approvals for some categories of low-skilled and some highly-skilled foreigners were also reduced. Nearly one year later, the government announced that it had identified more than 50 firms with "too few Singaporean professionals" and that it was setting up a jobs bank to ensure that employers should advertise jobs for Singaporeans first before opening them up to foreigners. The government had also declared that discriminatory hiring practices biased against Singaporeans were most widespread in the banking, services and information technology sectors.[19] The same report noted that the Minister for Manpower tried to calm the nerves of foreign investors with existing investments in Singapore, assuring them that no further curbs were likely to be implemented. To this assurance, the Chief Executive of the Singapore International Chamber of Commerce, Philip Overmyer voiced his approval of the PAP government's calibrated response to the Singaporean public's labour anxieties.[20]

This prolonged uneasiness of Singaporeans over the admission of foreign talent goes to show that global flows introduce tremendous side effects into national labour markets. There is now significant social polarisation between the Singaporean worker and his foreign counterpart who has now emerged in the popular imagination as an economic threat. This foreign talent threatens Singaporean jobs even while it substantiates the government's macro-economic claim that high economic growth rates can only be healthily sustained with large injections of foreign talent. There is therefore a second level of fear atop the first: there appears to be a psychological disconnection between the government's scientific management of borderless flows of foreign manpower and the physical and mental discomforts experienced by the average Singaporean. The PAP state has appeared — most strongly in the perception of those Singaporeans who had suffered from discriminatory hiring practices — as bending excessively to accommodate the needs of foreign capital at the expense of its own nationalist rhetoric over the past three decades. Indeed, if one scans the various controversies over workplace discrimination against Singaporeans reported on blogs, there appears to be a worrying trend of xenophobia that is increasingly driving Singaporeans to vote for opposition parties willing to give voice to their protests against an inequitable globalisation that has deeply dented the aspirations of the Singaporean middle class. As some scholars put it, the PAP's pandering to the need to harness the global economy has produced a scenario where popular insecurities arise from pursuing pragmatism over culture.[21]

Transnational Terrorism Erodes Sovereign Security

Singapore has also encountered the terrorist fallout from others' civil conflicts since independence. It was a direct by-product of globalisation that other people's struggles for their respective political causes sought to involve Singapore as either a target or a convenient location from which to stage a dramatic political act. Terrorism is always an act of political publicity intended to dramatise a particular plight or to convey a vivid form of anger. In this sense, Singapore was a legitimate target by extension of its deliberate enmeshment in global capitalism. Additionally, it is in the nature of terrorist plots to pick either a soft target, in the sense that it offers less resistance to armed attacks due to lax security, or select a proxy in substitution for a primary target; or to choose a counter-intuitive target of commensurate political value in order to show up the enemy's defences even further. In this sense, many pre-existing reflections on Singapore's counter-terrorism and national security strategies evade deeper analysis in conjunction with globalisation. These mainstream analyses postulate Singaporean security agencies' operational readiness, vigilance in patrolling and the reiteration of the Republic's long-standing "Total Defence" national strategy.[22] Total Defence is supposed to provide the doctrinal roadmap for integrating political, psychological, social, economic and military defences in a harmonious "whole-of-government" approach that is partnered with a vision of a "cohesive multiracial, multi-religious population" standing united in the face of threats to the collective nation.[23]

Transnational terrorism of the post-9/11 form of fundamentalist Islamic networks of shadow warriors and "lone wolf" jihadists challenge Singaporean national security because it poses a sharp ideological challenge to the sovereign boundaries that the Singaporean nation- and state-building projects have tried to protect since independence in 1965.[24] Fundamentalist Islamist terror groups ply their appeal by openly polarising the nascent global society into believers and "infidels". Muslims everywhere, according to this construction, need to return to a pastoral and disciplined past in order to correct the injustices of the present global order, whether it is poverty, exploitation or insults vented by secular Western modernity against the legacies of Prophet Mohammed. For the citizens of Singapore, it is actually a struggle of rationalising how local and rival Islamic universal beliefs should coexist. The theological struggle for Malay Muslims lies within intrareligious debate. This is surely an aspect of ideational globalisation that cannot be contained comprehensively within sovereign Singaporean frontiers. This much is even conceded by then-Prime Minister Goh Chok Tong and reiterated by his successor.[25] Multiple interviews with officials involved in religious rehabilitation and counter-terrorist experts connected with the Singapore government suggest that it is very much an ideological war of religious interpretation.

Additionally, Singapore's police, military and intelligence agencies have been saddled with the monumental task of securing globalisation against Al-Qaeda, Jemaah Islamiyah and now ISIS, in and around the Republic's sovereign borders. In this regard, Singapore's deployment of more security scanners and random security checks at sea, air and land entry points mirror Western security paranoia. This appears to be a form of security globalisation by imitation.[26] In many ways, Singaporean officialdom have very little choice other than to respond commensurately to their American and European Union trading partners' concerns for securing trade, finance and information flows if global capitalism is to sustain itself under the ever-threatening cloud of transnational terrorism. Take for instance, the official alarms rung through the main government-aligned English newspaper in Singapore, *The Straits Times*, in the wake of the horrendous spate of terrorist strikes in Sydney, Peshawar and Paris in December 2014 and January 2015. A three-page spread in the newspaper highlighted the proliferation of closed circuit television cameras in cafes and other public spaces, reminders of the need to practice social resilience amongst ordinary residents and local government committees, improved counter-terrorism vigilance by civilian and commercial security personnel, and the tightening of border controls on the trafficking of bomb-making chemicals. The same report noted that Singapore's traditionally strict gun and border controls already act to keep out firearms, but warned that determined terrorists could theoretically smuggle the requisite weaponry into Singapore even under the noses of the tightest of surveillance systems.[27] One might argue that the threat of transnational terrorism forces Singapore's government to embrace ever more intimately the security concerns of its trading partners as a case of inevitable interdependence. Moreover, it is also a case of Singapore performing security through mimicry: terrorist strikes in urban centres anywhere in the world are necessarily potential blue-prints for terrorist violence against Singapore and parts of its population.[28] The consequence of this is a structural contagion of amplified fears of the fundamentalist Islamic terrorist cycled through all parts of the global net-work of modernising states, cities, ethnicities and individual persons. Public proclamations of the need for vigilance against terrorism reproduce in their train hyper-rated disaster imaginations. Singapore's counter-terrorist plan-ning ought to be highly praised, judging by the standards of New York, London, Paris, Madrid, Jakarta, Bali, Peshawar and Mumbai, but one must also recognise this vigilance as an ingratiating performance *for* the sake of embracing globalisation.

The Little India Riot of 2013 and Its Insights into Public Security in Singapore under Globalising Conditions

The influx of large numbers of foreign workers annually into Singapore, num-bering in the tens of thousands at their height, also correspondingly strained the ability of local managers and police to cope with a transient population that shared very divergent perceptions of law and order. This situation ironically recalled the very similar situation confronted by the British colonial authorities: should the transients be integrated into local society, and if so, how? This was a key finding of the Committee of Inquiry's Report on the riot, and this in turn suggests Singapore's lack of preparedness for hosting global flows of human traffic landing on its shores. The landing of foreigners would be sure to arouse sentiments of social stratification, especially if cultural empathy is not built up early on. In tandem, the foreigners will be introducing their own cultural bag-gage in dealing with Singaporeans, and vice versa. The public perception of good and bad foreigners compels both the ordinary Singaporean and his government to resort to sanitising global flows. Consequently, problems at the interface between the local and the foreigner will lead Singaporeans to evaluate the risks arising from intense interconnectedness with the outside world. Incidentally, the position of foreigners in the workforce needs to be viewed in the context of Singapore's total population of 5,469,700 persons, of which 3,870,700 are formally citizens and "permanent residents" (PRs).[29] This statistic therefore counts 1,599,000 as foreigners on fully work permit status. Some sections of Singaporean public opinion might further delineate "permanent residents" as long-staying foreign labour hankering after full citizenship. This category of "PRs" add another 527,700 persons to the list of "non-citizenry". In a simplistic snapshot, one might therefore conclude that two out of every five persons living in Singapore for work or maintaining a home here are technically unintegrated as formal citizens.

According to news reports, the Little India riot broke out on 8 December 2013 when a South Asian construction worker, Sakthivel Kumaravelu, was fatally run over by the bus that was supposed to have transported him and his co-workers home to their dormitories after a night out in an entertainment nightspot around Serangoon Road popular with South Asian workers. This area was dubbed "Little India" long before the arrival of South Asian expatriates given its exceptionally high concentration of restaurants, shops and residences catering to the tastes and lifestyles of citizens and non-citizens of South Asian origin. Interestingly, there was a class dimension to the fracas. The majority of the 400 South Asian workers involved in the riot were overwhelmingly from the construction industry and categorised as hailing from the lower-skilled and rural backgrounds in the countries of origin. The Committee of Inquiry Report duly phrased it as a problem of foreigner-produced crime with a nod towards labour globalisation:

> This accident occurred in Little India on a Sunday evening. This was a time in the week when tens of thousands of South Asian workers, mostly from Tamil Nadu [province in India], would usually go to shop, eat, socialise, and run errands in the area. The accident occurred near a bus boarding open area, where hundreds of workers were waiting to catch a bus back to their dormitories. The rioters were male foreign workers primarily from the construction industry. Not a single citizen of Singapore was involved in the riot.[30]

The riot lasted two hours and the immediate response from the Singapore Police Force (SPF) was analysed as weak and underpowered in the face of rioting by 400 persons. Although the initial police personnel, in tandem with Singapore Civil Defence Force (SCDF) members, rescued the bus driver and the workers' timekeeper from the trapped vehicle, and also removed the body of Sakthivel Kumaravelu from the scene, the rioters returned in force and started attacking the SPF and SCDF personnel. Some 23 police cars, police motorcycles, ambulances and other vehicles were torched in the ensuing violence. Furthermore, 37 SPF officers, 12 SCDF officers, five private security officers from Certis CISCO and eight members of the Singaporean public were injured in the rioting.[31] It appeared as if the rioters held the police and SCDF personnel responsible for their co-worker's death, and were assumed to be shielding the "culprits" and potentially covering up the matter. It was only when troops from the SPF's Special Operations Command, trained in riot control, had arrived on the scene that the rioters dispersed for good. Interestingly, the Committee of Inquiry decided that three factors explained the riot: a crowd intoxicated by intense consumption of alcohol; the misperception that the early police and SCDF responders were protecting the culprits instead of attending to the victim; and that the rioters were acting out a premeditated sense of "street justice".[32] These varied findings meshed with the initial range of Singaporean public reactions to the riot, some of which bordered on the xenophobic or criticisms of the country's openness to global flows.[33]

Following in the train of the earlier case illustrations, the Committee of Inquiry both sanitised the social dangers provoked by transnational labour flows into Singapore and attempted to assuage Singaporean fears about foreigners working in Singapore fomenting civil violence according to the "traditions" and "politics" of their countries of origin. In this regard, paragraphs 119–123 of the Committee's Report bear unmistakable hallmarks of deliquescent (in)security and therefore merit quotation in full:

119. Following a review of scientific literature on crowd psychology in addition to all of the available evidence, the [Behavioural Analysis] Group [convened by Dr Majeed Khader, Senior Consultant Psychologist at the Home Team Behavioural Sciences Centre, at the request of the COI Investigation Team] postulated the following view in their report:

'The Behavioural Analysis Group is of the view that the Little India incident was fuelled by a misperception on the part of the foreign workers who may have felt that the situation on the day (loss of a fellow countryman), and the ensuing events that occurred was indicative that the responding authorities were against them. The events of the night had violated their expectations that the responding agencies ought to be fair and to respond to the deceased first rather than to the locals.

...

Certain members of the crowd could have had erroneous misperceptions, since the responding forces did in fact extricate the deceased before attending to the locals. In addition, the responding forces did not use unreasonable force, did not fire any shots, and did not injure any workers.'

120. Another factor which the Group identified as contributing to the riot was a desire for "street justice" or "retributive justice" on the part of the rioters:

'Street justice involves punishment meted out by members of the public to people who are perceived as "wrong doers" (even though this may not actually be true)... In many countries and especially in rural and suburban settings, there is a "retaliatory ethic" and a sense of the need for retribution for "wrongdoing".

...

Sometimes, victims may feel that street hustles cannot be formally taken to legal authorities ... The idea then is to "teach a lesson" to the adversary directly by taking the law into their own hands and attacking the perpetrator(s).'

121. This argument is supported by the testimony which the COI heard from individuals who lived for many years or grew up in India. One of the witnesses, who was born and raised in India, testified at the public hearing of the *"law of the underdog"* in India:

'I venture to say my personal opinion, having known workers all my life here, as back in India and also knowing the way things are — or the mob effect in India, back in India. Back in college I was not directly party to a riot but I was caught in a riot several times while in college or while in public places when I lived in India.

My personal feeling is that the riot on that night, that unfortunate incident that happened that night, was purely a mob reaction to a sudden death that occurred. So there is this huge wave of sympathy towards a fellow brother or a comrade, and whether the other people know him or don't know him or whether the reason what went wrong, it becomes immaterial and then there is this mob angst that comes up and that's the reaction that showed up over the night. I do not think or do not feel that it was premeditated or planned or is a result of any worker inequality or injustice or suffering of that sort.

...

It can happen in any political rally, it can happen in any college gathering. It could happen in a street where — in a street culture in India, a pedestrian crossing the road wrongly, if hit by a scooter the mob would attack the scooter. If the scooter is in the wrong lane or direction and hit by a car, the mob would attack the car. If the car is hit by a bus, the mob would attack the bus. It goes by this hierarchy. So it is the law of the underdog, what the common man in the street perceives.'

122. Another witness, an Indian citizen now living in Singapore, gave testimony to the COI after the conclusion of the public hearing. In his view, clashing with the police was a sub-culture or counter-culture among some working class men in Tamil Nadu:

'They feel heroism is to disobey the law enforcers. When they see anybody else, police or any authority, in our place, whenever ... They directly will feel if you are not obeying the law, you are considered as a hero.'

123. The COI's view is that some of the workers at the scene that night could have carried elements of such cultural psychology with them, which had a part to play in the riot...[34]

Indeed, the conclusion a Singaporean citizen might draw immediately from this is that globalisation has introduced elements of hitherto distant mediated dangers — items familiar in the televised content of Channel NewsAsia's Asian insights or National Geographic documentaries — into Singapore's neighbourhoods. Globalisation is no longer abstract — it is a deadly serious "inner globalisation" that has securitised a new front for protecting the Singaporean national identity. The government's response to the Committee's Report went even further to assure Singaporeans of the possibilities of taming the wilder dimensions of foreign labour in Singapore. The Minister for Manpower, Tan Chuan-Jin drew the curtain on the high standards of hygiene, comfort and recreational facilities in privately run foreign worker dormitories where most foreign construction workers live, and drew attention to the fact that the vast majority of foreign workers in Singapore were content with their living conditions and the legal and social frameworks that supported their stay here.[35] The Minister understandably warned against speculating about unruly attitudes amongst foreign workers in Singapore and pledged to increase the number of dedicated recreation centres for foreign workers. Deputy Prime Minister and Home Affairs Minister, Teo Chee Hean promised to install more security cameras in Little India, ramp up police recruitment, improve police command, control and communications systems, and work closely with businesses and "community stakeholders" to dissipate crowds at strategic traffic junctions in the area.[36] It ought to be noted that the palliative measures announced in the aftermath of the Little India riot amount to the simultaneous need to clean up global labour flows into Singapore and to systematically police them with a mixture of rational legal protections and the softer blandishments of comfortable dormitories and recreational facilities. Nonetheless, the risks of violent interconnectedness between locals and foreigners are evidently sanitised by separating their social spaces with a friendly tone from the government. Additionally, the official response to the Inquiry Report reveals the unspoken need to gain enduring approbation from global economic intelligence agencies, investors, G7 and BRICS governments so as to keep Singapore's coveted position as an icon of successful globalisation.

Conclusion: Deliquescent Security Is Here to Stay

Deliquescent security is hard to grasp for the policy-maker since it is mostly about defending the metaphysical borders of national identity and an essentialist notion of a Singaporean comfort zone that has been cumulatively derived since the arrival of the British in 1819. What is to be protected, and the source of the threat, are both mobile and existential, even embedded in the design of taken-for-granted flows of labour, tourism, trade, finance and information. The object and referent of security under globalising conditions are therefore liquid; they dissolve, or exist in a latent state, until ignited by a confluence of flows that challenge the very essence of a Singaporean national identity. Like deliquescent chemical compounds such as water, hydrochloric acid or lavender vapours, varying in the levels of pain or pleasantness that they exude when placed in proximity with other materials, they can only be addressed if one appreciates that the insecurities arise out of a cumulative stage of development that is modern, and nested within an advanced state of globalised openness to transnational flows of ideas, goods and people.

This chapter could have selected an even wider sample of case illustrations, such as the emergence of home-grown xenophobia vented on social media against foreign domestic helpers and callous high-living and vandalising Western expatriates; "China Chinese chauvinism" amongst Singapore-sponsored Chinese university students studying on local campuses; disagreements between locals and foreigners living in Housing & Development Board flats over the aroma of curry; and the infamous SMRT bus strike in 2012 staged by drivers of Chinese nationality that contravened labour dispute laws in the country. But the principal point about Singapore encountering deliquescent insecurities in a modern stage of development that requires a border-sensitive nationalism to stay open to partnership and cohabitation with unruly global flows is an issue shared in common with the SARS epidemic, the "problem" of living with foreign talent, the incitement of Singaporean Muslims by foreign jihadists, and the Little India riot. Naturally, more research needs to be driven along the avenues of sociology, anthropology and political science. Nonetheless, policy-making relevance is likely to come out of it only if one problematises globalisation as a security frontier that demands a surgical policing, amounting to discourses of sanitisation for political correctness, and mindfulness that unnamed powers outside the country are always judging Singapore, in terms of both its people and their government, for variable notions of good national behaviour hospitable to external flows.

Notes

[1] Richard Clutterbuck, *Conflict and Violence in Singapore and Malaysia, 1945–1983,* Second Edition (Singapore: Graham Brash, 1984), p. 17.

[2] *Ibid.,* p. 19.

[3] Richard Wilkinson, "Old Singapore," in *150th Anniversary of the Founding of Singapore.* Issue 1 of *M.B.R.A.S Reprints* (Singapore: MBRAS, 1973), p. 52.

[4] Abdullah bin Abdul Kadir (a.k.a. Munshi Abdullah), *The Hikayat Abdullah.* Annotated and trans. A.H. Hill (Kuala Lumpur: Oxford University Press, 1970), pp. 159–60.

[5] Alan Chong, "Premodern Southeast Asia as a Guide to International Relations between Peoples: Prowess and Prestige in 'Intersocietal Relations' in the Sejarah Melayu," *Alternatives: Global, Local, Political,* 37(2), pp. 87–105.

[6] E. Kay Gillis, *Singapore Civil Society and British Power* (Singapore: Talisman Publishing, 2005).

[7] Wilkinson (1973), *op. cit.* See also Malcolm Waters, *Globalisation* (London: Routledge, 1995).

[8] Peter J. Taylor, Michael J. Watts and Robert Johnson, "Global Change at the End of the Twentieth Century," in Robert Johnston, Peter J. Taylor and Michael J. Watts (eds.), *Geographies of Global Change: Remapping the World in the Late Twentieth Century* (Oxford: Blackwell Publishers, 1996), p. 3.

[9] Zygmunt Bauman, *Globalisation: The Human Consequences* (New York: Columbia University Press, 1998).

[10] Zygmunt Bauman, *Liquid Modernity* (Oxford: Polity Press, 2000).

[11] James N. Rosenau, *Along the Domestic–Foreign Frontier: Exploring Governance in a Turbulent World* (Cambridge: Cambridge University Press, 1997).

[12] Gayatri V. Spivak, *The Postcolonial Critic: Interviews, Strategies, Dialogues* (New York: Routledge, 1990), p. 126.

[13] Chua Mui Hoong, *A Defining Moment: How Singapore Beat SARS* (Singapore: Ministry of Information, Communications and the Arts, 2004), p. 31.

[14] *Ibid.,* pp. 102, 104.

[15] *Ibid.,* pp. 108, 135, 184.

[16] Yap Mui Teng and Christopher Gee, *Population Outcomes: Singapore 2050* (Singapore: Institute of Policy Studies, Lee Kuan Yew School of Public Policy, 2014), p. 82.

[17] *Ibid.,* p. 83.

[18] Patrick Tay, "Singaporeans First — Whither Labour Market Testing in Singapore?," *The Straits Times,* 18 September 2013, p. A25.

[19] Xue Jianyue, "Government Identifies More than 50 Firms with Too Few Singaporean Professionals," *Today,* 8 March 2014, p. 2.

[20] "No Further Curbs on Inflow of Foreign Manpower This Year: Chuan-Jin," *Today,* 8 March 2014, p. 2.

[21] Yang Peidong, "'Authenticity' and 'Foreign Talent' in Singapore: The Relative and Negative Logic of National Identity," *SOJOURN: Journal of Social Issues in Southeast Asia,* 29(2), pp. 400–437; see also Leong Yew's excellent critical treatment of the subject in his book *Asianism and the Politics of Regional Consciousness in Singapore* (Abingdon: Routledge, 2014).

[22] Norman Vasu and Bernard Loo, "National Security and Singapore: An Assessment," in Terence Chong (ed.), *Management of Success: Singapore Revisited* (Singapore:

Institute of Southeast Asian Studies, 2010), pp. 462–488; Yolanda Chin, "Community, Confidence and Security," in Chong (ed.) (2010), *op. cit.*, pp. 443–461; "Terror Test for Singapore Again (Editorial)," *The Straits Times*, 11 October 2014, p. A44.

23 Vasu and Loo (2010), *op. cit.*, pp. 474–476.

24 Chin (2010), *op. cit.*, pp. 450–453. See also Nur Asyiqin Mohamad Salleh, "Lone Wolves a Ticking Time Bomb," *The Straits Times*, 17 January 2015, p. D4.

25 Goh Chok Tong, *Winning against Terrorism: Speeches by Singapore Prime Minister Goh Chok Tong* (Singapore: Ministry of Information, Communications and the Arts, 2004).

26 *The Fight against Terror: Singapore's National Security Strategy* (Singapore: National Security Coordination Centre, Ministry of Defence Singapore, 2004), pp. 30–56.

27 Rachel Chang and Nur Asyiqin Mohamad Salleh, "Terrorism: How Prepared Is Singapore?," *The Straits Times*, 17 January 2015, pp. D2–D4.

28 *The Fight against Terror* (2004), *op. cit.*

29 "Population and Land Area," Department of Statistics, Singapore, 2014. Retrieved 20 March 2014, from http://www.singstat.gov.sg/statistics/latest-data#4.

30 COI, *Report of the Committee of Inquiry into the Little India Riot on 8 December 2013* (Singapore: Ministry of Home Affairs, 2014), p. 6. Retrieved 20 March 2015, from http://www.mha.gov.sg/Data/Files/file/Little%20India%20Riot%20COI%20report%20-%202014-06-27.pdf.

31 *Ibid.*

32 Amanda Lee, "Main Spark of Little India Riot Was Accident: Inquiry Panel," *Today*, 1 July 2014. Retrieved 20 March 2015, from http://www.todayonline.com/singapore/main-spark-little-india-riot-was-accident-inquiry-panel.

33 COI (2014), *op. cit.*, p. 7.

34 *Ibid.*, pp. 39–41.

35 Ng Jing Yng, "Little India Riot: More Self-Contained Dorms for Foreign Workers," *Today*, 7 July 2014. Retrieved 20 January 2015, from http://www.todayonline.com/singapore/little-india-riot-more-self-contained-dorms-foreign-workers.

36 Nur Asyiqin Mohamad Salleh, "Little India Riot: Government Accepts All 8 Recommendations from the COI," *The Straits Times*, 7 July 2014. Retrieved 20 January 2015, from http://www.straitstimes.com/news/singapore/more-singapore-stories/story/little-india-riot-government-accepts-all-8-recommendatio.

Chapter 4

Singapore and Global Governance: Free-Rider or Responsible Stakeholder?

Tan See Seng

The notion that Singapore "punches above its weight" has become common-place.[1] Reportedly boasting the highest gross domestic product (GDP) per capita in the world today and projected to maintain its pole position up till 2050,[2] Singapore's economic success and its strategies to ensure its success have invited accusations that the city-state has continually reaped the benefits of global governance but contributed little to it. For example, Singapore's ostensible efforts at "leapfrogging" and transcending the ASEAN region — its "dual track" approach of negotiating multilateral and bilateral free trade agreements (FTAs) is the offending instance in question[3] — have led critics to dismiss Singapore as a "free-rider" in global governance.[4] A similar charge has been made concerning "Singaporisation," a convenient label for critics in regard to the form of "assertive regionalism" that has purportedly been adopted by pro-independence parties in the Basque and Catalan parts of Spain.[5] Fairly or otherwise, some Europeanists see such enthusiasm for the (as they see it) Singapore model of preferential economic regionalism as evidence of the lack of "real political responsibility" in post-crisis Europe.[6]

For that matter, what Singaporeans have long regarded as prudence in the exercise of their foreign policy, especially when offering financial assistance to other countries, has elicited the occasional criticism that Singapore is insincere and overbearing. The derisive label of Singapore as an inconsequential "little red dot," which former Indonesian president Bacharuddin Jusuf Habibie famously introduced in 1999, constitutes one of the most memorable examples to date.[7] Investments made or sought after in Southeast Asia by Singapore's sovereign wealth fund vehicles, particularly Temasek Holdings, have at times triggered nationalistic backlash from countries such as Thailand regarding Singapore's "economic imperialism".[8] Nor has the aspiration of its leaders to make Singapore "a first world oasis in a third world region"[9] necessarily improved the city-state's image among its immediate neighbours. If anything, the impression some in the region have of Singapore is that it is egotistical, conceited and uncaring. "Singapore doesn't really care about the opinion of its neighbours," as Malaysia's former Prime Minister Mahathir bin Mohamad complained in 2007, "Singapore believes the most important thing is what profits Singapore."[10]

Is Singapore, as its critics believe, freeriding in the international system, reaping the benefits supplied by its respective providers of collective or public goods, be they of an economic, political or security nature, without playing its part in contributing to it? The argument against freeriding goes something like this: if others are cooperating for mutual benefit and we benefit from their cooperation, then we have an obligation to do our share.[11] The criticism against Singapore as a free-rider presupposes that Singapore has achieved a certain level of economic (and possibly political) development as a nation-state such that it ought now to bear particular obligations and responsibilities as an active contributor to, rather than a mere consumer of, global governance. Accordingly, Singapore is thereby obliged to behave as a "responsible stakeholder" — to borrow the term popularised by Robert Zoellick, the former US Deputy Secretary of State and World Bank President.[12] (It is worth noting that Zoellick's conception of responsible stakeholder, introduced in the context of what the United States (US) expected of China's international behaviour given its rising power and influence, goes beyond mere fulfilment of the basic expectations of membership in the international community.) Indeed, as veteran Singapore diplomat Tommy Koh has averred, Asia on the whole, as a major beneficiary of globalisation, should "behave as a responsible stakeholder and not as a free-rider" through sharing its wealth, knowledge, expertise and experience with other less developed regions of the world, shouldering a larger burden in the maintenance of international peace and security — United Nations (UN) peacekeeping missions are mentioned in particular — and contributing leadership and intellectual capital to global governance.[13] Although Koh's appeal putatively applies to Singapore as well, the question of global governance and Singapore's part in it — as free-rider or responsible stakeholder — is considerably more complicated, however.

Global Governance, Its Discontents and the Free-Rider Problem

Global governance, broadly understood, refers to the way in which global affairs are managed. With no global government, global governance typically involves a range of actors — world bodies, regional organisations and states. While the UN remains the closest thing to a comprehensive institution for global governance, the reality is that the practice of global governance is undertaken along functional lines where different institutions, many of which are affiliated to the UN, are responsible, if only nominally, for different and quite specific issue areas.[14] In the world of global finance, for instance, international financial institutions (IFIs) such as the International Monetary Fund (IMF), the World Bank (WB) and the Financial Stability Board (FSB), among others, collectively furnish the principles, rules and norms of the global financial regime from which central banks and commercial financial institutions (ostensibly) take guidance. In the world of global trade there is the World Trade Organization (WTO), whereas in the area of global health issues, the World Health Organization (WHO) is the "go to" institution. By and large, the functional governance furnished by these institutions involves consensus building on rules and norms that are either legally binding or non-binding on member nations of those arrangements.[15]

Despite its currency, global governance is a debated concept and issue.[16] On the one hand, its advocates see it as the logical response to globalisation through harnessing its potential and growing its rewards while managing and mitigating its discontents. On the other hand, its critics see it as the neoliberal ideology of globalisation — what has been termed the Washington Consensus[17] — and hence the system used by Western and other developed countries to ensure their continued dominance of the global economy at the expense of developing nations.[18] IFIs such as the IMF and the WB, whose leaderships and voting power have continually been controlled by Western powers, have long been seen as bastions of the Washington Consensus — a situation that, in the view of some, did not end even with the apparent effort by the IMF to revise its orthodox lending policy in the wake of the 2008–2009 Global Financial Crisis.[19] And although the crisis exposed key financial players such as Britain and the US as lax regulators which exerted little regulatory surveillance of their large internationally connected financial institutions, the reality is that getting them to accept greater international regulatory oversight will be diffi-cult precisely because of their power in the international regulatory domain.[20] In the UN Security Council, membership of the Permanent Five (P5), particu-larly the place and role of countries such as France and the United Kingdom, has been increasingly seen as anachronistic and irrelevant to the challenges and developments of the contemporary era.[21] Nor has the Group of Twenty (G20), a forum for the governments and central bank governors from 20 major economies which inaugurated in 1999,[22] escaped similar criticisms despite the presence within its ranks of emerging economies such as

Argentina, China, India, Indonesia and Mexico, along with the usual suspects from the developed world.[23]

At the heart of criticisms of global governance is the longstanding debate between equity (also referred to as representativeness) and efficiency. On the one hand, institutions for global governance are deemed effective and legitimate if they are comprehensively represented by all members of the international community. In this respect, institutional design — how members are selected, the procedures by which decisions are made and power exercised and so on — matters and to the extent they ensure all states in the international system enjoy equal stakes within the institution and their interests are adequately represented therein, input-oriented legitimacy is guaranteed.[24] Multilateral standing institutions such as the UN and the WTO, with their global memberships, are typical illustrations of input-oriented legitimacy (or, if you will, democratic legitimacy given its emphasis on representativeness). On the other hand, institutions are regarded as effective on the basis of the relevance and quality of their performance (i.e., their efficiency).[25] Typically, such emphasis on output-oriented or performance-based legitimacy is an implicit criticism against large institutions such as the UN, whose input-oriented or democratic legitimacy does not guarantee that institution's output-oriented or performance legitimacy.

For example, the formation of the G20 was welcomed precisely by those who favour efficiency over equity given, in their view, the aptness in gathering 20 economic powers which together account for nearly 80% of the world's wealth and resources.[26] In another argument against equity, the death of the Doha Round of world trade talks has been attributed by the former US trade representative, Susan Schwab, to the "lumping together of all emerging and developing economies in the Doha negotiating structure", which in her view allowed emerging economies disinclined to open their markets — free-riders in short — to undermine any prospect for progress.[27] But while the logic of collective action presupposes that numbers matter when enforcement is essential to interstate cooperation within international institutions,[28] the exclusiveness of output-oriented global institutions, no matter how efficient they might be, understandably invites criticisms from those outside their ranks regarding their undemocratic nature and their occasional propensity, inadvertent or otherwise, to replicate East–West and/or North–South divides (both inside and outside the institutions).[29] The situation is compounded further by the apparent inability or unwillingness of performance-oriented institutions and their exclusive, even elitist, memberships to manage, much less resolve, serious international diplomatic and/or economic crises as a result of political differences among them — as evidenced, say, by the strategic divergences among the

UN Security Council P5 members over the crisis in Syria and the relative weakness of the G20 in its response to the Global Financial Crisis. Ultimately, true democratic legitimacy depends on both these conceptions of legitimacy.[30]

The tension between equity and efficiency complicates further the freeriding problem in global governance. Typically, actors who accuse rising powers of free-riding are developed nations that carry the lion's share of the burdens of global governance.[31] The changing global distribution of wealth and economic power has also meant that countries like China, which overtook Japan in 2010 as the world's second largest economy[32] — face growing demands from the international community to do more. At the 2013 Munich Security Conference, China's Vice Foreign Minister Song Tao argued that emerging economies such as the BRICS countries are not free-riders in global governance given that they have ostensibly contributed to over 50% of global economic growth over the past five years, supplied five times more peacekeepers than the seven major industrialised countries in support of UN peacekeeping missions, and helped prop up a world economy plagued by international financial crisis and the European debt crisis.[33]

As Table 1 suggests, there is a wide disparity in the amounts of financial support for UN peacekeeping activities (2013–2015) given by the US and the other nine highest funder countries. There also appears to be an implicit division of labour between rich countries that finance UN peacekeeping activities and considerably poorer countries — the hewers of wood and drawers of water, if you will — that supply the boots on the ground. This raises the question of whether by active contribution to global governance — or for that matter, being

Table 1. UN Peacekeeping Funders and UN Troop Contributors: Top 10.

Top 10 UN Peacekeeping Funders (2013–2015)[34]		Top 10 UN Troop Contributors (June 2014)[35]	
United States*	28.38%	Bangladesh	8,766
Japan	10.83%	India	8,123
France*	7.22%	Pakistan	7,203
Germany	7.14%	Ethiopia	7,188
United Kingdom*	6.68%	Nepal	4,740
China*	6.64%	Nigeria	4,717
Italy	4.45%	Rwanda	4,650
Russia*	3.15%	Senegal	2,965
Canada	2.98%	Ghana	2,932
Spain	2.97%	Egypt	2,659

Notes: * = P5 member.

a responsible stakeholder — critics of freeriding mean playing by the rules set by others or, as some advocates for input-oriented legitimacy insist, actual involvement in the rule-making process itself. For example, as a pundit has opined about China's prospective participation in the Trans-Pacific Partnership (TPP), getting the rules of the TPP set before inviting China to join the party is a strange way of encouraging China to be a responsible stakeholder.[36]

Others have pointed to a similar occurrence in the Organization of Economic Cooperation and Development (OECD), when new and prospective members are expected to accept OECD membership requirements and align their policies with a now vast array of instruments and conditions they had no role in creating. As John West has noted, "From an OECD point of view, this means becoming a 'responsible stakeholder'. From an emerging country point of view, it means being a 'rule-taker', that is, swallowing an OECD agenda now increasingly questioned in light of recent financial crises".[37] Furthermore, Chinese leaders have been known to view external attempts to define China as a responsible international actor as a normative constraint for which they are still reluctant to accept, in the belief that it holds China to behavioural standards to which it may not be ready to live up to.[38] All of which makes China a "dissatisfied" great power, responsible or otherwise.[39]

Singapore: Beyond Its Developmental and Garrison State Mentality?

Great powers today, whose economic and political leadership have been essential to the establishment and maintenance of global governance, were rising powers and not yet the responsible stakeholders they now have become. For example, the US, which really began making its mark as a rising power at the genesis of the 20th century, proved then to be as protectionist as any other nation.[40] In a sense, Asian countries that emerged in the context of the Asian Economic Miracle (a contested phenomenon, admittedly[41]) were no different.[42] Developmental states are primarily concerned with their own economic modernisation and are presumably not ready to adopt broader perspectives of the sort international relations scholars refer to as "enlightened self-interest" or "a logic of appropriateness" out of concern that they may lose out economically to others.[43] For example, a Chinese Vice Minister recently argued, in the context of responsibility in global governance, that emerging economies ought to "shoulder common but differentiated responsibilities" since they ostensibly lag behind developed or established economies in socio-economic terms.[44]

Thus understood, that Singapore's history as a developmental state involved freeriding is therefore not particularly surprising. Indeed, in the

1970s, an effort by Singapore and others to press for collective responsibility failed partly due to the primacy of self-interest not least that of Singapore. Following the oil crisis of 1973, a group of developing countries used the UN Conference on Trade and Development (UNCTAD), which had been set up in 1964 as a counterweight to the General Agreement on Tariffs and Trade (GATT), the forerunner of the WTO, to press for changes in the management of the international economic system. Their demands were embodied in the Declaration for the Establishment of a New International Economic Order (NIEO), adopted by the UN General Assembly in May 1974.[45] As Aggarwal and Weber have noted, the changes called for today by advocates of reform of the IMF and the WB to reflect the shifting global balance of wealth bear a striking resemblance to those urged by the architects of the NIEO.[46] The push for the NIEO lost steam for a number of reasons that are beyond the scope of this paper.[47] One of them was likely the successful ability of the so-called four "tigers" or "dragons" — Taiwan, Hong Kong, South Korea and Singapore — at avoiding the middle-income trap.[48] However, their very success led indirectly to the collapse of the NIEO consensus since it implied, contrary to the assumptions of the NIEO, that developing economies can, under the right conditions, achieve developed status under the existing international economic order. This historical episode suggests that while developing countries might press for greater stakes in the world economy so long as they believe they are disadvantaged by its rules and mechanisms relative to developed countries that have had a hand in rule-making, they readily break ranks with their counterparts when they stand to gain under the existing system.

With its growing economic stature has come increasing demands on Singapore to contribute to global governance. In a sense, it is not difficult to see why facets of Singapore's external behaviour are interpreted by observers as evidence of freeriding. Not unlike the Chinese example cited earlier, Singapore has at times resisted such calls on the premise that it is not ready to assume greater responsibilities. For example, when Singapore was invited to join the OECD, it demurred on the basis that it was still dependent on direct foreign investment, multinational corporations, and borrowed science and technology, given that its research and development purportedly lacked in both a local talent pool and market base.[49] That being said, Singapore has sought to adhere to specific OECD requirements.[50] Furthermore, in response to the failure of the Third WTO Ministerial Conference held in Seattle in 1999, Singapore established a number of bilateral FTAs — to date, Singapore's suite of FTAs now includes 18 bilateral and regional FTAs in force with 24 trading partners and all consistent with and permissible by WTO rules, according to the Singapore

Ministry of Foreign Affairs website — that has earned it the ire of neoclassical trade economists who see economic bilateralism as anathema to the global multilateral trade regime. As Fred Bergsten, the influential Washington-based economist, argued in 2006:

> The indefinite suspension of the Doha round of world trade talks creates big risks for the world economy. A new explosion of discriminatory bilateral and regional agreements is likely to substitute for global liberalization. This will inevitably erode the multilateral rules-based system of the World Trade Organization (WTO). The backlash against globalisation will generate more protectionism in the vacuum left as momentum toward wide-ranging reduction of barriers ceases, especially as the world economy slows and global trade imbalances continue to rise. Financial markets will become more unstable as international economic cooperation breaks down further.[51]

Singapore's official position, on the other hand, has long been that bilateralism and multilateralism are neither mutually exclusive nor necessarily mutually competitive, but could in fact complement and reinforce each other.[52] As the logic undergirding Singapore's role as part of the founding "P4" (together with Brunei Darussalam, Chile and New Zealand) of the Trans-Pacific Strategic Economic Partnership — which got rebranded as the TPP — has it, the trade pact is not an impediment to but rather a building block for the Asia-Pacific-wide free trade area originally envisioned by the architects of the Asia-Pacific Economic Cooperation (APEC).[53] Needless to say, not all are convinced that the TPP will become the "gold standard" for FTAs as promised by the Obama administration, with some warning against US involvement should a poorly negotiated TPP inadvertently allow intellectual property theft, non-tariff barriers, discriminatory government procurement practices and other such practices among its members[54] — a putative warning, perhaps, that the TPP, if not handled properly, could end up as an enterprise of free-riders rather than responsible stakeholders.

While other developmental states appear to have succeeded in making the cognitive shift — say, Mexico, which joined the OECD in 1994, or Chile, which joined in 2010 — part of the reason why Singapore has hitherto avoided such commitments might have to do with the persistence of its garrison state mentality. Singapore's leaders have had a reputation for their hard-nosed security outlook, self-help philosophy and firm belief in the need for a stable balance of power in the Asia-Pacific.[55] A difficult early history — ejected from the Federation of Malaysia in 1965 after two tumultuous years whilst still in the throes of Confrontation (or *Konfrontasi*), the Sukarno-led Indonesia's undeclared war against Malaysia and Singapore (1963–1966) — facilitated the emergence of a foreign and security policy rooted in a strategic culture of insecurity, vulnerability arising from geopolitical and size-related factors, as well as a siege mentality.[56] As recent as in 2012, Prime Minister Lee Hsien Loong observed that "without the strategic ballast of bigger, more mature economies", Singapore "will always be vulnerable to the vagaries of external events. We must always fend for ourselves. No one will bail us out if we falter. In a rapidly changing world, this is one fact that will not change for Singapore".[57] The result of such an outlook has been, in tandem with an unremitting focus on economic development, the formation and enhancement of a robust military deterrent and an equally robust national resolve to prove that Singapore is not to be trifled with. "Singapore is not the 'Israel of Southeast Asia'", according to Tim Huxley, "but it has sent strong signals since the late 1960s that it is willing, *in extremis*, to risk assuming that status".[58]

Thus understood, there are presumably ample reasons why Singapore might prefer to forgo international responsibility in favour of freeriding. But as this discussion has highlighted, the issue of freeriding in global governance has become considerably complicated in the light of the tensions between equity and efficiency in institutionalism, on the one hand, and that between rule-making and rule-taking where conceptions of responsible stakeholder are concerned. The remainder of this essay examines four illustrations of how Singapore has arguably sought to adopt a more responsible engagement with global governance.

Singapore's Leadership of the Global Governance Group (3G)

A plausible example of global responsibility is Singapore's leadership of the Global Governance Group (3G), which acts as a "pressure group" comprising like-minded non-G20 states, whose collective aim is to "render the G20 process more consultative, inclusive and transparent".[59] The formation of the G20 in 1999 — and particularly its upgrading to a heads of state/government forum in 2008 — was viewed with concern by Singaporean leaders, who felt that the grouping, if treated as an alternative framework for global governance to the UN (the G20 has been informally viewed by some as "the other UN"[60]) could lead to the degrading and erosion of the UN's credibility, not to mention the marginalisation if not exclusion of non-G20 countries from the decision-making process in world affairs. (By contrast, criticisms have also been levelled at the G20 by those who fear that this larger body would dilute the power and influence of the more exclusive G8!)

In its proposal to strengthen the framework for engagement between G20 members and non-G20 countries, the letter to the UN Secretary-General from Singapore's permanent representative to the UN on behalf of the 3G countries (document A/64/706 dated 11 March 2010) made the following five points. First, it argued that the G20 process should recognise the UN as "the only global body with universal participation and unquestioned legitimacy" and reflect that recognition through ensuring that its actions and decisions complement and strengthen the UN rather than compete with and weaken it. Second, it called for the G20 to consult and engage with the UN and its member countries before G20 summits in order to allow non-G20 countries (especially small states) to raise issues of concern and make their views known to the G20. Third, it urged the G20 to formalise the participation of the UN Secretary-General and Sherpa at G20 summits and preparatory meetings. Fourth, it argued for the adoption of a "variable geometry" and flexibility by the G20 to allow non-G20 countries to participate in G20 ministerial meetings and working groups in discussions on specialised issues. Fifth and finally, while welcoming the G20's inclusion of regional organisations (e.g., APEC, ASEAN, African Union, European Union, New Partnership for Africa's Development [NEPAD]) in previous G20 summits, it argued that such participation should be effectively institutionalised and regularised within the G20 and its ancillary processes.[61]

Singapore has continued to plead the foregoing and ancillary arguments on behalf of the 3G. For example, averring that "global problems require global solutions", Singapore, acknowledging the G20's relative effectiveness in tackling short-term contingencies arising from the 2008–2009 financial crisis, nonetheless issued the following statement in 2013:

> In the 3G's view, the United Nations must continue to lead the effort in shaping the global governance framework. As the only global body with universal participation and unquestioned legitimacy, the United Nations has a central role in global governance. Other international institutions and informal groupings have important roles to play as meaningful complements to the United Nations; their relationship should be based on cooperation, avoiding duplication and competition … The 3G believes that strengthening the relationship between the United Nations and G20 is key to enhancing global economic governance. Although the G20 contains the largest developed and emerging economies in the world, G20 outcomes must have the support of non-G20 members for them to be implemented globally and effectively. A global economic governance framework cannot be the sole function of any single entity. It is therefore important that the G20 engages the United Nations through more institutionalised, predictable and regular channels.[62]

Whether Singapore's efforts in arguing for the UN as the relevant and representative framework for global governance constitute a commitment to international responsibility and distributive justice is debatable. At the very least, it reflects the concern over the prospect that the majority of countries in the world, Singapore included, could end up as mere "rule-takers" should the G20 overtake the UN as the lead global governance body. It also reflects a readiness on Singapore's part to exercise international leadership, albeit in an informal fashion, to highlight and voice the shared concerns of a disparate majority of states whose views and interests could well be marginalised should the UN lose out to the G20 in the high stakes game of global governance.

Singapore's Involvement in the Small Five (S5)

Another example of Singapore's growing awareness of sovereignty as responsibility is in its disposition towards the principle of "the responsibility to protect" (R2P), which argues that states have a fundamental responsibility to protect their populations from mass atrocity crimes, namely, genocide, crimes against humanity, war crimes and ethnic cleansing. First introduced in a groundbreaking 2001 Report by the Canadian-sponsored International Commission on Intervention and State Sovereignty (ICISS),[63] the R2P concept has since been adopted by the UN and refined a number of times.[64] Not unlike its ASEAN counterparts, Singapore, which supported the R2P at the UN World Summit in 2005,[65] has avoided fully embracing the norm presumably due to its long-standing concern over potential intervention in Southeast Asia by outside powers, but also out of regard for its neighbours' deeper circumspection with the R2P. However, that has not precluded its active involvement with the Group of Friends of R2P, an informal cross-regional group of UN member states that share a common interest in the R2P and in advancing the norm within the UN system.

It is in this context that Singapore's involvement in a group informally known as the "Small Five" (S5) — the others being Costa Rica, Jordan, Liechtenstein and Switzerland — has gained a measure of attention. The S5 submitted a draft resolution at the UN General Assembly in May 2012, which sought to amend the working methods of the UN Security Council.[66] Among the items called for in the draft resolution, one in particular stood out: described as "the responsibility not to veto", the S5 urged the P5 members of the Security Council — Britain, China, France, Russia and the US — to "[refrain] from using a veto to block Council action aimed at preventing or ending genocide, war crimes and crimes against humanity".[67] In essence, the S5's appeal for restraint in the use of the veto implicitly reiterated the recommendation made in the 2001 ICISS

Report for a "code of conduct" among the P5 regarding their veto powers.[68] Ultimately, the S5 was forced to withdraw its draft resolution. But it showed a willingness by Singapore and its compatriots, not to mention their courage, to remind the great powers of their grave responsibility to the international system in ensuring its stability and security rather than merely watching out for their own self-interests.

Singapore's Participation in International Disaster Relief and Peacekeeping

In contrast to some of its ASEAN counterparts, such as Indonesia and Malaysia, Singapore historically has been less active in UN peacekeeping efforts. That began to change in the post-Cold War era along with the broadening conception of security and the greater policy attention to non-conventional issues — food, climate, environment, economics and the like — which are often transnational in reach or have a transnational impact. This was accompanied by the recognition that states and societies can no longer handle such challenges on their own, but likely need to rely on multinational approaches and/or multilateral solutions.[69] In response to these concerns, militaries as such have had to embrace multilateral cooperation and dialogue on issues of security concern ranging from piracy to disaster relief.[70] They have had to retool themselves for a range of new and diverse roles lumped under the rubric "operations other than war" (OOTW), such as humanitarian and disaster relief efforts, peacekeeping duties and greater engagement in defence diplomacy efforts.[71] That being said, the apparent novelty of such missions is not something that warrants exaggeration. The contingencies facing militaries might well be new but their roles, conventional and non-conventional, might not necessarily be new.[72] As an eminent student of war once opined, "Future war will include both change and continuity from the past".[73]

The Singapore defence establishment and its armed forces have also been making the requisite adjustments in keeping pace with the ongoing transformation of their remits and roles. While there is no question regarding the continued importance of providing for the military deterrence and defence of Singapore from its enemies, Singapore has broadened and deepened its engagement in international OOTWs as a key facet of its self-conscious contributions as a responsible stakeholder. As the then-Defence Minister (now President) of Singapore, Tony Tan, put it in July 1997, "As a responsible member of the world community, Singapore shows its commitment to the principles enshrined in the UN Charter through its participation in UN peacekeeping and peace-making operations".[74] Similarly, a team of Singapore Armed Forces

(SAF) officers has explained their institution's growing involvement in OOTW as a reflection of Singapore's identity "as a responsible member of the international community".[75]

The SAF's maiden foray into UN peacekeeping missions began with the UN Transition Assistance Group (UNTAG) in Namibia in 1989. The first time the SAF entered a combat theatre involved the sending of a medical mission to the Persian Gulf during Operation Desert Storm. Since then, Singaporean military personnel have participated in medical missions to Guatemala and East Timor; observation missions in the Middle East and in Africa; reconstruction missions in Iraq; strategic lift and humanitarian and disaster relief (HADR) missions in Southeast Asia (including during the Indian Ocean tsunami in 2004); interdiction and anti-piracy operations in the Persian Gulf; Gulf of Aden and the Malacca Straits; HADR missions in New Zealand (Christchurch earthquake in 2011), the US (Hurricane Katrina in New Orleans in 2005) and in the Philippines (Typhoon Haiyan/Yolanda in 2013); and peace support and reconstruction missions as part of the NATO-led International Security Assistance Force (ISAF) in Afghanistan. While most of the aforementioned missions elicited well wishes and pride among Singaporeans for the SAF's accomplishments, the mission to Afghanistan — Operation Blue Ridge, which lasted six years and involved close to 500 SAF personnel[76] — evoked disquiet from some quarters over the risking of Singaporean lives in a war in which some felt their country had no business being involved.[77] Noting the growing import of HADR, Singapore's Defence Minister, Ng Eng Hen, has argued that the involvement of militaries in HADR is no longer the exception but has increasingly become the norm.[78] It has also been argued that while the SAF should work on developing its capabilities in niche areas and seeking new areas in which Singapore can contribute to global peacekeeping, at the same time, it needs to be selective and participate in missions where it has the means and ability to make an effective contribution.[79]

Finally, relative to what the leading funding countries are giving in support of UN peacekeeping (see Table 1), Singapore's contribution of 0.36% for the 2013 to 2015 period is small by comparison.[80] Nonetheless, when compared to the contributions by other countries, particularly G20 member countries, over the same period — Mexico (0.37%), Argentina (0.09%), India (0.13%) or Indonesia (0.07%) — Singapore's contribution is by no means small.

Singaporeans in the Portals of Global Power

For a country as small as Singapore, its contributions to global governance in terms of providing personnel who play key leadership roles has been no less than remarkable. Tommy Koh, whose opinion on Asia as a free-rider or responsible stakeholder was cited in this essay's introductory section, has served and represented both Singapore and the UN in areas as diverse as international law, environmental policy, trade, and dispute resolution. From 1981 to 1982, Koh served as President of the Third United Nations Conference on the Law of the Sea (UNCLOS). As James Sebenius and Laurence Green have noted in their Harvard Business School case study on Koh's efforts to mobilise disparate parties with competing interests to cobble together a collective agreement in the UNCLOS process:

> Carefully introducing outside experts while balancing formal meetings with non-binding gatherings, Koh incrementally built both momentum and consensus for a remarkably creative agreement on seabed mining. In 1980, Koh's group reached agreement on a text used directly by the convention. His unexpected success led the grateful LOS [Law of Sea] delegates to elect him to be president of the overall LOS conference, which finally produced a treaty — a "constitution for the oceans" — ultimately ratified by 165 nations and signed by an additional 15 countries.[81]

From 1990 to 1992, Koh chaired the Preparatory and Main Committees of the UN Conference on Environment and Development (the so-called Rio "Earth Summit") before serving in 1993 as the special envoy of the UN Secretary-General to the Russian Federation and Estonia, Latvia and Lithuania. During his Chairmanship of the Earth Summit — which comprised over 7,000 delegates representing 172 countries and covered a wide array of complex issues ranging from climate change and biodiversity to the rights of indigenous peoples to energy consumption — Koh and his colleagues successfully overcame intense opposition to produce a series of documents and agreements (such as the Rio Declaration of Principles, Agenda 21, the Forest Principles, the Convention on Biological Diversity, the United Nations Framework Convention on Climate Change and the United Nations Convention to Combat Desertification) which continue to serve as part of the foundation for international environmental policy.[82]

Another Singaporean who has arguably wielded considerable influence in global governance by virtue of his responsibility as Chairman of the International Monetary and Financial Committee (IMFC) is Tharman Shanmugaratnam, the Deputy Prime Minister and Finance Minister of Singapore. Originally selected to serve a three-year term from 2011 to 2014, Shanmugaratnam has agreed, at the urging of the IMFC, to extend his term by an additional year following the conclusion of his current term in March 2014.[83]

Conclusion

This paper has sought, in the light of criticisms that Singapore has not done enough to contribute to global governance, to assess whether Singapore has been a free-rider or a responsible stakeholder. Far from simple, the issue is complicated by a number of tensions within global governance. Debates have arisen over equity and efficiency as the more relevant foundation for the legitimacy and effectiveness of global bodies. Differences in opinion over responsible participation in global governance as primarily a matter of rule-making (or the chance to do so) and rule-taking have also arisen in tandem with the evolving global distribution of wealth and influence. Against this backdrop, Singapore's efforts at a greater — and presumably more responsible — engagement with global governance are a marked improvement relative to the perspective and policy it historically adopted as a post-colonial developmental and garrison state. From the standpoint of international relations theory, social constructivists might attribute such efforts to Singapore's pragmatic quest to gain international legitimacy through "mimicking" what others do rather than it being driven by some Kantian categorical imperative.[84] Even so, the behaviour implies that Singaporean leaders comprehend sovereignty as about a state's acknowledgement (and the exercise) of its responsibilities as the assertion of its rights.[85] At the very least, the evidence presented here suggests that the criticism of Singapore as a free-rider in global governance, while not incorrect from a historical perspective — indeed, all emerging powers, bar none, engage in freeriding — becomes a lot more tenuous once Singapore's evolving foreign policy disposition and behaviour are taken into consideration.

Notes

[1] Robyn Kingler Vidra, "The Pragmatic 'Little Red Dot': Singapore's US Hedge against China," in Nicholas Kitchen (ed.), *The New Geopolitics of Southeast Asia* (London: LSE IDEAS, 2012), p. 67; Andrew T. H. Tan, "Punching above Its Weight: Singapore's Armed Forces and Its Contribution to Foreign Policy," *Defence Studies*, 11(4), 2011, pp. 672–697.

[2] According to "The World Wealth Report 2012" by Knight Frank and Citi Private Bank, as cited in Surekha A. Yadav, "Singapore Tops the GDP Charts," *Forbes*, 14 August 2012. Retrieved 15 April 2015, from http://www.forbes.com/sites/surekhaayadav/2012/08/14/singapore-tops-the-gdp-charts/.

[3] Takashi Terada, *The Making of Asia's First Bilateral FTA: Origins and Implications of the Japan–Singapore Economic Partnership Agreement*, Pacific Economic Papers no. 354 (Canberra, ACT: Australia–Japan Research Centre, Australian National University, 2006).

4   Salil Tripathi, "Temasek: The Perils of Being Singaporean," *Far Eastern Economic Review*, May 2006. Retrieved 15 April 2015, from http://www.singapore-window.org/sw06/0605FEER.HTM.

5   Ulrike Guérot, "Europe and the Future of Global Governance." Paper presented at the Council of Councils Regional Conference on Europe and the Future of Global Governance, Italian Ministry of Foreign Affairs, Rome, 8–10 September 2013.

6   Ulrike Guérot, "The Continentalist: Regionalism as the Basis for a Post-Crisis EU," *World Politics Review*, 22 October 2012. Retrieved 15 April 2015, from http://www.worldpoliticsreview.com/articles/12438/the-continentalist-regionalism-as-the-basis-for-a-post-crisis-eu.

7   Mohan Srilal, "Singapore–Indonesia Ties Sink to Chilly Depths," *Asia Times Online*, 5 March 1999. Retrieved 15 April 2015, from http://www.atimes.com/se-asia/AC05Ae01.html.

8   Tripathi (2006), *op. cit.*

9   Seth Mydans and Wayne Arnold, "Lee Kuan Yew, Founder of Singapore, Changing with Times," *The New York Times*, 29 August 2007. Retrieved 15 April 2015, from http://www.nytimes.com/2007/08/29/world/asia/29iht-lee.1.7301669.html?pagewanted=all&_r=0.

10 Cited in Wayne Arnold and Thomas Fuller, "Singapore and Neighbours Just Can't Get along," *The New York Times*, 15 March 2007. Retrieved 15 April 2015, from http://www.nytimes.com/2007/03/15/world/asia/15iht-singapore.4922379.html?pagewanted=all&_r=0.

11 H. L. A. Hart, "Are There Any Natural Rights?," *Philosophical Review*, 64(2), 1955, pp. 185–186; John Rawls, *A Theory of Justice* (Cambridge, MA: Harvard University Press, 1971), p. 96. However, philosophers like Robert Nozick feel that this proposition is not as straightforward as it sounds because it assumes that others could impose an obligation on us by dint of their acting cooperatively to provide some good from which we also benefit. Robert Nozick, *Anarchy, the State, and Utopia* (New York: Basic Books, 1974), pp. 90–95.

12 Robert B. Zoellick, "Whither China: From Membership to Responsibility?." Remarks to National Committee on U.S.–China Relations, New York City, 21 September 2005, US Department of State Archives. Retrieved 15 April 2015, from http://2001-2009.state.gov/s/d/former/zoellick/rem/53682.htm.

13 Tommy Koh, "In Conversation with Professor Toming Koh," in *Rapporteur*, Lee Kuan Yew School of Public Policy, National University of Singapore, Singapore, February 2009, pp. 18–19.

14 Ian Hurd, *International Organisations: Politics, Law, Practice* (Cambridge: Cambridge University Press, 2010); Volker Rittberger, Bernhard Zangl and Andreas Kruck, *International Organization*, Second Edition (Basingstoke: Palgrave, 2012); Timothy J. Sinclair, *Global Governance* (Oxford: Polity Press, 2012); Thomas G. Weiss, *Global Governance: Why? What? Whither?* (Oxford: Polity Press, 2013).

15 Martha Finnemore and Kathryn Sikkink, "International Norm Dynamics and Political Change," *International Organization*, 52(4), Autumn 1998, pp. 887–917.

16 Robert O'Brien, Anne Marie Goetz, Jan Arte Scholte and Marc Williams, *Contesting Global Governance: Multilateral Economic Institutions and Global Social Movements* (Cambridge: Cambridge University Press, 2000); Philipp Pattberg, *Global Governance: Reconstructing a Contested Social Science Concept*, GARNET Working Paper no. 04/06, March 2006 (UK: University of Warwick, 2006).

17 The term was originally coined to summarise the form of economic orthodoxy to which both the IMF and WB adhered in their policy reform advice to indebted Latin American countries. John Williamson, "What Washington Means by Policy Reform," in John Williamson (ed.), *Latin American Adjustment: How Much Has Happened?* (Washington, DC: Institute for International Economics, 1990), pp. 7–20. Also see, John Williamson, "The Strange History of the Washington Consensus," *Journal of Post-Keynesian Economics*, 27(2), 2004/05, pp. 195–206.

18 Devin Joshi and Roni Kay O'Dell, "Global Governance and Development Ideology: The United Nations and the World Bank on the Left-Right Spectrum," *Global Governance: A Review of Multilateralism and International Organisations*, 19(2), April–June 2013, pp. 249–275.

19 Susanne Lütz and Matthias Kranke, *The European Rescue of the Washington Consensus? EU and IMF Lending to Central and Eastern European Countries*, LSE "Europe in Question" (LEQS) Discussion Paper Series no. 22/2010, May 2010 (UK: LSE, 2010).

20 Miles Kahler, "Asia and the Reform of Global Governance." Paper prepared for Asian Economic Policy Review conference — Asia Reshaping the Global Economic Order: Trade and Finance, Tokyo, 10 April 2010, p. 9.

21 Sabine Hassler, *Reforming the UN Security Council Membership: The Illusion of Representativeness* (Abingdon, Oxon: Routledge, 2012); Bardo Fassbender, *UN Security Council Reform and the Right of Veto* (Leiden: Martinus Nijhoff, 1998).

22 The G20 members are Argentina, Australia, Brazil, Canada, China, France, Germany, India, Indonesia, Italy, Japan, Republic of Korea, Mexico, Russia, Saudi Arabia, South Africa, Turkey, the United Kingdom, the US and the European Union.

23 Andrew F. Cooper, "The G20 and Its Regional Critics: The Search for Inclusion," *Global Policy*, 2(2), May 2011, pp. 203–209.

24 Andrew Potter, "Two Concepts of Legitimacy," *MacLean's*, 3 December 2008. Retrieved 15 April 2015, from http://www.macleans.ca/general/two-concepts-of-legitimacy/.

25 Dingxin Zhao, "The Mandate of Heaven and Performance Legitimation in Historical and Contemporary China," *American Behavioral Scientist*, 53(3), November 2009, pp. 416–433.

26 Moisés Naím, "Minilateralism: The Magic Number to Get Real International Action," *Foreign Policy*, 22 June 2009. Retrieved 15 April 2015, from http://www.foreignpolicy.com/articles/2009/06/18/minilateralism.

27 Susan C. Schwab, "After Doha: Why the Negotiations Are Doomed and What We Should Do About It," *Foreign Affairs*, 90(3), 2011, p. 104.

28 Judith Kelley, *The Role of Membership Rules in Regional Organisations*, ADB Working Paper Series on Regional Economic Integration no. 53, June 2010 (Manila: Asian

Development Bank, 2010), p. 4. Also see, James M. Buchanan, "An Economic Theory of Clubs," *Economica*, 32(125), February 1965, pp. 1–14; and Mancur Olson, *The Logic of Collective Action* (Cambridge, MA: Harvard University Press, 1965).

29 Joe Murphy, "Divided They Stand: G20 Ends with East and West Still Split over Syria Action," *The Independent*, 7 September 2013. Retrieved 15 April 2015, from http://www.independent.co.uk/news/world/middle-east/divided-they-stand-g20-ends-with-east-and-west-still-split-over-syria-action-8802598.html; Thomas Fues and Peter Wolff (eds.), *G20 and Global Development: How Can the New Summit Architecture Promote Pro-Poor Growth and Sustainability?* (Bonn: German Development Institute [DIE-GDI], 2010).

30 Daniel Gaus, "Two Kinds of Democratic Legitimacy for the EU? Input- and Output-Oriented Legitimacy as a Case of Conceptual Misformation." Paper presented at the conference Democracy as Idea and Practice, Oslo, 14–15 January 2010.

31 Stewart Patrick, "Irresponsible Stakeholders? The Difficulty of Integrating Rising Powers," *Foreign Affairs*, 89(6), 2010, pp. 44–53.

32 Andrew Monahan, "China Overtakes Japan as World's No. 2 Economy," *The Wall Street Journal*, 14 February 2011. Retrieved 17 April 2015, from http://online.wsj.com/news/articles/SB10001424052748703361904576142832741439402.

33 Song Tao, "Emerging Economies Not Free-Riders Says China," *The BRICS Post*, 4 February 2013. Retrieved 15 April 2015, from http://thebricspost.com/emerging-economies-not-free-riders-says-china/.

34 The figures are taken from "Implementation of General Assembly Resolutions 55/235 and 55/236," United Nations General Assembly A/67/224/Add.1, 27 December 2012.

35 "Monthly Summary of Contributions (Police, UN Military Experts on Mission and Troops)," (as of 30 June 2014), in *Contributors to UN Peacekeeping Operations*. Retrieved 11 June 2015, from http://www.un.org/en/peacekeeping/contributors/2014/apr14_1.pdf.

36 Stephen Grenville, "The Trans-Pacific Partnership: Where Economics and Geopolitics Meet," *The Lowy Interpreter*, 4 March 2014. Retrieved 17 April 2015, from http://www.lowyinterpreter.org/post/2014/03/04/Trans-Pacific-Partnership-Where-economics-and-geopolitics-meet.aspx?COLLCC=3559796430&.

37 John West, "The OECD and Asia: a Cold War Organisation in the Age of Globalisation," *East Asia Forum*, 11 January 2012. Retrieved 17 April 2015, from http://www.eastasiaforum.org/2012/01/11/the-oecd-and-asia-a-cold-war-organisation-in-the-age-of-globalisation/.

38 Kai He, "A Tale of Three Fears: Why China Does Not Want to Be No. 1," *RSIS Commentaries* no. 104/2014, 2 June 2014. Retrieved 17 April 2015, from http://www.rsis.edu.sg/publications/Perspective/RSIS1042014.pdf.

39 Shaun Breslin, "China's Emerging Global Role: Dissatisfied Responsible Great Power," *Politics*, 30(1), 2010, pp. 52–62.

40 President William McKinley, for instance, was known for his robust advocacy of protectionism. Quentin R. Skrabec Jr., *William McKinley, Apostle of Protectionism* (New York: Algora, 2008).

[41] Paul Krugman, "The Myth of Asia's Miracle: A Cautionary Fable," *Foreign Affairs*, 73(6), 1994, pp. 62–79.

[42] James Fallows, *Looking at the Sun: The Rise of the New East Asian Economic and Political System* (New York: Vintage, 1995).

[43] Kjell Goldman, "Appropriateness and Consequences: The Logic of Neo-Institutionalism," *Global Governance*, 18(1), 2005, pp. 35–52.

[44] Song (2013), *op. cit.*

[45] "Declaration on the Establishment of a New International Economic Order," United Nations General Assembly no. A/RES/S-6/3201, 1 May 1974.

[46] As Aggarwal and Weber have observed, "It's stunning today to read the NIEO demands — because they are almost exactly the same as what Supachai Panitchpakdi, head of UNCTAD and previously Director General of the WTO (2002–2005), is now calling for. Then as now, the emerging market players called for management of volatile commodity markets, preferential trade access to rich country markets, greater stability in exchange rates, monitoring of trans-border capital flows, greater aid to the least developed, favourable debt rescheduling, and regulation of multinational corporations to ensure that they comply with national laws and foster technology transfers. All this represents a considerable turn away from anything resembling a Washington Consensus and towards a more highly managed system favouring preferential terms for developing countries and redistribution over competition and efficiency." Vinod K. Aggarwal and Steve Weber, "The New New International Economic Order," *Harvard Business Review Blog Network*, 18 April 2012. Retrieved 17 April 2015, from http://blogs.hbr.org/2012/04/the-new-new-international-econ/.

[47] Robert Cox, "Ideologies and the NIEO: Reflections on Some Recent Literature," *International Organization*, 33(2), 1979, pp. 257–302.

[48] Haruhiko Kuroda, "The Role of Asia in a Globalized Era," *Asia-Pacific Review*, 20(2), November 2013, pp. 101–115.

[49] Linda Low, "Between a Rock and a Hard Place," in Linda Low (ed.), *Developmental States: Relevancy, Redundancy or Reconfiguration?* (Hauppauge, NY: Nova Science, 2004), p. 164.

[50] Michael Hennigan, "Switzerland, Singapore Join OECD Agreement to End Bank Secrecy for Tax Evasion," *FinFacts Ireland*, 7 May 2014. Retrieved 15 April 2015, from http://www.finfacts.ie/irishfinancenews/article_1027638.shtml; "Singapore Joins the OECD White List," Baker and McKenzie, n.d. Retrieved 17 April 2015, from http://www.bakermckenzie.com/RRSingaporeJoinsOECDNov09/.

[51] Fred Bergsten, "Plan B for World Trade: Go Regional," *Financial Times*, 16 August 2006. Retrieved 17 April 2015, from http://www.ft.com/cms/s/0/f5eec3f8-2cc3-11db-9845-0000779e2340.html#axzz3A4tDNtyw.

[52] Margaret Liang, "Singapore's Trade Policies: Priorities and Options," *ASEAN Economic Bulletin*, 22(1), 2005, pp. 13–14.

[53] The point is made in Shawn Donnan, "Trade Ministers Seek to Kick-Start Pacific Rim Pact," *Financial Times*, 18 May 2014. Retrieved 17 April 2015, from http://www.ft.com/intl/cms/s/0/7d996164-dea5-11e3-b46b-00144feabdc0.html#axzz3A4tDNtyw.

[54] Stephen J. Ezell and Robert D. Atkinson, *Gold Standard or WTO-Lite? Shaping the Trans-Pacific Partnership*, ITIF Report, May 2011 (Washington, DC: Information Technology and Innovation Foundation, 2011).

[55] Barry Desker and Mohamed Nawab Mohamed Osman, "S. Rajaratnam and the Making of Singapore Foreign Policy," in Kwa Chong Guan (ed.), *S Rajaratnam on Singapore: From Ideas to Reality* (Singapore: World Scientific, 2006), p. 4.

[56] Michael Leifer, *Singapore Foreign Policy: Coping with Vulnerability* (London: Routledge 2000); Derek da Cunha, "Defence and Security: Evolving Threat Perceptions," in Derek da Cunha (ed.), *Singapore in the New Millennium: Challenges Facing the City-State* (Singapore: Institute of Southeast Asian Studies, 2002), pp. 133–153.

[57] "Speech by Prime Minister Lee Hsien Loong at Economic Society of Singapore Annual Dinner," Singapore Prime Minister's Office, 8 June 2012. Retrieved 17 April 2015, from http://www.pmo.gov.sg/mediacentre/speech-prime-minister-lee-hsien-loong-economic-society-singapore-annual-dinner.

[58] Tim Huxley, *Defending the Lion City: The Armed Forces of Singapore* (NSW: Allen and Unwin, 2000), p. 249.

[59] Iftekhar Ahmed Chowdhury, *The Global Governance Group ('3G') and Singaporean Leadership: Can Small Be Significant?*, ISAS Working Paper no. 108, 19 May 2010 (Singapore: Institute of South Asian Studies, National University of Singapore, 2010), p. 2.

[60] Dorothy-Grace Guerrero, "The Broken 'New Normal' and the G20 Mirage," *Focus on the Global South*, n.d. Retrieved 17 April 2015, from http://focusweb.org/content/broken-new-normal-and-g20-mirage.

[61] "Letter Dated 11 March 2010 from the Permanent Representative of Singapore to the United Nations Addressed to the Secretary-General," United Nations General Assembly no. A/64/706, 11 March 2010, pp. 2–3.

[62] "Statement by Mr. Albert Chua, Permanent Representative of Singapore to the United Nations, on Behalf of the Global Governance Group (3G) at the High-Level Thematic Debate on the United Nations and Global Economic Governance, 15 April 2013," Singapore Ministry of Foreign Affairs, 15 April 2013. Retrieved 17 April 2015, from http://www.mfa.gov.sg/content/mfa/overseasmission/newyork/nyemb_statements/global_governance_group/2013/201304/press_20130415.html.

[63] *The Responsibility to Protect*, Report of the International Commission on Intervention and State Sovereignty, December 2001 (Ottawa, ON: International Development Research Centre, 2001).

[64] See, "Resolution Adopted by the General Assembly: 60/1," 2005 World Summit Outcome, United Nations General Assembly A/RES/60/1, 24 October 2005. Retrieved 17 April 2015, from http://daccess-dds-ny.un.org/doc/UNDOC/GEN/N05/487/60/PDF/N0548760.pdf?OpenElement; "Implementing the Responsibility to Protect," Report of the Secretary-General, United Nations A/63/677, 12 January 2009. Retrieved 17 April 2015, from http://www.un.org/preventgenocide/adviser/pdf/SG%20Report%20R2P.pdf; "Resolution 1674, United Nations Security Council S/

RES/1674," 28 April 2006. Retrieved 17 April 2015, from http://daccess-dds-ny.un.org/doc/UNDOC/GEN/N06/331/99/PDF/N0633199.pdf?OpenElement.

65   "Resolution adopted by the General Assembly: 60/1."

66   Yang Razali Kassim, "S5 vs P5: The Rise of the Small States?," *RSIS Commentaries* no. 187/2012, 8 October 2012.

67   Recommendation 20 in "Enhancing the Accountability, Transparency and Effectiveness of the Security Council," United Nations General Assembly no. A/66/L.42/Rev.1, 3 May 2012, p. 5.

68   *The Responsibility to Protect* (2001), *op. cit.*, p. 51.

69   Mely Caballero-Anthony, *Non-Traditional Security and Multilateralism in Asia: Reshaping the Contours of Regional Security Architecture?*, Policy Analysis Brief, June 2007 (Muscatine, IA: The Stanley Foundation, 2007).

70   Colonel Jimmy Tan, "Unclenching the Fisted Hand: Globalisation and Military Multilateralism," *Pointer: Journal of the Singapore Armed Forces*, 28(1), 2002. Retrieved 17 April 2015, from http://www.mindef.gov.sg/safti/pointer/back/journals/2002/Vol28_1/5.htm.

71   Charles W. Hasskamp, *Operations Other than War: Who Says Warriors Don't Do Windows?*, Air War College Maxwell Paper no. 13, March 1998 (Maxwell, AL: U.S. Air War College, 1998).

72   Samuel P. Huntington, "New Contingencies, Old Roles," *JFQ: Joint Force Quarterly*, (2), Autumn 1993, pp. 40–43.

73   Colin S. Gray, "War — Continuity in Change, and Change in Continuity," *Parameters*, 40(2), Summer 2010, p. 7.

74   Cited in Captain Jeremy Lim, "UN Peacekeeping and the SAF," *Pointer: Journal of the Singapore Armed Forces*, 27(2), 2002. Retrieved 17 April 2015, from http://www.mindef.gov.sg/safti/pointer/back/journals/2001/Vol27_2/3.htm.

75   Lieutenant Colonel Yeong Chee Meng, Major Aaron Tan, Major Dean Tan and Captain Jerediah Ong, "RSAF [Republic of Singapore Air Force] in Operations Other than War — The Challenges," *Pointer: Journal of the Singapore Armed Forces*, 33(1), 2007. Retrieved 17 April 2015, from http://www.mindef.gov.sg/imindef/publications/pointer/journals/2007/v33n1/feature4.html.

76   Fabian Koh, "Singapore Armed Forces Concludes Deployment in Afghanistan," *The Straits Times*, 25 June 2013. Retrieved 17 April 2015, from http://www.straitstimes.com/breaking-news/singapore/story/singapore-armed-forces-concludes-deployment-afghanistan-20130625#sthash.TxSj3uD1.dpuf.

77   Jermyn Chow, "Should S'pore's Military Bear Open Arms?," *The Straits Times/ANN*, 16 January 2014. Retrieved 17 April 2015, from http://www.thejakartapost.com/news/2014/01/16/should-spores-military-bear-open-arms.html.

78   Teo Jing Ting, "Dr Ng Visits Exercise Wallaby," *Cyber Pioneer*, 3 January 2014. Retrieved 17 April 2015, from http://www.mindef.gov.sg/imindef/resourcelibrary/cyberpioneer/topics/articles/features/2014/jan14_cs.print.img.html.

[79] Lieutenant Colonel Deep Singh, "The SAF's Experiences in Peace Support Operations," *Pointer: Journal of the Singapore Armed Forces*, 31(1), 2005. Retrieved 17 April 2015, from http://www.mindef.gov.sg/imindef/publications/pointer/journals/2005/v31n1/features/feature4.html.

[80] The figure is taken from "Implementation of General Assembly Resolutions 55/235 and 55/236".

[81] James K. Sebenius and Laurence A. Green, *Tommy Koh: Background and Major Accomplishments of the "Great Negotiator, 2014"*, Working Paper no. 14-049, 13 February 2014 (Cambridge, MA: Harvard Business School, Harvard University, 2014), p. 3.

[82] Sebenius and Green (2014), *op. cit.*, pp. 4–5.

[83] "IMFC Extends Term of Chairman Tharman Shanmugaratnam by One Year," International Monetary Fund (IMF) Press Release no. 13/525, 18 December 2013. Retrieved 17 April 2015, from http://www.imf.org/external/np/sec/pr/2013/pr13525.htm.

[84] Hiro Katsumata, "Mimetic Adoption and Norm Diffusion: 'Western' Security Cooperation in Southeast Asia?," *Review of International Studies*, 37(2), April 2011, pp. 557–576.

[85] Alex J. Bellamy and Mark Beeson, "The Responsibility to Protect in Southeast Asia: Can ASEAN Reconcile Humanitarianism and Sovereignty?," *Asian Security*, 6(3), 2010, pp. 262–279; See Seng Tan, "Providers Not Protectors: Institutionalizing Responsible Sovereignty in Southeast Asia," *Asian Security*, 7(3), 2011, pp. 201–217.

Chapter 5

The Challenge of Strategic Intelligence for the Singapore Armed Forces

Kwa Chong Guan

Singapore was born by constitutional fiat on 9 August 1965 as a defenceless city-state vulnerable to external predatory powers in a rough neighbourhood beset by wars and communist insurgencies. Facing the prospect of the withdrawal of British armed forces from east of Suez, particularly from their bases in Singapore, and uneasy at the prospect of being dependent on the Malaysian armed forces for its protection, Singapore embarked on an accelerated build-up of its own armed capability, with the help of Israeli advisers and experts from Commonwealth countries. That build-up, including the enlistment and training of National Servicemen to provide the mind and muscle of the nascent army, proceeded at a sharp pace under the leadership of Dr Goh Keng Swee, the first Defence Minister.[1]

But the capability and willingness of an emerging Singapore Armed Forces (SAF) to defend the island-state had to be underpinned by a strategic intelligence capability to make sense of the neighbourhood and warn of threats which the SAF may be deployed against. Dr Goh and his colleagues have personal memories of the consequences of American and British intelligence underestimating Japanese capability and intention to challenge their hegemony of the Asia-Pacific, which led to the Pacific War. In particular, they would recall how the US ignored signals and warnings of the Japanese attack on Pearl Harbour and the invasion of Malaya on 8 December 1941. Dr Goh would also have learnt from the Israeli advisers of the need for a military and strategic intelligence capability to complement an effective armed force.

The Israeli advisers advised Singapore on not only the setting up and formation of the armed forces and its combat doctrines, but also the organisation of a centralised and integrated Ministry of Defence and its intelligence service.[2] By 1971s, this external intelligence service known as the Security and Intelligence Division (SID) was sufficiently well-established to need some streamlining of its organisation. S. R. Nathan, who had pioneered Singapore's nascent foreign service was appointed by Dr Goh to become director of SID and remained in the job for the next seven years[3] before being succeeded by Eddie Teo.[4]

Dr Goh and his senior colleagues would have watched with deep concern the failure of the Israeli Defense Force's much vaunted G2 and the intelligence service Mossad to provide early warning of Egypt's surprise attack on 6 October 1973, though they were not the first, nor the last, to fail to do so.

Why Has Intelligence Failed in Anticipating Surprise Attacks?

The track record of intelligence services in providing its policy-makers early warning of a surprise military attack in an escalating diplomatic crisis has been dismal. Successful surprise military attacks in three Arab–Israeli Wars (two in which Israel achieved surprise and the third in which Israel was surprised); the Argentinean invasion of the Falklands; and the 1990 invasion of Kuwait by Iraq, have to a large part been attributed to intelligence failure to anticipate the incentives and opportunities for a surprise attack in a political crisis.[5] Broadly, four categories of failures have been identified.

The first category of failures is the inability of intelligence to see through the fog of deception issued by the adversary in the build-up to a crisis. Central to penetrating the fog of deception is uncovering the adversary's actions to cover and conceal his movements to launch a surprise attack. The Soviets successfully covered and concealed much of their shipment of their missiles to Cuba from the CIA until 14 October 1962, when they were about to complete it. The lesson that intelligence services have drawn is that deception and denial of information by the adversary of their intentions and actions are a major obstacle they are up against in their efforts to provide better assessments and estimates to their policy-makers. But to what extent is it feasible or possible to develop counter-deception strategies[6] given that successful deception feeds into, and exploits the adversary's expectations and preconceptions to "see what they expect to see"? It is easy to preach as Sunzi did some two millenniums ago, that success in battle depends upon knowing one's enemy and knowing oneself first, but practicing that maxim is not easy.

The second category of explanations for intelligence failures are cognitive biases driving intelligence analysis. As CIA veteran Richards J. Heuer, Jr.[7] has advised his staff, there are biases in the evaluation of evidence; biases in perception of cause and effect; biases in estimating probabilities; and finally hindsight biases in evaluating the quality and value of intelligence products. Studies by a generation of scholars have all lamented the inevitability of cognitive failures in anticipating a crisis which could lead to a surprise attack. For these analysts, surprise is inevitable.

The third category of reasons for intelligence failures to forecast crisis and surprise attacks is attributed to the management and organisation of the intelligence services. This has been the finding of most Commissions of Inquiry from the Congressional Hearings into Pearl Harbor to the Agranat Commission on failures in Israeli intelligence leading to Israel being surprised in 1973. More recently, the 9/11 Commission Report and the July 2004 Butler Report on Iraq called for reform of not only the intelligence community, but much of the entire government.[8] The challenge in reforming the intelligence services is the delicate check on over-centralisation and balance with decentralisation and pluralism.[9]

Finally, failure of intelligence to warn their policy-makers of an impending crisis may lie in their relations to their policy-maker.[10] The mainstream expectation of the intelligence analyst is that he is to provide an objective and accurate picture of "what is out there" to his policy-maker. The analyst is not a part of the policy process to ensure that his estimates and assessments are not skewed to the biases of the policy-maker. The 2004 Butler Report into Iraq's weapons of mass destruction (WMD) documents the consequences of the politicisation of the intelligence process.[11] As Richard Betts argued back in 1982,[12] intelligence may correctly anticipate a crisis, but the policy-maker either chooses to ignore it or is reluctant to authorise a military response. Was US intelligence "wrong for the right reasons on the issue of WMD in Iraq"?

If we accept that intelligence failures are inevitable, then should we resign ourselves to being surprised, or examine how to reframe our understanding of an international crisis and expectations of intelligence in the management of an international crisis?[13]

Understanding International Crises

Surprise attacks are not a singular problem. They are an option for states locked in a diplomatic crisis or stand-off with one or more other states. Anticipating and preventing a surprise attack therefore starts with recognising that normal diplomatic relations have broken down and events are taking an unexpected and surprising turn of events, creating a crisis.[14] Surprise attacks are the culmination of an escalating diplomatic crisis in which one party never expected the other to resort to the military option to resolve the impasse in their relations and is therefore *fundamentally* surprised.[15] America was fundamentally surprised by the audacity of the Japanese attack on Pearl Harbor. In contrast, the British anticipated an increasingly aggressive Japan may attack Malaya and prepared its defences and made contingency plans against a Japanese invasion. Consequently, the British were not fundamentally surprised by the Japanese attack on the evening of 8 December 1941, but were tactically surprised by its timing and the capability of the Japanese to sink two of their capital ships, the *Prince of Wales* and the *Repulse*.

For Singapore and its ASEAN partners, the collapse of the Saigon government in March 1975 following the ignominious withdrawal of US forces was a fundamental surprise. It raised the spectre of the falling South Vietnamese domino toppling other dominos which could eventually hit Singapore. It spurred another round of accelerated defence planning in the SAF. Then-Prime Minister Lee Kuan Yew admitted to an American news audience that "I would frankly like to say that perhaps never in all our scenarios that we envisaged such a catastrophic collapse of will and morale which led to this terrible disaster".[16] The crisis galvanised ASEAN to finally convene a Heads of Government Meeting in Bali to deliberate on its response to a victorious Socialist Vietnam. Four years later, Singapore and its ASEAN partners were again fundamentally surprised that Vietnam's deteriorating relations with Cambodia escalated into a Vietnamese blitzkrieg invasion and occupation of Cambodia. For Lee Kuan Yew, the Vietnamese invasion of Cambodia was so "startling, so unexpected, so bold, so audacious that the significance and implications of what had been done is only being gradually grasped". Singapore rallied its ASEAN partners to respond as a group to the Cambodian occupation for the next 12 years.[17]

Responding to the threat of a surprise attack is then about how to manage the spiralling diplomatic crisis and maintain control over events to avoid war.[18] Intelligence is expected to provide policy-makers the foreknowledge of events taking an unpredicted turn leading to a crisis. In this dismal record of intelligence failures, the Cuban Missile Crisis of 1962 and the earlier Berlin Blockade of 1948–1949 and possibly, the Sino–Soviet border crisis of 1969 stand out as cases of diplomatic crises which could, but did not, lead to war.

The Cuban missile crisis has been, and continues to be, the locus case of successful crisis management[19] and about the role of US intelligence in shaping the crisis. The evaluations of US intelligence performance in the crisis have usually focused on the failure to estimate the Soviet intent to deploy strategic missiles on Cuba. Special National Intelligence Estimate (SNIE 85-3-62) issued on 19 September 1962 argued against Soviet deployment of missiles on Cuba because the risks involved were "incompatible with Soviet practice to date and with Soviet policy as we presently estimate it".[20] However, it was monitoring of the Soviet build-up on Cuba, especially the U-2 aerial reconnaissance, which confirmed the construction of ballistic missile sites at San Cristobal and precipitated a crisis. Declassified records now enable us to assess the support US intelligence subsequently provided to their policy-makers during the crisis by monitoring the levels of Soviet build-up on Cuba and globally, while also attempting to estimate Soviet reactions to possible US options against their missiles deployed on Cuba. In contrast, the opening up of the Soviet archives shows that Soviet intelligence were cut out of the Soviet decision-making, leading to their deployment of missiles on Cuba, and during the crisis had no information on US options and response to this deployment of missiles on Cuba.[21]

For Kennedy, the crisis over Soviet deployment of missiles erupted on 14 October 1962 when U-2 aerial photographs confirmed the construction of missiles sites on Cuba, undermining the Special National Intelligence Estimate 85-3-62. Kennedy and his colleagues who had been assured by the Special National Intelligence Estimate 85-3-62 were thus fundamentally surprised that Khrushchev would act so irrationally against what they, the White House policy group, perceived to be Soviet national interests and clear US warnings of its interests.[22] But for Khrushchev, the outbreak of a crisis would be over whether the US will discover the deployment of Soviet missiles before they had completed it and so present the US with a *fait accompli*. Apparently, Khrushchev thought Kennedy would do nothing because the US was already vulnerable to Soviet intercontinental missiles, and Soviet missiles in Cuba were therefore not a new or escalating threat. Further, Khrushchev may have assessed that the Soviet Union could withstand any diplomatic pressure from the young US President. Were both Kennedy and Khrushchev wrongly advised by their intelligence services about the intentions and resolve of each to challenge the other?

Emergent Issues in Crisis Management

The current and dominant framework for crisis management, whether political-military,[23] industrial or corporate,[24] is that a crisis may be occurring once the warning signals that an international actor is out to challenge the international order and flaunting diplomatic protocols (or industrial safety standards are being breached; or the production system is under stress and about to breakdown) are disregarded or missed. The challenge for policy-makers (and industry or corporate chiefs) is to recognise that the actor challenging the international order has crossed the rubicon (or the safety valves of the industrial plant are about to blow) and a crisis is in progress, and contingency plans to contain the damage and limit the crisis must be launched. The successful containment and de-escalation of a crisis (or termination of an industrial accident) in large part depends upon how the policy-maker (or corporate chief) makes sense of, and grasps, the crisis as it unfolds.[25]

Equally important, if not more intractable, is avoiding being surprised by a transnational terrorist suicide attack post-9/11. Anticipating and pre-empting the surprise of a terrorist threat has traditionally been an internal security issue. For Singapore, this has been the responsibility of the Internal Security Department (ISD), descendent of the old British Special Branch (SB) established in 1916 to monitor and act against a series of subversive threats against the colony.[26] Anticipating a transnational terrorist suicide attack in Singapore however presents a rather different set of challenges from monitoring a clandestine communist party network planning to plant a series of time bombs, as happened in December 1974.

But diplomatic crises which could escalate into a surprise attack today are unlikely to be a slow build-up of carefully considered moves and exchanges signalling changes of policy and political positions. It is more likely that a diplomatic crisis may erupt over an unplanned and unanticipated incident such as the detention of a foreign fishing trawler for poaching inside the territorial waters of a country.

It is unlikely that any early warning system can anticipate the actions of the skipper of a fishing vessel or the Captain of a naval patrol boat in the South China Sea when it is confronted by another naval vessel challenging its right to be where it is. Neither can intelligence anticipate the nature and extent of "blowback" which will follow that naval confrontation or detention of a fishing vessel. Making sense of the crises which followed the 26 March 2010 sinking of a South Korean patrol vessel, or the 7 September 2010 collision of a Chinese trawler with a Japanese Coast Guard patrol boat near the Senkaku Islands, and more recently, the 7 November 2011 Japanese Coast Guard detention of a Chinese fishing vessel within Japanese waters, is difficult. The issue for intelligence is what is their role in these crises over such incidents at sea?

The unintended consequences of an incident at sea between competing naval vessels or detention of fishing vessels are "wild cards" that are unpredictable and indicative of a complex and chaotic world. The instinctive reaction of the skipper to being pursued by a coast guard vessel cannot be anticipated and may trigger a series of reactions which culminates in a diplomatic crisis, the outcome of which is totally unpredictable.

Information technology today has created a new matrix of real-time information flows, enabling an unprecedented number of not only participants in a crisis, but also observers to bear witness to what is happening.[27] The response time for officials and policy-makers to respond to the detention of their fishing vessels or collusion of their naval vessels is contracted to single-digit hours as the unfolding crises are captured and broadcast by participants on their mobile applications. The policy-maker today will not have the time which Kennedy and his advisers had in 1962 to reflect on their proposed responses to Khrushchev.

Revising the Role of Intelligence in International Crisis Management

A leader must first *act* to establish order in a crisis, sensing where stability is present and where it is absent, and then respond by working to transform the situation from chaos to complexity, where the identification of emerging patterns can both help prevent escalating the crises and discern new opportunities for management of the crisis".[28] Making sense of the catastrophe and ensuing crisis following the meltdown of the Fukushima Daiichi Nuclear Power Plant after it was hit by the 11 March 2011 earthquake and tsunami was complicated and difficult, involving a number of "known-unknowns" about the technology of what was happening in the reactor core. But making sense of the crisis in governance after the catastrophe has been complex, involving the internal politics of the ruling Democratic Party, and tensions between the politicians and bureaucrats and central and local governments, making for uncertainty and unpredictability in Japanese leadership and policy-making.[29]

Has intelligence a role in supporting policy-makers to *act* to seize control of events and impose some order at the onset of a diplomatic crisis following a collision between a Japanese and Chinese coast guard vessel in the East China Sea? Yes, but it will be a different role from the old one of attempting to provide expert judgment of worse-case/warning-focused assessments based on incoming operational intelligence. The new role for intelligence will be a more complex analysis, probing and trying to make sense of "unknown-unknowns" of how the Chinese and Japanese leaders are reading the other's actions and intentions in their perception of the emerging crisis, and deciding how to respond.

A diplomatic crisis is an ascending stairway to war, on which there is at every step opportunities to de-escalate and return to normal, achieve a stand-off with no resolution of the crisis or climb up the next step of the crisis (Figure 1). This decision of whether to escalate or de-escalate the crisis or go for a stand-off is shaped by a range of cognitive biases attempting to instinctively

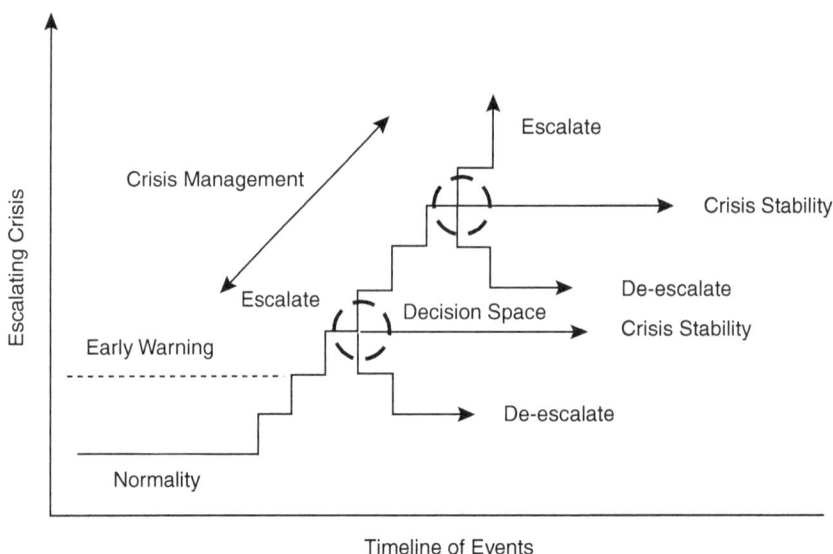

Figure 1. Timeline of Crisis Development.

make sense of the chaos of a crisis.[30] Our minds, as Daniel Kahneman has demonstrated, are wired to think fast and slow.[31] Fast thinking enables us to balance on a bicycle without falling, multiply 2x2, or orient to the source of a sudden sound and detect hostility in a voice. It is this system of fast thinking that usually drives our reactions to the world around us, and in this case, actions to try to control a crisis. The slower, more deliberative and logical system of our mind is only activated when fast thinking confronts a problem it has no immediate response to, like multiplying 17x24.

The role of intelligence must be to support the slow thinking reflective system of the policy-maker's mind. Arguably, intelligence support for the fast thinking system of the policy-maker's mind has been its nemesis when it provided the policy-maker desired evidence — for example, of the presence of WMD in Iraq. Intelligence should feed the slow thinking system of the policy-maker's mind to break the instinctive fast thinking system's move to action because that action will feed into the crisis and may escalate it.

But decision-making in a crisis is not a static single choice. Rather, it is a dynamic decision problem requiring the policy-maker to make sequential risky choices in a rapidly evolving and complex environment. The policy-maker has to make sense of the feedback and consequences of his choice and decide how to respond to the next round of the crisis. Further, the policy-maker can try to anticipate, but cannot control how a decision he makes now will impact on his options later in the unfolding crisis. The sequential risky choices made by adversaries in a crisis create an uncertain and unpredictable environment not under their control. The challenge for intelligence is to advise their policy-makers on the adversary's capacity for risk, sensitise the policy-maker to the possible consequences of his own risky choices on the adversary, and open up the policy-maker's mindset to divergent outcomes of the crisis.

There is not one predictable outcome of a crisis or aim in resolving it. Rather there are multiple possible outcomes as competing parties in the crisis manoeuvre and act out their scenarios to contain (or prolong, if not escalate) the crisis. The Chinese term for crisis, *weiji,* refers to a possible disaster or danger while also offering opportunities, as the word *ji* refers, for China to exploit to further its interests. This makes the prospect of possibility of crisis management with China more complex, as China chases conflicting targets of preventing an escalation of a crisis while exploiting it to maximise its national interests.[32] This is in contrast to European and American norms of containing the dangers of a crisis through mediation and, where necessary, compromise.

Dave Snowden has pointed out that in a complex and chaotic world there is not one future we are working towards. Rather, there are multiple futures we could work towards which we need to probe, make sense of and then respond to. The starting point of policy is not necessarily the past leading into the known present, and from here to then work towards the knowable future. Rather, the more useful starting point may be the multiple futures which a crisis could lead to and probing for whether there are patterns among them which can then be worked back to our present. Understanding China's position on its claims to the South China Sea will, as a first step, involve identifying the various Chinese agencies who have emerged or are emerging as interested parties claiming a stake in the issue, and trying to make sense of their different claims and core interests in the South China Sea.[33] But we need to go beyond discerning the bureaucratic politics of Chinese agencies to try to make sense of what China wants and work backwards to how China's actions are shaped by what it wants.

The mainstream understanding of China's narrative underpinning its response to the various crises in which it is involved in the South and East China Seas is the narrative of China's rise after a century of humiliation[34] and the continuation of a Cold War strategy of containment enacted in a series of treaties at San Francisco at the end of World War II. But, as the historian Paul

A. Cohen has argued, there is a deeper narrative of suffering humiliation, sometimes externally inflicted, occasionally self-imposed, "in order to carry out an important task" enshrined in the proverb *renru fuzhong*. This story is about a fifth century BCE king who, to save his beleaguered kingdom, went into self-exile and servitude in his rival's kingdom to buy time to rebuild his kingdom and eventually avenge himself in conquering his rival. Cohen has demonstrated the relevance of this story to understanding how Chiang Kai-shek identified himself with this fifth century BCE Yue King Goujian and its influence in his sensing of the political crisis of Republican China in the 1920–1930 period, and after World War II, his decamping to Taiwan.[35] Are we today experiencing China's quest for revenge for its century of humiliation now that China through patience, hard work, and foresight triumphed against the odds and is now ready to avenge the humiliation inflicted upon it?

For the Association of Southeast Asian Nations' 10 members, the challenge is not only making sense of Chinese narratives of the South China Sea, within which they are framed, but also the stories the US leaders are telling about themselves, and shaping their perception of developments in the South and East China Seas and their responses to supporting their allies — Japan or the Philippines — in their next confrontation with China. Would watching the first run of the 1960's television and movie serial *Star Trek* help to understand the self-image of the US from then, up to perhaps even today?[36] Strategic intelligence has to revise its modus operandi of simplifying and reducing the "number of dots" to form a pattern to increasing the number of dots and the possible patterns they could form within different stories adversaries in a crisis tell themselves. The challenge for the intelligence analyst is to discern how these foundational narratives are being appropriated, adapted and asserted by different parties in an emerging crisis for different agendas.

Traditional data processing, as Max Boisot and Bill McKelvey[37] have argued, is hierarchic, in which the mountains of data are processed upwards through the layers of a pyramid of "experts" into a single agreed assessment. In the intelligence world this is the Intelligence Estimate, SNIE 85-3-62, issued by the CIA assessing it unlikely the Soviets would deploy missiles on Cuba. But in the emergent complexity leading to a chaotic world of crisis management, this pyramid has to be inverted in a search for multiple and divergent patterns. Predictive warning may then be more a process of socialising the policy-maker into understanding and accepting that there are multiple futures, the "dots" of which need to be connected into various patterns that could form probable futures or scenarios which the analyst and policy-maker then need to keep in view as they work out of their present into their preferred future.

This involves more than just acquiring the current intelligence which enables the analyst to reconstruct how the other side sees the world and is making sense of it. It involves a deep empathy and reading of the stories the other side is telling itself about its place in the world and making sense of any crisis within these implicit stories. This is not about how the other side is "learning the lessons of history" but about the evolving self-identify of the other party in a crisis.

The conventional reductive analysis of inductive pattern recognition to predict a warning of a crisis will have to change to a more open warning system that probes and attempts to make sense of possible multiple crises and, together with the policy-maker, judge and assess which are the more probable crisis scenarios they should be responding to. Such a change amounts to a paradigm shift in intelligence practice.

Conclusion

The SAF in 2015 is operating in a more complex and demanding regional and international environment than at its inception in 1965.[38] Back then, and for much of the next decade-and-a-half, the SAF could contend with being a force-in-waiting to be mobilised on reception of early warning of an imminent threat to Singapore. Providing early warning of threats which could escalate and erupt into a surprise attack on Singapore was then a critical imperative of the Security and Intelligence Division and the various military intelligence branches of the SAF. By 1990, the SAF could look back and reflect on its continuing relevance as a force-in-waiting. It had developed a combined arms conventional war capability and was moving to a joint service capability. The SAF is no longer a force-in-waiting, like a porcupine raising its spines when it senses a threat. The SAF has become a more active force responding to a variety of demands thrust upon it. These ranged from demands to contribute to a variety of United Nations Peacekeeping Operations to supporting an increasing number of Humanitarian and Disaster Relief operations and naval deployments in the Straits of Malacca and the Gulf of Aden to combat piracy. The SAF could think of itself as a dolphin, intelligent and capable of swimming with the sharks.

The fear of being crushed by falling dominos is gone with the end of the Cold War, the opening up of China and Vietnam joining ASEAN. The establishment of the ASEAN Regional Forum marked a new era of regional security cooperation. The paradigm of avoiding surprise by searching for indicators and signs of emerging and escalating threats that warrant issuing early warning of imminent danger and declaration of alert states, which appears to have worked well for much of the past 50 years, may need to be changed to account for a more uncertain, complex, chaotic and unpredictable world we cannot assume to be able to influence, much less shape, the future of.

Post-Cold War globalisation is drawing us closer and making us more interdependent in a tightly networked and complex world.[39] Information technology is dragging us from our current world to a new world of more complex flows of information and knowledge that is changing our world and how we relate to each other, to governments and to markets. Unforeseen events, this essay argues, can reverberate through our tightly networked world with catastrophic consequences, escalating minor events or issues into a crisis. An overload of fragmentary and contradictory information enabled by exponential development of information technology contributes to the confusion of the crisis, challenging the power and effectiveness of governments to be more transparent, responsive and accountable for their actions. A new, more intuitive and metaphor-rich approach to intelligence support is needed to help policy-makers make sense of a crisis they are caught in.

Notes

[1] See, *inter alia*, Bernard F. W. Loo, "Goh Keng Swee and the Emergence of a Modern SAF: The Rearing of a Poisonous Shrimp," in E. Chew and C. G Kwa (eds.), *Goh Keng Swee: A Legacy of Public Service* (Singapore: World Scientific, 2012), pp. 127–151, on the build-up of the SAF in relation to its threat perceptions.

[2] The Israeli recollection of their contribution to the formation of the SAF is summarised in a 16 July 2004 article by Amnon Barzilai titled "A Deep, Dark, Secret Love Affair" in *Haaretz*. Retrieved 23 February 2015, from http://www.haaretz.com/a-deep-dark-secret-love-affair-1.128671. They recall preparing a "Brown Book" (because of the colour of its cover) dealing with combat doctrine, followed by the "Blue Book" dealing with the creation of the Defence Ministry and intelligence bodies.

[3] S. R. Nathan, *An Unexpected Journey: Path to the Presidency* (Singapore: Editions Didier Millet, 2011), pp. 321–325. See also Tim Huxley, *Defending the Lion City; The Armed Forces of Singapore* (St Leonards, NSW: Allen & Unwin, 2000), pp. 89–91, on the SAF's intelligence asserts and capabilities.

[4] Eddie Teo, "Reflections on Thirty Five Years of Public Service: From Espionage to Babies," *Ethos,* January 2006, pp. 2–7. Retriered 21 April 2015, from http://www.cscollege.gov.sg/knowledge/ethos/ethos%20january%202006/Pages/Reflections%20on%20Thirty-Five%20Years%20of%20Public%20Service%20From%20Espionage%20to%20Babies.aspx.

[5] Klaus Knorr and Patrick Morgan (eds.), *Strategic Military Surprise: Incentives and Opportunities* (New Brunswick, JJ: Transaction Books, 1983).

⁶ Michael Bennett and Edward Waltz, *Counter Deception Principle and Applications for National Security* (Boston: Artech House, 2007); and earlier, Donald C. Daniel and Katherine L. Herbig (eds.), *Strategic Military Deception* (New York: Pergamon Press, 1982).

⁷ Richard J. Heuer Jr., *Psychology of Intelligence Analysis* (Washington, DC: Center for Study of Intelligence, CIA, 1999)

⁸ Daniel Byman, "Strategic Surprise and the September 11 Attacks," *Annual Review of Political Science,* 8, 2005, pp. 145–170; and Robert Jervis, *Why Intelligence Fails: Lessons from the Iranian Revolution and the Iraq War* (US: Cornell University Press, 2011).

⁹ Richard K. Betts, *Enemies of Intelligence: Knowledge and Power in American National Security* (New York: Columbia University Press, 2007), pp. 124–158.

¹⁰ An issue that also worries strategic intelligence analysts and their managers; see for example, Jack Davis, "Tensions in Analyst–Policymaker Relations: Opinions, Facts and Evidence," Sherman Kent Center for Intelligence Analysis, *Occasional Papers*, 2(1). Retrieved 21 April 2015, form https://www.cia.gov//library/kent-center-occasional-papers/vol2no.1.htm; and Jack Davis, "Improving CIA Analytic Performance: Analysts and the Policymaking Process," Sherman Kent Center for Intelligence Analysis, 1(2), September 2002. Retrieved 21 April 2015, from https://www.cia.gov/library/kent-center-occasional-papers/vol1no2.htm which reviews five US government post-mortem critiques of intelligence process. The British perspective on this issue is summed up by Sir David Omand (who retired after a long service in various intelligence capacities as Intelligence and Security Coordinator in the Cabinet Office from 2002–2005) in his book *Securing the State* (London: Hurst, 2010), pp. 171–208.

¹¹ Mark Phythian, "Political Interference in the Intelligence Process: The Case of Iraqi WMD," in R. Dover and M. S. Goodman (eds.), *Learning from the Secret Past: Cases in British Intelligence History* (Washington, DC: Georgetown University Press, 2011), pp. 101–132 and reproduced Annex B of the Butler Report on "Intelligence Assessments and Presentation: From March to September 2002". Also Richard J. Aldrich, "Intelligence and Iraq; The UK's Four Enquiries," reprinted in C. Andrew *et al.* (eds.), *Secret Intelligence: A Reader* (London: Routledge, 2009), pp. 229–244.

¹² Richard K. Betts, *Suprise Attack: Lessons for Defense Planning* (Washington, DC: Brookings Institution Press, 1982), p. 4.

¹³ See the response of veteran CIA analyst Jack Davis, "Strategic Warning: If Surprise Is Inevitable, What Role for Analysis?," Sherman Kent Center for Intelligence Analysis, *Occasional Papers,* 2(1), January 2003. Retrieved 21 April 2015, from https://www.cia.gov/library/kent-center-occasional-papers/vol2no1.htm; an abbreviated version of which is in "Strategic Warning: Intelligence Support in a World Uncertainty and Surprise," in Loch K. Johnson (ed.), *Handbook of Intelligence Studies* (London: Routledge, 2009), pp. 173–188. See also David Omand's advice on "living with surprise" in Omard (2010), *op.cit.*, pp. 221–250.

14 Michael Handel has distinguished military surprise as an integral part of military planning from diplomatic surprise. Surprise in military planning is to gain a strategic advantage over the adversary who must be deceived and deprived of knowledge of moves against him. In contrast, diplomatic surprise is about moves and signals to the adversary of planned changes in foreign policy which may surprise the other. The 1971 US–Chinese rapprochement is an instance of a major diplomatic surprise de-escalating US–China tensions. See Handel, *The Diplomacy of Surprise* (Cambridge, Massachusetts: Harvard University Press, 1981).

15 Zvi Lanir, *Hahafta'a Habsisit: Modi'in Bemashber* [Fundamental Surprise: The National Intelligence Crisis] (Tel Aviv: Hakibutz Hama'ukhad, 1983) makes this critical distinction between *fundamental* and *tactical* surprise. I thank Zvi Lanir, who served in the Israeli Defense Force G2 at the time of the 1973 war, for discussing his work with me in the late 1980s.

16 Quoted in Ang Cheng Guan, *Lee Kuan Yew's Strategic Thought* (London: Routledge, 2013), p. 38.

17 Ang (2013), *op. cit.*, p. 49. Ang Cheng Guan, *Singapore, ASEAN and the Cambodian Conflict, 1978–1991* (Singapore: NUS Press, 2013).

18 Alexander L. George (ed.), *Avoiding War: Problems of Crisis Management* (Oxford: Westview Press, 1991) and earlier, Phil Williams, *Crisis Management: Confrontation and Diplomacy in the Nuclear Age* (New York: Wiley, 1976) make this point about crisis management being about maintaining control over events to avoid war.

19 Graham Allison and Philip Zelikow, *Essence of Decision; Explaining the Cuban Missile Crisis,* Second Edition (New York: Longman/Addison-Wesley, 1999) remains the benchmark study, with this second edition reiterating the Rational Actor Model of decision-making argued for in the first edition of the text published some 25 years earlier.

20 CIA History Staff, *CIA Documents on the Cuban Missile Crisis 1962* (Washington, DC: CIA, 1992)

21 James G. Blight and David A. Welch (eds.), *Intelligence and the Cuban Missile Crisis* (London: Frank Cass, 1998).

22 Both Williams (1976), *op.cit.*, Chapter. 7 and A. L. George and W. E. Simons (eds.), *The Limits of Coercive Diplomacy,* Second Edition (Boulder, Colorado: Westview Press, 1994) acknowledge that successful crisis management is about recognising the limits and need to moderate coercive diplomacy.

23 Arjen Boin *et al., The Politics of Crisis Management: Public Leadership under Pressure* (Cambridge: Cambridge University Press, 2005).

24 On the growing business management literature on managing industrial and corporate crises, see *Harvard Business Review on Crisis Management* (Boston: Harvard Business School, 1999) which indicates how thinking on crisis management has evolved from 1994 to 1999 in eight classic articles. Much of the literature are "how to manage a crisis" manuals, on which see Steven Fink, *Crisis Management: Planning for the Inevitable* (US: Backinprint.com, 2002) while Ian I. Mitroff *et al.,*

The Essential Guide to Managing Corporate Crises (UK: Oxford University Press, 1996) provides a more analytical approach outlining various qualitative techniques for crisis management.

[25] The CIA appears to be exploring the corporate practice of crisis planning in a category of "exotic" organisations called "high reliability organsations" (HROs) such as nuclear power plants, oil rigs, and refineries where there is a high risk of accidents, and are therefore expected to be preoccupied with warning systems and signals of breakdowns and accidents — see Warren Fishbein and Gregory Treverton, "Making Sense of Transnational Threats," Sherman Kent Centre for Intelligence Analysis, *Occasional Papers*, 3(1), October 2004. Retrieved 23 April 2015, from http://cia.gov/library/keng-center-occasional-papers/vol3no1.htm.

[26] Ban Kah Choon, *Absent History: The Untold Story of Special Branch Operations 1915–1942* (Singapore: Raffles/SNP Media Asia Pte Ltd, 2001). Throughout the 1950s and 1960s the SB/ISD was in the forefront of an undeclared war against an internationally inspired Malayan Communist Party attempt to subvert an anti-colonial and nationalist struggle for independence in Singapore as part of a wider armed struggle to establish a Communist Malaya and Singapore, on which see Leon Comber, *Malaya's Secret Police 1945–60: The Role of the Special Branch in the Malayan Emergency* (Clayton: Monash Asia Institute/Singapore: Institute of Southeast Asian Studies, 2008).

[27] This challenge of decreasing response time to an increasing volume of real-time information confronts not only the intelligence analyst and their policy-makers, but also traditional media editors as BBC anchor commentator Nik Gowing explains in *'Skyful of Lies' and Black Swans; The New Tyranny of Shifting Information Power in Crises,* RISJ Challenges (Oxford: Reuters Institute for the Study of Journalism/University of Oxford, 2009).

[28] David J. Snowden and Mary E. Boone, "A Leader's Framework for Decision Making," *Harvard Business Review,* November 2007. Retrieved 21 May 2015, from https://hbr.org/2007/11/a-leaders-framework-for-decision-making.

[29] Yoichi Funabashi and Heizo Takenaka (eds.), *Lessons from the Disaster: Risk Management and the Compound Crisis Presented by the Great East Japan Earthquake* (Tokyo: Japan Times, 2011).

[30] K. E. Weick, "Enacted Sensemaking in Crisis Situations," *Journal of Management Studies*, 25(4), 1988, pp. 305–317 and *Sensemaking in Organizations* (Thousand Oaks, CA: Sage, 1995).

[31] Daniel Kahneman, *Thinking, Fast and Slow* (London: Penguin/Allen Lane, 2011) sums up his work with his late colleague Amos Tversjy on decision-making and uncertainty, for which he received the Nobel Prize in Economics in 2002.

[32] See the National Institute for Defense Studies, Japan, "NIDS China Security Report 2013" attempt to understand and make sense of crisis management in China. Retrieved 23 April 2015, from http://www.nids.go.jp/english/publication/chinareport/.

[33] See the International Crisis Group, "Stirring up the South China Sea (I)," Asia Report N° 223, 23 April 2012, on trying to make sense of Chinese policies and positions on the South China Sea. Retrieved 21 May 2015, from http://www.crisisgroup.org/en/regions/asia/north-east-asia/china/223-stirring-up-the-south-china-sea-i.aspx. The issue maybe more complex than poor or lack of coordination between China's different state agencies claiming an interest in the South China Sea, as this report suggests, but a more complex issue of each of these agencies having a different justification and narrative for their stake in the South China Sea.

[34] See Julia Lovell, *The Opium War: Drugs, Dreams and the Making of China* (London: Picador, 2011) for a historiographic analysis of the myths of the Opium Wars and its legacy in shaping China's relations with the West.

[35] Cohen, *Speaking to History: The Story of King Guojian in Twentieth-Century China* (Berkeley: University of California Press, 2009). Cohen has since widened his thesis to reconstruct how often forgotten stories like the fall of Masada has been recalled as a leitmotif in modern Jewish memory, or Lawrence Oliver's film re-enactment of William Shakespeare's *Henry V* helped restore and unify English faith in itself towards the end of World War II in *History and Popular Memory: The Power of Story in Moments of Crisis* (New York: Columbia University Press, 2014).

[36] Nicholas E. Sarantake, "Cold War Pop Culture and the Image of US Foreign Policy: The Perspective of the Original Star Trek Series," *Journal of Cold War Studies,* 7(4), 2005, pp. 74–103, and more recently, Aaron D. Miller, "To Boldly Lead from behind? How Star Trek's Prime Directive Explains Obama's Foreign Policy," *Foreign Policy,* 8 January 2014. Retrieved 21 May 2015, from http://foreignpolicy.com/2014/01/08/to-boldly-lead-from-behind/.

[37] Max Boisot and Bill McKelvey, "Speeding up Strategic Foresight in a Dangerous and Complex World: A Complexity Approach," in Gabriele G. S. Suder (ed.), *Corporate Strategies under International Terrorism Adversity* (Cheltenham: Edward Elgar, 2006).

[38] See Bernard F. W. Loo, "Maturing the Singapore Armed Forces: From Poisonous Shrimp to Dolphin," in Bridget Welsh *et al.* (eds.), *Impressions of the Goh Chok Tong Years in Singapore* (Singapore: NUS Press/Lee Kuan Yew School of Public Policy/Institute of Policy Studies, 2009), pp. 178–199.

[39] Well-analysed by Manuel Castells in his now classic *The Rise of Network Society*. This is the first of a three volume study *The Information Age: Economy, Society and Culture* (Oxford: Blackwell Publishers, 1996).

Chapter 6

Desecuritisation and after Desecuritisation:
The Water Issue in Singapore–Malaysia Relations

S. R. Joey Long

On 16 November 1970, the Singaporean government dispatched a sharply worded memorandum to the Malaysian government. The diplomatic note remonstrated against Kuala Lumpur's delay in informing the Asian Development Bank (ADB) that Malaysia would back Singapore's plans to enhance the capacity of the reservoirs in Johor to supply more water to the island.[1] Singapore had in April 1968 sought the bank's support to develop a reservoir in Kranji and to expand the water works in Johor. Under the terms of the 1962 water agreement signed between the government of Johor and the city council of Singapore (an arrangement incidentally guaranteed by the 1965 Separation Agreement), Singapore was entitled to extract up to 250 million gallons of raw water daily from the Johor River. By the late 1960s, Singapore was drawing some 30 million gallons per day from the Johor river, and planned to extract more to meet the needs of its people and expanding industries. A loan from the ADB would permit Singapore to expand the existing waterworks in Johor and pump more water to the island. But the bank would only agree to release the funds if the Malaysian government endorsed the proposal. Dragging their feet, the federal and Johor authorities in Malaysia were ostensibly "disinclined to let Singapore make off with water that the developments round Johore Bahru might need".[2] The Malaysians were also miffed that the Singaporean government had apparently submitted its plans to the ADB without first consulting them.[3]

The disagreement generated much annoyance in Kuala Lumpur and Singapore. According to British High Commissioner to Singapore Samuel Falle, some Malaysian leaders accused the politicians across the causeway of being intransigent and that it was "impossible for them to deal with Singapore so long as Lee Kuan Yew is in power".[4] The Singaporean Prime Minister, conversely, was indignant and believed the Malaysians were attempting to exploit

Singapore's dependence on Malaysia for water for political leverage.[5] Echoing Lee, Singapore's Minister for Foreign Affairs Sinnathamby Rajaratnam thought the Malaysians were "obstructive" and that the "more extreme Malays" were influencing those who were "not themselves ill-intentioned…to adopt an unfriendly policy towards Singapore".[6]

The Singaporean politicians were undoubtedly cognisant of the threat made by Malaysian officials that if Singapore's policy "became prejudicial to Malaysia, they [the Malaysians] could bring pressure to bear by threatening to turn off the water in Johore". Lee's position was that if Kuala Lumpur attempted to disrupt the water supply, he would regard it as "an act of war" and Singapore would respond accordingly. As Singapore met 80% of its daily water needs in 1970 by importing water from Johor, any disruption to the supply would critically undermine the viability of the state. British analysts estimated that "Singapore could only exist from her own sources for about three to six months".[7] To safeguard the resource, Singapore might intervene militarily and undertake an "occupation of a minimum of 500 to 600 square miles [of territory] in southern Johore State". The British observers had come up with those numbers after computing the distances separating the water intake and treatment facilities at the Johor River, the Pontian Kechil Reservoir, and the Singapore-run waterworks in Tebrau and Scudai that channelled water to the island. They nevertheless did not think Singapore would undertake such an operation since the "cost of such an operation in [the] face of a united Malaysia…would seem likely to be more expensive than the attainment of self-sufficiency in supply". But "serious misjudgments" were certainly possible.[8]

As far as Singaporean policy-makers were concerned, the resort to coercive means to secure the city-state's rights was not something that they totally ruled out.[9] Yet, while the recurring idea that was expounded in their private conversations with British envoys in Singapore was that bilateral agreements should be honoured, there was also a steely resolve to ensure that the island should progressively reduce its dependence on Malaysia for water. The British High Commissioner in Singapore best summed up the Singaporean attitude and motivation: "It must be exceedingly unpleasant to have one's main water supply controlled by a potentially hostile neighbour".[10] Thus, while Minister for Defence Goh Keng Swee had indicated that "Singapore intends to stand fast on what it regards as its clear, existing rights", Lee had privately declared to Falle his "determination to make Singapore independent of Malaysian water".[11]

A body of scholarship has emerged on Singapore's efforts to address its water concerns. Scholars have focused on governance and state policies,

arguing that the Singaporean government has implemented effective regulatory procedures and efficiently managed the water cycle to enhance the country's water supply.[12] Other analysts have studied the subject in the context of
Malaysia–Singapore relations. On one side are those who contend that if
Malaysia deliberately disrupted the water supply to Singapore, the latter might
employ military means to forcibly restore the water flow.[13] On the other side
are those who argue that the water issue in Malaysia–Singapore relations
should no longer be viewed in military and security terms since the island has
since the 2000s achieved a significant measure of water self-sufficiency.[14]

Building on the extant scholarship, this essay argues that Singapore's
endeavours to loosen its dependence on Malaysian for water have been
successful. It holds to the position that the water issue in Malaysia–Singapore
relations should no longer be perceived as a hard security matter, requiring the
use of military force to ensure that the water from Malaysia, as contracted,
continues to flow to Singapore. Diplomacy and political action would suffice to
address any deliberate interruption of the supply. Yet, apart from undercutting
the need for Singapore to respond militarily to any hostile and intentional disruption of the water flow, the city-state's policies and encouragement of private
enterprise to develop the thriving local water industry since the 2000s have
also enhanced the capacity of the state and society to cope with the prospective
trauma or strains generated by a severe disruptive change to the status quo. The
policies and programmes, in other words, have hardened the resilience of
Singapore and Singaporeans to any politically-induced water crisis.

What follows is an elaboration of the contentions. This essay first examines
the endeavours pursued by the Singaporean state to enhance the island's water
resources. It then discusses the endeavours and private–public partnerships
that Singapore has pursued since the mid-2000s to build up its capacity to further adapt to unanticipated changes in the status quo. It concludes by reflecting
on the significance of the Singaporean experience in turning a limitation into
an innovative and growing sector of the economy.

Desecuritising the Water Issue

Since attaining independence, Singapore has pursued three broad strategies to
develop and sustain its access to adequate supplies of water. First, it has sought to
maximise the yield from the hydrological cycle. Second, Singapore has endeavoured to diversify and expand the number of sources from which it obtains its
supply of water. And third, Singapore has worked to manage the way water is
supplied to and consumed by the population and the city-state's industries. These

strategies combine to enable Singaporeans to obtain access to adequate volumes of high quality drinkable water, facilitate the socio-economic development of the country, lessen Singapore's dependence on Malaysia for water and reduce the likelihood of conflict between the two states.

Located just north of the equator and in a region where the tropical climate is wet and humid, Singapore consistently receives annual rainfall totals approximating 2,400mm.[15] The issue for Singapore is therefore not that it is situated in a harsh and dry environment, where the availability of water is low. The issue is how much water it is able to collect, store, and purify for its population and industries to consume. The amount of water that Singapore is able to dispense, in turn, determines how many people and industries it is able to accommodate and sustain on the island. Without sizeable water reserves, the city-state would not be able to sustain population sizes large enough to maintain a credible military force that could preserve the country's security. Without sizeable water reserves, the city-state would not be able to expand the labour force and grow the economy. Without sizeable water reserves, the city-state would likewise not be able to develop new sectors of the economy crucial to Singapore's development. Water shortages might also compel industries to cap or curtail production. Essential to the quality of life, security, and the economy, water and its adequacy were core concerns that exercised the minds of Singaporean decision-makers. As Lee Kuan Yew remarked, "This (water) dominated every other policy. Every other policy had to bend at the knees for water survival".[16]

Building a robust domestic water supply and storage system rather than becoming dependent on Malaysia for a large part of Singapore's water requirements was thus a challenge that the Singaporean government addressed. In 1965, three reservoirs (MacRitchie, Peirce and Seletar) stored the water collected in Singapore or piped from Johor. Tensions with Malaysia and the need to expand the water supply for demographic and economic reasons provided the impetus for the government to embark on an intensive reservoir construction programme. Between 1965 and 1986, Singaporean planners expanded existing reservoirs and completed the construction of 11 additional reservoirs. They included the Lower Seletar (1969), Pandan (1974), Kranji (1975), Upper Peirce (1977), Pulau Tekong (1979), Murai (1981), Poyan (1981), Sarimbun (1981), Tengeh (1981), Jurong Lake (1983) and Bedok (1986) Reservoirs. Thereafter, Singapore had to wait some 20 years for the clean-up of the rivers and advancements in filtration technology to harness the water flowing from the Kallang River, Rochor Canal and Singapore River. Officially opened in 2008, the Marina Reservoir became the 15th reservoir contributing to Singapore's water supply. Following Marina, two other reservoirs, formed by damming the Punggol and Serangoon rivers in the northeast of the island, were completed in 2011 to augment Singapore's fresh-water supply. These reservoirs have raised the total holding capacity of the city-state's reservoirs to more than 150 million cubic metres or 33 billion gallons.[17]

Further maximising the yield from the hydrological cycle, the authorities in Singapore constructed and connected a network of canals, drains, and storm water collection depots across the island to capture and channel storm water to the reservoirs. Sixteen of these storm water ponds had been built across Singapore by 2014.[18] And directing the rainwater to the ponds as well as the reservoirs are the drains that traverse across the island, including heavily built-up areas. Strict anti-littering laws and anti-pollution measures provide the first safeguards against contaminants entering the water harvesting cycle. Together with the reservoirs, then, the network of collection systems enable Singapore to maximise the amount of water it can collect from the rainwater that falls on the island throughout the year. Despite its urban setting, Singapore has managed to use some two-thirds of the island to capture and store water, making it less dependent on Malaysia for its water requirements.[19]

Apart from creating the infrastructure to enable almost the whole island to harvest storm water for human and industrial consumption, the national water agency, the Public Utilities Board (PUB), has also diversified and expanded the number of sources from which the city-state obtains its supply of water. One of those sources is the sea. For years, Singapore, which is surrounded by seawater, has explored opportunities to develop its water supply from rainfall-independent sources. Desalination processes that employed evaporation and distillation techniques did not appear to the Singaporean government to be feasible as they consumed a lot of energy, and were expensive to operate and maintain. Breakthroughs in reverse osmosis methods during the 1990s and 2000s, however, moved the government to exploit the advancements in technology to enhance the robustness of the city-state's water supply.

In 2003, the PUB awarded a multimillion-dollar contract to a private contractor, Hyflux, to build and operate a desalination plant that employed membrane rather than thermal technology to purify seawater. Becoming operational in 2005, the first desalination plant in Singapore had the capacity to generate 30 million gallons of potable water daily. Each cubic metre of puri-fied water was also priced at S$0.78. With further improvements in technology, the price of each cubic metre of desalted water had decreased to S$0.45 in 2013. Charged by the operators of the second desalination plant, this water was also obtained by passing seawater through semi-permeable membranes. More energy efficient systems, however, helped to lower the costs of operating the plant, which has been able to produce 70 million gallons of potable water daily. Together, these desalination plants enable Singapore to supplement the water it harvests from the hydrological cycle.[20]

In addition to reverse osmosis desalination, the PUB has also exploited advances in membrane technology to recycle wastewater and boost the water supply. Singaporean policy-makers had mooted the possibility of treating wastewater and using the treated product in the 1970s. But they eventually abandoned the project as the treatment process was prohibitively expensive. The quality of the reclaimed water, furthermore, was not consistently high. Policy-makers revived the idea from the late 1990s, however, when less expensive and more reliable treatment methods became available. Following a review, the PUB decided to build and operate two recycling plants at Bedok and Kranji in 2003. They are respectively capable of producing 18 million and 17 million gallons of what the PUB terms NEWater daily. In 2007 and 2010, the PUB welcomed the opening of two more NEWater plants at Ulu Pandan and Changi respectively. Constructed and managed by private contractors, their production capacities are respectively 32 million and 50 million gallons of NEWater daily. By 2016, another plant at Changi, run again by a private consortium and capable of generating another 50 million gallons of purified water per day, will become operational.[21]

All these installations employ reverse osmosis and ultraviolet germicidal irradiation techniques to treat wastewater, and make them potable or usable again. The purified water would either be discharged into reservoirs for remineralisation, or sold to industries that require water containing minimal amounts of minerals and nutrients. Because the treatment of wastewater requires less energy than the purification of seawater, the PUB appears to have invested more heavily in building NEWater rather than desalination plants in Singapore. Further advancing the reclamation efforts, the PUB has spent billions of dollars to construct a tunnel system that will channel the used water and sewage across the island to centralised water reclamation plants for preliminary treatment before subjecting the water to purification at the NEWater factories. Called the Deep Tunnel Sewerage System, the tunnel works would close the loop on how storm water that falls on Singapore could be used, reclaimed and purified, and reused again rather than for the wastewater to be merely treated and pumped out into the sea.[22] By 2020, with the sewerage system and the NEWater plants becoming fully operational, Singapore is expected to have the capacity to generate some 200 million gallons of recycled water daily. They alone will be sufficient to meet about half of Singapore's water requirements and to further reduce the city-state's need to continue to import water from Malaysia.[23]

While Singaporean policy-makers have invested in desalination and reclamation technologies to enhance the city-state's water reserves, they have also been mindful of the need to ensure that the water collected or produced is used prudently. Legislation, management, persuasion and incentives characterise the endeavours the Singaporean government pursues to influence the way water is used. To check water use, legislation promulgated since the 1990s require the installation of low capacity flushing cisterns in all commercial, industrial and residential developments. The 2008 regulations mandate that cisterns should discharge 4.5 litres of water for a full flush and 3.0 litres for a reduced flush.[24] Public urinals should likewise discharge no more than 0.5 litres per flush.[25] Apart from checking the use of products that consume significant volumes of water, the authorities could also bring to court individuals or organisations that illegally siphon off water from the pipelines. Under the Public Utilities Act, these individuals or organisations could be fined and imprisoned.[26]

In addition to strict laws against the misuse of water, Singapore also closely manages and regularly maintains the water supply network. About 5,300 kilometres of pipelines run across the island. The PUB has since the 1980s used copper and stainless steel pipelines to transport water to consumers. Galvanised iron pipes, which were deployed prior to the 1980s, were dug up and replaced with the cooper and stainless steel pipes. Unlike galvanised iron pipelines, the new pipes are more durable and better able to resist corrosion. These help keep leaks to a minimum. The PUB, furthermore, routinely checks the underground pipeline system for leaks. Cracks and damages to the pipes are immediately fixed, minimising the volume of water that is wasted. As a consequence of these efforts, the number of leaks has significantly decreased from 95 leaks per 100 kilometres of pipelines per year in 1985 to less than six leaks per 100 kilometres of pipelines per year in 2010. Freshwater, in other words, is being efficiently transported to consumers rather than being wasted.[27]

Besides maintaining the pipeline network, the PUB combats water wastage through persuasion campaigns. It promotes the prudent use of the resource in schools and among the public. Integrated into the geography and science curricula are topics related to water conservation and environmental science. Students are taught why water should be conserved and how. Pamphlets and posters describing ways to cut down on water use are also distributed to households. They are advised to reduce the time taken for showers, use water efficiently when doing the laundry and address damages to the water pipes in their homes swiftly.[28]

Reinforcing those messages are monetary incentives and disincentives that the PUB employs to shape consumer behaviour. Water tariffs are comparatively high and set at a level that compels consumers to think twice before they go overboard in their use of water. In addition to the tariffs, consumers in Singapore pay a water conservation tax and a so-called waterborne fee when they buy water from the local water agency. These charges motivate consumers to make the best use of the resource as the consequence would be an expensive water bill. They also encourage the people in Singapore to purchase household appliances that consume water efficiently.[29]

Remarkably, the PUB's persuasion campaigns and charging system have made a significant impact on water consumption patterns on the island. In 1998, the per capita domestic consumption of water in Singapore was 166 litres. In 2013, the number had declined to 151 litres. By 2030, the PUB aimed to bring the number to a more sustainable 147 litres per capita domestic consumption. In restraining the growth in the per capita volume of water being consumed in Singapore, the water agency had helped ease the demand pressure on the reservoirs on the island and reduced the amount of water it needs to import from Malaysia.

Singapore's efforts to increase its water reserves, diversify the sources from which it obtains water and manage consumption have worked collectively to significantly reduce its dependence on Malaysia for water. The endeavours have made the possibility of conflict between the two especially remote. Some historical perspective is useful. In 1970, the reservoirs in Singapore were capable of generating 30 million gallons of water per day to meet the daily demand of 10 million gallons. Against those numbers, British consultants speculated that if Malaysia–Singapore relations soured and Johor abruptly terminated its water supply to Singapore, the city-state could "carry on in comparative comfort for 4–6 months" if some rationing was introduced and if the hydrological cycle was not disrupted by extraordinary changes to the weather patterns.[30] Israeli consultants, who called on Lee Kuan Yew in November 1970 and discussed Singapore's water constraints, had even calculated that "by strict rationing", "increasing reservoir capacity", and some augmentation of the water supply via desalination, Singapore could eventually "survive without outside water".[31] Even so, observers believed that Singaporean policy-makers would resort to "diplomatic action" to resolve their problems with Malaysia. Military action to reopen the water supply was the last resort.[32] Affirming that analysis was the research department of the Foreign and Commonwealth Office's South and Southeast Asia section, which adjudged that armed violence between Malaysia and Singapore over water, while possible, nevertheless made little economic sense.[33]

If the observation in the 1970s was that water could still serve as a likely proximate cause of armed conflict between Malaysia and Singapore, the situation in the 2000s had made that a null possibility. The billions of dollars spent on building reservoirs, desalination plants, and NEWater factories have enhanced Singapore's water reserves and made the city-state capable of enduring a sudden termination of the water supply from Johor. In 2011, while consumption stood at 380 million gallons of water daily, the reservoirs as well as the desalination and NEWater factories were capable of adding 217 million gallons of water daily to the billions of gallons of water cached in Singapore's 17 reservoirs.[34] More installations will become operational over the next decades as the city-state invests in building more water purification plants, or enhancing the capabilities of the extant NEWater and desalination factories. Singapore need not and will have no incentives to employ violent measures to uphold its legal access to the reservoirs and waterworks in Johor.

In fact, so robust and diversified have the water reserves in Singapore become that the city-state had decided to allow the 1961 water agreement with Johor to lapse. In August 2011, as the agreement came to an end, Minister of the Environment and Water Resources Vivian Balakrishnan witnessed the official handover of the treatment plants and pump house in Sungei Tebrau and Sungei Skudai, and the four reservoirs in Gunung Pulai to Sultan of Johor Ibrahim Iskandar. From September 2011, Singapore will no longer be able to draw 86 million gallons of water from Johor. Yet, that has not adversely affected Singapore's capabilities to provide water for its citizens and industries. Rather than becoming a likely proximate cause of armed conflict between the two neighbouring states, then, the water issue remains desecuritised. Singapore has achieved a measure of self-sufficiency in water, and has no strong material reasons to forcibly and violently ensure that Malaysia maintains the flow of water to the city-state.

After Desecuritisation

Indeed, as Singapore expands its water reserves and becomes more self-reliant, it has implemented policies to strengthen the resilience of the state and society to sudden and disruptive changes to its water supply. The PUB envisages that imported water from Malaysia will remain one of the four national taps supplying the liquid resource to Singapore. The other three are water from the reservoirs and catchment facilities in Singapore, reclaimed water, and desalinated water. As far as the water from Malaysia is concerned, a second agreement, signed in 1962 and expiring in 2061, still enables the PUB to run the Linggiu

Dam and a treatment plant in Johor. It also permits the PUB to import up to 250 million gallons of raw water daily.[35] If hotheads ever come to power in Malaysia and violate that agreement, the two states will certainly be caught up in a diplomatic wrangle. But there will remain no incentives for Singapore to respond violently. The city-state appears resilient enough and has sufficient water reserves for policy-makers to employ diplomatic and other non-violent means to resolve any disputes with Malaysia. Singapore's large investments in cutting-edge research on water technology and management techniques, the close private and public cooperation in strengthening the water infrastructure, as well as the PUB's continued efforts to build up a water conservation culture in Singapore have enhanced the city-state's capacity to confront disruptions to the city-state's water supply.

Singapore's approach to dealing with its water challenges stems from its recognition that human societies are dynamic and complex social systems. The city-state's policy-makers appreciate that dealing with the "wicked problems" — issues which may not be easily recognisable or determinable — that arise from such systems require whole-of-government — even whole-of-nation — approaches. As one of the government's strategists acknowledged: "Developing policies and plans to deal with wicked problems requires the integration of diverse insights, experience and expertise". "People from different organisations, both inside and outside government," the policy official acknowledged, "have to come together and pool their knowledge so as to find potential solutions."[36] Singapore's water supply is one area where such whole-of nation approaches apply.

Significant public monies being set aside to spur innovations in water technology and management accompanied the move to the whole-of-nation approach in dealing with Singapore's water issues. Singapore has invested heavily in research on water technology and the management of water issues to make itself resilient to disruptive changes to its water supply. In June 2006, the Singaporean government established the Environment and Water Industry Programme Office. The office aims to build up the city-state's capacities in cutting-edge water research. It also supports the creation of start-up companies and the establishment of an industry capable of adding value to innovations in water technology. A National Research Foundation, led by government ministers, senior civil servants, academics, and industry players, disbursed close to half a billion Singaporean dollars to the office to spearhead the development of the water industry, control energy costs, and further enhance the city-state's water resources.[37]

The Environment and Water Industry Programme Office has managed the monies to fund research and development in water-related projects. It helps organise the Singapore International Water Week — a gathering for government officials, policy analysts, and private enterprise to debate ideas on emerging water technologies, the creation of more drought-proof water supplies, and close business deals (worth S$13.6 billion in 2012, for example). It funds research on water-related projects undertaken by public sector agencies, academics in the local universities and private enterprise via a competitive process. It has also helped establish an array of centres of excellence to identify best practices, undertake research and train people to support the water industry. These centres include the Nanyang Environment and Water Research Institute at the Nanyang Technological University, the Environmental Research Institute at the National University of Singapore, and the Environmental and Water Technology Centre of Innovation at Ngee Ann Polytechnic.[38]

Together with industry, these centres have helped generate new research and products that have strengthened the ability of Singapore to deal with unexpected disruptions to its water supply. For example, grants have been awarded to fund a joint project involving the PUB, Nanyang Technological University, and private company memsys clearwater to develop membranes that last longer and are capable of resisting oil droplets in seawater during the desalination process. Research projects that lead to the commercialisation of ideas which can reduce the amount of energy needed to purify water have also been funded. One of these include research on the aquaporin-based biomimetic membrane, undertaken jointly by the Singapore Membrane Technology Centre at Nanyang Technological University, Aquaporin A/S, and DHI Water & Environment. As less energy is required to push wastewater or seawater through these highly permeable membranes, the cost of purifying water with the technology would fall. With significant advancements in the development of low-energy and greener desalination and water purification techniques, the overall cost of enhancing Singapore's water reserves would thus decline. All of these developments would ultimately strengthen the city-state's capacities to efficiently run its water recycling and desalination factories, and appropriately respond to unexpected disruptions to its water supply.[39]

Apart from funding research, the Singaporean government, via various agencies, has also been collaborating closely with private enterprises to enhance the city-state's water supply. The Environment and Water Industry Programme office financially supports the commercialisation of the research. It also funds projects undertaken by companies to more efficiently manage their usage of water. For example, the office has financially backed a private company, Meiden Singapore, to develop ceramic membranes to treat commercially-generated wastewater.

It funded a consultancy, DHI Environment & Water, to work with the Singapore Refining Company to improve its water and wastewater infrastructure. And it disbursed a grant to the Silicon Manufacturing Company in Singapore to help it recycle the wastewater that it uses more efficiently, reducing daily water consumption "equivalent to the amount of water used in 1,500 4-room HDB [Housing & Development Board] homes daily".[40] All in all, the water industry in Singapore has expanded significantly during the 2000s as the government moved to encourage its development. In 2003, the water industry contributed S$500 million and 5,500 jobs to the economy. In 2011, the sector was worth S$1.4 billion, providing jobs to 12,400 people.[41]

More important than the economic data, however, is the story the numbers tell about Singapore's dynamic and innovative water supply and management system. A dense and extensive network of private and public partnerships has developed since the 2000s to enhance the capacity of Singapore to meet its own water requirements. Much of those partnerships have undoubtedly focused on the refinements to and the leveraging of technology to generate sustainable supplies of water for the city-state. But commercial entities and the government have also worked to reduce water wastage. All of these endeavours have helped to enhance the capacity of Singapore to absorb and adapt to any sudden disruptions to its water supply from across the causeway or even unexpected changes in the weather patterns.

Despite the important role that new research and technologies play in making more robust and diversified Singapore's water supply, they alone are not sufficient to prepare the city-state to meet and rebound from a water crisis. The resilience of the society depends not only on the sturdiness of its infrastructure. It also depends on a range of other more ethereal and softer factors such as affinity, confidence, empathy and legitimacy. In Singapore's case, the PUB has of course been at the forefront in promoting water conservation campaigns and managing the demand for water in the city-state. Such efforts are expected to continue as the PUB seeks to reduce Singapore's per capita daily water consumption to 140 litres, if not lower, by 2030.[42] Significantly, however, what the PUB has also done from the mid-2000s was to expand its efforts to further engage citizens in its national mission.

In 2006, the PUB unveiled the Active, Beautiful, Clean Waters (ABC Waters) Programme. This aimed at transforming its water catchment infrastructure into appealing community and recreational spaces. The PUB has not left the network of drab, grey drains and canals as they were. The reservoirs and the spaces surrounding them have also not been isolated to serve merely their water catchment purposes. Instead, the PUB has attempted to enhance their aesthetic appeal and create green oases, drawing citizens to the landscaped places. The aim of the programme is clearly to develop among the citizenry a sense of identification with what the state is doing about Singapore's water supply, its importance and its value. By developing an affinity for the water catchment infrastructure, citizens are more likely to develop a stake in protecting it, prudently using it, and ensuring its recovery should adversities strike. As a PUB report stated: "Drains, canals and reservoirs are integrated with parks and green spaces, creating places for recreation and community bonding". "This," the report continued, "improves the aesthetics of the waterways and also brings people closer to water, creating opportunities for them to better appreciate and cherish this precious resource."[43] The ABC Waters Programme, in sum, marks a concerted attempt by the Singaporean government to further give Singapore's citizens a vested interest in minimising the wastage of water, to keep it clean and to adapt to any sudden disruptions to the supply.

In sum, Singapore's establishment of a vibrant and innovative water industry, its investments in private–public sector cooperation on water innovations, and its efforts to strengthen its citizens' affinity for the city-state's water resources have combined to harden the resilience of the state and society to unanticipated disruptions to its water supply. Indeed, Malaysia's supply of water to Singapore can be intentionally disrupted, and the 1962 water agreement between Malaysia and Singapore can continue to generate interstate discord. The price of raw water that Johor sells to Singapore, in particular, has generated disquiet in Malaysia. Significant economic development and demographic changes in Johor have put pressure on the Malaysian state's water resources. While Johor charges Malacca RM0.30 for every 1,000 gallons of raw water the latter draws from the former, the Malaysian state is unable thus far to revise the rates it charges Singapore for a similar volume of the liquid resource. Comparison has bred contempt, with former Malaysian Prime Minister Mahathir Mohamad publicly and acerbically criticising the different manner in which Johor has had to deal with a Malaysian state and a foreign country. The prospect for discord between Malaysia and Singapore over the 1962 water agreement thus remains.[44]

Yet, despite the persistence of disagreement, it is safe to continue to assert that the prospect for armed violence in Malaysia–Singapore relations over water is remote. Singapore has developed vast intellectual and technological know-how to augment the water cached in the island's reservoirs. Although Singapore's existing recycling and desalination factories are efficient, they are continually being reworked to produce potable water more cheaply and efficiently. Those initiatives would ultimately enable the city-state to swiftly overcome any disruption to the water resources it imports from Malaysia. They create the conditions for negotiations and other types of non-violent state action. They could even enhance the likelihood of cooperation between Malaysia and Singapore over the water resources and their management in Johor. Cooperation after desecuritisation is certainly possible between the states.

Concluding Thoughts

This survey of Singapore's concerns and policies with regard to water brings into focus several things. First, the securitisation of the water issue in Malaysia–Singapore relations had been premised on the notion that the deliberate disruption of the water supply from Johor to Singapore would severely undermine the city-state's ability to function as a viable sovereign state. By treating the matter as such, the establishment had been able — perhaps rightly — to legitimise the use of coercive power to correct any deliberate and hostile change to the status quo. Attention was thus focused on the security dimensions of the water relationship between Malaysia and Singapore, accentuating the potential for armed conflict. Still, what the securitisation of the Malaysia–Singapore water relationship did also do was to bring top-level attention to bear on the problem. No less than the Prime Minister of Singapore oversaw the build-up of the city-state's water reserves and capabilities. And by addressing one of the main causes of Singapore's insecurity, in this case the overdependence of the city-state on Malaysia for the resource, Singaporean policy-makers have dramatically decreased — even made remote — the prospect for armed conflict between the two states.

Indeed, the desecuritisation of the water issue has decisively swung the focus away from the likelihood of interstate violence between Malaysia and Singapore. The desecuritisation of the water issue has instead swung the focus in Singapore from reactive to more dynamic and preventive strategies of securing the resource, and strengthening the capacity of the state and society to absorb and rebound from any disruption to the water supply. Fifty years after independence, public discourse about water in Singapore is furthermore less concerned with how it may limit the city-state's ability to grow. Instead, it has become one of the drivers of Singapore's economic growth. Water, or more precisely the catchment, recycling, and desalination of it, has predominantly become the object of business, scientific, and technocratic inquiry in the city-state.

Finally, nothing in Singapore's development of its water capabilities precludes continued cooperation with Malaysia over the use and conservation of the resource. A common challenge that confronts both states such as climate change could induce the two states to review their calculations of their national interests, and create the conditions for mutually advantageous bargains and agreements to be negotiated and sanctioned. In so doing, they would have enhanced the collective well-being of the two societies.

Notes

1 Confidential Singapore Note, 16 November 1970, attached to John K. Hickman, High Commissioner to Singapore, to David P. Aiers, Foreign and Commonwealth Office, 21 November 1970, FCO24/1208, The National Archives, London (hereinafter TNA).

2 Binnie and Partners Note, 1 September 1970, attached to John K. Hickman, High Commissioner to Singapore, to David P. Aiers, Foreign and Commonwealth Office, 21 November 1970, FCO24/1208, TNA.

3 H. C. White, High Commissioner to Malaysia, to D. F. Le Breton, Foreign and Commonwealth Office, 19 November 1970, FCO24/1208, TNA.

4 Samuel Falle to Sir Alec Douglas-Home, 1 January 1971, FCO24/1209, TNA.

5 Samuel Falle Memorandum, 11 February 1971, FCO24/1209, TNA.

6 Samuel Falle to David P. Aiers, 17 March 1971, FCO24/1209, TNA.

7 Research Department Report, South and South-East Asia Section, Foreign and Commonwealth Office, 1 June 1971, FCO24/1208, TNA.

8 Research Department Report, South and South-East Asia Section, Foreign and Commonwealth Office, 19 July 1971, FCO24/1208, TNA.

9 Lee Kuan Yew, *From Third World to First, The Singapore Story: 1965–2000* (Singapore: Times Media, 2000), pp. 258, 276 and 287–288.

10 Samuel Falle to David P. Aiers, 4 March 1971, FCO24/1208, TNA. See also A. A. Duff to David Aiers, 29 March 1971, FCO24/1208, TNA.

11 Goh's remarks are in John Hickman to David P. Aiers, 21 November 1970, FCO24/1208, TNA; for Lee, see Samuel Falle Memorandum, 11 February 1971, FCO24/1209, TNA. See also Samuel Falle to David P. Aiers, 19 March 1971, FCO24/1208, TNA.

12 See Cecilia Tortajada, Yugal Joshi and Asit Biswas, *The Singapore Water Story: Sustainable Development in an Urban City State* (Oxon: Routledge, 2013); Cecilia Tortajada and Yugal K. Joshi, "Water Resources Management and Governance as Part of an Overall Framework for Growth and Development," *International Journal of Water Governance,* 1, October 2013, pp. 285–306; Lee Poh Onn, "The Four Taps: Water Self Sufficiency," in Terence Chong (ed.), *Management for Success: Singapore Revisited* (Singapore: Institute of Southeast Asian Studies, 2010), pp. 417–442; Ivy Bee Luan Ong, "Singapore Water Management Policies and Practices," *International Journal of Water Resources Development*, 26(1), March 2010, pp. 65–80; Teng Chye Khoo, "Singapore Water: Yesterday, Today and Tomorrow," in Asit Biswas, Cecilia Tortajada and Rafael Izquierdo (eds.), *Water Management in 2020 and beyond* (Berlin:

Springer, 2009), pp. 237–250; Tan Yong Soon, Lee Tung Jean and Karen Tan, *Clean, Green and Blue: Singapore's Journey towards Environmental and Water Sustainability* (Singapore: Institute of Southeast Asian Studies, 2009); and Cecilia Tortajada, "Water Management in Singapore," *International Journal of Water Resources Development*, 22(2), June 2006, pp. 227–240.

[13] See, for example, Muhammad Fuad Mat Noor, "Konflik Malaysia & Singapura: Analisis Kritikal Kekuatan Angkatan Tentera Dan Keupayaan Dalam Konflik (Malaysia & Singapore Conflict: A Critical Analysis of the Armed Forces to Deal with the Conflict)," *Perajurit*, 12 November 2000, pp. 3–9; Tim Huxley, *Defending the Lion City: The Armed Forces of Singapore* (St Leonards, NSW: Allen & Unwin, 2000), pp. 58–63; and Tim Huxley, "Singapore and Malaysia: A Precarious Balance?," *The Pacific Review*, 4(3), 1991, pp. 204–213.

[14] Joey Long, "Desecuritising the Water Issue in Singapore-Malaysia Relations," *Contemporary Southeast Asia,* 23(3), December 2001, pp. 504–532. Lee also alludes to this in Lee (2010), *op. cit.*, pp. 417–442.

[15] Chang Chian Wui, "Meeting the Challenges of Climate Change: Singapore," in Carol Howe, Joel B. Smith and Jim Henderson (eds.), *Climate Change and Water: International Perspectives on Mitigation and Adaptation* (Denver, CO: American Water Works Association & IWA Publishing, 2010), p. 241.

[16] Quoted in Lee (2010), *op. cit.*, p. 417.

[17] J. L. Teh, "From Creative Vision to Reality," *The New Paper*, 4 November 2008, p. 8.

[18] Joanna Seow, "Work to Enhance Stormwater Collection Pond in Bukit Panjang Starts," *The Straits Times*, 20 July 2014. Retrieved 26 May 2015, from http://www.straitstimes.com/news/singapore/environment/story-work-enhance-stormwater-collection-pond-bukit-panjang-starts-201407.

[19] See Tortajada, Joshi and Biswas (2013), *op. cit.*, Chapters 3–4.

[20] See "Singapore Opens First Desalination Plant to Cut Dependence on Malaysia," *Agence France Presse*, 13 September 2005. Retrieved 26 May 2015, from http://www.singapore-window.org/sw05/050913af.htm. Woo Sian Boon, "New Desalination Plant Brings S'pore Closer to Self-Sufficiency," *Today*, 19 September 2013. Retrieved 26 May 2015, from http://www.todayonline.com/singapore/new-desalination-plant-brings-spore-closer-self-sufficiency.

[21] "Using Each Drop More than Once." Retrieved 28 October 2014, from http://www.pub.gov.sg/LongTermWaterPlans/wfall_3rdtap.html; David Ee, "Consortium to Build Second NEWater Plant in Changi," *The Straits Times*, 18 September 2014. Retrieved 26 May 2015, from http://www.straitstimes.com/news/singapore/environment/story/consortium-build-second-newater-plant-changi-20140918.

[22] "Deep Tunnel Sewerage System Phase 2, Tuas Water Reclamation Plant and Integrated Waste Management Facility to Reap Potential Benefits from Water–Energy–Waste Nexus," 3 June 2014. Retrieved 28 October 2014, from http://www.news.gov.sg/public/sgpc/en/media_releases/agencies/pub/press_release/P-20140603-1/AttachmentPar/0/file/Media%20Release_PUB%20DTSS2%20Signing%20Ceremony_NEA%20IWMF.pdf;

"Deep Tunnel Sewerage System (DTSS), Singapore." Retrieved 28 October 2014, from http://www.water-technology.net/projects/deep-tunnel-sewerage-system-dtss/.

23 "Newater to Meet 40 Percent of Singapore's Needs," *The Straits Times*, 4 May 2010. Retrieved 26 May 2015, from http://www.lexisnexis.com.ezlibproxy1.ntu.edu.sg/ap/academic.

24 Public Utilities Act (Chapter 261), Public Utilities (Water Supply) (Amendment) Regulations 2008. Retrieved 15 November 2014, from http://www.pub.gov.sg/general/Documents/MWELS%20Regulations_31Dec08.pdf.

25 "Requirements for Urinal Flush Valves under Water Efficiency Labelling Scheme (WELS)." Retrieved 15 November 2014, from https://app.pub.gov.sg/WaterFittings Users2/WaterWsFitting_URINAL_FLUSH_VALVE.aspx?fd=Requirements%20 for%20Urinal%20Flush%20Valves%20under%20Water%20Efficiency%20 Labelling%20Scheme%20(WELS)&l1=2&l2=8&l3=4-2&l4=5.

26 PUB, *Ensuring Low Unaccounted-for-Water: PUB Singapore's Experience.* Retrieved 16 November 2014, from http://www.pub.gov.sg/general/watersupply/Documents/UFW_Guidebook.pdf.

27 *Ibid.*

28 "Good Water Saving Habits to Meet the 10-Litre Challenge." Retrieved 17 November 2014, from http://www.pub.gov.sg/conserve/Households/PublishingImages/PUB-7water%20English.jpg.

29 For specific details, see "Water Pricing in Singapore," PUB, Singapore's National Water Agency. Retrieved 1 October 2014, from http://www.pub.gov.sg/general/Pages/WaterTariff.aspx.

30 Binnie and Partners Note, 1 September 1970, attached to John Hickman to David Aiers, 21 November 1970, FCO24/1208, TNA.

31 Samuel Falle to David Aiers, 4 March 1971, FCO24/1208, TNA.

32 Binnie and Partners Note, 1 September 1970, attached to John Hickman to David Aiers, 21 November 1970, FCO24/1208, TNA.

33 Research Department Report, South and South-East Asia Section, Foreign and Commonwealth Office, 19 July 1971, FCO24/1208, TNA.

34 For the water consumption rate, see Tortajada, Joshi and Biswas (2013), *op. cit.*, p. 9.

35 Salbiah Said, "Singapore Will Not Renew 1961 Water Agreement: Goh," *Bernama*, 5 August 2002. Retrieved 26 May 2015, from http://www.singapore-window.org/sw02/020805bn.htm; "PUB to Hand over Water Assets to Johor," *New Straits Times*, 26 August 2011. Retrieved 26 May 2015, from http://www.news.asiaone.com/News/AsiaOne+News/Singapore/Story/A1Story20110826-296255.html; Esther Ng, "Waterworks Handover Won't Affect Singapore's Water Supply: Dr Vivian," *Today*, 31 August 2011. Retrieved 26 May 2015, from http://www.lexisnexis.com.ezlibproxy1.ntu.edu.sg/ap/academic.

36 Peter Ho, "Governments Must Thrive in Complex World," *The Straits Times*, 21 August 2012. Retrieved 26 May 2015, from http://www.straitstimes.com/breaking-news/singapore/story/governments-must-thrive-complex-world-20120821.

[37] Jessica Cheam, "Additional $140 Million for Water Research," *The Straits Times*, 5 July 2011. Retrieved 26 May 2015, from http://www.nccs.gov.sg./news/straits-times-additional-140-million-water-research.

[38] See *Handbook on Industrial Water Solutions for the Petrochemical and Refinery Sector*. Retrieved 20 November 2014, from http://www.pub.gov.sg/ewi/documents/handbook_on_iws_for_the_petrochemical_and_refinery_sector.pdf.

[39] See *Handbook on Industrial Water Solutions for the Petrochemical and Refinery Sector, op. cit.*; PUB Singapore, *Innovation in Water Singapore* (Singapore: PUB, 2013); and PUB Singapore, *Innovation in Water Singapore* (Singapore: PUB, 2011). A list of other innovations arising from the huge investment in water research and development can be obtained from the other *Innovation in Water Singapore* volumes: Retrieved 20 November 2014, from http://www.pub.gov.sg/mpublications/Innovation/Pages/default.aspx.

[40] *Handbook on Industrial Water Solutions for the Petrochemical and Refinery Sector, op. cit.*

[41] Grace Chua, "Industrial Water Solutions Sector Ripe for Tapping," *The Straits Times*, 5 September 2013. Retrieved 26 May 2015, from http://www.news.asiaone.com/news/singapore/industrial-water-soultions-sector-ripe-tapping.

[42] PUB Singapore, *Innovation in Water Singapore* (Singapore: PUB, 2014), p. 5. For more details, see Tortajada, Joshi and Biswas (2013), *op. cit.*, Chapter 5.

[43] *Ibid.*

[44] Pau Khan Khup Hangzo and J. Jackson Ewing, "Will Rapid Development in Johor Impact Water Access, Quality or Price in Singapore?," *NTS Insight*, IN13-06 (Singapore: RSIS Centre for Non-Traditional Security Studies, 2013).

Chapter 7

Singapore's Security in the Context of Singapore–Malaysia–Indonesia Relations

Bilveer Singh

Introduction

History, geography and demography have condemned Singapore, Malaysia and Indonesia to be permanent neighbours. This geopolitical relationship is often framed in the context of ASEAN Kecil or the Small ASEAN.[1] In turn, this has had serious security implications for the "Malay World" neighbours' security, leading many to describe the triangular relationship as one of security indivisibility and where the three states are seen as the "ASEAN core".[2] Yet, in different ways, each is also concerned with the security dilemma brought about by developments across the borders of the three states, including military modernisation and internal conflicts.[3] While there are many facets to the triangular relationship, it would be far more useful to analyse the bilateral relationships, namely, Singapore–Malaysia, Singapore–Indonesia and Malaysia–Indonesia, and how these have affected ties among the three states. In general, despite being inseparable from various geopolitical and geostrategic dimensions, relations among the three states have shifted from the initial turbulence, best evident from Confrontation (1963–1966),[4] to one that is defined by intense cooperation, both bilaterally and multilaterally through ASEAN. Still, there are many hiccups in bilateral ties that often sour relations and in turn affect the wider regional security climate.

Ties That Bind and Unbind — The Key Determinants

The many key factors that have helped to create a situation of "ties that bind" are also behind why ties tend to break down sometimes. Essentially, what characterises the triangular relationship is the ubiquitous factor of all-round asymmetry (see Table 1). What has affected the Singapore–Malaysia–Indonesia relationship is the sum total of a number of enduring factors that are affected

Table 1:   Basic Data: Indonesia, Malaysia and Singapore.

State	Land Area (km²)	Population 2013	GDP (US$ Million) 2013	GDP Per Capita (US$ Million) 2013	Total Trade (US$ Million) 2013	Foreign Direct Investments Inflow (US$ Million) 2013
Indonesia	1,860,360	248,818,100	862,567,9	3,466.7	369,180.5	18,443.8
Malaysia	330,290	29,948,000	312,071,6	10,420.5	434,261.6	12,297.4
Singapore	715	5, 399.200	297,945,8	55,183.3	783,265.5	60,544.9

Source: "ASEAN Community in Figures (ACIF) 2013."[5]

by leaders or personalities in power, in turn, giving a positive or negative twist to bilateral ties.

History

What is Singapore, Malaysia and Indonesia today was part of the historical Malay world made up of far-flung empires such as the Srivijaya, Majapahit, Mataram and Malacca Empires. For the most part, it was largely Hindu-Buddhist until Islam came to dominate the region from the 11th to the 12th centuries onwards. While mainland Southeast Asia remained largely Buddhist, maritime Southeast Asia was Islamised, creating the modern Islam–Buddhist fault line in the region to this day.

Geography

Singapore, Malaysia and Indonesia are essentially a single geographical territory joined by maritime narrows. Today, Singapore is joined with the Malaysian mainland by two land bridges despite the seas remaining the major "highway" for the movement of people and goods in the region. Of the three states, Indonesia is a mammoth nation with more than 17,500 islands, stretching some 5,000 kilometres from the northern tip of Sumatra to the easternmost corner of Papua. Malaysia is split into East and West Malaysia, with both territories separated by 500 kilometres of the South China Sea. Malaysia and Indonesia share a 2,000 kilometres land border in Kalimantan. West Malaysia is separated from the island of Sumatra by the Straits of Malacca, one of the most important sea lines of communications. Indonesia is also in control of three other critical maritime chokepoints, namely, the Lombok, Sunda and Makassar Straits, connecting the maritime traffic that flows from the Indian to the Pacific Oceans.

Compared to Indonesia and Malaysia, Singapore is the smallest state, the only island nation in the region, hemmed between the two states, Malaysia to the north and Indonesia to the south. As it is located on the southern tip of the Straits of Malacca, through astute policies that were first started by the British colonialists, Singapore has emerged as a major air and maritime trading hub. What this means in reality is that the Republic will always be under a "border pressure" situation and what transpires in its immediate north and south would have direct implications for Singapore's security. The lack of "geographical strategic depth" is one of the most enduring security realities of Singapore as far as Malaysia and Indonesia are concerned.[6] Recalling his experience as Prime Minister, Lee Kuan Yew, commented on how difficult ties with Malaysia, for instance, can make life difficult for Singapore:

> We are not vulnerable? They can besiege you. You'll be dead. Your sea lanes are cut off and your businesses come to a halt. What is our reply? Security Council, plus defence capabilities of our own plus the Security Framework Agreement with the Americans. They stopped sand. Why? To conscribe us. As Mahathir says, 'even at their present size they are trouble, you let them grow some more they will be more trouble.' We got friendly neighbours? Grow up.[7]

Demography

Singapore, Malaysia and Indonesia are located in what is often referred to as the "Malay World". Indonesia is the world's largest Muslim nation, with about 90% of its 250 million people adhering to the Islamic faith. Malaysia is also a Muslim majority nation. In this regard, despite being part of the "Malay World" and originally a part of the Johor, due to British colonial practices, Singapore is a Chinese majority nation suffering from a double minority syndrome where its Malays are a national minority but a regional majority and its Chinese population a national majority but a regional minority. This also means that while the Malaysians and Indonesians often talk of belonging to the same "Malay ethnic stock" (*Rumpun Melayu*),[8] Singapore is seen as the "alien" nation, being made up of "imports" from China. While ethnicity is an important factor, it is by no means the sole determinant nor implies that the "*Rumpun Melayu*" nations will always act in unison against Singapore. As was observed by Lee Kuan Yew:

> You take the Malays in Malaysia. They thought: *serumpun* (familial ethnic stock) towards the Indonesians. The Indonesians now have more hatred for the Malaysians than for us because they are quarrelling over oil fields

in Ambalat (a sea block in the Sulawesi Sea). We are not quarrelling over that. And they nearly went to war when their ships clashed near Ambalat … It [*serumpun*] cuts no ice with the Indonesians. I'm the big brother. They say *serumpun*, that means you surrender to me as the elder brother.[9]

Political-Diplomatic

From the perspective of political and diplomacy, relations among the three "ASEAN Core" states have seen ebbs and flows, often strongly influenced by personalities that led the nations. Hence, Sukarno's relations with Tunku Abdul Rahman were largely tense, as were Tunku's relations with Lee Kuan Yew. While Suharto's relations were largely cordial with Lee Kuan Yew from 1973 to the early 1990s, Mahathir's relations with Suharto and Lee Kuan Yew were essentially difficult. While the Cold War period elicited a particular kind of bilateral ties between the three states, since 1990 with the end of the Cold War and especially in post-Suharto Indonesia, many new uncertainties have been injected into the bilateral ties between Indonesia and Malaysia, under Habibie, Wahid, Megawati, Yudhoyono and now Jokowi. The same can be said of Indonesia's relations with Singapore.

Economic

An important source of positive or negative relations was in part due to the state of economic ties between the three states. Of the three states, even though Singapore is devoid of natural resources, it is also the one that has performed well and outstripped both its neighbours in terms of per capita income and purchasing power. As Singapore is heavily dependent on the two neighbours for resources, it has led to accusations of Singapore's exploitation of its neighbours, often interpreted as nothing more than a "Chinese Singapore" exploiting its "Malay neighbours" in a colonial fashion. The fact that Singapore's economy is essentially in Chinese hands and the leading economic players in Indonesia and Malaysia are also ethnic Chinese has not helped the situation.

Military-Strategic

The overall state of political, economic and social relations has affected the tenor of military-security relations between the three states. Here, the key factor has been the issue of trust and the extent to which each is viewed as a threat by the other. While Malaysia and Indonesia do not view Singapore as a direct threat, the same cannot be said of Singapore's perceptions of its two immediate Malay neighbours.[10] In fact, if anything, the national security and defence policies of Singapore have been largely premised on the perception that the key external security threat to Singapore will emanate from Malaysia and Indonesia. At the same time, the state of security relations between Malaysia and Indonesia has not been warm, in part, due to the legacy of *Konfrontasi*, where Indonesia launched limited war against Malaysia (including Singapore) as well as the continuing unresolved issues between both states, especially over their maritime boundaries. This has had the effect of limiting military-security cooperation between the three states. Still, there are different types of military cooperation among the three states, with extensive land, air and naval exercises between the armed forces of the three member states, including coordinated patrols of the Malacca Straits to counter the threats of piracy.

Challenges in the Singapore–Malaysia–Indonesia Relationships

The three states have experienced many difficult issues with limited war breaking out from 1963 to 1965 when Sukarno's Indonesia sought to dismantle the planned establishment of Malaysia that incorporated Singapore, Sarawak and Sabah into Malaya. Since then, there have been many bilateral issues, especially between Singapore and Malaysia, on the one hand, and Malaysia and Indonesia, on the other. While many issues have been settled bilaterally, despite the existence of ASEAN and its dispute settlement mechanisms, never has ASEAN as an organisation been used to settle disputes. Instead, all three states have referred some issues to international bodies such as the International Court of Justice (ICJ) to resolve their differences.

Singapore–Malaysia

As Singapore was formerly a state in Malaysia (September 1963–August 1965), many legacy issues have continued to sour ties. Both states have in the past, at one time or another, expressed differences over various issues, including the price of water which Singapore imports from Malaysia; the issue of a Malaysian naval base in Singapore (KD Malaya); the problem associated with the Malaysian Railway Land and Station at Tanjong Pagar in Singapore; the differences over the visit by Israeli President Chaim Herzog to Singapore; the issue of Singapore granting military bases to the United States (US); complaints over Singapore fighter jets trespassing into Malaysian airspace; the setting up of a new Customs, Immigration and Quarantine (CIQ) checkpoint in Woodlands, Singapore; and

Singapore's reclamation works in Tekong island and its detrimental impact on Johor. While many of these issues have been resolved, such as the Malaysian Railway Land and the location of the CIQ checkpoint in Woodlands, one of the most serious issues was the territorial conflict over Pedra Branca.

The issue over the ownership of Pedra Branca (*Pulau Batu Puteh*) broke out in December 1979 following the publication of a new map by Malaysia which showed that Pedra Branca was within Malaysian territorial waters. This led to a series of protests from Singapore and official discussions to resolve the issue, including calls for the exchange of documents to ascertain the ownership of the island and two adjoining islets, Middle Rocks and South Ledge. In February 2003, both sides signed a Special Agreement to refer the dispute to the ICJ and in July 2003, the ICJ was notified of this agreement. Nearly five years later, on 23 May 2008, the ICJ ruled that Pedra Branca was under Singapore's sovereignty while Middle Rocks belonged to Malaysia. As for South Ledge, the ICJ ruled that it belonged to the state in the territorial waters of which it is located. Since then, both sides have established a Joint Technical Committee to delimit their maritime boundary around Pedra Branca and Middle Rocks but to no avail thus far.

Malaysia–Indonesia

Having a longer history of independence, the differences between Malaysia and Indonesia are also long-standing in nature. While many issues have soured relations, including the establishment of Malaysia and Indonesia's limited war to dismantle what was dubbed a "neo-colonial scheme", other issues, such as Malaysia' treatment of Indonesian workers, especially illegal workers, have continued to affect bilateral ties. However, the most serious disputes have been over territorial boundaries, especially involving Sipadan-Ligitan and Ambalat.

While Malaysia and Indonesia share land and maritime borders, with most of the boundaries amicably demarcated, the region bordering eastern Sabah and Kalimantan, adjacent to the Sulawesi Sea is still subject to dispute between the two states. The islands of Sipadan and Ligitan, off the coast of Sabah and Kalimantan, were claimed by both Indonesia and Malaysia. While both states succeeded in settling their continental shelf border in 1969, they could not agree on the sovereignty of the two scenic islands. As with the Malaysia's 1979 map which claimed Pedra Branca, it also claimed Sipadan and Ligitan, which Indonesia protested against. After failing to settle the dispute bilaterally, in May 1997, both countries signed a special agreement to refer the matter to the ICJ and the court was notified of this agreement in November 1998. In December 2002, Malaysia was awarded ownership of the two islands.

This, however, did not settle the issue of the maritime border, including the delimitation of territorial waters. This has led the conflict over the maritime spaces, including the Ambalat area, believed to be rich in hydrocarbons (especially in the Ambalat Block and East Ambalat), in the Sulawesi Sea.[11] Both countries have awarded exploration contracts to oil companies in the Ambalat region and this led to tensions, with both sides dispatching naval vessels to protect what they consider to be their territorial waters, with tensions reaching a high point in May 2009.[12] While intermittent negotiations have been held since 2009, the dispute remains unresolved.

Role of Foreign Powers

A major issue in the foreign policy of the three states has been over relations with external powers. This mainly stemmed from their perceptions of external threats, the role of major powers in the region as well as the particular threat the three states were believed to pose to each other, especially from Singapore's perspective, which viewed both its large Malay neighbours as an existential threat to its security. This in turn conditioned the adoption of a particular foreign policy outlook, with Singapore essentially believing in the embedded presence of major powers in the region. In contrast, Malaysia and Indonesia, despite close ties with major powers, believe that the region should not be dominated by any major powers and no state in the region should facilitate the military presence of the great powers in the region, as this not only promoted great power rivalries in the region but created the potential for these powers to dominate and interfere in the internal affairs of the region and states within it.

Singapore's Security in the Context of the Triangular Singapore–Malaysia–Indonesia Relations

All being equal, neighbours tend to have a more cooperative than conflicted relationship. This is especially true of Singapore, Malaysia and Indonesia. Their close political, economic, security and social-cultural ties have brought immense benefits to all of them and from the perspective of Singapore, it has been particularly useful. A cooperative and peaceful relationship is not only beneficial from the manifold synergies it generates but is also less costly in terms of the expenditure in financial and human costs that an enmity-based relationship would have incurred. Hence, the benefits of a connected relationship stemming from close political, economic, security and social-cultural relations.

The peace dividends from a cooperative relationship are self-evident. This is especially so for Singapore, a trading nation, heavily dependent on international trade for its economic survival and where regional peace is a key prerequisite. While both Malaysia and Indonesia are well-endowed with natural resources and arable land, Singapore is a net-importer nation. Yet, in 2010, Singapore was the "14th largest exporter and the 15th largest importer in the world".[13] Singapore also has the highest trade to GDP ratio in the world at 407.9%.[14] While Singapore's geostrategic location, developed port and airport facilities, and skilled labour force have accounted for a huge volume of international trade to pass through Singapore, without regional peace, this would not be possible, especially where the bulk of the international trade moves through the strategic international sea lanes of trade controlled largely by Malaysia and Indonesia.

For instance, speaking at the Singapore–Malaysia Business Forum in September 2014, Mr Lim Hng Kiang, Singapore's Minister for Trade and Industry stated that "Singapore and Malaysia enjoy a deep and longstanding relationship. Over the years, bilateral trade, investment and people-to-people flows have continued to deepen. In 2013, Malaysia remained Singapore's top export destination while Singapore was correspondingly Malaysia's top export destination".[15] Singapore is also one of Indonesia's top trading partners, being the fourth largest exporter to Indonesia in 2013.[16] Malaysia–Indonesia economic relations are also very close despite being competitors in key exports such as rubber and palm oil. Despite problems of migrant labourers, Malaysia is also heavily dependent on Indonesia workers to drive its economy.

The political-security ties between the three states have also improved markedly. In addition to close top-level visits, one of the best indicators of improved relations is the regular holding of military exercises between the three states (Table 2). These have been going on since the 1970s. For instance, the first bilateral air force and navy exercises between Singapore and Malaysia were held in 1984, with the army exercises starting in 1989. Singapore's military exercises with Indonesia have a longer history, with the navy exercises starting in 1974, the air force in 1980 and the army in 1989. Malaysia and Indonesia had an even longer history of conducting bilateral military exercises, with the navy beginning in 1973, the air force in 1975 and the army in 1977. Since 1982, Malaysia and Indonesia have also been conducting combined arms military exercises involving all three services.

The single most important evidence of a peace dividend in bilateral ties is the warming relations between Singapore and Malaysia, especially since 2009, when Najib Tun Razak became Prime Minister. While past imperatives of

Table 2: Bilateral Military Exercises.

Singapore–Malaysia Bilateral Military Exercises	
Army	Ex Semangat Bersatu
Air Force	Ex Sarex
Navy	Ex Malapura
Singapore–Indonesia Bilateral Military Exercises	
Army	Ex Safkar Indopura
Air Force	Ex Elang Indopura
Navy	Ex Eagle
Malaysia–Indonesia Bilateral Military Exercises	
Army	Ex Kekar Malindo
	Ex Tatar Malindo
	Ex Kripura Malindo
Air Force	Ex Elang Malilndo
Navy	Ex Malindo Jaya
Joint Services	Ex Darsasa Malindo

history, geography and demography remain relevant, most dominant in the new narrative has been the personal warmth between the two Prime Ministers and the strategic nature of their bilateral ties. Most of the past issues have been addressed or settled, such as relocation of the CIQ complex, land reclamation and even water. Most importantly, these include the breakthroughs that both leaders have made vis-à-vis two issues, namely, the resolution of the Tanjong Pagar Railway Station and the land exchange deal, as well as Singapore's support for the Iskandar Development Project in Johor. Other positive developments in ties include the holding of annual leader's retreats, re-establishment of links between both countries' stock exchanges, Malaysia's agreement to sell electricity to Singapore, the agreement to build a high speed train link between Kuala Lumpur and Singapore, the amicable post-Pedra Branca technical talks to resolve legacy issues over the islands' dispute and finally, the establishment of a Singapore consulate in Johor Bahru.

If there is one key factor that has brought bilateral ties to a new height, it is the cooperation in the Iskandar Project. Not only is the Singapore government supporting investments in the project through government-linked companies such as Temasek Holdings but it is also playing an important role in encouraging the private sector to invest in the project. Additionally, thousands of Singaporeans are expected to be permanently based in the Iskandar region and Johor as a whole, bringing interdependence to a level that was never seen before. To that extent, Iskandar has been the key game changer in Singapore–Malaysia bilateral ties of late, providing the key trigger for the emergence of a security community between Malaysia and Singapore as the future of both states will be tightly enmeshed.

The breakthrough in bilateral ties was a function of a number of factors. First, the decision by both sides to adopt a new approach to bilateral ties in order to garner win-win results. Second, the personal warmth between the top leaders was extremely helpful. Third, the calculation of the mutual benefits that would be gained by both sides in view of the increasing regional and global competition. Fourth, over the last two decades or so, there has also been increasing economic interdependence with Singapore as one of the top investors in Malaysia. Two-way trade and investments are among the highest between the two states. Fifth, there is also the realisation of increasing security indivisibility of both states. Finally, the ideological pragmatism of both sides has also helped in boosting bilateral ties.

While one can expect the warming of ties to continue, this cannot be taken for granted. First, the warm ties between the two Prime Ministers, both of whom are sons of two former Prime Ministers who were not close, may not survive personalities if a more nationalistic Prime Minister takes over in Singapore or Malaysia. Second, tensions could surface if the promised cooperation proves futile or produces one-sided benefits, say in the Iskandar Project. Finally, growing domestic tensions in Malaysia, especially among the Malay and Chinese communities in Johor or in Malaysia could spill over into Singapore–Malaysia relations and undermine the newly gained warmth.

Singapore–Malaysia–Indonesia: The Elusive Peace Dividend and Rising Insecurity

Despite vast improvements in bilateral ties among the three states, many problems with potential security implications continue to colour ties among them. One issue that has continued to sour ties is the persistence of racial and religious politics in the three states. Indonesia and Malaysia, especially the latter, have envisioned themselves as the protectors of Malays in the region. This has the potential to harm bilateral ties in states where Malay minorities exist, especially in Thailand, the Philippines and Singapore. While Malaysia may pursue a Malay-first policy nationally, this has direct consequences for Singapore when champions of Malay rights accuse Singapore of being anti-Malay and of ignoring the plight of the "sons of the soil" in the Republic. As Singapore pursues a totally different approach to race relations and nation-building, and does not adopt affirmative action policies, this, for many Malay nationalists is tantamount to being anti-Malay and hence, the surfacing of tensions in bilateral relations resulting from domestic politics of Malaysia. An external factor that is often enjoined to this aspect of race relations is Singapore's ties with Israel, which Malaysia and Indonesia do not recognise officially, leading to the description of Singapore as the "second Israel", implying that it is anti-Muslim, just as Israel is accused of being anti-Arab in its domestic and foreign policy orientations.[17]

Of greater concern is the difference and lack of convergence among the three states in their external relations, including conflicts resulting from territorial conflicts. Among the three states, the most serious territorial conflicts are between Malaysia and Indonesia, especially in the Ambalat region. While economic competitiveness has been ongoing, more stark are the differences in foreign policy orientations and defence policies that are perceived to be directed at each other. What makes contested territorial claims dangerous is the possession of military wherewithal to enforce one's claims, something that has been growing due to the aggressive military modernisation programmes of all three states. Following the Asian Financial Crisis, all three states have adopted a posture to modernise their armed forces with offensive-oriented modern weapon systems, including submarines, advanced fighter jets and even missiles strengthening their respective arsenals.

There are also differences over each other's foreign policy orientations, especially in aligning with the great powers. Of the three states, Singapore has developed the closest military relationship with the US, cemented through three major military agreements, including the 1990 MOU that permitted the US to undertake rotational basing of its air force and navy assets, and the 2000 and 2004 agreements that further entrench the US in Singapore.[18] The US has also exported cutting-edge weapon systems to the Republic, including the export of littoral combat ships, the first of which (*USS Freedom*) arrived in April 2013.[19] While Malaysia and Indonesia also have close ties with the US, due to domestic considerations, these are often unspoken or kept low key, leading to the impression that it is Singapore that is facilitating the American military presence in the region, with maligned intentions towards its two neighbours.

A perpetual fear in Singapore's policy-makers' mind is the possibility of Malaysia and Indonesia, two large Malay neighbours, ganging up to harm Singapore, often referred to as Singapore being a "Chinese nut in a Malay nut-cracker".[20] This fear of a "Malay pincer movement" against a "Chinese island" has driven many aspects of Singapore's strategic outlook, which include among others, the development of a strong National Service-based military capability that for a long period excluded the local Malays; a strong, pre-emptive, offensive oriented military strategy; a strategic policy of establishing close ties with strong military powers such as the US, engaging with all great and middle powers to ensure that "overwhelming power is always on Singapore's side"; and giving every state, including Malaysia and Indonesia, a direct tangible stake in Singapore's survival and where harming Singapore and its interests would result in a lose-lose outcome for all.

The Road Ahead

Regardless of how close and synergetic Singapore's relations with its immediate neighbours develop, Singapore's first Prime Minister, Lee Kuan Yew's warning that "your neighbours are never your best friends wherever you are"[21] will continue to influence Singapore's policies toward them. This stems not just from the sharp demographic fault lines but also the immense all-round asymmetry between Singapore and its two immediate Malay neighbours. In the same vein, Malaysia's relations with Indonesia will be coloured by the asymmetrical differences that exist between them and if not anchored by convergences, any divergence can lead to the sense of fear and potential threat, especially in an Indonesia that has been increasingly nationalistic and one that would like to flex its political-military muscles and gain influence in commensurate terms to its size in the region. In such a scenario, there would be serious implications for Singapore's security, confirming the view that a small state such as Singapore must always be prepared, be it through its own material resources or through adept diplomacy to safeguard its security. After 50 years of independence, a security community remains a distant dream with security dilemma remaining as a key feature in Singapore's security as far as Malaysia and Indonesia are concerned.

Notes

[1] Tim Huxley, *Defending the Lion City* (Australia: Allen and Unwin, 2000), p. 52. While ASEAN encompasses 10 states, the fulcrum of the regional organisation is believed to be Singapore, Malaysia and Indonesia, and hence, the description of the trio as the core of ASEAN or ASEAN Kecil.

[2] See Shaun Narine, *Explaining ASEAN Regionalism in Southeast Asia* (Boulder, Colorado: Lynne Rienner, 2002).

[3] Clark D. Neher, "The Security Dilemmas of Southeast Asia," *The Journal of Asian Studies,* 60(4), November 2001, pp. 1236–1238.

4 Also known as *Konfrontasi*, this was a violent conflict from 1963 to 1966, an unde-clared war, resulting from Indonesia's opposition to the creation of Malaysia, viewed as a British colonial plot to maintain its influence in the newly created state while being anti-Indonesian at the same time. While most of the military conflict was in Kalimantan, along the borders of Sabah and Sarawak, there was also intermittent violence in West Malaysia and Singapore. In addition to Malayan, later Malaysian forces, British, Australian and New Zealand troops were also mobilised to defend Malaysia (including Singapore). The fall of Sukarno following the September 1965 coup de-escalated the conflict and *Konfrontasi* ended with Indonesia's recognition of Malaysia in August 1966.

5 "ASEAN Community in Figures (ACIF) 2013," The ASEAN Secretariat, Jakarta, 2014. Retrieved 11 June 2015, from http://www.asean.org/images/resources/Statistics/2014/ACIF%202013.PDF.

6 Huxley (2000), *op. cit.*, p. 29.

7 Han Fook Kwang, Zuraidah Ibrahim, Chua Mui Hoong, L   ydia Lim, Ignatius Low, Rachel Lin and Robin Chan (eds.), *Lee Kuan Yew: Hard Truths to Keep Singapore Going* (Singapore: Straits Times Press, 2011), p. 27.

8 See Khoridatul Anissa, *Malaysia Macan Asia; Ekonomi, Politik, Sosial-Budaya & Dinamika Hubonganya dengan Indonesia* [Asian Tiger Malaysia: Political, Social and Cultural Dynamics with Indonesia] (Jogjakarta: Garasi, 2009), pp. 173–78.

9 Han *et al.* (2011), *op. cit.*, p. 312.

10 See Tim Huxley, "Singapore and Malaysia: A Precarious Balance," *Pacific Review*, 4(3), 1991, p. 210.

11 See Taufik Adi Susilo, *Indonesia vs Malaysia: Membandingan Peta Kekuatan Indonesia & Malaysia* [Indonesia versus Malaysia: Comparing the Power Map of Indonesia and Malaysia] (Jogjakarta: Garasi, 2009), p. 106.

12 Resistensia Kesumawardhani, "Dispute between Indonesia–Malaysia over Ambalat Block," *Yuridika*, 23(3), 2008, pp. 1–19.

13 See "Singapore Exports, Imports and Trade," *Economy Watch*, 18 March 2010. Retrieved 28 April 2015, from http://www.economywatch.com/world_economy/singapore/export-i.

14 *Ibid.*

15 See Speech by Mr Lim Hng Kiang, Minister for Trade and Industry, at the Singapore–Malaysia Business Forum at Raffles City Convention Centre on 4 September 2014. Retrieved 28 April 2015, from http://www.mti.gov.sg/NewsRoom/Pages/Mr-Lim-Hng-Kiang-at-the.

16 See Daniel Workman, "Singapore's Top Import Partners — World's Top Exporters," 1 November 2014. Retrieved 28 April 2015, from http://www.worldstopexportspcom/Singapore-top-import-partner/2539.

17 Jim Sleeper, "Blame the Latest Israel–Arab War on … Singapore," *The Huffington Post*, 17 January 2013. Retrieved 28 April 2015, from http://www.huffingtonpost.com/jim-sleeper/blame-the-latest-israelar.

18 See "Singapore and the US: Security Partners, Not Allies," *ISN ETH Zurich*, 27 August 2013. Retrieved 11 June 2015, from http://www.isn.ethz.ch/layout/set/print/content/view/full/24620?id=168339.

19 *Ibid.*

20 Huxley (2000), *op. cit.*, p.50.

21 Transcript of a speech made by the Prime Minister, Mr Lee Kuan Yew at a seminar on "International Relations" held at the University of Singapore on 9 October 1966.

Chapter 8

Singapore's Relations with Malaysia and Indonesia

Theophilus Kwek and Joseph Chinyong Liow

The Malay word for "neighbourhood", *kejiranan*, not only implies a geographical "quarter" or "precinct" but also, in a more communal sense, an interdependent society of individuals and interests. Singapore's immediate neighbourhood, held together by both history and proximity, contains three states whose relations have been complex at best, and contentious at worst. From the — political and personal — tumult of separation, through the violence of *Konfrontasi* and the trials of early cooperation, the intrigues which have shaped the attitudes of Singapore, Malaysia, and Indonesia toward each other are often murky to their own inhabitants and impervious to the outside observer. Yet, in addition to hosting the world's highest cargo traffic in their ports, the three form the core of many new security initiatives in the Asian-Pacific region, and front a region of increasing political salience in today's world.

This essay explores Singapore's relations with Malaysia and Indonesia through the administrations of three Prime Ministers, whose approaches to Singapore's immediate neighbours reflect a continuity of outlook tempered with strategic and personal adaptation. While the key influences through five decades of their leadership were, undoubtedly, the three state's underlying bilateral complexities coupled with momentous changes in Southeast Asia's broader security context, each Premier also brought a sense of his own style and convictions to the role, which lent Singapore's foreign policy under each administration a flavour distinctive to its time. Thus, rather than presenting a straightforward assessment of whether Singapore is more secure today than before, and keeping to the theme of this collection of essays, this chapter will explore the new and old security perspectives of each administration in relation to its closest neighbours.

The Lee Kuan Yew Years

As Prime Minister of independent Singapore from 1965–1990, Lee Kuan Yew not only oversaw the tremendous development and modernisation of Singapore, he also led the island-state through some of the most challenging and tumultuous episodes in its short history. Many of these challenges involved bilateral relations with two of Singapore's closest neighbours, Malaysia and Indonesia.

Singapore's separation from Malaysia in August 1965 has been described by historian Albert Lau as "a moment of anguish". Even after separation, Singapore's then-foreign minister S. Rajaratnam noted that "there is something unreal and odd about lumping our relations with Malaysia under foreign relations".[1] Beneath the veneer of what was then talked of as being "inseparable fates", the reality was that both Singapore and Malaysia were evolving fundamentally different socio-political cultures, between a "Malay Malaysia" and a "Malaysian Malaysia", the latter of which Lee Kuan Yew was a main proponent. More to the point, the notion of a "Malaysian Malaysia" built not on the supremacy of one particular race but on the principle of meritocracy was one that the Malaysian leadership categorically rejected, resulting in the separation:

> They (the Alliance leaders) fear us — what an effective, efficient administration which is not bogged down by corruption can do and which, by its results, will convince millions around us that they (the Alliance leaders) should do likewise. This is what really goes deep into their bones. Basically this was the reason they refused to cooperate even after merger . . . and that they said in the end, 'get out!' . . . So we have been sacrificed. Logic, history, geography, economics, all have been sacrificed to preserve the orchid from within.[2]

Needless to say, the difficult experience of separation coloured the early years of bilateral relations. Furthermore, given the dominant role that Lee Kuan Yew played in the merger and separation, there was also a tendency — which remains today — among Malaysian leaders to narrow their explanations of bilateral tensions to the personal role of Singapore's first Prime Minister.[3] Not long after separation, then-Malaysian Prime Minister Tunku Abdul Rahman accused Singapore as being "another state next door to us which has been carrying out policies with the intention of bringing hardship to Malaysian citizens".[4] This marked the inception of a Malaysian political narrative that alleged Singapore with pursuing a "beggar thy neighbour" policy, and that served only to sour relations further. This narrative was subsequently picked up in earnest by Dr Mahathir Mohamad when he became Prime Minister.

A major longstanding irritant for bilateral relations throughout these early years was Singapore's reliance on Malaysia for its supply of water. Problems resulting from this dependence were compounded by the fact that Malaysian politicians, including then-Prime Minister Tunku Abdul Rahman, frequently used this reliance as strategic leverage.[5] Needless to say, this aggravated the sense of vulnerability on the part of the newly independent island-state, and triggered a quest for water self-reliance that culminated in the implementation and construction of advanced water management and planning policies and facilities.

Another major difficulty for Singapore's relations with Malaysia was the visit by Israeli President Chaim Herzog in November 1986. Despite requests by Malaysia and Indonesia that the visit be cancelled, Singapore decided to proceed with the plan to host Persident Herzog in recognition of the close and invaluable defence cooperation that it enjoyed with Israel. In response to the Herzog visit, Malaysian politicians remonstrated against what they described as Singapore's lack of sensitivity towards its Muslim neighbours (including Indonesia and Brunei). Meanwhile, Malaysia recalled its diplomats in Singapore, and protests were staged outside the Singapore High Commission, including the burning of the Singapore flag and effigies of Lee Kuan Yew.

An equally challenging relationship that confronted Singapore in the early years of independece was that which they sought to forge with Indonesia.[6] Given that Indonesia under President Sukarno had launched its policy of Confrontation against the formation of the Federation of Malaysia, of which Singapore was a part at its inception in September 1963, it was not surprising that it was viewed as an existential threat to Singapore at independence. Asked by journalists about Indonesia on 9 August 1965 at the pronouncement of independence, Lee responded: "We want to be friends with Indonesia. We have always wanted to be friends with Indonesia. We would like to settle any differences and difficulties . . . But we must survive . . . we have a right to survive. And to survive we must be sure that we cannot just be overrun . . . In other words, we must have the capacity to prevent a successful invasion."[7] Singapore's concerns for the threat posed by Indonesia were not unfounded at the time. Even though Confrontation would be brought to a halt a year later, there was no indication in 1965 that would be the case. In fact, the Indonesian architect of Confrontation, Foreign Minister Subandrio, had expressed that Indonesia would not accept the independence of Singapore unless its British bases were removed.[8] This prompted the following retort from Lee: "If the British government does this not only Singapore will be destroyed by the Indonesians, I think the Federation of Malaysia will also be crushed."[9]

Indonesia eventually recognised Singapore's independence with no pre-conditions in June 1966. Confrontation between the two countries was brought to an end in August 1966, with full diplomatic relations established in September 1967 with the opening of embassies in both countries. Notwithstanding the upturn in relations, residual security concerns towards Indonesian intentions remained. In fact, the instability in Indonesia as a result of a communist coup, military counter-coup and the emergence of a new regime under General Suharto in Indonesia during this period served to amplify threat perceptions. Bilateral tensions threatened to take a turn for the worse in October 1968, when Singapore announced it planned to execute two Indonesian marines convicted of terrorist acts — the 1965 bombing of McDonald House — in Singapore during Confrontation. Despite a personal appeal for clemency lodged by President Suharto, Singapore proceeded to hang the two marines. The executions sparked widespread protests in Indonesia calling for retaliation and the reinstatement of "Confrontation" against Singapore. Mindful of the repercussions that the execution would trigger in Indonesia, the Singapore government under Lee nevertheless also saw that the executions had a strategic significance — it was an important demonstration of a small state's independence and resolve even if it meant antagonising its large neighbour. The storm clouds soon passed, and the 1970s saw an upturn in bilateral relations. Economic cooperation was deepened with several Singapore investment missions to Jakarta, many led by then-Finance Minister Goh Keng Swee, while political and diplomatic relations also received a boost with both parties agreeing to hold periodic talks on issues such as safety of navigation and pollution in the Straits of Malacca. In May 1973, Lee Kuan Yew made a visit to Indonesia which would prove to be a turning point in relations.[10] In September 1974, Singapore and Indonesia held their first bilateral naval exercise, Exercise Eagle.

Built on the back of the strong personal relationship that Lee had cultivated with Suharto, bilateral relations strengthened even further in the 1980s as private Singaporean investments in Indonesia increased, most notably with the joint development of the island of Batam. But it was in the military sphere that bilateral developments were most significant. Defence relations were enhanced with the inauguration of Exercise Elang Indopura (which involved the air forces of both countries), Exercise SAFKAR Indopura (between the armies of the two countries) and the joint development of an air weapons range in Sumatra. Indonesia also permitted Singaporean troops to train in the country in return for Singapore's agreement to share defence technology.

The Goh Chok Tong Years

When Goh Chok Tong took over from Lee Kuan Yew as Prime Minister in November 1990, he inherited a stable but nevertheless tricky set of bilateral relationships with the two immediate neighbours. After several years of relative calm, relations with Malaysia had begun to look volatile in the preceding years as a result of Malaysian opposition to the visit of Israeli President Chaim Herzog to Singapore in November 1986. Malaysian sensitivities were riled further by a series of incidents involving accusations of spying and military intrusion by elements of the Singapore Armed Forces (SAF) into Malaysian territory. Relations with Indonesia were on comparatively firmer footing on the eve of Goh's ascension to power. As noted earlier, this was the product of two decades of efforts to cultivate close personal relations between Singapore's political leadership, particularly Prime Minister Lee Kuan Yew and President Suharto, which in turn translated to sound ties between Singapore and Jakarta. Given that both Malaysia and Indonesia are strategically and politically crucial to the continued stability of Singapore, it was clear that, not unlike the Lee administration before him, Goh would have to devote much time, manpower, and resources to nurturing these two bilateral relationships.

Relations with Malaysia started off on the right foot with Goh proposing and fronting the "Growth Triangle" to tie the economies of Singapore, Johor and the Indonesian island of Batam, which won the support of the Malaysian federal government and the Johor state government, then led by the Menteri Besar, Muhyiddin Yassin, who is currently Deputy Prime Minister. The year 1990 also saw the Goh administration sign a water agreement supplementary to the existing agreements of 1961 and 1962, relating to the building of the Linggiu Dam on the Johor River, and the purchase by Singapore of treated water in excess of the 250 million gallons per day from this river. This cooperation was cemented with Goh's visit to Malaysia in January 1991. That said, relations in the early years did experience several hiccups. This included counter-claims to ownership of Pedra Branca and the arrest of several Singaporean fishermen in that vicinity by Malaysian authorities, as well as the implementation of a levy on Malaysian cars entering Singapore. Bilateral relations took a turn for the worse and a number of unresolved issues carried over from the previous administration resurfaced. The Malaysian media and local politicians played up bilateral disputes by criticising Singapore, and the spectre of war was even bandied about on occasion as relations in the late 1990s saw some of the most tumultuous episodes since November 1986.[11]

Relations began to turn decidedly sour in 1996 over remarks made by Lee Kuan Yew, who at the time was Senior Minister, about the possibility of a re-merger between Singapore and Malaysia. This issue, which sparked a minor debate within Singapore that required various ministers to clarify to their local constituencies the context of the Senior Minister's remarks, was nevertheless latched upon by Malaysian politicians as an example of an opportunistic pre-election broadside on the part of the PAP government. Later, in 1997, underlying tensions boiled over into a diplomatic crisis yet again when Lee sought to discredit a claim by an opposition politician that he was forced to flee to Johor for his life by suggesting that Johor was "notorious for shootings, muggings, and car-jackings". While he subsequently apologised unreservedly for those remarks, the Malaysian media did not relent on its criticisms. Conscious of the sensitivity of the situation and its own domestic constraints, the Malaysian government responded cautiously, and then-Foreign Minister Abdullah Badawi commented that though Kuala Lumpur accepted Lee's apologies, the restoration of relations to previous levels "would take time". Indeed, this remark proved portentous. The Asian Financial Crisis that struck the region soon after in 1997 and disagreements over water supply drove yet another wedge into an already tenuous relationship.

The issue of water was tabled when Goh met his Malaysian counterpart, Dr Mahathir Mohamad, in February 1998 in an attempt to ensure its long-term supply. Later, during their meeting on the sidelines of the December 1998 ASEAN Summit in Hanoi, Mahathir mooted the idea of dealing with all outstanding bilateral issues as a package, rationalising that "if you … leave the other problems outstanding then the relationship would still be affected. So it is better that we resolve everything all at once". Goh was receptive to this suggestion, opining in response that "you can't discuss water without Singapore giving something in return".[12] In principle, terms for the continued supply of water to Singapore were to be linked in a package that included the settlement of differences over the Points of Agreement on Malayan Railway land in Singapore; the location of Malaysia's Customs, Immigration and Quarantine facilities in Tanjong Pagar; Kuala Lumpur's claims of intrusions into Malaysian airspace by Singapore military aircraft; the status of Central Provident Fund savings of Malaysian workers employed in Singapore; and the migration of Clob-traded Malaysian shares from Singapore to the Malaysian Central Depository. This conciliatory approach, however, could barely veil fundamental differences in interpretation of the 1961 and 1962 water agreements, and these surfaced to the detriment of the package negotiations.

The water issue had in fact surfaced as both states found themselves in the throes of a financial crisis that threatened to slow their respective economies. Goh had to defend Singapore against accusations that Singapore was "insensitive", "arrogant" and conducted "unneighbourly" relations. He rejected suggestions that Singapore was pursuing a "beggar thy neighbour" policy by arguing that a faltering Malaysia was detrimental to the island-state's own economic health. To drive home this point, Goh revealed that Singapore still held on to several billion ringgits in its foreign policy reserves despite the depreciation of the Malaysian currency. Goh was purportedly also prepared to extend a S$6.57 billion loan to Malaysia, which Mahatir had initially requested but subsequently retracted.[13] Under the Goh administration, Singapore also refrained from commenting on the controversial sacking of Malaysian Deputy Prime Minister Anwar Ibrahim in 1998. Instead, Senior Minister Lee Kuan Yew's expression of sympathy for Mahathir went against the grain of the international outcry sparked by Anwar's removal. Conscious of the sensitivity of the time, Goh publicly chastised a Singapore newspaper for suggesting at the height of *Reformasi* that the time had come for Mahathir to step down.[14]

Relations with Indonesia during the early years of the Goh administration, on the other hand, benefitted from close ties that his predecessor had established with the Jakarta leadership, particularly President Suharto. Before his appointment, Goh had held the important position of Defence Minister for six years. This afforded him numerous opportunities to work closely with his Indonesian counterparts. The Goh administration also played an instrumental role in supporting several major Indonesian economic and industralisation initiatives, including the development of Batam. Despite sound foundations, however, ties with Indonesia were not impervious to strain. In fact, a number of issues soon arose that tested the bilateral relationship. The more pressing of these included the haze problem and piracy in Indonesian territorial waters. The advent of the financial crisis heralded a major shift in Indonesian domestic politics that would prove to have a significant impact on bilateral relations as well. Restoring relations with Indonesia to the levels enjoyed during the Suharto administration would prove to be one of the most taxing tasks for the Singapore government under Goh Chok Tong.

Issues in the bilateral relationship began to surface when the financial crisis first struck the Indonesian economy. Several Indonesian leaders (but not Suharto) accused Singapore of providing a safe haven for Indonesians who had committed economic crimes, demanding that the city-state extradite them to face charges of corruption. Echoing criticisms from Kuala Lumpur, Jakarta further accused Singapore of deliberately enticing much-needed local capital away from the Indonesian economy with attractive interest rates.[15] The situation deteriorated further after the fall of Suharto. His immediate successor, B. J. Habibie, criticised Singapore for being an unhelpful neighbour during the financial crisis, referring to it as a "little red dot" and echoing denigrations by Malaysian politicians of the SAF's allegedly discriminatory policies that blocked ethnic Malay Singaporeans from holding high positions. It was thought that Habibie's attacks on Singapore were motivated by Senior Minister Lee Kuan Yew's remarks on 7 February 1998 that "the market was disturbed by his (Suharto's) criteria for the vice-president that required mastery of science and technology ... If the market is uncomfortable with whoever is the eventual vice-president, the rupiah would weaken again".[16] This remark was believed to have been interpreted by Habibie as a veiled personal criticism. Singapore's delay in sending congratulations to Habibie also did not go unnoticed by the Indonesian President.

Many of Habibie's criticisms were repeated by his successor Abdurrahman Wahid, who in November 2000 accused Singapore of profiteering, and charged that the latter was manipulative and racist. Moreover, it was reported that Wahid had, in a closed-door discussion, suggested to Mahathir that Indonesia and Malaysia withhold the water supply to "teach Singapore a lesson".[17] As Habibie did before him, Wahid expressed resentment at allusions made by Lee that he may not be in power for long.[18] Part of this disdain towards Singapore, it seemed, stemmed from the lack of prudence on the part of the city-state's political leadership. As Ganesan (2005) noted, "flushed by success, its elite displayed what some regional elite regarded as unacceptable or unbecoming behaviour, especially since it came from a state that was hardly representative of the region in terms of its size and domestic contours".[19]

The strategic centrality of Indonesia, coupled with concern for any ripple effect its collapse might have on the region in general and Singapore's interest in particular, compelled the Goh administration to cautiously rebuild relations with Jakarta in the post-Suharto era. The primary objective of this policy was to restore political and economic normalcy and stability to Indonesia as soon as possible. A pragmatic approach to handling Indonesian sensitivities was required, which included the building of ties via less public channels. Economic incentives, for example, included the establishment of an investment fund to buy over assets of bankrupted Indonesian companies being held by the Indonesian Bank Restructuring Agency. Goh was, however, mindful of the political dangers if Singapore was being seen to be buying over Indonesian assets, and noted in announcing the policy that "we are a close and good neighbour of Indonesia and we don't want to risk any misunderstanding that Singapore is acquiring assets cheap when Indonesia is in distress".[20] Likewise, Goh reacted to further criticisms of Singapore's reluctance to assist by responding that while it was in Singapore's interest to help the Indonesian economy, any assistance would be limited because it was a "little red dot" and not in the league of Japan, the United States (US) or Australia. Singapore proceeded to offer assistance in the form of a US$5 billion pledge to the IMF-led assistance plan for Indonesia, and dispatched humanitarian aid to several parts of Indonesia in a demonstration of goodwill. Following the impeachment of Wahid and the rise of Megawati Sukarnoputri, relations improved somewhat. Even so, Indonesian leaders, given to nationalist aspirations, continued barbed verbal attacks and accusations against Singapore.[21] This included a recurring row over the release of trade statistics stemming from discrepancies between Singapore's figures of exports to Indonesia and Jakarta's data of imports coming in from the Republic.

As Goh's term approached its conclusion, broader geopological shifts brought a new security context to the region. The Iraq War, in particular, heralded some of these changes. Speaking shortly after the campaign, Goh acknowledged that it had "catalysed opposition to US pre-eminence", and "raised grave questions about the future of the UN".[22] The former affected Singapore because as one of America's foremost allies, and an often unqualified supporter of Bush's "War on Terror", anti-US sentiment in the region placed it in a uniquely dangerous position, as Tony Tan acknowledged in January 2004.[23] These changes were coupled with the seemingly inexorable rise of China and India, which the elder Lee predicted would "shake the world".[24] Both Goh and his successor Lee Hsien Loong described this as a shift in the "centre of gravity of the world economy" towards Asia, which would bring both promise and peril for Singapore.[25] With a new global economic and strategic context, a new approach to Singapore's immediate neighbours was required — spearheaded by a new Prime Minister.

The Lee Hsien Loong Years

The start of Lee Hsien Loong's premiership was framed by emergent global security concerns which shifted great power presence in the region toward the end of Goh's term. There is a sense in which Singapore's relations with its immediate neighbours under the younger Lee's administration must be understood through the prism of its relations with the rest of the world. At the same time, any consideration of this fifth decade of interactions between the three nations must account for the losses and lessons of the previous four, in light of the region's (and ASEAN's) growth. This section will first consider some of the changes Lee's appointment brought in Singapore's position towards Indonesia and Malaysia, especially in light of global strategic developments. It will then look at issues arising more recently between the three states and what they mean for Lee's foreign policy.

Soon after his swearing-in in August 2004, the SAF played a swift and successful role in delivering aid supplies to tsunami-hit Aceh. Lee personally visited Aceh on 4 January 2005, and described the "massive, spontaneous outpouring of compassion" of ordinary Singaporeans on a "scale unlike any [we] have ever witnessed".[26] This not only demonstrated a degree of fellowship among the countries, but helped to soften Singapore's image in the eyes of Indonesians. While regional economies reeled from the disaster, Singapore was the biggest investor in Indonesia from January to June of 2005, with 108 simultaneous projects amounting to US$591 million — enlarging its prior position as among the country's top five investors. With regard to Malaysia, Lee resolved the outstanding bilateral dispute over Singapore's reclamation projects in Tuas and Pulau Tekong soon after his appointment, arriving at a "full and final settlement" in April 2005.[27] Both sides saw this development with a hopeful eye to the future: Foreign Minister George Yeo described a "basis of mutual benefit and mutual respect" which could help resolve other differences, and his counterpart Syed Hamid Albar commented that "nothing [was] impossible if we put our hearts and minds together".[28] The exchange of memorials from 2004 to 2005 at the International Court of Justice, to which both sides had referred the Pedra Branca disagreement, seemed to affirm their commitment to "civil and civilised" dispute resolution.[29]

Taking global developments into account, these moves can be seen to reflect Singapore's dedication to a collective response to shifts in the region's strategic overlay. The limits of a bilateral response to the rise of China and India had been revealed by Lee's unofficial visit to Taiwan before assuming the premiership, which swiftly drew China's ire despite its long-term engagement with Singapore. Beijing froze official economic exchanges and a Foreign Affairs Spokesperson said in no uncertain terms that this had "damaged China's core interest",[30] forcing Lee to affirm the One China Policy during his first National Day Rally: "If Taiwan goes independent, Singapore will not recognise it."[31] Signalling his shift toward a multilateral approach, he said later that it was Singapore's aim to "help China establish enduring good relations" with ASEAN members.[32] There had also been other signs that Singapore would not be able to take on China and India alone. Singapore's trade with India, for example, fell far short of the initial estimate of US$50 billion in 2010 — amounting only to US$25 billion in 2011–2012 even after the conclusion of CECA (Comprehensive Economic Cooperation Agreement) in 2005.[33] Singapore's approach to build a strong regional front rather than relying on "traditional" great power partners was perhaps best illustrated by its decision not to enter into a formal alliance with the US. It preferred to remain a "Major Security Cooperation Partner", hoping that this special relationship would appease its neighbours, who for domestic political reasons had always been somewhat uncomfortable with its close ties with the US.

One aspect of this regional security response was the continuation of extensive defence diplomacy with Singapore's immediate neighbours from Goh's leadership. At a retreat in Bali in October 2005, immediately after questions of regional security were uncomfortably raised by the second terrorist attack there, Lee brought a Defence Cooperation Agreement and a Counterterrorism Agreement to the table with President Yudhoyono. Earlier that year, Singapore's willingness to work with Indonesia on issues of regional security had already been reaffirmed by a joint surveillance system to complement Indo–Singaporean Coordinated Patrols. Malaysia joined the two countries in December to establish an air surveillance system and a set of operational procedures to help the pursuit of maritime offenders across sea borders under three-way coordinated patrols. Speaking in 2008, President S. R. Nathan acknowledged the function of defence diplomacy in "building confidence and mutual trust with the neighbouring armed forces and their key personalities".[34] This augmented the defence diplomacy which Singapore undertook with both the US and rising regional powers, like the Singapore–India Maritime Exercises, inaugurated in 2005 in the South China Sea.

Beyond neighbourly cooperation, the other aspect of a regional response involved strengthening the ASEAN collective. As Lee recently put it, "when something happens in our region…it affects the tone for the whole neighbourhood".[35] Deepening relations with Indonesia and Malaysia was seen to be crucial to this end. Indeed, if cooperation with its immediate neighbours was important for a coordinated response to China and India, Singapore's leaders were acutely aware that stronger ties with the rest of ASEAN were also in order: George Yeo, among others, articulated the imperative to position "Southeast Asia [as] a major intermediary between China and India".[36] The inaugural East Asian Summit in December 2005, for example, brought India, along with Australia and New Zealand, into dialogue with the "ASEAN Plus Three" grouping, which included China, Japan and South Korea. This, in the older Lee's words, would "be a useful balance to China's heft" and keep the dialogue's "centre of gravity" in Southeast Asia.[37] Singapore's immediate neighbours were crucial in this process, with Malaysia hosting the 2005 East Asia Summit (EAS) and Indonesia joining Singapore to lobby for the inclusion of India. Singapore's improved diplomacy with Malaysia and Indonesia, in turn, was based on a new common understanding about how they would interact. Singapore and Indonesia agreed earlier in 2005 not to engage in "megaphone diplomacy" — announcing decisions through the media, and waiting for the other's reaction — while "negotiations on sensitive issues and future cooperation were ongoing";[38] megaphone diplomacy with Malaysia had, with Prime Minister Badawi's appointment, also been curtailed. This paved the way for cooperation on both cross-strait and ASEAN issues, and relations became less adversarial.

Despite these gestures of solidarity, more recent developments have not only revealed cracks in the surface of ostensibly positive relations, but also points of divergence between official goodwill and public opinion in the three states. The annual exchanges between Singapore and Indonesia over haze from Sumatran forest fires provide a case in point. While Yudhoyono's apology was received "wholeheartedly" by Lee in 2013, for example,[39] he was widely censured at home for "shaming the nation",[40] and Coordinating Minister for People's Welfare, Agung Laksono, accused Singaporeans "behaving like a small child" over the haze.[41] Laksono also construed Singapore's offer of assistance as an insult, telling a press conference that "if it [was] just half a million [dollars], better we use our own budget [sic]".[42] Though it is possible to see this incident and others simply as "teething troubles" in efforts to mount a regional response to worsening environmental problems, they are telling of residual negative sentiments that exist between Singapore and ts neighbours. Environment Minister Vivian Balakrishnan's comment that "no country has the right to pollute air at the expense of Singaporeans' health and well-being"[43] received the sharply-worded response that "Indonesian citizens also need to be looked after".[44] Tensions like this which bear directly on ASEAN initiatives (in this case, the 2002 ASEAN Agreement on Transboundary Haze Pollution) also threaten to undo past regional gains — or to reveal their weaknesses, with implications for regional efficacy.

Speaking at the Woodrow Wilson International Center for Scholars in 2014, Lee attempted to play down the impact of recent bilateral disagreements on ASEAN solidarity: although there will "always be differences in ... perspectives and postures", he stressed that ASEAN comprised "ten independent countries making common cause", and that "speaking together" was an integral part of remaining "relevant in a regional architecture".[45] He also specifically praised the Yudhoyono administration for the "stability and predictability and restraint" it brought.[46]

Other issues showed that notwithstanding the general upturn in Singapore's relations with Indonesia and Malaysia, unresolved issues remained that would occasionally surface as irritants in bilateral relations. In 2014, for example, Singapore and Malaysia engaged once again in tit-for-tat commuter fare increases, with toll increases on both sides after Singapore raised its levy on foreign-registered vehicles.[47] With regard to regional security, the recapture of escaped terrorist Mas Selamat in 2009 by Malaysian police, with information given by Singapore's Internal Security Division, showed that cooperation between the two, at least, remained strong where security concerns were mutually imbricated.[48] But latterly, the naming of an Indonesian ship after the two executed Indonesian marines responsible for the McDonald House bombing in 1965 reopened old wounds and dealt a fresh blow to bilateral ties and Singaporean insecurity. Though Indonesian Foreign Minister Marty Natalegawa tried to repair relations, Military Chief Moeldoko added salt to the wound by saying that he "could not accept if Usman and Harun are represented as terrorists (by Singapore) — they were marines".[49] In response, Singapore barred the ship from entering its ports and rescinded the invitations of more than 100 Indonesian delegates to the Singapore Airshow — Asia's largest defence trade show.[50] If anything, this incident reflects that as the younger Lee's term enters its 11th year, advances made in defence diplomacy remain plagued by unpredictability even as history continues to weigh on relations. To borrow Lee's words from a press statement after Mas Selamat's arrest: "the price of security is eternal vigilance."[51]

Conclusion

Singapore's relations with Indonesia and Malaysia, its two neighbours and two of the most important states for Singapore's security, have come a long way in the 50 years since the difficult and turbulent years of separation and independence. Through adroit, and oftentimes quiet, diplomacy and engagement, political leaders in all three countries have managed to keep the focus on mutual interests and shared concerns for regional stability and development, and in the process managed to keep frequent bilateral disagreements from boiling over. At the same time, Singapore's management of relations with Malaysia and Indonesia have also increasingly been shaped by regional and global imperatives in the wake of globalisation and regional integration. This has been the consequence of a clear-eyed realisation that the security interests of all three states are no longer merely intertwined, but increasingly susceptible to broader strategic, economic and political trends. Hence, the next 50 years, *kejiranan* between Singapore and its immediate neighbours will have to hew much more closely, and be even more sensitive, to developments in an even larger neighbourhood.

Notes

1. Speech by the Minister of Foreign Affairs (Mr S. Rajaratnam), Singapore Legislative Assembly, 17 December 1965.
2. Transcript of a speech by the Prime Minister, Mr Lee Kuan Yew, at the 15th Anniversary Celebrations of the Singapore Printing Employees' Union on 17 October 1965, held at the Chinese Chamber of Commerce, lky\1965\lky1017a.doc. Retrieved 23 April 2015, from http://www.nas.gov.sg/archivesonline/data/pdfdoc/lky19651017a.pdf, p. 15.
3. See for example, Kadir Mohamad, *Malaysia–Singapore: Fifty Years of Contentions 1965–2015* (Kuala Lumpur: The Other Press, 2015).
4. "Tengku Attacks Work Permits," *The Straits Times*, 23 January 1966, p. 1.
5. See Joey Long, "Desecuritizing the Water Issue in Singapore–Malaysia Relations," *Contemporary Southeast Asia*, 23(3), December 2001, p. 506.
6. Parts of this section were drawn from Terence Lee, "Explaining Singapore's Relations with Indonesia 1965–1990," MSc thesis, Institute of Defence and Strategic Studies, Singapore, 1999.
7. Transcript of a press conference given by the Prime Minister, Mr Lee Kuan Yew, at Broadcasting House, 9 August 1965, lky\1965\lky0809b.doc. Retrieved 23 April 2015, from http://www.nas.gov.sg/archivesonline/data/pdfdoc/lky19650809b.pdf, pp. 1–2.
8. Lee Kuan Yew, *The Singapore Story: Memoirs of Lee Kuan Yew* (Singapore: Singapore Press Holdings, 1998), p. 652.
9. Transcript of a press conference of the Prime Minister, Mr Lee Kuan Yew, with Malay journalists at the studio of Television Singapura, 11 August 1965, lky\1965\lky0811a.doc. Retrieved 23 April 2015, from http://www.nas.gov.sg/archivesonline/data/pdfdoc/lky19650811a.pdf, p. 4.
10. It was during this visit that Lee sprinkled flowers on the graves of the two executed marines.
11. S. Jayakumar, Speech to Parliament, 25 January 2003. Retrieved 20 May 2015, from http://www.nas.gov.sg/archivesonline/speeches/view-html?filename=2003012508.htm.
12. "S'pore, KL to Settle Issues as a Package," *The Straits Times*, 18 December 1998, p. 3.
13. This loan would have amounted to a substantial outlay for the Singapore government during the height of an economic crisis which already witnessed the implementation of a S$10.5 billion cost-cutting package in Singapore. It should also be noted that the loan was to have been tied to Malaysia's continued supply of water to Singapore.
14. "Goh Chok Tong: Finally Being His Own Man," *Asiaweek*, 3 December 1999. Retrieved 20 May 2015, from http://www.singapore-window.org/sw99/91203aw.htm.

15 The fact that interest rates are set by banks and are beyond the control of the central government did not seem to prevent Indonesian criticism of Singapore's political leadership.

16 Lee Kuan Yew, *From Third World to First: The Singapore Story: 1965–2000* (Singapore: Times Academic Press, 2000), p. 315. B. J. Habibie was a qualified engineer.

17 Derwin Pereira, "Singapore Wants Only Profits, Says Gus Dur," *The Straits Times*, 27 November 2000, p. 3.

18 "Indonesia's Wahid Launches Tirade against Singapore,"*Agence France-Presse*, 26 November 2000. Retrieved 20 May 2015, from http://global.factiva.com.

19 N. Ganesan, *Realism and Interdependence in Singapore's Foreign Policy* (London: Routledge, 2005), p. 93.

20 "Singapore's Goh Unveils Investment Package to Help Indonesia," *Asian Political News*, 17 January 2000. Retrieved 20 May 2015, from http://global.factiva.com.

21 The Minister for Foreign Affairs (Professor S. Jayakumar), "Estimates of Expenditure for the Financial Year 1st April, 1999 to 31st March 2000," 15 March 1999, Singapore Parliament Reports (Hansard).

22 Goh Chok Tong, Speech to the Asia Society, 7 May 2003. Retrieved 20 May 2015, from http://www.mfa.gov.sg/content/mfa/overseasmission/washington/newsroom/press_statements/2003/200305/press_200305_03.html.

23 Tien Chung Ping, "Singapore Lays out Plans to Beat Airline Terrorists," *The Straits Times,* 5 January 2004, p. 3.

24 "Managing Globalization: Lessons from China and India," speech by Minister Mentor Mr Lee Kuan Yew at the Official Opening of the Lee Kuan Yew School of Public Policy, Shangri-La Hotel, 4 April 2005. Retrieved 20 May 2015, from http://mfa.gov.sg/content/mfa/overseas/mission/pretoria/press_statements_speeches/2005/200504/press_200504_07.html.

25 "Riding the Asian Tide," speech by Senior Minister Mr Goh Chok Tong, at the Nomura Singapore Seminar, 8 November 2005. Retrieved 20 May 2015, from http://www.bis.org/reviews/r051214b.pdf; "Moving ASEAN Forward: Sustaining Momentum," speech by Prime Minister Lee Hsien Loong at the Third Asean Business and Investment Forum, Shangri-La Hotel, Kuala Lumpur, 11 December 2005. Retrieved 20 May 2015, from http://www.mfa.gov.sg/content/mfa/overseasmission/wellington/press_statements_speeches/2005/200512/press_200512_4.html.

26 See for example, "Speech by Prime Minister Lee Hsien Loong at the Tsunami Disaster Memorial Service on 9 January 2005." Retrieved 31 March 2015, from http://www.mfa.gov.sg/content/mfa/overseasmission/tokyo/press_statements_speeches/2005/200501/press_200501_2.html.

27 See for example, "Remarks in Parliament by Singapore Foreign Minister George Yeo on the Settlement Agreement between Singapore and Malaysia on Land Reclamation, 16 May 2005." Retrieved 31 March 2015, from http://www.mfa.gov.sg/content/mfa/media_centre/special_events/pedrabranca/resource_center/remarks_in_parliament/2005/200505/press_200505_1.html.

28 "Singapore and Malaysia Resolve Land Reclamation Dispute," *Channel NewsAsia*, 26 April 2005. Retrieved 31 March 2015, from http://global.factiva.com.

29 *Ibid.*

30 See "Spokesperson Zhang Qiyue's Statement on Singaporean Deputy Prime Minister Lee Hsien Loong's Visit to Taiwan," 11 July 2004. Retrieved 31 March 2015, from http://www.china-embassy.org/eng/fyrth/t142801.htm.

31 Chi Su, *Taiwan's Relations with Mainland China: A Tail Wagging Two Dogs* (UK: Routledge, 2008).

32 "Future of Singapore–China Relationship Bright: FM," *Xinhua News Agency*, 29 December 2005. Retrieved 1 April 2015, from http://global.factiva.com.

33 See for example, "India–Singapore Bilateral Relations," January 2013. Retrieved 1 April 2015, from http://www.aseanindia.com/wp-content/uploads/2013/51/Brief__for_MEA_s_website_-_Jan_2013-1.pdf.

34 Speech by President S. R. Nathan at the MFA Diplomatic Academy's Inaugural S. Rajaratnam Lecture, Shangri-La Hotel, Singapore, 10 March 2008. Retrieved 20 May 2015, from http://www.mfa.gov.sg/content/mfa/overseasmission/manila/press_statements_speeches/speeches_by_sg_leader/2008/200803/press_200803.html.

35 Transcript of "Singapore Prime Minister Lee Backs Trans-Pacific Partnership and Stronger US Ties: A Conversation with Lee Hsien Loong," 24 June 2014. Retrieved 1 April 2015, from http://www.cfr.org/singapore/singapore-prime-minister-lee-backs-trans-pacific-partnership-stronger-us-ties/p35663.

36 Address by George Yeo, Minister for Foreign Affairs, at the Global Leadership Forum in Kuala Lumpur, 6 September 2005.

37 Simon Elegant, Michael Elliot and Zoher Abdoolcarim, "Lee Kuan Yew Reflects," *TIME*, 12 December 2005. Retrieved 20 May 2015, from http://content.time.com/time/magazine/article/0,9171,1137705,00.html.

38 "Ties with Jakarta Good, but Some Issues Need Time," *The Straits Times*, 18 October 2005. Retrieved 20 May 2015, from http://global.factiva.com.

39 Lee Hsien Loong, Statement from the Prime Minister's Office, 25 June 2013. Retrieved 20 May 2015, from http://www.pmo.gov.sg/mediacentre/statement-prime-ministers-office-4.

40 "Yudhoyono: Haze Apology Was Needed, Not Excessive," *The Malay Mail Online*, 27 June 2013. Retrieved 1 April 2015, from http://www.themalaymailonline.com/malaysia/article/yudhoyono-haze-apology-was-needed-not-excessive.

41 "Indonesian Minister Says Singapore 'Behaving Like a Small Child' over Haze," *The Straits Times*, 20 June 2013. Retrieved 20 May 2015, from http://www.straitstimes.com/breaking-news/se-asia/story/haze-update-indonesian-minister-hits-out-singapore-20130620.

42 *Ibid.*

43 Vivian Balakrishnan's Facebook page, accessed 1 April 2015. Retrieved 23 April 2015, from https://www.facebook.com/permalink.php?id=30332546206&v=wall&story_fbid=10151420624816207. Also cited in Amar Toor, "Suffocating in Singapore," *The Verge*

27 June 2013. Retrieved 1 April 2015, from http://www.theverge.com/2013/6/27/4471184/singapore-indonesia-smog-crisis-palm-oil-companies-behind-it.

44 U-wen Lee, "Indonesia: 'Stop Behaving Like Children'," *The Business Times,* 21 June 2013. Retrieved 20 May 2015, from http://global.factiva.com.

45 Transcript of "Singapore Prime Minister Lee Backs Trans-Pacific Partnership and Stronger US Ties: A Conversation with Lee Hsien Loong," 24 June 2014. Retrieved 1 April 2015, from http://www.cfr.org/singapore/singapore-prime-minister-lee-backs-trans-pacific-partnership-stronger-us-ties/p35663.

46 *Ibid.*

47 "Commuters to Pay the Price While Singapore, Malaysia Quarrel," *Ejinsight,* 11 August 2014. Retrieved 1 April 2015, from http://www.ejinsight.com/20140811-singpoare-malaysia-crossing/.

48 "Mas Selamat in Detention: Malaysia Home Minister," *AsiaOne,* 8 May 2009. Retrieved 1 April 2015, from http://news.asiaone.com/News/AsiaOne%2BNews/Singapore/Story/A1Story20090508-140192.html.

49 Satish Cheney, "Ship's Name Ignites Singapore–Indonesia Spat," *Al Jazeera,* 18 February 2014. Retrieved 1 April 2015, from http://www.aljazeera.com/indepth/features/2014/02/ship-name-ignites-singapore-indonesia-spat-201421710114344164.html.

50 *Ibid.*

51 "Comments by PM Lee on the Re-Arrest of Mas Selamat," *AsiaOne,* 9 May 2009. Retrieved 1 April 2015. http://news.asiaone.com/News/AsiaOne%2BNews/Singapore/Story/A1Story20090509-140400.html.

Chapter 9

International Missions of the Singapore Armed Forces: How Far Would You Go?

Katie Tan and Ong Weichong

Introduction

Since its first international mission to then-East Pakistan (now Bangladesh) in 1970, the Singapore Armed Forces (SAF) has participated in more than 30 overseas missions, ranging from civil assistance (CA), peace support operations (PSOs), counter-piracy operations, humanitarian assistance and disaster relief (HADR) to stabilisation, security, transition and reconstruction (SSTR) missions.[1] Singapore's contribution to United Nations (UN) peacekeeping missions started with the UN Transition Assistance Group (UNTAG) in 1989, when the SAF sent a small contingent of SAF Officers, policemen and civil servants to support Namibia's election. While still relatively new to international PSOs, SAF commanders and command teams have assumed command leadership roles as Force Commander of the UN Mission of Support in East Timor (UNMISET) and led the counter-piracy Combined Task Force 151 in the Gulf of Aden (GOA) on three occasions.

Despite the SAF's increased experience and expertise in overseas missions, such missions do not fall neatly under the ambit of the armed forces — particularly in one that is primarily geared towards homeland defence with citizen soldiers at its core. These "non-war" operations — under the broad category of Operations Other Than War (OOTW) — are conducted beyond the traditional security paradigm where the application of kinetic military force may be the exception rather than the norm. In the case of the SAF, the focus appears to be on the following: HADR, PSO, non-combatant evacuation operations (NEO) and CA. These missions are often conducted away from home and increasingly, out of Singapore's immediate region of Southeast Asia. From closer to home in Southeast Asia to more than 6,000 kilometres away from home in Afghanistan and more than 7,000 kilometres away in the GOA, the SAF and its servicemen and servicewomen have been deployed in overseas missions away from the comforts of home.

In 2014, the Singapore Army ran a series of recruitment advertisements centred on the question "How Far Would You Go?" — from the Australian outback, to the jungles in Brunei and to the plains of Germany — the series showcased National Servicemen (NSmen) of various vocations and backgrounds training in overseas locations far from home. Although this narrative was very much set in the context of homeland defence, the question "How Far Would You Go?" is also a useful one to ask of the SAF's overseas operations and international missions. In fact, the other questions raised around the advertisement's theme of going "around the world to protect our home" are just as relevant; such as, how far would you go "to meet challenges head on", "to safeguard our nation and our future", "to overcome all threats and earn respect" and "to make a difference".[2]

In light of the SAF's considerable overseas experience of the past few decades, how far would the SAF go in future international missions? Would they be a significant departure from the scale and scope of present day deployments? This chapter shall attempt to take stock of the SAF's contributions to international missions since its first foray in 1970 and explore its prospects for further development and change.

Deploying around the World to Protect Our Home

The first large-scale and long-term contribution to an international peace operation was Singapore's deployments to Timor Leste in 1999. Singapore was among the first countries to participate in the UN-sanctioned International Force for East Timor (INTERFET) peace enforcement mission, with three Landing Ship Tanks (LSTs), an SAF liaison team and a medical detachment. When the United Nations Transitional Administration in East Timor (UNTAET) took over, tasked to maintain law and order and set up an effective administration, the SAF contributed medical teams and staff officers for the UNTAET Headquarters as well as a platoon of peacekeepers. After the country's independence, Singapore continued to participate in UNMISET to help see Timor Leste through its next phase of nation-building, to which the SAF committed a company of peacekeepers and staff officers. From 2006 to 2012, the SAF also contributed military observers, as well as liaison and staff officers to the UN Integrated Mission in Timor-Leste (UNMIT) HQ.[3]

Singapore's participation in the various UN missions in East Timor, from 1999 to 2003, marked an important chapter in the SAF's history. It saw the SAF's first deployment of peacekeepers and was also the first time Singapore had Full-Time National Servicemen (NSFs) as well as Operationally Ready National Servicemen (ORNS) volunteering to serve as peacekeepers. Additionally, BG Tan Huck Gim was appointed Force Commander of

UNMISET in the first ever appointment of a Singapore officer to lead a UN peace support mission.

Prior to the East Timor mission, Singapore's commitment to the UN was already formalised back in 1997 with the signing of the Memorandum of Understanding (MOU) on the UN Standby Arrangements System (UNSAS). Under the MOU, Singapore was committed to placing "planning officers, military observers, medical personnel and police officers on standby to support UN peacekeeping (PKO) missions".[4] At that time, Singapore was the seventh nation to have signed on. Since then, as of 2013, 57 countries have signed the UNSAS MOU.[5] In addition to Singapore's pledge to UN peacekeeping missions, the SAF is also committed to certain PSOs led by other countries.

More recently, in June 2013, the SAF concluded its longest and most extensive overseas mission after six years of operations in Afghanistan in support of the "multinational reconstruction and stabilisation efforts". The SAF operated as part of the International Security Assistance Force (ISAF) — "to help the local people regain back their country and run it themselves."[6] As part of their operations, the SAF improved health and medical care for the civilians, helped to build infrastructure for transportation and education, and provided critical support to ISAF's security and intelligence operations.[7]

In the wake of an earthquake and a tsunami that devastated many coastal populations around the Indian Ocean on 26 December 2004, the SAF mounted its largest-scale operation to date. Operation Flying Eagle (OFE) was launched, with deployments at multiple locations, including Phuket in Thailand, and Banda Aceh, Meulaboh and Medan in Indonesia. More than 1,500 personnel were deployed, including three LSTs, 12 helicopters and eight fixed-wing transports. Working together with the local authorities and the host countries' armed forces, landing beaches were established, lines of communications opened, field hospitals were set up, relief supplies delivered and air traffic control restored.[8]

Under the category of NEOs, the largest operation was undertaken when political violence broke out in Cambodia in May 1997. In Operation Crimson Angel, the SAF evacuated more than 400 Singaporeans out of the country. During this operation, the Singapore Ministry of Defence (MINDEF) worked closely with the Singapore Ministry of Foreign Affairs (MFA). Together with Singapore's Phnom Penh embassy staff, they planned and executed the "Warden System" — a call-up system similar to the SAF's mobilisation system as well as the first phase of the evacuation.[9] The operation demonstrated the ability of MINDEF and the SAF to work closely with their MFA counterparts in NEOs — particularly in situations where interagency cooperation is crucial to mission success.

A summary of some of the other more notable OOTW missions the SAF had participated in is outlined in Table 1.

Table 1. Peace Support Operations (PSOs).

Mission	Duration	Type	Personnel and Equipment	Remarks
UN Transition Assistance Group (UNTAG) in Namibia	October 1989–November 1989	Election observers	14 SAF officers, 48 police officers and 20 civil servants	First UN mission
Operation Nightingale	20 January–13 March 1991	Medical team	30 SAF medics and medical officers	Part of the UN support to the Allied forces in the Gulf War
Operation Blue Torch	April 1991–March 2003	Singapore's contribution to UN peacekeeping mission UNIKOM (UN Iraq–Kuwait Observation Mission)	88 SAF personnel as military observers — to help enforce the ceasefire and the DMZ between Iraq and Kuwait	SAF personnel held key appointments such as the Deputy Force Commander of the UN missions and the Deputy Chief Operations Officer in the UNIKOM HQ
UN Angola Verification Mission II (UNAVEM II)	July 1991–December 1992	Military observers	16 SAF personnel	
Operation Blue Angel (UNTAC in Cambodia)	20 May–20 June 1993	Assist the UNTAC to conduct elections and aerial policing	Helicopter (Super Puma) detachment	First Republic of Singapore Air Force (RSAF) UN peacekeeping
Operation Blue Cross in Guatemala	February–May 1997	Medical support	Medical team	Part of UN-sponsored Misión de las Naciones Unidas en Guatemala (MINUGUA)
UN Special Mission in Afghanistan (UNSMA)	May 1997–May 1998	Military adviser	One SAF officer	First time SAF participates in a *peacemaking* mission, rather than a post-conflict peacekeeping mission

Table 1. (*Continued*)

Mission	Duration	Type	Personnel and Equipment	Remarks
INTERFET (International Force East Timor)	September 1999–February 2000	Logistics, medical teams and liaison	In theatre: up to three Landing Ship Tanks (LSTs), one C-130 transport aircraft and about 370 personnel	
United Nations Transitional Administration in East Timor (UNTAET)	February 2000–May 2002	UNTAET HQ medical team and combat peacekeepers	In theatre: up to 330 SAF personnel, Light Strike Vehicles (LSVs) deployed for mobility patrols	145 police officers joined the UN Civilian Police Mission
UNMISET (UN Mission of Support in East Timor)	May 2002–November 2003	Combat peacekeepers, staff officers in Force Commander Group, helicopter (UH-1H) detachment and LST deployment	In theatre: up to company-sized task forces, four UH-1H and one LST	First deployment of NSFs in combat peacekeeping duty; included 17 reservists and 10 conscripts who volunteered
Operation Blue Orchid Part of US-led Multi-National Force (Iraq)	October 2003–December 2008	Maritime security operations, logistics support operations and air-to-air refuelling missions	In theatre: up to 998 personnel, one RSN LST, one RSAF C-130 detachment and one RSAF KC-135 detachment	Tasks included protecting the waters around key oil terminals, conducting patrols and security sweep operations, logistics support for coalition vessels and helicopters
Aceh Monitoring Mission	August 2005–December 2006	Election monitors and military observers	19 SAF personnel over two rotations, together with three police officers	At invitation of Indonesian government, as part of EU–ASEAN Aceh Monitoring Mission

Table 1. (*Continued*)

Mission	Duration	Type	Personnel and Equipment	Remarks
UNMIT (UN Mission in Timor)	September 2006–September 2010	Military observers, and liaison and staff officers	Typical rotation of two SAF officers	
Operation Blue Ridge	2007–2013	Peace support operations, security operations and reconstruction efforts	Total of 492 personnel; equipment include Weapon Locating Radar and Unmanned Aerial Vehicle	Deployment include providing dental, medical and surgical treatment, enhancing security of the International Security Assistance Force (ISAF), Imagery Analysis Teams, Military Institutional Trainers to train the Afghan National Security Forces
Operation Blue Sapphire	Five deployments since April 2009 (last deployment was from March–June 2014)	Counter-Piracy Operation CTF 151 patrols the Internationally Recommended Transit Corridor in the Gulf of Aden[10]	In theatre: up to ~300 personnel, one LST or one Frigate with Seahawk naval helicopter, two SP helicopters, one Fokker-50 Maritime Patrol Aircraft	Operations were conducted in conjunction with the NATO and the EU Naval Force Somalia, and other independently deployed naval ships SAF led CTF 151 on three of the five deployments
Operation Palm	December 1970	East Pakistan (now Bangladesh) Cyclone	47-men medical team	First HADR

Table 2. HADR Operations.

Mission	Duration	Disaster/Location	Personnel and Equipment	Remarks
Operation Thunderstorm	May 1975	To provide medical aid to refugees from South Vietnam stranded near Singapore waters	Six mobile medical teams	
Operation Lionheart	July–August 1990	Baguio Earthquake (Philippines)	Medical team comprised mainly of SAF volunteers	First collaboration with SCDF
Operation Flying Eagle	September–October 1999	Taiwan Earthquake	Medical relief for disaster victims	
Operation Flying Eagle	June 2000	Bengkulu Earthquake (Sumatra, Indonesia)	Medical relief for disaster victims	SAF was the first foreign military to respond
Operation Flying Eagle	December 2004–January 2005	Asian tsunami	In theatre: over 1200 personnel, three LSTs, six Chinooks, two Super Puma helicopters, and eight support aircraft (C-130 and Fokker 50)	At invitation of Indonesian government
Operation Flying Eagle	April–June 2005	Nias Earthquake (Bantul, Indonesia)	Medical relief and medical evacuation	
Operation Flying Eagle	May–June 2006	Yogjakarta Earthquake	Medical relief and Disaster Assistance and Rescue	Collaboration with SCDF
Operation Swift Lion	October 2009	Indonesia Sumatra Earthquake	54-strong medical team, supported by medical staff from MOH and SCDF	Code-named "Swift Lion", to distinguish between purely medical relief operations from Operation Flying Eagle's broader HADR scope

Source: Compiled from Singapore Ministry of Defence website — http://www.mindef.gov.sg/imindef/press_room/official_releases/sp/1997/23nov97_speech.html.

Challenges in Sustaining Commitment to OOTW

Involvement in NEO, HADR and CA operations can be understood, easily enough, from the angle of moral obligation to serve and responsibility to protect (R2P). As a result, even though natural-civil disasters may not have direct relevance and connectivity with the mission of the armed forces, militaries generally have the capabilities to support the critical needs of emergency relief and substantially contribute to restoring normalcy after the immediate disaster. In the case of missions that are perceived as military interventions, an even stronger justification and buy-in is necessary when it comes to engaging public opinion.

This was particularly the case for the SAF's overseas missions in Afghanistan (2007–2013) and Iraq (2003–2008). In both cases, the SAF contributed to the post-combat stabilisation and reconstruction phases of non-UN sanctioned military campaigns. In fact, Ms Irene Ng, Member of Parliament (MP of Tampines), had asked the Minister for Defence if the SAF was justified in getting involved in Iraq, which could be interpreted as supporting an arguably "unjust" war (2002 Iraq War) — especially when "weapons of mass-destruction have not been found".[11] Furthermore, military operations are necessarily conducted "amongst the people" — not just in the "cities, towns, streets and their houses",[12] but also through the media (to people) in cafes and homes, all over the world. Governments, when deciding to contribute military troops to such operations, would inevitably have to take into consideration public opinion on the direction and scope of the military involvement.

In the case of Singapore, scaling up of the SAF's contributions can raise many issues — beyond operational ones. Participation in such military operations may involve high costs in resources to sustain the missions. For a conscript armed force such as the SAF, there are also the socio-political risks associated with the deployment of NSmen. International missions — even non-combat deployments — bear with them the risk of injury and harm to personnel deployed. Although there are no known casualties so far, the *raison d'être* of Singapore's citizen soldier model remains that of homeland defence and not expeditionary missions. Indeed, from time to time, questions have been raised in parliament about the government's rationale for sending SAF servicemen to overseas missions — particularly considering the high costs and risks involved.[13]

Some parliamentarians, including Mr Sin Boon Ann (on 16 May 2002)[14] and Mr Steve Chia Kiah Hoong (on November 10 2003),[15] have questioned if parliament should have been consulted before the government decides on troop contributions to Iraq and other missions that are not purely "humanitarian missions" per se. Singapore's constitution does not require parliamentary approval for the overseas deployment of the SAF — these matters fall under the purview of the cabinet.[16] However, such issues would be of particular concern to Singaporeans, given that they touch not only on Singapore's relationship with other countries, but also on the risks involved for the troops as well as the financial and human resources. Accordingly, these matters would be regularly discussed and debated on in parliament, and the government had made it a point to provide parliament and the public with adequate information about such deployments; including explanations of how the SAF's participation in these overseas operations contribute to securing Singapore's interests.[17]

More recently, Minister for Defence Ng Eng Hen reinforced the central motivation behind Singapore's contribution to such overseas operations in explaining the need for the SAF participate in the coalition against ISIS. He pointed to the transnational nature of the threat, and how, as an international hub, Singapore is especially vulnerable to the spread of terrorism. In relation to the scope of the SAF's contribution, he referred to the niche areas that the SAF has established in its previous deployments to such operations, such as providing planning/liaison officers, an imagery analysis team and air-to-air refuelling. In addressing the risks involved, he reassured parliament that SAF troops will conduct its operations outside of the war zone, in neighbouring countries. Moreover, the risks would be mitigated by ensuring "that our servicemen are well equipped, and receive additional training in weapon handling, dealing with Improvised Explosive Devices (IEDs), as well as reacting to hostile elements".[18]

With regard to the broader challenges, Deputy Prime Minister, Mr Teo Chee Hean, underlined the importance of supporting multinational efforts that aim to combat ISIS's brand of jihadist terrorism, in addition to continued international engagements with our neighbours. Recognising that such issues cannot be handled by security agencies alone, Associate Professor Dr Yaacob Ibrahim, Minister-in-Charge of Muslim Affairs, emphasised the ongoing efforts by the various religious and civil organisations in Singapore to promote social harmony and unity amongst different religions, and reiterated the need to maintain such engagements to continue to build confidence between countries and also between different races and religious groups.[19]

While recongnising the global character of the ISIS threat, OOTW missions in far-flung places could still be seen as an unnecessary distraction from the SAF's primary purpose of defending Singapore. Reflecting this

perception, Dr Lim Wee Kiak, MP of Nee Soon, requested MINDEF to provide updates on Singapore's "contributions to humanitarian and peacekeeping
missions", the amount of resources required for such missions, and if all those
contributions would "distract MINDEF from the primary role of defending
Singapore".[20] At the same Committee of Supply's debate on the Defence
Budget, Ms Ellen Lee, MP of Sembawang, noted the perceptible shift in
MINDEF's role, and also questioned the relevance of having the SAF to participate in this wide gamut of OOTWs, pointing out that "it is hard to believe
that all these efforts, directly or indirectly, impact Singapore's safety".[21] As such,
overseas deployments increasingly have to be rationalised by its relevance to
the defence of Singapore, and justified with the assurance that not only would
the SAF's primary role not be compromised, but its operational readiness
should be enhanced with these costly experiences.[22] With limited manpower,
the SAF would not be able to deploy large contingents, and it must be selective
of the type of missions it can commit to. There are political constraints placed
on a largely conscript force such as the SAF when it comes to international
missions. Consequently, it is necessary to understand the political context and
motivations for the SAF's increasing involvement in international OOTWs.

International Missions — "Not a Soldier's Job, but Only a Soldier Can Do It"[23]

Underlining Singapore's role in the international community, Minister for
Defence, Dr Ng Eng Hen, reiterated the need for Singapore to "continue to play
our role judiciously as a responsible member of the global community to ensure
peace and stability in our region".[24] More recent sizeable deployments also hint
at greater confidence in the SAF's operational capabilities and sophistication of
its equipment and training, as well as a long-standing desire to develop greater
interoperability with multinational partners in complex missions. While initially
Singapore tended to deploy only with UN-led missions, in recent years the SAF
has been deployed increasingly in US-led coalitions of the willing operating in
Iraq and Afghanistan as well as the GOA.

   With regard to UN missions, the respect for international norms is important for small states like Singapore. Then-Prime Minister Goh Chok Tong
underscored this in a speech to the UN General Assembly in 1995, saying:
"Small countries like Singapore need the UN, and must play a constructive role
in supporting it." Echoing this point in 1997, Dr Tony Tan Keng Yam, then-
DPM and Minister for Defence, stressed the need for the SAF to actively
participate in UN peacekeeping missions. He argued that it was necessary to

demonstrate Singapore's commitment to the UN's role in safeguarding international law and order, and Singapore's role as a "firm believer of the principles of the UN Charter".[25] The same year saw the SAF participating in its first peace-making mission in the UN Special Mission in Afghanistan (UNSMA), set up to facilitate negotiations between warring parties towards national reconciliation. The decision to commit defence resources to more than peacekeeping was explained by Dr Tony Tan as a necessary and logical development for the SAF to contribute effectively in the riskier but more vital phase of peacemaking.[26]

The transnational character of threats (such as terrorism and piracy) faced by Singapore today means that instability elsewhere in the world can affect the security of Singapore and its immediate region. This point on how a specific security threat could affect countries all over the world was emphasised by then-Defence Minister Teo Chee Hean in November 2009 — that as a result of "the increasing interconnectivity of the world that we live in, instability in one part of the world has far-reaching consequences for other regions".[27] More recently, in June 2013, Minister for Defence, Dr Ng Eng Hen reinforced the need to *defend forward* as he explained why the SAF needed to support the ISAF's stabilisation and reconstruction operations in Afghanistan, to defend against the transnational threat of terrorism. He explained that the SAF was there "to prevent extremists from using Afghanistan as a base to export terror-ism to the rest of the world".[28] Underpinning this point, it was the intelligence obtained from the US operations in Afghanistan that led to the interception and subsequent break-up of a terrorist plot that targeted Singapore.[29]

The Defence Minister further expanded on the idea of forward defence, when he expounded on the SAF's continued involvement in international and regional counter-piracy efforts, such as with the CTF-151 in the GOA some 4,000 nautical miles away. As one of the world's major shipping lanes, approxi-mately 20% of Singapore's trade and 11% of the world's petroleum flow through the GOA each year. Noting the interconnectedness of economies all over the world, and given how Singaporean's livelihood is dependent on global trade, Dr Ng Eng Hen highlighted the need for the SAF to help ensure the "freedom and safety of navigation (along) vital sea routes".[30] To that end, CTF-151, for example, has contributed to the significant reduction of piracy attacks in the GOA over the past few years by patrolling the Internationally Recommended Transit Corridor (IRTC) between the coasts of Somalia and Yemen.[31]

OOTW missions also play a function in defence diplomacy, which is criti-cal in enabling Singapore to "punch above its weight". One example is Singapore's relationship with Bahrain in the Middle East. Bahrain had provided valuable support to the SAF's deployment in the GOA. In 2010, Bahrain ratified the Gulf Cooperation Council (GCC)–Singapore Free Trade Agreement (FTA) that would enhance Singapore's growing economic ties with the Gulf nations. Singapore would continue to support dialogues and opportunities for further military cooperation with Bahrain as the two countries share common military interests in dealing with the Gulf region's security challenges, particularly the "transnational threats such as terrorism and maritime security threats".[32]

Another case in point is the SAF's participation in the reconstruction efforts in Afghanistan and Iraq. On one hand, the significant rationale behind the SAF's involvement in Iraq and Afghanistan can be understood by examining the implications of instability in the Gulf region, which could seriously impact "the supply of oil and the spread of terrorism".[33] On the other hand, Singapore also needs to be seen playing a proactive and constructive role in promoting international security. By participating in international missions, the SAF has established itself to be a credible and respected armed force, built international goodwill and provided valuable opportunities to foster relationships with foreign counterparts. Such confidence-building forms of defence diplomacy are essential to promoting greater understanding and mutual trust amongst militaries and countries, and allow Singapore to be a player in shaping the international security environment.

Other than diplomacy, the SAF's varied participation in such operations could be seen as an opportunity to showcase its ability to effectively handle multiple crises simultaneously. In 2005, the SAF conducted a large-scale HADR operation in January in response to the Asian tsunami. A few months later in April, the SAF deployed medical relief and evacuation teams to the Bantul earthquake in Indonesia — whilst concurrently managing Operation Blue Orchid deployments in Iraq. More recently, in 2009, the SAF again demonstrated this ability to command and control a range of overseas operations, some running back-to-back, and some simultaneously. In 2009, SAF dispatched medical relief and humanitarian aid to earthquake victims in Padang, supported ongoing reconstruction and humanitarian efforts, and security and force protection operations in Afghanistan (from 2007 to 2013), as well as coordinated deployments in the GOA as part of CTF-151 (five deployments between April 2009 to June 2014).

The SAF's ability to respond to a wide spectrum of security challenges is testament to its confidence and proficiency. At the same time, NSmen's and NSFs' participation in such operations have demonstrated not only their competency, operation-readiness and professionalism — but also their ability to operate effectively with regular soldiers. Increasingly, the SAF's full-spectrum capabilities demonstrated in various overseas missions are to be found not only in the SAF regulars, but the citizen soldiers who serve with them. This is especially crucial for a conscript armed force like the SAF, where NSmen and NSFs constitute the bedrock.

HADR: Finding a Regional Response and Niche Role

Singapore is located in the world's most disaster-prone region. Between 2004 and 2013, over 40% of the world's natural disasters occured in the Asia-Pacific region resulting in "economic damages of over US$560 billion".[34] Moreover, studies have indicated an upward trend from natural disasters arising from extreme weather and rapid urbanisation, with corresponding rising economic costs and disaster-related deaths.[35] Given the interdependence between Singapore's economy and the fortunes of the Asia-Pacific region, Singaporeans will be increasingly exposed to the cost of such disasters. As explained by Minister for Social and Family Development and then-Second Minister for Defence, Mr Chan Chun Sing, "Militaries have unique capabilities such as strategic airlift and are on 24/7 operational footings, able to rapidly mobilise and deploy".[36] In the event of regional natural disasters, the SAF would be expected to step in to contribute towards providing disaster-aid relief and maintaining stability in the aftermath of the disaster.

The scope of the SAF's involvement in such operations is typically limited to the immediate aftermath of the disaster. As the operations on the ground transit from "emergency relief" to "recovery phase", Singapore's contributions would, similarly, transit from government to non-governmental organisations and other volunteer agencies. For example, the SAF's deployment to Aceh, in the aftermath of the Boxing Day tsunami in 2004, lasted for only three weeks. During that time, the Singapore Army's Combat Engineers, supported by the Republic of Singapore Navy's LSTs, constructed beach landing points, helicopter landing sites, and field hospitals in Meulaboh and Bandar Aceh, so that relief supplies and medical aid could be delivered to the populace otherwise cut off from the rest of Sumatra. In addition, the Republic of Singapore Air Force set up a mobile air traffic control tower that was critical in helping the Bandar Aceh International Airport to resume operations. After which, as the relief work transitioned to the recovery phase, the SAF pulled out most of its personnel and assets — except for three Chinook helicopters, which the Indonesian authorities requested to remain in support of the recovery operations.[37]

Furthermore, contributions to such regional HADR missions provide a "show-case" of the SAF's expeditionary capabilities in a low-profile manner, and serve to reinforce our servicemen's confidence in one another, in their training, in their equipment and in the NS system. Similarly, HADR's operational requirements provide for capability development in "dual-use" platforms. For example, larger capacity platforms such as the Joint-Multi-Mission Ships (JMMS) would — according to Defence Minister, Dr Ng Eng Hen — give the SAF the capability to project larger forces to "crisis-hit areas" and support "extended helicopter operations".[38] Increasingly, the SAF lift assets such as LSTs, Chinook heavy-lift helicopters and the planned JMMS are proving their flexibility in both OOTW missions and conventional scenarios.

The SAF can play a niche role in strengthening military-to-military coordination between Asia-Pacific countries and assist in building a regional capability that would enhance the effectiveness of multinational HADR operations. To that end, Singapore offered to host the Regional HADR Coordination Centre (RHCC), which had commenced operations on 12 September 2014. The centre was set up with the aim to "contribute towards a more effective regional response to disasters by facilitating military-to-military coordination".[39] According to then-Second Minister for Defence, Mr Chan Chun Sing, it would be designed to enhance information sharing and operational C2 (command and control) amongst militaries and their respective operational centres, and interfacing existing HADR coordinating mechanisms such as the ASEAN Coordinating Centre for Humanitarian Assistance (AHA Centre) and the UN Office for the Coordination of Humanitarian Affairs (OCHA).[40] On a broader level, HADR missions offer a common platform in terms of confidence building amongst nations and forging closer relationships between militaries. More importantly, as noted by Defence Minister Ng in his Third Putrajaya Forum Speech: "no country has the resources or ability to provide all the solutions. But … we will be able to meet the challenges before us as long as we pool resources and synergise efforts; as long as we continue together based on shared interests, aspirations and principles."[41]

Trends Analysis

Even as the SAF continues to focus its training and development on building a credible conventional force, it is more likely that the SAF would be expected to undertake a range of OOTW missions in the Asia-Pacific region and beyond. Consequently, the SAF would find itself devoting more resources and efforts to the planning and preparations for OOTW missions far from home. Notwithstanding, this evolution of the SAF into a more "global" and "visible" force is an iteration of the search for relevance in times of peace, reinforcing the notion of an "always ready" SAF, capable of overseas deployment, while not compromising Singapore's safety and security.[42]

From the angle of relevance, Singapore typically adopts a pragmatic approach to its international missions — an approach that balances the responsibility of a citizen of the world, while seeking tangible returns in both the military and political realms.[43] Certainly, the "pragmatic" approach is adopted with regard to the SAF's contribution to Iraq, by putting aside the debate on whether the Iraq War in 2003 was justified, and focusing on the reconstruction and stabilisation of the country, so as to bring about security and stability to the Gulf region. At the same time, in undertaking Operation Blue Orchid, Singapore had not just "accumulated invaluable operational experience and professional expertise that will stand us in good stead for missions that are directly relevant to safeguarding Singapore's peace and security in the future",[44] but also underscored the value Singapore perceives of its partnership with global and regional partners.

With regard to planning and preparations, the SAF would have to ensure that, in terms of capabilities and training, it would be able to continue to effectively address requirements placed by overseas missions. These entail making sure that SAF personnel (both regular and citizen soldiers) would be adequately equipped, trained and prepared for such missions. In terms of force structuring and capability development, Minister for Defence Dr Ng Eng Hen highlighted the need to "build an SAF with capabilities for a wide spectrum of operations, primarily to protect our nation against direct threats and also respond flexibly to transnational security challenges posed by terrorism, piracy, the proliferation of weapons of mass destruction and natural disasters".[45] Over the years, the SAF has leaned on the Guards formation to lead in overseas operations, which most notably include the UN PKO in Timor Leste, 2004 tsunami OFE and participation in ISAF from 2007 to 2013.[46] They led in the building up of SAF's PSO and HADR capabilities, ranging from less-lethal weapons and ammunition, to logistics support capabilities.

Looking forward, in light of the SAF's considerable overseas experience over the past few decades, how far would the SAF go in future international missions? Judging from global and regional trends as well as the sizeable expertise that the SAF has developed in OOTW, the SAF can be expected to shoulder a greater role in terms of size, scope, frequency, duration and distance of missions. There is however the question of societal attitudes toward such missions — which is particularly salient for a citizen force like the SAF. Will societal attitudes and political appetite allow for the higher risk missions of the OOTW spectrum that may entail the employment of kinetic force? The trends analysed in this chapter suggest that whilst OOTW missions in the immediate region and beyond will be a growing concern for the SAF, the primary role of the SAF will nevertheless remain that of homeland defence rather than an expeditionary force.

Notes

[1] Ng Eng Hen, "Speech by Minister for Defence Dr Ng Eng Hen at the Overseas Service Medal Pressentation Ceremany," 19 July 2013. Retrieved 15 May 2015, from http://www.mindef.gov.sg/imindef/press_room/official_releases/sp/releases/sp/2013/19jul13_speech.html#.VV1SfrmqpHx.

[2] Our Singapore Army, "Our Army: How Far Would You Go?," 19 August 2014. Retrieved 19 December 2014, from https://www.youtube.com/watch?v=HcYJNeZl4No, https://www.youtube.com/watch?v=6tRmJdKDdug, and https://www.youtube.com/watch?v=8Ir513jQaok.

[3] Singapore Ministry of Defence, "SAF Participation in Peacekeeping Operations in Timor-Leste," 11 July 2003. Retrieved 19 December 2014, from http://www.mindef.gov.sg/content/imindef/press_room/official_releases/nr/2003/jul/11jul03_nr/11jul03_fs2.html#.VIHNkjGUeSo.

[4] Singapore Ministry of Foreign Affairs, "International Peace Keeping Efforts." Retrieved 20 August 2014, from http://www.mfa.gov.sg/content/mfa/international_issues/intl_peace_keeping_efforts.html.

[5] UN Library, *United Nations Stand-By Arrangements System Military Handbook Edition 2003*. Retrieved 19 August 2014, from https://cc.unlb.org/UNSAS%20Documents/KEY%20DOCUMENTS/UNSAS%20Handbook%20%202003.pdf. The MOU on Stand-by Arrangements with the UN specifies resources provided, response times and conditions for employment.

[6] Singapore Ministry of Defence, "SAF to Round up Afghan Deployments by June," *Cyberpioneer*, 8 February 2013. Retrieved 23 August 2014, from http://www.mindef.gov.sg/imindef/resourcelibrary/cyberpioneer/topics/articles/news/2013/feb/08feb13_news.html#.VK541yuUeSo.

[7] Singapore Ministry of Defence, "Two Thousand Two Hundred and Sixty Three Days 2007–2013: Operation Blue Ridge — The SAF's Six-Year Mission in Afghanistan." Retrieved 23 November 2014, from http://www.mindef.gov.sg/imindef/mindef_web-sites/atozlistings/army/Our_Stories/OBR.html.

[8] Singapore Ministry of Defence, *Reaching out: Operation Flying Eagle — SAF Humanitarian Assistance after the Tsunami* (Singapore: SNP International, 2005), pp. 54–96.

[9] Matthias Yao Chih, "Speech by Mr Matthias Yao Chih, Minister of State for Defence, at the Grassroots Leaders' Visit to Tuas Naval Base," 23 November 1997. Retrieved 23 November 2014, from http://www.mindef.gov.sg/imindef/press_room/official_releases/sp/1997/23nov97_speech.html.

[10] See Combined Maritime Forces. Retrieved 15 November 2014, from http://combinedmaritimeforces.com/ctf-151-counter-piracy/. Combined Task Force 151 (CTF-151) is one of three task forces operated by Combined Maritime Forces (CMF). In accordance with United Nations Security Council Resolutions and in cooperation with non-member forces, CTF-151's mission is to disrupt piracy and armed robbery

at sea, and to engage with regional and other partners to build capacity and improve relevant capabilities in order to protect global maritime commerce and secure freedom of navigation. CMF is a multinational naval partnership, and the 30 nations that comprise CMF are not bound by either a political or military mandate; participation is purely voluntary.

[11] Hansard, Oral Answers to Questions over Singapore Armed Forces Contingent to Iraq, 10 November 2003, column 3272. For instance, Ms Irene Ng Phek Hoong (MP of Tampines) raised this issue in parliament — "I want to ask the Minister whether he thinks the cause is justified in this case because, as we know, the weapons of mass destruction have not been found and the occupation of the US forces has provoked resistance and violence in some quarters by Iraqi groups."

[12] Rupert Smith, *The Utility of Force: The Art of War in the Modern World* (New York: Vintage Books, 2008), p. 281.

[13] Hansard, Oral Answers to Questions over Singapore Armed Forces Contingent to Iraq, 10 November 2003, column 3273; Debate on Ministry of Defence Budget, 5 March 2010, columns 3093 and 3094. Other Members of Parliament (MPs) who had questioned the rationale for sending SAF troops to Iraq included Mr Chiam See Tong, MP of Potong Pasir, when he asked, "in what way is our sending of troops to Iraq, which (the Minister) admits is a nation very far away from Singapore, in the interest of Singapore?". Similar concerns were raised again, when in 2006, the SAF expanded its deployments in the "Greater Middle East" to Afghanistan. MPs, once more, questioned the rationale for Singapore's involvement in such far away missions. For example, a few years into Operations Blue Ridge, as the SAF increased its scope of operations in Afghanistan, Dr Lam Pin Min, MP of Ang Mo Kio pointed out in parliament — "Singapore's involvement in international humanitarian and peace-keeping missions has increased over the years …[and] such missions are not without risk to the lives of our servicemen: (a) What is the rationale for Singapore's involvement in missions situated far way, such as in the Middle East and beyond?; (b) Are our servicemen adequately trained and equipped to operate in these hostile conditions?".

[14] Hansard, Debate on Ministry of Defence Budget, 16 May 2002, column 1378. Mr Sin Boon Ann, MP of Tampines, asked whether parliament should be the appropriate forum to discuss Singapore's participation in such risky missions.

[15] Hansard, Oral Answers to Questions over Singapore Armed Forces Contingent to Iraq, 10 November 2003, column 3271. Mr Steve Chia Kiah Hoong, Non-Constituency MP, asked, "Why did our Government and our Defence Minister not get the consent of our Parliament before committing the lives of our Singapore soldiers to this high risk in Iraq? What is the role of the Parliament if not to debate on important issues like sending our young boys to the war zone where lives are at risk?". He further pointed out that British parliament approval was required to send British troops to Iraq, but consent was not sought in MINDEF's commitment of troops to Iraq.

[16] See Singapore Attorney General's Chambers, "Constitution of the Republic of Singapore." Retrieved 22 October 2014, from http://statutes.agc.gov.sg/aol/search/

display/view.w3p;ident=12209485-937f-473e-8afa-317ca0462aff;page=0;query=Do cId%3A%22cf2412ff-fca5-4a64-a8ef-b95b8987728e%22%20Status%3Ainforce%20 Depth%3A0;rec=0#P1III. Singapore's constitution allows for "participation in cooperative international schemes beneficial to Singapore".

[17] Hansard, Oral Answers to Questions over Singapore Armed Forces Contingent to Iraq, 10 November 2003. For example, then-Defence Minister, RADM Teo Chee Hean, took pains to provide the rationale for SAF's troop contributions to Iraq in 2003, during a parliament session on the SAF contingent to Iraq.

[18] See, for instance, Dr Hakim and Dr Wee Teck Young, "In Singapore, Afghanistan and the Arena of Ideas," 10 November 2014. Retrieved 10 December 2014, from http://www.theonlinecitizen.com/2014/11/in-singapore-afghanistan-and-the-arena-of-ideas/. Other comments are available from online posts such as "therealsingapore.com" and "theonlinecitizen.com". For example, Giong Goh posted his comment on 1 December 2014, "Are you out of your mind Mr Ng?? What can a 50-60 SAF personal [sic] do there?? And you wanted to make our country into ISIS target as well??". Retrieved 21 December 2014, from http://therealsingapore.com/content/ng-eng-hen-we-will-be-sending-50-60-saf-personnel-fight-isis-middle-east.

[19] Hansard, Oral Answers to Questions over Singapore Armed Forces' Contribution to Fight against ISIS, 3 November 2014.

[20] *Ibid*. Minister for Defence, Dr Ng Eng Hen's answers to questions on "SAF's Contribution to Fight against ISIS".

[21] "Singapore Will Join Coalition against Islamic State," *Channel NewsAsia*, 3 November 2014. Retrieved 13 December 2014, from http://www.channelnewsasia.com/news/singapore/singapore-to-join/1450248.html.

[22] Hansard, Committee of Supply debate on Ministry of Defence, 5 March 2012.

[23] *Ibid*.

[24] Hansard, Debate on Ministry of Defence Budget, 2 March 2011, column 3353. Stressing on similar points, MP Ms Indranee Rajah raised queries about SAF's deployments in Afghanistan, and how they might benefit Afghanistan, the SAF and Singapore.

[25] Borrowing and adapting an oft-quoted phrase from former UN Secretary-General, Dag Hammarskjöld, who was then, referring more specifically to "peacekeeping" missions.

[26] Hansard, Addendum to the President's Address by Ministry of Defence, 10 October 2011.

[27] Dr Tony Tan Keng Yam, "Speech by Dr Tony Tan Keng Yam, at the Medal Presentation Ceremony for 5th SAF UNIKOM Team," 7 January 1997. Retrieved 17 July 2014, from http://www.mindef.gov.sg/imindef/press_room/official_releases/sp/1997/07jan97_speech.html#.VK56dyuUeSo.

[28] Dr Tony Tan Keng Yam, "Speech by Dr Tony Tan Keng Yam, Deputy Prime Minister and Minister for Defence, at the Medal Presentation Ceremony for Blue Torch 6 and Send-Off Ceremony for the Military Adviser to United Nations Special Mission in Afghanistan," 20 May 1997. Retrieved 2 November 2014, from http://www.mindef.gov.sg/imindef/press_room/official_releases/sp/1997/20may97_speech.print.img.html.

[29] Teo Chee Hean, "Speech by Deputy Prime Minister and Minister for Defence Teo Chee Hean at the Overseas Service Medal Presentation Ceremony," 25 November 2009. Retrieved 15 November 2014, from http://www.mindef.gov.sg/imindef/press_room/official_releases/sp/2009/25nov09_speech.html#.VIMEgzGUeSo.

[30] Dr Ng Eng Hen, "Speech by Minister for Defence Dr Ng Eng Hen at the Overseas Service Medal Presentation Ceremony," 19 July 2013. Retrieved 29 November 2014, from http://www.mindef.gov.sg/imindef/press_room/official_releases/sp/2013/19jul13_speech.html#.VK57KSuUeSo.

[31] "Intelligence from Afghanistan Breaks Singapore Plot," *CNN.com,* 11 January 2002. Retrieved 21 August 2014, from http://edition.cnn.com/2002/US/01/11/ret.singapore.plot/index.html.

[32] Dr Ng Eng Hen, "Speech by Dr Ng Eng Hen, Minister for Defence, at the Overseas Service Medal Presentation Ceremony," 27 June 2014. Retrieved 17 November 2014, from http://www.mindef.gov.sg/imindef/press_room/official_releases/sp/2014/27jun14_speech.html#.VJLydCuUeSo.

[33] See International Chamber of Commerce, "Somali Pirate Clampdown Caused Drop in Global Piracy, IMB Reveals," 15 January 2014. Retrieved 9 August 2014, from https://www.icc-ccs.org/news/904-somali-pirate-clampdown-caused-drop-in-global-piracy-imb-reveals. "Piracy at sea has reached its lowest levels in six years, with 264 attacks recorded worldwide in 2013, a 40% drop since Somali piracy peaked in 2011, the International Chamber of Commerce (ICC) International Maritime Bureau (IMB) revealed today. 15 incidents were reported off Somalia in 2013, down from 75 in 2012, and 237 in 2011."

[34] Dr Mohamad Maliki Bin Osman, "Minister of State for Defence Attends 10th Manama Dialogue in Bahrain," 7 December 2014. Retrieved 27 December 2014, from http://www.mindef.gov.sg/imindef/press_room/official_releases/nr/2014/dec/07dec14_nr.html#.VK57fCuUeSo.

[35] See Singapore Ministry of Defence, *Partnering to Rebuild: Operation Blue Orchid — The Singapore Armed Forces Experience in Iraq* (Singapore: MINDEF Public Affairs, 2010), p. 8. According to the statement by then-Minister for Defence Teo Chee Hean.

[36] UN, "Asia-Pacific Report: World's Most Disaster Prone Region Experiences Three-Fold Rise in Deaths," 18 December 2014. Retrieved 28 December 2014, from http://www.un.org/apps/news/story.asp?NewsID=49642#.VJWAnV4AKA.

[37] The World Bank, "To the Brink: Climate Change Will Increase Frequency and Severity of Disasters, Stress Food and Energy Production in South Asia," 24 June 2013. Retrieved 14 September 2014, from http://www.worldbank.org/en/news/feature/2013/06/24/climate-change-natural-disasters-stress-food-energy-production-south-asia.

[38] Mr Chan Chun Sing, "Closing Address by Minister for Social and Family Development and Second Minister for Defence Mr Chan Chun Sing at the Regional Conference on 'Building Civil-Military Capacity for Disaster Relief Operations,'" 12 September 2014. Retrieved 21 October 2014, from http://www.mindef.gov.sg/content/imindef/press_room/official_releases/sp/2014/12sep14_speech.html#.VK6BDCuUeSo.

[39] See Ministry of Defence, *Reaching out: Operation Flying Eagle — SAF Humanitarian Assistance after the Tsunami* (Singapore: SNP International, 2005), p. 106.

[40] Dr Ng Eng Hen, "Dr Ng: SAF and NS Well Poised to Tackle Future Challenges," *Cyberpioneer*, 1 July 2014. Retrieved 11 October 2014, from http://www.mindef.gov.sg/imindef/resourcelibrary/cyberpioneer/topics/articles/news/2014/jul/01jul14_news.html#.VK6C2yuUeSo.

[41] Singapore Ministry of Defence, "The Philippines Expresses Strong Support for the Changi Regional HADR Coordination Centre," 25 September 2014. Retrieved 15 November 2014, from http://www.mindef.gov.sg/imindef/press_room/official_releases/nr/2014/sep/25sep14_nr2.html.

[42] Singapore Ministry of Defence, "SAF Working with Partner Militaries to Strengthen Disaster Relief Coordination," 12 September 2014. Retrieved 22 November 2014, from http://www.mindef.gov.sg/imindef/press_room/official_releases/nr/2014/sep/12sep14_nr2.html#.VK586yuUeSo.

[43] Ng Eng Hen, "Speech by Dr Ng Eng Hen, Minister for Defence, at the 3rd Putrajaya Forum, at Seri Pacific Hotel Kuala Lumpur," 14 April 2014. Retrieved 15 May 2015, from http://www.mindef.gov.sg/imindef/press_room/official_releases/sp/2014/14/apr14_speech.html#. VV14X7mqpHx.

[44] Yee-Kuang Heng and Weichong Ong, "The Quest for Relevance in Times of Peace in Asia-Pacific Nations," in Chiyuki Aoi and Yee-Kuang Heng (eds.), *International Peace Support and Stability Missions* (NY: Palgrave MacMillan, 2014), p. 144.

[45] Ong Weichong, "Peripheral to Norm? The Expeditionary Role of the Third Generation Singapore Armed Forces," *Defence Studies*, 11(3), September 2011, p. 555.

[46] According to then-Deputy Prime Minister and Minister for Defence, Mr Teo Chee Hean. Quoted in Singapore Ministry of Defence (2010), *op. cit.*, p. 7.

[47] Hansard, Addendum to the President's Address by Ministry of Defence, 10 October 2011.

[48] Singapore Ministry of Defence, "Guardsmen Showcase Capabilities from Overseas Operational Experience," 19 September 2014. Retrieved 29 November 2014, from http://www.mindef.gov.sg/imindef/press_room/official_releases/nr/2014/sep/19sep14_nr.html#.VK5_cyuUeSo.

Chapter 10

Why the FPDA Still Matters to Singapore

Ralf Emmers

Introduction[1]

As Singapore celebrates 50 years of independence, ongoing regional and domestic crises around the world provide a stark reminder to the city-state of the vulnerability of national security. Singapore's innate sense of vulnerability has derived from its physical size, geostrategic location, history and its lack of natural resources.[2] As a small state, it has traditionally focused on deterrence and diplomacy as the twin pillars of its national security policy. Central to Singapore's national strategy has been the preservation of its sovereignty and independence. Among the vast array of deterrence and diplomatic instruments that Singapore possesses to deal with its own vulnerability lies a "relic of the past": the Five Power Defence Arrangements (FPDA). The latter has enabled Singapore to both strengthen its own military capabilities as well as to follow a policy of external balancing through association with external powers.

Established in 1971, the FPDA involves Malaysia, Singapore, Australia, New Zealand (NZ) and the United Kingdom (UK). It operates as a loose structure focusing on both traditional and non-traditional security issues, such as maritime security, terrorism, and humanitarian assistance and disaster relief (HADR), which are of direct concern to its participants. The FPDA is arguably the oldest institutional expression of defence diplomacy in Southeast Asia today, and predates other military-to-military institutions such as the Association of Southeast Asian Nations' (ASEAN) ASEAN Defence Ministers' Meeting (ADMM) by at least 35 years.

The FPDA was created amidst fears and uncertainties stemming from the 1967 announcement by the British Labour government of its new policy of military withdrawal from East of Suez. The British decision to disengage militarily was of particular concern to both Singapore and Malaysia as both states relied heavily on their military ties with London. The 1967 decision was tempered somewhat as the subsequent British Conservative government sought to maintain some military engagement in the Southeast Asian region and thereby proposed to replace the 1957 Anglo–Malayan Defence Agreement (AMDA) with the FPDA. With this origin in mind, it is clear that the FPDA was an instrument created to deal with the concerns of the time and especially with the insecurity felt by its Southeast Asian participants at an early stage of their independence.

More than 40 years on, Singapore remains an interested participant in this "relic of the past" despite having invested heavily in its own defence and developed a close strategic partnership with the United States (US). Therein lies an interesting puzzle: why does the FPDA remain relevant to Singapore? This paper argues that the FPDA remains important for the city-state for three main reasons, namely: its confidence-building role in bilateral relations between Singapore and Malaysia; its existence as a channel for direct relations with three external parties (Australia, NZ and the UK) and for indirect relations with the US, and finally, its contribution to Singapore's regional defence diplomacy. This paper will first briefly cover the historical and institutional evolution of the FPDA before delving into an elaboration on each of the three reasons outlined in the argument.

History of the FPDA

The FPDA was created amidst a tense situation in Southeast Asia. Apart from security concerns arising from the disengagement of British military in the region, the formation of the FPDA also followed the Indonesian opposition to the formation of the Federation of Malaysia in 1963. Sukarno started a campaign of Confrontation or *Konfrontasi* to oppose the Federation as it was perceived in Jakarta as a British neocolonial design. While the end of the Sukarno era in 1965 and the establishment of ASEAN in 1967 signified the end of *Konfrontasi*, regional relations continued to be tense and were characterised by mistrust. Despite political reconciliation between Malaysia and Indonesia, the former remained fearful of the latter. Likewise, Singapore, having suffered attacks during *Konfrontasi*, mistrusted Indonesia. Indonesia's annexation of East Timor in 1975 was another issue that further complicated Singapore–Indonesia relations. Singapore, at the time, remained fearful of Jakarta's regional intentions and potential hegemonic aspirations.[3]

Indonesia and its potential regional ambitions were therefore a clear referent of the FPDA during the 1970s and 1980s.[4] Jakarta itself would for a long period remain sceptical about the FPDA. It perceived it as inappropriate as the arrangements represented an "insurance against Indonesia's possible reversion to her old ways".[5] As late as 1990, the former Indonesian foreign minister, Mochtar Kusmaatmdja, called for the FPDA to be abolished and replaced by a trilateral defence relationship between Indonesia, Malaysia and Singapore. A few years later, Indonesia gradually softened its approach, and the former Defence Minister General Benny Murdani eventually declared in 1994 that "if the FPDA makes its members feel secure, then regional security is enhanced and Indonesia is happy".[6]

As iterated earlier, the FPDA was born out of the British Labour government's decision to disengage militarily. As the subsequent Conservative government opted to maintain some military involvement in the region, the FPDA was created to replace the AMDA. East Malaysia was excluded from the ambit of the FPDA as Australia wanted to refrain from getting involved in territorial disputes with the Philippines and Malaysia over Sabah on the island of Borneo. The commitments undertaken by the FPDA were restricted to mere consultations. In fact, it simply linked the security of Singapore and Malaysia to a loose and consultative defence arrangement with Australia, NZ and the UK, and did not provide concrete security guarantees. This is in contrast to the automatic commitment within the AMDA for members to respond to an external attack. In the FPDA, this commitment was replaced by an obligation to consult in such an event, for the purpose of deciding on the appropriate measures to take. Finally, the FPDA did not include any commitment to station troops in Singapore and Malaysia.[7] The original military structures found under the AMDA were gradually reduced in the 1970s.[8] Canberra withdrew its battalion from Singapore in February 1974 and the UK removed its naval and ground troop presence by 1975 and 1976 respectively. The New Zealand military battalion eventually left Singapore at the end of 1989.

The FPDA's consultative nature and lack of clear military commitments suggest that it has little "bite". With that said, however, it does not belittle the deterrence effect that the FPDA possesses. In spite of the absence of clear military commitments, analysts have often pointed to the political and psychological deterrence provided by the FPDA towards Singapore and Malaysia. For example, Ang (2008) explains that the "multilayered interests of military powers outside the region would complicate the plans of any would-be aggressor and thus provide a valuable psychological deterrent".[9]

Despite the long life of the FPDA, the arrangements have remained exercise-centric and have not evolved on the same scale as other regional institutions such as ASEAN. Throughout the 1970s and 1980s, the structure and activities of the FPDA remained limited.[10] The Joint Consultative Council (JCC) was initially established to act as a senior consultative group, bringing together senior officials from the defence ministries of Singapore and Malaysia, as well as the High Commissioners of Australia, NZ and the UK.[11] In the event of an external threat to the security of Singapore and Malaysia, the JCC would function as a "convenient forum for initial consultation between the Five Powers".[12] Additionally, the FPDA was organised around a regular series of combined but limited exercises. While air defence exercises had been held annually since 1972, regular land and naval exercises only commenced in the 1980s.[13] This was in response to Vietnam's occupation of Cambodia and the Soviet invasion of Afghanistan.[14] The FPDA's central operation structure was the Integrated Air Defence System (IADS), located at the Royal Malaysia Air Force Base Butterworth in Malaysia, which was placed under the command of an Australian commander and the supervision of the Air Defence Council. The IADS was established as part of the FPDA framework to safeguard the air defence of the two Southeast Asian participants. In short, despite the JCC and IADS, the FPDA remained underinstitutionalised throughout most of the Cold War period. Rolfe (1995) explains that in "the first 10 years of the organization's existence, for example, Ministers had never met, and there were only four meetings of the JCC".[15]

Nevertheless, the role of the FPDA has been expanded since the end of the Cold War. The threat perception of Singapore and Malaysia has moved away from Indonesia to transnational terrorism and the uncertain distribution of power in the Asia-Pacific region. The Soviet collapse in 1991 and its own budgetary constraints obliged the US to reduce its military deployments in Asia. In addition, the US had to withdraw from its Subic Bay Naval Base and Clark Air Base in the Philippines by November 1992 due to a Philippine senate vote. In contrast, the influence of China grew more significantly. Some Southeast Asian states, Singapore being the prime example, feared that the withdrawal of US military from East Asia might encourage China to fill the "power vacuum" left by the retreating external power.[16] Separately, the September 11 terrorist attacks and the Bali bombings in 2002 also transformed the perception of the nature of threats in Southeast Asia. There was an increased fear of transnational terrorism in the region which overshadowed other sources of regional instability. Jemaah Islamiyah, the terrorist group that had planned attacks on several embassies in Singapore, was identified as a significant group with links to the Al-Qaeda. Additionally, the threats of piracy and maritime terrorism in the Straits of Malacca and Singapore were further securitised in post-9/11.[17] Hence, the five powers in the FPDA saw the emergence of an uncertain multipolar structure and changing strategic conditions in the Southeast Asian region to be prime sources of concern.

In response to these changes in the strategic environment, the FPDA has, since the late 1980s, gradually widened its institutional structures and activities.[18] In 1988, it was decided that the FPDA Defence Ministers' Meeting would be held every three years while the FPDA Defence Chiefs' Conference would meet more regularly. Since 2001, the latter has coincided with the Shangri-La Dialogue, held annually in Singapore. By 1994, the JCC and the Air Defence Council were transformed into the FPDA Consultative Council, which brings together senior diplomats and defence ministry officials from the five powers. The FPDA Activities Coordinating Council was formed the following year while the IADS was upgraded into the Integrated Area Defence System, integrating air, land and naval forces with its headquarters in Butterworth in the late 1990s. Since 1997, Singapore and Malaysia have also alternatively hosted the FPDA Professional Forum, which has become "the main format in which members of the arrangements come together to discuss new ideas, concepts and the way ahead, including the future shape of the operational element of the FPDA and the role of HQ IADS".[19]

These institutional changes have been matched by more sophisticated and encompassing military exercises. Tan (2008) writes that from "a basic single-service air defence focus, FPDA exercises evolved throughout the 1990s and early 2000s to include complex combined exercises involving major platforms".[20] In 2004, the Defence Ministers from the five powers announced that the FPDA would broaden its military exercises to address terrorism, maritime security and a number of other non-traditional threats.[21]

In sum, in light of the post-Cold War developments and shift in focus to new security challenges, Thayer is right to define the FPDA as "the 'quiet achiever' in contributing to regional security".[22] Through today, this "quiet achiever" has remained a low-key institution with no full secretariat. The lack of institutionalisation of the FPDA does not mean that the FPDA is of low importance to the five powers. In fact, Singapore remains an interested and involved participant in the arrangements for reasons that will be explored in the following section.

The FPDA's Continuing Relevance to Singapore

Role in the Singapore–Malaysian Relationship

From its inception, the FPDA was expected to act as a confidence-building measure in Singapore–Malaysian relations. Saravananuttu (2011) explains that this function "should be understood not just in security and defence terms but in the broader sense of ameliorating an often strained and choppy relation-ship between the two countries".[23] Singapore's traumatic separation from the Federation of Malaysia in 1965 severely affected its ties with Kuala Lumpur. As such, Singapore perceived the FPDA as an additional means to regulate relations with Malaysia and to constrain any potential aggressive disposition towards the city-state. In the many years that followed the formation of the FPDA, recurrent tensions occurred between the two states due to a number of bilateral issues "ranging from the denial of sand exports, the use of airspace to the island republic and a territorial dispute over a small atoll".[24] Nonetheless, through the FPDA, defence cooperation has been sustained and the combined military exercises have continued. For instance, while Malaysia withdrew from the annual Stardex exercise in 1998 due to the consequences stemming from the Asian Financial Crisis and a worsening of relations with Singapore, it resumed its participation the following year.

Furthermore, historically, the FPDA has defined the security of Singapore and Malaysia as indivisible. The FPDA has operated on the premise that pursu-ing the security of one nation separately and at the possible expense of the other would be counter-productive. From its inception therefore, the FPDA was meant to act as a set of arrangements that permitted parties to consult one another regarding the joint external defence of Singapore and Malaysia. Leifer explains that the arrangements were "predicated on the indivisibility of the defence" of the two Southeast Asian nations and that they were intended to enhance regional stability by engaging them both "in a structure of defence cooperation".[25] It is in this context that the FPDA has, over the years, succeeded in playing a significant confidence-building role in bilateral ties between Singapore and Malaysia. When examined in that light, the FPDA and its flexi-ble consultative model, based on the premise of indivisible security, have enhanced ties between the two states.

The military exercises undertaken as part of the FPDA have also bolstered the arrangements' confidence-building role. One of the primary outcomes has been to maintain channels of communication open between the armed forces of Malaysia and Singapore, independently of variations in the climate of bilat-eral relations.[26] Peter Ho, former Permanent Secretary of Defence of Singapore, argues that the training opportunities have provided a "platform for the two defence establishments of the two countries to keep channels of communica-tion open and to maintain a level of contact not possible in a bilateral setting".[27]

Over the years, the complexity and scope of the FPDA exercises have been significantly expanded to address the type of challenges faced by Malaysia and

Singapore. To illustrate this point, the military exercises have since adopted a stronger maritime and non-traditional security dimension. Bateman explains that the last 10 years have seen increased "concern in the FPDA for asymmetric threats, particularly piracy, terrorism and to some extent, the proliferation of weapons of mass destruction (WMD)".[28]

The combined exercises have also enabled participants to enhance professionalism, personal relationships, capacity building, as well as interoperability, especially in the areas of maritime security.[29] Having independently developed their own respective defence capabilities, Singapore and Malaysia have therefore continued to regard the FPDA as an instrument "to promote professionalism, rapport and to deepen knowledge of one another's strengths, capabilities and organizations".[30] In short, the FPDA has enabled the armed forces of Singapore and Malaysia to maintain links with each other and thereby improve the climate of their bilateral relations. The military exercises, conducted as part of the arrangements, have provided an ongoing channel of communication between the respective defence and security establishments.

Still, while the FPDA has certainly acted as a useful confidence-building exercise in Singapore–Malaysia relations, its overall impact on defence ties should not be overstated, as some level of mutual mistrust and competition remains in the relationship. For example, Zakaria Ahmad notes that the command of the IADS has continued to be held by an Australian commander, as assigning the position to a Malaysian or Singaporean continues to be unacceptable to the other party, and that land exercises in Malaysia involving the Singapore Armed Forces (SAF) are still not possible due to the "political sensitivities" involved.[31] Furthermore, the notion of indivisibility in the security of both Malaysia and Singapore has to some extent been diluted over the years, as the armed forces of both countries have had to address different needs and priorities.[32] The fact that Malaysia's and Singapore's defence are no longer interlinked in all circumstances is perhaps unsurprising given the complex strategic environment characterised by a mix of both conventional and transnational security challenges. Nonetheless, the FPDA is still highly regarded in Singapore, as it has allowed the city-state to maintain an open defence relationship with Malaysia.

FPDA as a Channel for Relations with External Powers

Singapore has traditionally followed a policy of balancing through external association to deter any form of aggression against its sovereignty and territorial integrity. This has involved strengthening its own relative position through diplomatic and military alignments with the US and to a lesser extent Australia, the UK and other external powers. This same logic has been applied to the FPDA. The historical function of the arrangements as a psychological deterrent against external aggression has been dependent on strategic commitments, albeit of a consultative nature, from the extra-regional powers. Likewise, the confidence-building role in the Singapore–Malaysian relationship has been supported by their participation.

In the post-Cold War era, the uncertain power distribution in the Asia-Pacific, combined with a dynamic strategic environment, has further encouraged Singapore to cultivate ties with external powers with the aim of deepening their benign involvement in Southeast Asian security. As a result, Singapore has actively strengthened relations with the US and other external powers with security interests in the region. For example, Singapore and its Ministry of Foreign Affairs played an important role in the establishment of the ASEAN Regional Forum in 1994, eventually bringing together the US, China, India, Japan and others into a structure for security cooperation led by ASEAN. It can be argued that the FPDA has played a similar "cultivating" role with regard to Australia, NZ and the UK. Moreover, the close ties linking Canberra and London to Washington are an additional reason why the FPDA has remained attractive to Singapore.

Australia is important to Singapore as a result of its deep interest in regional stability. During his visit to Australia in March 2007, then-Minister Mentor Lee Kuan Yew indicated that Singapore and Australia share "a common strategic view".[33] Singapore–Australian military ties are robust and based on complementary security interests and outlooks. This is best exemplified by Canberra making training facilities available to the SAF in Australia. Leifer (2000) writes that Singapore values its relationship with Australia due to "the professional competence in training and advice of Australia's armed forces and diplomatic service set within a common strategic perspective" as well as due to "Australia's sustained strategic partnership with the USA".[34] Arguably, the FPDA complements existing bilateral defence links, as it enables Australia and Singapore to practice diplomacy through their respective militaries and further strengthen bilateral relations. Still, it is important to note that the bilateral defence ties would likely be strong even if the FPDA ceased to exist, given the shared security outlooks of the two powers. The complementary nature of the FPDA, rather than its ability to substitute or replace bilateral ties, should thus be stressed.

For Singapore, the UK remains a significant partner in light of historical ties, close diplomatic and trade links, as well as the UK's permanent seat at the

United Nations Security Council. Britain's role and interest in the FPDA has been substantial. As its founding participant, it played a leading role in the negotiation and formation of the FPDA and its participation was also critical in persuading Australia and NZ to join the arrangements. Additionally, the UK has been committed to the FPDA and its exercises, as it has continued to provide it with a legitimate, albeit limited, defence role in the Southeast Asian region. The consultative nature of the FPDA has significantly reduced the British commitment to Singapore's defence, making it both politically acceptable and sustainable in terms of cost. The FPDA should thus be viewed in the context of sustaining the Singapore–UK relationship, as the arrangements are the only formal defence agreement that links the city-state to its former colonial master.

NZ is less significant to Singapore in strategic terms. Still, the FPDA has provided a means for the city-state to preserve a security engagement with Wellington and to maintain its commitment to Southeast Asian security. The "Defence White Paper 2010" identified the FPDA as NZ's "most significant operational security link to Southeast Asia" and stressed that it would "continue to provide a valuable anchor for the presence of our defence assets in the region".[35] In light of its limited capabilities, Wellington's contribution to the joint exercises has traditionally been modest. That said, in the post-9/11 context, New Zealand has been committed to broadening the exercises to address non-traditional maritime security concerns critical to Singapore.[36]

In addition to facilitating direct defence relations with external powers, the FPDA has arguably served as a channel for indirect relations between Singapore and the US through two of its closest allies — Australia and the UK. Singapore has historically considered continued US involvement in the region as critical to its own security. This strategic consideration has often been translated into tangible policies. For example, in response to the American withdrawal from its bases in the Philippines, Singapore offered in 1990 the US Navy and Air Force the use of its military facilities more extensively. By offering Washington compensating facilities, Singapore sought to mitigate the consequences of American withdrawal from the Subic Bay Naval Base and Clark Air Base. Additionally, in 1998, Singapore declared that US aircraft carriers would have access to Changi Naval Base after its completion. In more recent years, Singapore has further developed strong military relations with the US Pacific Command and worked closely with the US in addressing non-traditional security issues, especially terrorism and maritime piracy. Perhaps most significantly, the Strategic Framework Agreement for a Closer Cooperation Partnership in Defence and Security (SFA), signed by Singapore Prime

Minister Lee Hsien Loong and then-US President George W. Bush in July 2005, recognised the Southeast Asian nation as a major strategic partner of the US and provided a framework for bilateral defence cooperation.

Nevertheless, in contrast to Canberra and London, Singapore is not a formal ally of Washington and an American military response to an external attack against the city-state is therefore not guaranteed. The defence ties that Australia and the UK maintain with the US have arguably made the FPDA even more attractive to Singapore. It might even have provided the city-state with an additional diplomatic and psychological deterrent against any potential aggression. Finally, the FPDA and the bilateral defence ties that Singapore maintains directly with the US have, over the years, focused on similar traditional and non-traditional threats, more recently transnational terrorism and maritime security. Indubitably, the FPDA's role, as a channel for direct and indirect relations with significant external parties, has therefore been a major reason for Singapore's sustained involvement with the arrangements.

FPDA's Contribution to Singapore's Defence Diplomacy

The third reason for Singapore's sustained involvement in the FPDA is attributable to its contribution to the city-state's defence diplomacy in the region, in part due to the arrangements' complementary nature to other forums such as the ADMM and the ADMM+. While the FPDA could be referred to as a "relic of the past", its continued presence in the regional security architecture suggests that it may actually help augment the newer structures that are in place. Bristow rightly argues that:

> [T]he FPDA is a hangover from a bygone era, which is being overtaken by other regional structures, and is diminished in importance by the strength of U.S. commitments. Another way of looking at it is that the FPDA overlaps with existing bilateral alliances, exercise programmes and other security structures, rather than competes with them, and helps to strengthen regional security as a result.[37]

As discussed above, the FPDA helps strengthen and complement bilateral ties between Singapore and external powers. Likewise, the FPDA complements other forums that Singapore helped create to promote regional defence diplomacy, such as the ADMM and the ADMM+.

The ADMM was inaugurated in Kuala Lumpur in May 2006 as an expression of defence regionalism in Southeast Asia. The forum seeks to enhance dialogue as well as practical cooperation between the various Southeast

Asian militaries and defence establishments, especially in the area of HADR.[38] The ADMM needs to be examined in the wider context of ASEAN and its security community project. The Association was not formed as a direct response to an external adversary and has never evolved into a formal or tacit alliance. It has traditionally rejected any form of military cooperation and concentrated instead on confidence building, dialogue and conflict avoidance rather than dispute resolution. For example, a proposal by Indonesia to create an ASEAN peacekeeping force was duly rejected and downplayed by the other ASEAN members, most notably Singapore and Vietnam. In the absence of joint military capabilities and a common external threat perception, the ASEAN member states have sought to enhance their domestic socio-economic security and to generally improve the climate of relations in Southeast Asia. Still, in response to a series of transnational threats, the various Southeast Asian leaders announced at an ASEAN Summit in Bali in October 2003 the formation of an ASEAN Security Community (ASC) by 2020 (later set at 2015). The latter stresses the willingness of the member states to "rely exclusively on peaceful processes in the settlement of intra-regional differences".[39]

The FPDA naturally complements the ADMM by offering Singapore a conventional defence component still lacking in this defence diplomacy process and its focus on non-traditional security issues. Further, it is precisely in the overlapping area of military preparedness and HADR that the FPDA can be most relevant to the ADMM in terms of information sharing. The FPDA is well ahead of ASEAN in this particular area. Following the tsunami disaster in December 2004, the FPDA Defence Ministers had already decided to further widen the scope of the arrangements by including HADR as well as incorporating non-military agencies into future exercises.[40] At the 2006 FPDA meeting, then-Singapore Defence Minister Teo Chee Hean declared that the ministers had agreed to explore how the five powers could cooperate "in developing capacity for humanitarian assistance and disaster relief so that if in future should member countries participate in such missions, capacity building and interoperability can be developed and will enhance effectiveness".[41]

Likewise, the FPDA supplements the nascent forum that is the ADMM+ (also referred to as the ADMM-Plus or ADMM+8). The ADMM+ is the very latest arrangement that overlaps with the FPDA structures. The ADMM+ was established in 2010 and comprises the 10 ASEAN member states and eight extra-regional powers (Australia, China, India, Japan, South Korea, NZ, Russia and the US). ASEAN's aim of including extra-regional partners was to help build regional capacity by drawing on the expertise and resources of the defence establishments of the regional major and middle powers.[42] At its launch in 2010, it was decided that the ADMM+8 participants would collaborate on non-traditional security concerns over that of conventional security due to the perception that the former was less sensitive than the latter.[43] In 2011, five Experts' Working Groups were established to focus on the areas of maritime security, counter-terrorism, humanitarian assistance and disaster relief, peacekeeping operations and military medicine. In 2013, a Sixth Experts' Working Group focusing on Humanitarian Mine Action was established and the year also marked the first time the military of ASEAN and the Plus countries jointly conducted practical exercises in the areas of maritime security, counter-terrorism, humanitarian assistance and disaster relief, military medicine. Despite the advances in practical cooperation, the ADMM+ arrangement has not yet moved beyond confidence building. As such, the FPDA complements the ADMM+ much like how the FPDA works as a "military exercise" counterpart to the ADMM: by bolstering Singapore's defence with a military arrangement that focuses on traditional and transnational security, albeit in a consultative nature.

Taken as a whole, the FPDA contributes to Singapore's defence diplomacy by providing more tangible military cooperation that, at present, is still missing from the multilateral security architecture in the Asia-Pacific. Additionally, the FPDA, having existed for a longer time as compared to other regional forums with the exception of ASEAN itself, has helped foster relations between states which therein have allowed Singapore to address challenges and threats, such as maritime security, terrorism and humanitarian assistance.

Conclusion

As Singapore celebrates its 50 years of independence, it is reminded, by ongoing and emerging threats, of the vulnerability of national security. The FPDA is one of many instruments that Singapore possesses to safeguard its defence. Few at the time of the FPDA's inception would have expected it to last so long and to continue contributing to the stability of the Southeast Asian region more than four decades after its establishment. The FPDA has endured, in large part due to its flexibility as well as its consultative and complementary attributes. As Huxley (2011) notes, the FPDA is a "non-provocative form of hedging and confidence-building, and it would be surprising if any of the participating member-states chose to discard their FPDA commitments or role".[44]

On the part of Singapore, the FPDA has maintained its relevance due to three main reasons outlined in this paper. First, the FPDA has functioned as a significant confidence-building measure in Singapore–Malaysian relations. Training opportunities have offered both states with a continuing channel of communication between their respective defence and security establishments. Second, the FPDA has provided Singapore with a conduit with which to reach out directly to extra-regional partners namely Australia, NZ and the UK, and to reach out indirectly to the US, thus complementing its own bilateral relationship with Washington. This, in turn, has allowed Singapore to maintain military relations with significant players on the world stage and has sustained the arrangements' role in psychological deterrence. The third and final reason is that the FPDA has contributed to the city-state's defence diplomacy in the region, and has complemented other forums such as the ADMM and the ADMM+. In light of the aforementioned reasons and the changing strategic environment that it operates in, Singapore's involvement in the FPDA has endured and is likely to endure for years to come.

Notes

[1] This chapter draws from Ralf Emmers, "The Five Power Defence Arrangements and Defence Diplomacy in Southeast Asia," *Asian Security*, 8(3), November 2012, pp. 271–286; and Ralf Emmers, "The Role of the Five Power Defence Arrangements in Southeast Asian Security Architecture," in William T. Tow and Brendan Taylor (eds.), *Bilateralism, Multilateralism and Asia-Pacific Security: Contending Cooperation* (London: Routledge, 2013), pp. 87–99.

[2] For a discussion on Singapore's sense of vulnerability, see Michael Leifer, *Singapore's Foreign Policy: Coping with Vulnerability* (London: Routledge, 2000).

[3] See Leifer (2000), *op. cit.*, pp. 43–67.

[4] Jim Rolfe, "Anachronistic Past or Positive Future: New Zealand and the Five Power Defence Arrangements," Working Paper, Centre for Strategic Studies (CSS), Victoria University of Wellington, 1995, p. 14.

[5] Chin Kin Wah, "The Five Power Defence Arrangements: Twenty Years after," *The Pacific Review*, 4(3), 1991, p. 201.

[6] General Benny Murdani, former Indonesian Armed Forces Commander and former Minister of Defence and Security at a seminar on Australia's Defence White Paper, Australian Defence Forces Academy, December 1994.

[7] Khoo How San, "The Five Power Defence Arrangements: If It Ain't Broke …," *Pointer: Quarterly Journal of the Singapore Armed Forces*, 26(4), October–December 2000, pp. 107–114, Internet edition.

8   Michael Leifer, *Dictionary of the Modern Politics of Southeast Asia* (London: Routledge, 1995), p. 106.

9   Ang Wee Han, "Five Power Defence Arrangements: A Singapore Perspective," *Pointer: Quarterly Journal of the Singapore Armed Forces*, 24(2), April–June 2008, pp. 49–59, Internet edition.

10 *Ibid.*, pp. 49–59.

11 Rolfe (1955), *op. cit.*, p. 7.

12 Five Power Ministerial Meeting on Defence: Five Power Consultative Arrangements after 1971, FPM (L) (P) 2/71, in Ministry of Defence file 1/2/4: Treaties and Agreements: Five Power Arrangements.

13 *Ibid.*, p. 7.

14 Leifer (1995), *op. cit.*, p. 106.

15 Rolfe (1995), *op. cit.*, p. 7.

16 Leszek Buszynski, "Post-Cold War Security in the ASEAN Region," in Gary Klintworth (ed.), *Asia-Pacific Security: Less Uncertainty, New Opportunities?* (New York: St Martin's Press, 1996), p. 121.

17 See Ralf Emmers, *Non-Traditional Security in the Asia-Pacific: The Dynamics of Securitization* (Singapore: Marshall Cavendish, 2004).

18 Andrew T. H. Tan, "The Five Power Defence Arrangements: The Continuing Relevance," *Contemporary Security Policy*, 29(2), 2008, p. 294.

19 Damon Bristow, "The Five Power Defence Arrangements: Southeast Asia's Unknown Regional Security Organization," *Contemporary Southeast Asia*, 27(1), April 2005, p. 6.

20 Tan (2008), *op. cit.*, p. 294.

21 "Second FPDA Defence Ministers' Informal Meeting," *Ministry of Defence News Release*, Singapore, 7 June 2004, Retrieved 1 February 2010, from http://www.mindef. gov.sg/imindef/news_and_events/nr/2004/jun/07jun04_nr.html.

22 Carlyle A. Thayer, "The Five Power Defence Arrangements: The Quiet Achiever," *Security Challenges*, 3(1), February 2007, p. 79.

23 Johan Saravananuttu, "Malaysian Foreign Policy and the Five Power Defence Arrangements," in Ian Storey, Ralf Emmers and Daljit Singh (eds.), *The Five Power Defence Arrangements at Forty* (Singapore: Institute of Southeast Asian Studies, 2011), p. 43.

24 *Ibid.*, pp. 43–44.

25 Leifer (2000), *op. cit.*, p. 106.

26 Tim Huxley, "The Future of the FPDA in an Evolving Regional Strategic Environment," in Storey, Emmers and Singh (eds.) (2011), *op. cit.*, p. 119.

27 Peter Ho, "FPDA Still Relevant at 40 Years on," *The Straits Times*, 7 December 2011. Retrieved 20 May 2015, from http://www.straitstimes.com/print/Review/Others/ STIStory_741998.html.

28 Sam Bateman, "The FPDA's Contribution to Regional Security: The Maritime Dimension," in Storey, Emmers and Singh (eds.) (2011), *op. cit.*, p. 73.

29 Kate Boswood, "Engaging Our Interests: The Five Power Defence Arrangements and Its Contribution to Regional Security," *Defence Magazine*, (9), August 2007, p. 36.

30 J. M. Jamaluddin, "FPDA Expanding Its Role Beyond Security Concerns," *Asian Defence Journal*, (5), July & August 2006, p. 7.

31 Zakaria Ahmad, "A Quasi-Pact of Enduring Value: A Malaysian Perspective on the FPDA," in Storey, Emmers and Singh (eds.) (2011), *op. cit.*, p. 102.

32 *Ibid.*; Saravananuttu (2011), *op cit.*, p. 46.

33 "Singapore and Australia Share Common Strategic View: MM," *The Straits Times*, 29 March 2007, p. 25.

34 Leifer (2000), *op. cit.*, p. 129.

35 Defence White Paper 2010 (Wellington: Ministry of Defence, November 2010), p. 30.

36 Mark G. Rolls, "The FPDA and Asia's Changing Strategic Environment: A View from New Zealand," in Storey, Emmers and Singh (eds.) (2011), *op. cit.*, pp. 107–108.

37 Damon Bristow, "The Five Power Defence Arrangements: Southeast Asia's Unknown Regional Security Organization," *Contemporary Southeast Asia*, 27(1), April 2005, p. 16.

38 See The Joint Declaration of ASEAN Defence Ministers on Strengthening ASEAN Defence Establishments to Meet the Challenges of Non-Traditional Security Threats. The Third ASEAN Defence Ministers' Meeting was held in Pattaya, Thailand, from 25 to 27 February 2009. Retrieved 20 May 2015, from http://cil.nus.edu.sg/rp/pdf/2009%20 Joint%20Dec%20ASEAN%20def%20Estb%20to%20Meet%20Challenges-pdf.pdf.

39 Declaration of ASEAN Concord II (Bali Concord II), Bali, Indonesia, 7 October 2003. Retrieved 20 May 2015, from http://www.asean.org/news/item/ declaration-of-asean-concord-ii-bali-concord-ii.

40 Tan (2008), *op. cit.*, p. 295.

41 Quoted in Tunku Ya'acob Tunku Abdullah, "FPDA Remains Relevant with Broadened Role to Reflect New Security Threats," *Asian Defence Journal*, (5), July & August 2006, p. 6.

42 Tan See Seng, "From Talkshop to Workshop: ASEAN's Quest for Practical Security Cooperation through the ADMM and ADMM-Plus Processes," in Bhubhindar Singh and Tan See Seng (eds.), *From Boots to Brogues: The Rise of Defence Diplomacy in Southeast Asia* (Singapore: S. Rajaratnam School of International Studies, 2011), pp. 28–41.

43 David Capie and Brendan Taylor, "Two Cheers for ADMM+," *PacNet,* (51), 20 October 2010. Retrieved 20 May 2015, from http://csis.org/publication/pacnet-51-two-cheers-admm.

44 Huxley (2011), *op. cit.*, pp. 118–121.

Chapter 11

Singapore in ASEAN's Quest toward a Security Community

Mely Caballero-Anthony

Introduction

The year 2015 marks a significant milestone for Singapore and the Association of Southeast Asian Nations (ASEAN). This is the year when Singapore celebrates its 50th anniversary as a nation. 2015 is also the year when ASEAN is supposed to have realised its vision of becoming a community after 48 years — an ASEAN Community anchored on the three pillars of economic community, socio-cultural community, and political and security community.

Singapore joined ASEAN in 1967, just two years after its independence from Malaysia in 1965. As one of five founding members of ASEAN, Singapore has been an integral part of ASEAN's development into becoming one of the most successful regional organisations in the world. Although Singapore is the smallest state of ASEAN, it stands tall among the rest of its ASEAN neighbours having transformed itself into one of the most advanced, industrialised economies in Asia. As a city-state known to "punch above its weight", Singapore's contribution in shaping ASEAN's regional agenda spanning the wide remit of socio-economic, political and security cooperation has been very significant.

At the outset, one would note that Singapore's engagement with ASEAN as a member of this regional security organisation is closely intertwined with its own historical narrative of a post-colonial state that went through a difficult period of separation from Malaysia to now become one of its leading members. Singapore is also one of the most politically stable states in the region. Similarly, ASEAN's history was born out of the painful post-colonial experience of enmity and amity among the newly independent states in Southeast Asia in the 1960s. After almost five decades, ASEAN has now become an established regional grouping that claims centrality in Asia's regional security architecture.

ASEAN is also one of the world's most vibrant economic regions. One could therefore argue that ASEAN's evolution as a successful regional organisation closely mirrors that of Singapore's success.

The interesting dynamics between ASEAN as a successful regional grouping and Singapore as an important member state can be seen throughout their respective historical experiences moving in tandem. From the historical perspective of ASEAN's political and security cooperation, the grouping has significantly evolved from a regional mechanism for peace and reconciliation in Southeast Asia during its formative years to becoming an ASEAN Political and Security Community (APSC) in 2015.[1] The Blueprint of the APSC adopted in 2009 spelt out the ambitious vision of a security community in Southeast Asia wherein member states would *"live at peace with one another and with the world at large, in a just, democratic and harmonious environment"*.[2]

The Blueprint also sets out five strategic thrusts, or areas of cooperation, aimed at bringing ASEAN's political and security cooperation to a "higher plane" and ensuring that the peoples and states of ASEAN live in peace with one another. These are: political development, norm setting and norm sharing, conflict prevention, conflict resolution, and post-conflict peacebuilding.[3] These new areas of cooperation indicate that the APSC is more than just an instrument of security cooperation, but is also fundamentally a political project, designed to shape the normative framework of the region based on the norms of democracy, the rule of law, transparency, good governance and respect for human rights.

The goal of an ASEAN Community living in peace, security and prosperity by 2015 is indeed a lofty one, given the kinds of security challenges faced by ASEAN over the last 48 years. Some of these challenges continue to persist till today. These include the unresolved territorial disputes between member states, challenges of political transitions in some member states, widening economic divides among and within states, as well as a slew of transborder non-traditional security challenges such as climate change, food security, energy security, terrorism, and religious extremism. Yet, it is precisely these challenges that underscore the need for ASEAN to more than ever strengthen the foundations of regionalism in Southeast Asia and compel its member states to continue to help ASEAN maintain regional peace and security. Singapore has and continues to play a significant role in steering ASEAN toward becoming a security community.

Against this background, the main objective of this chapter is to examine Singapore's important contribution to political and security cooperation in ASEAN. The chapter is therefore organised as follows. Following the introduction, Section Two of this essay proceeds to trace Singapore's contribution to regional peace and security as seen through some of the key policies it spearheaded during the formative years of ASEAN in the mid-'70s to the mid-'90s. The third and fourth sections further examine Singapore's role in ASEAN as the grouping deepens regional cooperation to achieving its goal of building a three-pillared ASEAN Community, particularly its vision of becoming an ASEAN Political and Security Community (APSC). Finally, the fifth section ends with some concluding thoughts on Singapore's role in an evolving ASEAN.

Singapore in ASEAN's Quest of Building Regional Peace and Security

Throughout its history, ASEAN member states have endeavoured to promote and advance the core norms of ASEAN in order to maintain regional peace and security. These norms, often referred to as the ASEAN Way, are the respect for sovereignty, non-interference, non-use of force and peaceful settlement of disputes. These norms were seriously challenged when ASEAN was confronted with the conflict that broke out in Cambodia in the late 1970s.

The Cambodian Conflict

The Cambodian Conflict (1978–1991) was a very significant issue in the contemporary history of international relations in Southeast Asia with important implications for the survival of Singapore and development of the Singapore Foreign Service. The conflict was regarded by Singapore founding leaders as a crucial issue for the Ministry of Foreign Affairs and the centrepiece of ASEAN diplomacy during the 1970s and 1980s. According to the late Professor Michael Leifer:

> [T]he Cambodian conflict ... was a defining period for ASEAN. It was the critical episode over and during which the Association attained and demonstrated the quality of a diplomatic community able to conduct itself up to a point, as a unitary international actor. Equally significant was the way in which Singapore assumed an increasingly active diplomatic role within the Association in upholding a corporate solidarity in challenging Vietnam's military occupation of Cambodia and the legitimacy of the government carried into Phnom Penh in the saddlebags of its army.[4]

Former Deputy Prime Minister Goh Keng Swee argued that the Cambodian issue is a life-and-death struggle, the outcome of which will have a profound impact on Singapore.[5] Meanwhile, former Permanent Secretary of the Ministry of Foreign Affairs and former President S. R. Nathan explained the importance of the issue to Singapore. The Cambodian conflict "was central to Singapore's policy. The principle involved was that no foreign military intervention should be allowed to overthrow a legally constituted regime".[6] Singapore believed that the violation of the principle would result in a dangerous precedent. Hence, Singapore was not willing to compromise. Singapore's position in the Non-Aligned Movement and in the UN General Assembly, along with that of its ASEAN fellow members, enabled ASEAN to raise the issue in the Paris Conference on Cambodia and helped restore Cambodia's independence.[7]

Former Deputy Prime Minister Wong Kan Seng, who was also the Foreign Minister between 1988 and 1994, explained that Singapore's extraordinary level of diplomatic activity with regard to the Cambodian issue was not an interference in the affairs of other states. Neither did Singapore support the Khmer Rouge regime. For Singapore, it was "an issue of principle" — "the invasion of a smaller country by a larger neighbour, the deposition of a legitimate government by external force and the imposition of a proxy by a foreign power" was a "direct challenge to the fundamentals" of Singapore's foreign policy.[8]

In his welcome address at the 10th ASEAN Ministerial Meeting in Singapore on 5–7 July 1977, Prime Minister Lee Kuan Yew asserted that the evolving political landscape in Southeast Asia required ASEAN states to establish their diplomatic relations with Vietnam, Laos and Cambodia "with the assurance that there would be non-interference in each other's internal affairs".[9] As such in October 1978, Vietnamese Prime Minister Pham Van Dong visited Singapore and assured its leaders that Vietnam would respect the sovereignty, territorial integrity and independence of all the countries in Southeast Asia, and would not interfere in their respective internal affairs. But not long after, in December 1978, Vietnam began the invasion of Cambodia with a mission to stop the ethnic cleansing being perpetrated by the Pol Pot regime. In January 1979, the Vietnam-installed government in Phnom Penh announced the establishment of the Khmer People's Revolutionary Party and subsequently, the People's Republic of Kampuchea. The Indonesian Foreign Minister, who was then-Chairman of the ASEAN, issued a statement expressing ASEAN's rejection of the invasion which violated the principles of the UN Charter and the Bandung Conference.[10]

Then-Defence Minister Goh Keng Swee accentuated the implication of the invasion for Thailand, a US ally and who had helped the American forces during the Vietnam War. According to Goh, "suddenly, Thailand found the

Vietnamese Army on her border … within easy range of Bangkok".[11] To have a discussion of the Vietnamese invasion of Cambodia at the ASEAN level, then-Foreign Minister S. Rajaratnam initiated a special ASEAN Foreign Ministers closed-door meeting, which was convened in Bangkok in January 1979. It was during this meeting that ASEAN decided how it would respond to the issue. Rajaratnam rallied his ASEAN colleagues. The Thais valued the support of Singapore in pushing for international support and rallying all ASEAN members to oppose Vietnam's action. Singapore's strong stand against the Vietnamese occupation was due to its "affinity of feelings" for Cambodia as "Cambodia's problems could become Singapore's problems in the future". In Lee Kuan Yew's perspective, ASEAN should be concerned as the conflict could spill over into Thailand. Thailand's long frontier with Cambodia and Laos made it likely that the conflicting aims of Vietnam, China and the Soviet Union would drag Thailand into the conflict, and later the rest of ASEAN.[12]

The ASEAN states were nervous as there were now communist regimes in Cambodia, Vietnam and Laos. The outflow of Vietnamese and the swell of Cambodian refugees pouring into Thailand further destabilised the region. The Chinese invasion of northern Vietnam added a global dimension. As a result of the Bangkok meeting by the ASEAN foreign ministers, ASEAN was able to issue a Joint Statement deploring Vietnamese intervention in Cambodia and calling for "the immediate and total withdrawal of all foreign forces", reflecting Singapore's consistent position. Hence, according to S. R. Nathan, the meeting turned out to be very significant as it signified the start of a longer phase of intense activity by Singapore's foreign ministry in opposing the Vietnamese occupation.[13]

To further articulate ASEAN's position, a joint communiqué was issued at the ASEAN Foreign Ministers' Meeting in Bali in June 1979, condemning Vietnam's occupation of Cambodia and its policy of expelling unwanted citizens. S. Rajaratnam reiterated Vietnam's efforts to destabilise ASEAN: "[E]ach junk-load of men, women and children sent to our shores is a bomb to destabilise, disrupt and cause turmoil and dissension in ASEAN states. This is a preliminary invasion to pave the way for the final invasion."[14]

ASEAN states laid the groundwork for a settlement by mobilising international opinion against Vietnam, motivating the Cambodian resistance movements to unite against Vietnam, and lobbying both Beijing and Moscow to accept a compromised settlement. Singapore pulled out all the diplomatic stops as its foreign service officers played a vital role to galvanise support for ASEAN's position. They worked effectively at the United Nations (UN), in international meetings and through other diplomatic channels. Their efforts had resulted in growing support from many member states of the UN to ASEAN's collective stance. The international condemnation of Vietnam unified a remarkable collection of states while the UN's votes against Vietnam's occupation increased each year. Throughout the 1980s, Singapore played an active role in attempting to forge a negotiated settlement. Singapore took the lead in hosting the tripartite negotiations among the leaders of the three Cambodian opposition groups.[15]

Former Deputy Prime Minister Wong Kang Seng explained that Singapore's campaign on the Cambodian issue at the UN was an equally important theatre, focused on denying Vietnam the opportunity to claim Cambodia's seat at the UN General Assembly. With intense lobbying, Singapore pushed through the ASEAN resolution in support of Cambodia year after year with increased majorities. Its goal was to keep the issue in international consciousness and persuade Vietnam to come to the negotiating table.[16]

The end of the Cold War facilitated the resolution of various regional conflicts; Singapore considered the withdrawal of Vietnamese forces from Cambodia and the signing of the Paris Peace Agreement in October 1991 as the most important regional development. It hailed the peace agreement as among the positive outcomes of the evolving post-Cold War landscape. Singapore's role in ensuring the international isolation of Vietnam had been the high point of its diplomacy. The agreement augured well for Singapore's strategic and economic interests in Asia-Pacific as it marked the end of the region's largest conflict.[17] The agreement also paved the way for UN-supervised elections. For Singapore's foreign ministry, it was a moment to relish.[18]

Post-Cambodia ASEAN: Engaging US Military Presence in Post-Cold War Southeast Asia

Despite the conclusion of the Cambodian conflict, Singapore remained concerned over equally important security issues that could undermine regional peace and order in ASEAN in the early 1990s. Its leaders perceived the danger of new regional conflicts, e.g., the South China Sea territorial disputes, the Korean Peninsula and Singapore's own dispute with Malaysia over Pedra Branca off the coast of Johor. For Singapore, these challenges could be ignored if the regional balance of power underpinned by US military presence remained intact. However, the closure of US military bases in the Philippines had created profound uncertainty in Southeast Asia.[19]

As a result of these post-Cold War regional concerns, Singapore's foreign policy entered into a "post-survival" phase. Singapore's survival concerns were reflected in its desire to preserve a favourable balance of power in Southeast Asia. It regarded no credible alternative security arrangement in the region that could be as reliable as the US military presence. Singapore's role in preserving the regional balance of power has been to provide military facilities to the US. In November 1990, Singapore and the US signed the Memorandum of Understanding Regarding United States Use of Facilities in Singapore (1990 MOU) which provides for increased use of maintenance and repair facilities that have been used by the US Navy for more than 25 years. The MOU is aimed at ensuring the continued security presence of the US in Southeast Asia. Singapore also viewed the agreement as a "way of tying the US more firmly to Singapore as a form of insurance".[20]

Having ensured continued US presence in the region, Singapore and the rest of ASEAN's members were nonetheless mindful of the risk of getting caught up in major power competition. To avoid such predicament, ASEAN emphasised the importance of keeping the region free from major power politics. As Chair of ASEAN in 1992, the Singapore Declaration stated that "ASEAN will seek to realise the Zone of Peace, Freedom and Neutrality (ZOPFAN) and a Southeast Asian Nuclear Weapon Free Zone (SEANWFZ)".[21]

ASEAN's Turn to Multilateralism: Charting Relations with Major Powers

As Chair of ASEAN in 1992, Singapore facilitated the institutionalisation of political and security cooperation in Southeast Asia and the wider region.

Singapore's Pivotal Role in Establishing the ASEAN Regional Forum (ARF)

The decade-long Cambodian issue had galvanised ASEAN, as no other issue had done, to collectively address a very sensitive political issue. ASEAN, then made up of Indonesia, the Philippines, Malaysia, Thailand and Singapore, actively led an intense lobbying effort at the UN to condemn Vietnam's invasion of Cambodia until the issue was successfully resolved with the withdrawal of Vietnamese troops. ASEAN countries had by then become more sensitised to the need to directly deal with regional security and political issues and to engage external players on these issues. This mindset helped forge ASEAN's response to the evolving regional landscape in the post-Cambodian crisis period. At the Fourth ASEAN Summit in Singapore in 1992, the ASEAN leaders decided that ASEAN should heighten its external discussions on political and security issues by using the ASEAN Post Ministerial Conferences (PMC). As the host of the 1993 ASEAN Ministerial Meeting (AMM)/PMC, Singapore felt that it was clearly in its interest to build on this idea. Singapore was concerned that ASEAN's dialogues partners might lose interest in participating in AMM/PMC meetings if their discussions were just limited to drug trafficking problems and requests for developmental aid. The Singapore foreign ministry worked hard to get the ASEAN senior officials to convene a special Post Ministerial Conference Senior Officials Meeting (PMC SOM) to send a clear signal to dialogue partners that ASEAN was already prepared to discuss political and security issues.[22]

In May 1993, ASEAN senior officials and their counterparts from dialogue partners started discussing political and security matters over an informal dinner in Singapore. Subsequently, the ARF was officially launched in Bangkok in July 1994 with the 18 founding members: six ASEAN member states (Brunei, Indonesia, Malaysia, Singapore, Thailand and the Philippines), its dialogue partners (Australia, Canada, European Union, Japan, South Korea, New Zealand and the US), its consultative partners (China and Russia) and observers (Vietnam, Laos and Special Observer Papua New Guinea).[23]

According to Former Deputy Prime Minister S. Jayakumar, Singapore played a key role in initiating the ARF process through the concept paper which was proposed by Singapore at the Bangkok ARF in 1994 and which was officially adopted at the Second ARF in Brunei in 1995. Singapore "proposed that the ARF should be realistic and not start trying to tackle all the potential security challenges, some of which were very sensitive and controversial, simultaneously".[24]

ARF members adopted Singapore's suggestion for a three-stage evolutionary process, namely: Stage 1: Promotion of Confidence Building Measures; Stage 2: Development of Preventive Diplomacy Mechanisms; and Stage 3: Development of Conflict Resolution Mechanisms. S. Jayakumar claimed that through ARF meetings, member states were able to discuss a wide range of both traditional and non-traditional security issues, ranging from peacekeeping, non-proliferation and disarmament, to disaster relief, maritime security, counter-terrorism and transnational crime.[25]

S. Jayakumar identified Singapore's national interests in promoting regional discussions on political and security matters, leading to the ARF. Singapore's primary objective was to develop and maintain a predictable pattern of political relationships in the Asia-Pacific region for a peaceful, stable geopolitical landscape. ARF meetings would be aimed at forging political discipline in the way regional countries conduct their relationships. As such, mutual confidence and trust were built over a period of time. More importantly for Singapore, "the underlying strategic purpose was not just to build up a network but also to engage China (then emerging out of isolation) within a predictable framework with the United States, which had eschewed multilateralism in such a way as to give ASEAN (and by extension Singapore) an ability to influence the regional agenda".[26]

Moving ASEAN Political and Security Cooperation to a Higher Plane

The ASEAN Charter

It was again during Singapore's Chairmanship of ASEAN when its leaders signed the ASEAN Charter at the 13th ASEAN Summit in Singapore on 20 November 2007. The Charter is significant as it provides ASEAN with a legal framework after 40 years of gradual institutionalisation. It establishes a set of rules and the new structures should strengthen the bloc's institutions through the formal role accorded to the ASEAN Summits as well as the establishment of three pillars of the ASEAN Community, comprising the ASEAN Security Community, ASEAN Economic Community and ASEAN Socio-Cultural Community.

The ASEAN Charter is a positive development; it moves ASEAN ahead. But it was also seen as a disappointment. ASEAN was at a crossroads, but with the adoption of the ASEAN Charter, the 10-member grouping decided to codify existing norms and maintain its historical identity as an intergovernmental organisation. ASEAN did less than it could have done. In fact in some areas, ASEAN had even gone backwards. The question arises whether ASEAN needed a Charter or whether its energies would have been better spent on increasing functional cooperation among its members.[27]

According to S. Jayakumar, Singapore's representative to the Eminent Persons Group (EPG) and former Deputy Prime Minister, Singapore cannot solely claim credit for the idea of the ASEAN Charter. The drafting of the ASEAN Charter underwent a two-stage process. First, an EPG was created to make key recommendations on the Charter to the ASEAN leaders. Following that, a High Level Task Force (HLTF) was formed to draft the actual Charter based on the EPG's recommendations.[28]

Nonetheless, Singapore actively pursued the drafting of the Charter. It was Singapore's idea to form an EPG. At the ASEAN Foreign Ministers' Retreat in Cebu in 2005, then-Foreign Minister George Yeo convinced the other Foreign Ministers to start developing a Charter through a top-down approach and they agreed to appoint an EPG. Subsequently, this proposal was endorsed by the ASEAN leaders and mentioned in the Kuala Lumpur Declaration on the ASEAN Charter in 2005. George Yeo appointed former Deputy Prime Minister S. Jayakumar to be Singapore's representative to the EPG.

As articulated by George Yeo and S. Jayakumar, Singapore's key contribution was to persuade the EPG to include strong dispute settlement provisions in the ASEAN Charter. Singapore thought that ASEAN needed a binding dispute settlement mechanism. In ASEAN, "there was a widening gap between taking decisions and the enforcement or implementation of those decisions. ASEAN needed a culture of compliance to focus on the implementation of decisions, timelines and action plans".[29]

With regard to more effective decision-making, S. Jayakumar notes that the EPG's approach was that consensus would be sought for more sensitive and critical issues. In the EPG, Singapore also made a stronger push for ASEAN to move towards a single market and closer economic integration. The EPG recommended various measures to buttress ASEAN's organisational effectiveness. Singapore proposed the formation of the Committee of Permanent Representatives (modelled after the EU's COREPER) and other measures to strengthen the office of the Secretary-General. Concerning the funding of the ASEAN, Singapore strongly recommended:

> [O]ur approach was that we should stick to compulsory contributions on an equal basis. Beyond that, member countries should have the flexibility to contribute more on a voluntary basis to assist newer members or less developed countries in the region. We were prepared to do more if necessary. In fact, Singapore had introduced the Initiative for ASEAN Integration (IAI) and helped to set up training centres in the CMLV countries (Cambodia, Laos, Myanmar and Vietnam).[30]

The EPG concluded its task within a year in 2006 and submitted its final report to the ASEAN leaders during the 12th ASEAN Summit in Cebu in January 2007. The High Level Task Force (HLTF) then drafted the Charter based on the recommendations of the EPG. According to Singapore representatives to HLTF, Tommy Koh and Walter Woon, apart from the two ideas which were dropped, all the other EPG's recommendations were adopted by the ASEAN leaders. S. Jayakumar writes that if then-Foreign Minister George Yeo had not proposed the top-down approach, with an EPG and HLTF, it was unlikely if the Charter could have been finalised within the short span of two years.[31]

Establishment of the ADMM and ADMM-Plus

Singapore is indeed a strong advocate of multilateral security forums. It believes that multilateralism would enhance regional security in the region.[32] As such, apart from the ARF, Singapore has also greatly contributed to the strengthening of the ASEAN Defence Ministers' Meeting (ADMM). At the Second ADMM in Singapore in 2007, the first three-year programme (2008–2010) which guided regional cooperation in security issues was adopted. It included activities in areas such as (1) promoting defence and security cooperation, (2) conflict prevention and resolution, and (3) norms setting and sharing.

To complement the Track 1 meetings of ADMM, Singapore, through the S. Rajaratnam School of International Studies (RSIS), took the initiative to inaugurate the Track II Network of ASEAN Defence and Security Institutions (NADI). Its inaugural meeting was held in Singapore in August 2007. NADI can contribute to the ADMM process by thinking ahead of the curve and anticipating possible security challenges, addressing emerging issues in security cooperation, as well as thinking of new ideas and recommendations for cooperation which would be relevant and timely for the ASEAN Defence Senior Officials Meeting (ADSOM) and the ASEAN defence track to consider.[33]

In addition, the Second ADMM in Singapore adopted a Concept Paper to establish the ADMM-Plus at the same meeting in Singapore, with the objective of promoting and strengthening engagement with ASEAN dialogue partners on security issues through triennial meetings and consultations of Defence Ministers of member states.[34] In October 2010, the ADMM-Plus was launched. ASEAN invited eight dialogue partners, namely, Australia, China, India, Japan, New Zealand, Republic of Korea, Russia and the United States (US) to the ADMM-Plus.

The inaugural ADMM-Plus agreed on five areas of practical cooperation to pursue under this new mechanism. These areas are maritime security, counter-terrorism, humanitarian assistance and disaster relief, peacekeeping operations and military medicine. To facilitate cooperation on these areas, five Experts' Working Groups (EWG) were established. Five sets of Co-Chairs have also been identified to lead the EWGs, namely, Australia and Malaysia to Co-Chair the EWG on maritime security, Indonesia and the US to Co-Chair the EWG on counter-terrorism, Vietnam and China to Co-Chair the EWG on humanitarian assistance and disaster relief, the Philippines and New Zealand to Co-Chair the EWG on peacekeeping operations, and Singapore and Japan to Co-Chair the EWG on military medicine.

The ADMM-Plus EWG on maritime security was the first to kick off the EWG series. The Inaugural Meeting was convened in Perth, Australia, on 20–22 July 2011. The Meeting aimed to identify areas of common interests across the spectrum of maritime security challenges with a view to exploring practical initiatives for defence and military cooperation and capacity build-ing. Some of the key shared maritime security challenges highlighted by member states in the meeting are as follows: sea piracy, maritime terrorism, people and drugs smuggling, illegal fishing, threats to marine environment, natural disasters, accidents at sea, and armed robbery at sea.

Non-Traditional Security Issues

Singapore has been deeply involved in addressing some of the non-traditional security challenges in ASEAN, particularly the transboundary haze, and humanitarian assistance and disaster relief. As Singapore's environment and pub-lic health are affected by transboundary haze coming from Sumatra, Singapore has been actively pushing for regional mechanisms to deal with this issue.

ASEAN has opted for cooperation, and the haze issue has been placed squarely on the regional agenda since acute episodes in 1997–1998. Singapore thought that for the past 10 years or so, actions have been focused on the ASEAN Transboundary Haze Agreement. But the so-called "ASEAN Way" of addressing the problem by political consensus rather than hard law among ASEAN countries has clearly not solved the haze problem. It even took more than 10 years for Indonesia before it ratified the Agreement.[35]

Singapore regularly attends the annual Meeting of the ASEAN Sub-Regional Ministerial Steering Committee on Transboundary Haze Pollution. In recent years, Singapore, through its Minister for Environment and Water Resources, Dr Vivian Balakrishnan, has sought clear deliverables from the meeting. He has urged member countries in the committee to submit their concession maps and agree to a date for the launch of a monitoring system that enables the identification of errant companies.[36]

As a concrete contribution to anti-haze efforts in the region, Singapore recently passed the Transboundary Haze Pollution Act. This legislation makes it an offence for any entity — Singaporean or non-Singaporean — to cause or to contribute to transboundary haze pollution in Singapore. It is not intended to replace the laws and enforcement actions of other countries, but it is to complement the efforts of other countries to hold companies accountable.[37]

Singapore generously contributes to enhancing regional efforts to effec-tively and promptly respond to disasters. Singapore established the Changi Regional HADR Coordination Centre or RHCC in September 2014, which seeks to facilitate military-to-military coordination in disaster response in the region. Singapore hopes that the RHCC can contribute to more effective multinational military responses to disasters by enhancing operational coordination among military responders.[38]

In June 2013, Singapore co-hosted with Brunei Darussalam the second edition of the ASEAN Militaries' Humanitarian Assistance and Disaster Relief (HADR) Exercise (AHX). The Ministry of Defence argues that disasters in the region have shown how difficult it is for a single country, no matter how big, to muster all its resources and capabilities necessary to attend to the needs of the disaster victims. Hence, it believes that an effective system to coordinate efforts across all aid agencies would need to be worked out and validated through joint military exercises such as the AHX.[39]

Beyond Political and Security Community to the ASEAN Economic Community

Achieving economic development has always been integral to building regional peace and security in ASEAN. The twin goals of economic prosperity and regional security have in fact defined ASEAN's strategies on regionalism in Southeast Asia. In this regard, Singapore has not only contributed to the security and political discussions at the ASEAN level but has also actively participated in ASEAN discussions on the creation of a regional economic community.

The focus on economic regionalism is an important development for Singapore. Its economic prosperity is anchored on its strategy of "globalisation". Singaporean leaders have seen economic regionalism as a vital response to the anaemic global economy. The ongoing economic slowdown in the West, the emergence of regional trade arrangements in Europe and North America, the trend towards market-oriented reforms in ASEAN, and the massive growth in trade and investment linkages between East Asia and Southeast Asia have driven Singapore to look more closely at regional trade and investment opportunities. This involves not only entering new markets in the region, but encouraging Singaporean investments in southern China, Vietnam and ASEAN. Singapore's perception on regional economic cooperation is broad and flexible — regional in the economic sense consists of three layers: ASEAN; a sub-regional layer consisting of Singapore, Malaysia and Indonesia; and a macroregional layer encompassing Eastern Asia and Asia-Pacific.[40]

Apart from the Growth Triangle concept incorporating Singapore, Riau Archipelago in Indonesia and Johor in Malaysia, the establishment of the ASEAN Free Trade Area (AFTA) assumed importance as the second tier of regional economic cooperation for Singapore. The AFTA was endorsed by the six heads of government at the Fourth ASEAN Summit held in Singapore on 28 January 1992.[41] As stated in the ASEAN's 1992 Singapore Declaration, "ASEAN shall establish the ASEAN Free Trade Area using the Common Effective Preferential Tariff (CEPT) Scheme as the main mechanism within a time frame of 15 years beginning 1 January 1993 with the ultimate effective tariffs ranging from 0% to 5%".[42]

In accordance with the AFTA Framework Agreement, ASEAN members had committed to establish a free trade area by 2008 by means of a Common Effective Preferential Tariff (CEPT) scheme. Taking effect from January 1993, this scheme would gradually reduce tariffs on capital goods, manufactured products and processed agricultural goods. The complete removal of ASEAN tariffs would substantially increase the share of Singapore's exports to ASEAN. So if the AFTA is fully implemented, the regional orientation of Singapore's economy would dramatically increase in the long run.[43]

Singapore was a strong advocate of the AFTA as then-Prime Minister Goh Chok Tong saw the proposed trade bloc as a timely ASEAN response to a changing international economic landscape that was marked by the emergence of new markets in Eastern Europe and regional economic blocs such as the Single European Market and the North America Free Trade Area. In addition, Goh felt that the intraregional competition brought about by the reduction of trade barriers would, in the long run, improve the efficiency and productivity of ASEAN economies. This would, in turn, increase ASEAN's attractiveness to foreign investments. Singapore was one of the first ASEAN countries to fulfil its AFTA commitment by lifting import tariffs on the goods listed under the CEPT scheme.[44]

However, AFTA's scope faces a number of barriers, including questions over the speed of sectoral liberalisation and concerns over unequal distribution of benefits. Hence, facilitating ASEAN economic cooperation through AFTA was not enough to counter the economic woes in the region in the 1990s. Moving forward, at the 2003 ASEAN Summit in Bali, Indonesia, ASEAN leaders agreed to establish an ASEAN Economic Community (AEC) by 2020. The idea of an AEC was first proposed by then-Prime Minister Goh Chok Tong in the previous year's ASEAN Summit in Phnom Penh, Cambodia. According to Prime Minister Goh, "Singapore's continued growth depended on establishing open links with regional and global partners, through which we could advance our economic and strategic interests. We did this by establishing a number of regional and inter-regional forums, as well as the ASEAN Economic Community".[45] Since 2003, the timeline for establishing the AEC has moved from 2020 to 2015.

Conclusion

ASEAN has come a long way since its formation in 1967. The chapter has traced how the grouping has significantly evolved from its aim of building regional peace and security to promoting its vision of an ASEAN Community. The discussion has also shown how critical the role of Singapore has been throughout the various stages of ASEAN's development. This role continues as ASEAN goes through the myriad transitions of becoming a community, and in particular — a political and security community.

This process of managing such a transition to a security community presents difficult challenges, even for an organisation that is almost 50 years old. These challenges include building a regional identity against the heterogeneity of the communities in each of the ASEAN member states, and managing the differences in the levels of economic development in a rapidly changing global environment. As such, building an ASEAN Political and Security Community would require much more work that what ASEAN had done in the past. It compels member states to reassess the basic foundations of what "secure" communities means in the current climate within and among ASEAN countries. This would also require bringing back the need to address the developmental and security challenges facing the region, as well as to bridge the societal divides and the deep fault lines that could impede the realisation of a meaningful ASEAN Community. Thus, in every step of becoming an ASEAN security community, Singapore is expected to continue with its proactive role in advancing this goal.[*]

Notes

[1] The first idea of an ASEAN Political Security Community was announced in 2003 with the adoption of the Bali Concord II during the Ninth ASEAN Summit held in Bali, Indonesia in 2003. It was first referred to as the ASEAN Security Community (ASC), and later on changed to ASEAN Political Security Community (APSC) in 2009.

[2] ASEAN, "Vientiane Plan of Action," 2004. Italics added for emphasis.

[3] See ASEAN, "ASEAN Political-Security Community Blueprint," in *Roadmap for an ASEAN Community 2009–2015* (Jakarta: ASEAN Secretariat, 2009), pp. 5–20.

[4] Michael Leifer, *Singapore's Foreign Policy: Coping with Vulnerability* (London: Routledge, 2000), pp. 84–85.

[5] Ang Cheng Guan, *Singapore, ASEAN and the Cambodian Conflict, 1978–1991* (Singapore: NUS Press, 2013), p. 5.

[*] Acknowledgment: The autor wishes to thank Julius Trajano for his valuable research support.

6   Ang Cheng Guan quoting extracts of Notes of Conversation between 1PS and Mr David Dodwell, *Financial Times* correspondent, MFA, 30 October 1979.

7   Ang (2013), *op. cit.*, p. 5.

8   "Lessons for Singapore Foreign Policy: The Cambodian Conflict." Transcript of the Speech by Former Deputy Prime Minister and Former Coordinating Minister for National Security Wong Kan Seng at the S. Rajaratnam Lecture at Shangri-La Hotel, 23 November 2011. Retrieved 27 April 2015, from http://www.mfa.gov.sg/content/mfa/overseasmission/phnom_penh/press_statements_speeches/embassy_news_press_releases/2011/201112/press_201112_06.html.

9   Joint Communiqué of the 10th ASEAN Ministerial Meeting, Singapore, 5–8 July 1977. Retrieved 27 April 2015, from http://www.asean.org/1762.htm.

10 Ang (2013), *op. cit.*, pp. 14–19.

11 Linda Goh (ed.), *Wealth of East Asian Nations: Speeches and Writings by Goh Keng Swee* (Singapore: Federal Publication, 1995), p. 321.

12 Ang (2013), *op. cit.*, p. 20.

13 *Ibid.*

14 Gretchen Liu, *The Singapore Foreign Service: The First 40 Years* (Singapore: Ministry of Foreign Affairs, 2005), p. 135.

15 *Ibid.*, p. 135.

16 "Lessons for Singapore Foreign Policy: The Cambodian Conflict" (2011), *op. cit.*

17 Amitav Acharya, *Singapore's Foreign Policy: The Search for Regional Order* (Singapore: World Scientific, 2008), p. 21.

18 Liu (2005), *op. cit.*, p. 135.

19 Acharya (2008), *op. cit.*, p. 57.

20 *Ibid.*

21 Singapore Declaration of 1992, Singapore, 28 January 1992. Retrieved 27 April 2015, from http://www.asean.org/news/item/singapore-declaration-of-1992-singapore-28-january-1992.

22 S. Jayakumar, *Diplomacy: A Singapore Experience* (Singapore: Straits Times Press, 2011), p. 81.

23 *Ibid.*, p. 83.

24 *Ibid.*

25 *Ibid.*, p. 84.

26 *Ibid.*, p. 85.

27 Barry Desker, "Is the ASEAN Charter Necessary?," *RSIS Commentaries,* S. Rajaratnam School of International Studies, 17 July 2008.

28 Jayakumar (2011), *op. cit.*, p. 94.

29 *Ibid.*, p. 97.

30 *Ibid.*, pp. 98–99.

31 *Ibid.*, p. 101.

32 "Strengthening Cooperation to Enhance Regional Security." Transcript of speech by Minister of Defence Ng Eng Heng at the Sherpa Meeting of the Shangri-La

Dialogue, Singapore, 26 January 2015. Retrieved 27 April 2015, from http://www.iiss.org/en/events/shangri%20la%20dialogue/archive/fullerton-forum-2015-b1ae/keynote-address-be5f.

33 Tan Seng Chye, "Purpose and Objectives of NADI," 28 July 2009. Retrieved 27 April 2015, from http://www.rsis.edu.sg/nadi/.

34 Joseph Liow, *Dictionary of the Modern Politics of Southeast Asia,* Fourth Edition (New York: Routledge, 2015), p. 67.

35 Transcript of parliament Q&As supplementary questions for the second reading of the Transboundary Haze Pollution Bill, Ministry of Environment and Water Resources, 5 August 2014. Retrieved 27 April 2015, from http://app.mewr.gov.sg/web/Contents/Contents.aspx?Yr=2014&ContId=2015.

36 S. Ramesh, "Vivian Balakrishnan, Grace Fu to Attend Transboundary Haze Meeting in KL," *Channel NewsAsia*, 17 July 2013. Retrieved 27 April 2015, from http://www.channelnewsasia.com/news/specialreports/mh370/news/vivian-balakrishnan-grace/746048.html.

37 Transcript of the opening speech by Dr Vivian Balakrishnan, Minister for the Environment and Water Resources, for the second reading of the Transboundary Haze Pollution Bill, 4 August 2014. Retrieved 27 April 2015, from http://app.mewr.gov.sg/web/Contents/Contents.aspx?ContId=2014.

38 "Strengthening Cooperation to Enhance Regional Security" (2015), *op. cit.*

39 Sheena Tan, "S'pore, Brunei Co-Host 2nd ASEAN Disaster Relief Exercise," 16 June 2013. Retrieved 27 April 2015, from http://www.mindef.gov.sg/imindef/resourcelibrary/cyberpioneer/topics/articles/news/2013/jun/16jun13_news.html#.VOLyDi6H_LU.

40 Acharya (2008), *op. cit.*, p. 25.

41 *Ibid.*, p. 27.

42 Singapore Declaration of 1992, Singapore, 28 January 1992, *op. cit.*

43 Acharya (2008), *op. cit.*, p. 27.

44 "ASEAN Leaders Agree to Create an ASEAN Free Trade Area," *HistorySG: An Online History Guide*, National Library of Singapore, 28 January 1992. Retrieved 27 April 2015, from http://eresources.nlb.gov.sg/history/events/bf07b77f-68fd-4473-9ccb-1197fe323cb8.

45 See "The Practice of Foreign Policy for Sustained Growth — The Singapore Experience." Transcript of speech by Emeritus Senior Minister Goh Chok Tong at S. Rajaratnam Lecture on Friday, Singapore, 17 October 2014. Retrieved 27 April 2015, from http://www.mfa.gov.sg/content/mfa/media_centre/press_room/pr/2014/201410/press_20141017.html.

Chapter 12

Singapore and the Great Powers

Khong Yuen Foong

A common refrain in Singapore's foreign policy towards the great powers — confined to the United States (US) and China in this essay — is that it does not want to choose between them. Singapore is far from alone in articulating this strategic preference: many of its ASEAN and Asian-Pacific neighbours, including US military allies such as Australia and Thailand, have voiced similar inclinations. This essay seeks to probe a little deeper into the "not wanting to choose" discourse to make three related points. First, I argue that Singapore has already chosen; it made a choice early on — in favour of the US — soon after the British withdrawal East of Suez. Second, I suggest that that choice has served Singapore well. Third, I argue that the dilemma Singapore faces after 15 years of a very successful foreign policy (vis-à-vis the great powers) is whether to stick with America, or gravitate towards China, given the shifting power distribution in Asia. Singapore's actions in recent years suggest that it continues to strongly favour America when it comes to military security; on the economic and political-diplomatic fronts, however, it appears to be more even-handed in engaging the US and China. We conclude with an observation: the fact that Singapore is a Chinese-majority state, constrains, rather than facilitates, how far it can move towards the China bandwagon.

The Context of Not Choosing

"We do not want to choose between China and the US."[1] The straightforward interpretation of the statement is that Singapore wants to maintain good relations with both the US and China.[2] That is undoubtedly the understanding of Singapore's policy-makers and they have been remarkably successful in doing that. Yet the recurrent asseveration of this not wanting to choose mantra by Singapore and its Asian-Pacific neighbours suggests that the security dynamics of the region is making it more challenging for them to maintain good relations with *both* the great powers. Choose they may have to in the coming years.[3]

The prospect of having to choose between China and the US — which side to align oneself with when push comes to shove — has become more acute since the turn of the century. It arises out of China's growing economic and military might — and its concomitant desire for political influence in Asia, if not globally — in a context where the US remains the preponderant military power in Asia. In such a situation, analysts and policy-makers expect to see a more competitive US–China relationship, analogous perhaps to US–Soviet rivalry during the Cold War.[4] The US–China competition might be more subdued, given their intense economic interdependence (absent in the US–Soviet case), or it could be more serious, given China's potential for achieving hegemonic status.

Whichever it is, it is foreseeable that the two great powers will seek the allegiance of partners, friends and neutrals as they try to outcompete the other across a spectrum of issues. The extreme manifestation of this expectation — albeit in an extreme circumstance — was US President George W. Bush's message to the world after the September 11 attacks: "you are either with us or against us." In this case, it was easy for most of humankind to be with the US, given Al-Qaeda's brutality and disregard for innocent lives. However, if the US and China, in their struggle for primacy in Asia, were to make the same demand of the states in the region, it would put the latter in a strategic quandary. Most in Asia would resist being put in that position and that is why they emphasise the importance of keeping US–China relations on an even keel. If the US–China competition remains friendly and manageable, Asia will be under less pressure to choose between them in the medium to long term.[5]

The "not wanting to choose" logic is unobjectionable and it certainly seems in accord with the national interests of Singapore and most of its Asian neighbours. But it begs a key question: has one already chosen in accepting the status quo? More pertinently, what is the status quo? The status quo, I submit, is one of American hegemony or preponderance. Singapore's leaders do not dissent from this description, having used terms like "sole superpower", and "preeminent in setting the rules of the game" to describe America in the 21st century.[6] The descriptors used by Singapore's leaders suggest that Singapore might have already chosen: it is more comfortable strategically with American hegemony than its alternatives. In his seminal volume on *Singapore's Foreign Policy*, Michael Leifer describes Singapore's disposition in the following way:

> Since Britain's withdrawal in the 1970s, and despite clashing with Washington over political values, the USA has long been the preferred primary source of external countervailing power … for Singapore, balance of power is a policy

which discriminates in favour of a benign hegemon as opposed to one which guards against any potential hegemonic state.[7]

What Leifer calls "balance of power", most international relations theorists would term hegemony. Balance of power policies best describe efforts to maintain a power equilibrium among the great powers to prevent a hegemon — who will supposedly threaten the political independence of others — from rising. A policy that "discriminates in favour of a...hegemon" is more accurately described as a preference for hegemony. But not just any hegemon. In Singapore's case, the identity of the hegemon is key. The critical adjective here is "benign": Leifer's description of Singapore's strategic leanings hits the nail in the head because "benign" is an adjective that Singapore has so far been comfortable conferring only to the US.[8]

From Singapore's perspective, the US was, and remains, a benign hegemon. When the British announced their military withdrawal East of Suez in 1967, Singapore had two existential concerns. One was strategic, the other economic; both related to its survival as a nation-state. The strategic concern was who would replace the British and help deter Singapore's potential adversaries? The Five Power Defence Arrangement (FPDA), although short of an alliance, was an ingenious but partial answer. By linking Singapore, Malaysia, Britain, Australia and New Zealand in the military-security arena, the FPDA served useful confidence-building roles for Singapore–Malaysia, and it also linked the "arrangement" to the US (via the Australia, New Zealand, United States Security Treaty or ANZUS Treaty).

As hinted by the FPDA link to the US, the real answer to the question of who was best suited to provide Singapore the security assurance it needed was the US. Despite some initial doubts about the reliability of the Americans, Prime Minister Lee Kuan Yew was a quick study when it came to the utility of America's military presence in East Asia. The US intervention in Vietnam demonstrated that the US was a serious and credible Asian-Pacific power, willing to risk lives and fortunes to prevent the spread of communism. Lee has also been the major proponent of the thesis that the US military intervention in South Vietnam from 1965–1973 bought time for the young, non-communist states of Southeast Asia (such as Singapore) and allowed them to get their houses in order.[9]

Even after the US military defeat in Vietnam, and the Vietnamese invasion of Cambodia (1978), the US remained sufficiently engaged with Southeast Asia by cooperating with ASEAN to delegitimise the Heng Samrin government and to pressure Vietnam to withdraw from Cambodia. Singapore took a lead role in these anti-Vietnam efforts because as a small and vulnerable state, it wanted to draw a line in the (regional) sands about what was permissible and was not permissible in Southeast Asia. In this case, Singapore wanted to emphasise the norm of respecting the territorial integrity and political sovereignty of states, a norm held dear not only by Singapore, but also routinised through a decade of intra-ASEAN diplomacy and enshrined in ASEAN's Treaty of Amity and Cooperation. America's strategic interests in Asia, in other words, seem to largely coincide with Singapore's — it is in that sense that the latter sees the former as benign.

Singapore's second existential concern, economic survival, was also addressed by the US, or rather, US multinational corporations. In the late 1960s, British military expenditure was responsible for 20% of Singapore's GDP, generating 30,000 front line jobs and an additional 40,000 in support services.[10] Britain's military withdrawal from Singapore therefore constituted "a blow to our economy".[11] Singapore's response was to go all out to invite foreign investment by providing investors with tax incentives, a business-friendly environment and solid infrastructure. The first wave of investors who came in the late 1960s and early 1970s were predominantly American technological companies, including Texas Instruments, National Semiconductor and Hewlett-Packard. This was followed in later years by Japanese and European investments. By the late 1970s, according to Lee Kuan Yew, this economic strategy had allowed Singapore to put "our old problems of unemployment and lack of investments behind us".[12]

Accounts of how Singapore's hungry and go-getting agencies (such as the Economic Development Board) went about persuading the Chief Executive Officers of multinationals to locate their manufacturing plants and/or to set up their (regional) headquarters in Singapore make for instructive reading on how to win and prosper in the capitalist world economy. Timing mattered (first mover advantage), as did a pro-business government, not to mention cheap and abundant labour (in the initial days). Today, there are 3,600 American firms in Singapore, and it would be correct to say that US multinationals forged a symbiotic relationship with Singapore early on. They came in search of a business-friendly and profit-generating environment and by providing that, Singapore not only secured good jobs for its growing population, but also set itself on the path of export-led growth that would come to characterise the growth strategy of the East Asian Newly Industrialising Countries (NICs). US multinationals, in other words, played an early and critical role in helping Singapore industrialise, and in time, also helped catapult Singapore to the forefront of prosperous trading states.

As Singapore grew more prosperous, it also came to appreciate a third component of US benignity: US soft power or its power to attract. The appeal of its innovative, network-based entrepreneurial culture, perhaps best manifested in its world-beating universities and Silicon Valley firms, have also encouraged the Singapore government to diversify its "investment portfolio" from the more familiar British icons (Oxbridge and Rolls Royce) to cutting-edge American concerns (Harvard–Yale–Stanford and Microsoft–Google). Thousands of Singaporeans — including many government scholarship holders who have gone on to hold top positions in the cabinet and ministries — have obtained their tertiary and advanced degrees from top US universities. Tie-ups between Singapore and US universities are common, as are internships and jobs for Singaporeans in the top Silicon Valley firms. In the finale to the Singapore–US Free Trade Agreement of 2003, the US threw in a "free gift", allowing 500 Singaporeans to work in the US without going through the arduous labour certification process required of non-citizens.

As the above account of the US military, economic and soft power roles suggests, the US has been benign for Singapore, and Singapore's alignment with the US has served it well. Crucially, Singapore takes the view that the US military and economic presence have been helpful not only for Singapore, but for the region writ large. The peace and stability enjoyed by Asia in the last 60 years, from Singapore's perspective, have been undergirded by the preponderant US military presence in the region.[13] Although Asia experienced wars in the 1950s (the Korean War) and 1960s (the Vietnam War), Singapore's position is that the US involvement in these two "hot wars" stalled the advance of communism — if the US had not intervened, the psychological blow to the non-communist governments of Southeast Asia would have been enormous, and would have made some of them more susceptible to communism.[14]

It is possible to argue that in the 1960s, with Britain's withdrawal from the region, Singapore had no choice but to move in the direction of the US. That would be incorrect. One need only take a cursory glance at the choices of small states and medium powers in Southeast Asia and beyond to see that different countries made different choices. Some chose to align themselves politically with the socialist-communist bloc, others tried to steer a middle course as in the Non-Aligned Movement, while another group aligned itself with the US (and the West). The political ideology of the leaders proved crucial in making these choices. The same is true on the economic front: there existed a vociferous debate in the 1960s and 1970s about the correct path to economic modernisation — dependency theorists argued that integration into the capitalist world economy and relying on foreign capital would entail exploiting one's working class and result in underdevelopment, while neo-liberals saw integration into the world capitalist economy and foreign capital as capable of generating growth. Singapore chose the neo-liberal path, and like its fellow travelers in East Asia, prospered.

If Singapore made an early and good choice in aligning itself with the US, and has reaped the benefits of that partnership in the last 40 odd years, why cannot it just continue with that policy? The reason is the great power that was factored out of Singapore's choice set then — China — has risen and Singapore needs to factor the new (power) dynamics into its foreign and security policies. Alignment with China in the 1960s and 1970s was never in the cards for Lee Kuan Yew's Singapore. Lee's government was staunchly anti-communist; China was providing moral and material support for communist insurgents in Southeast Asia, and China itself was going through the throes of the Cultural Revolution. Moreover, even if China had been perceived as less threatening, Lee would have exercised great caution, given the importance he placed on reassuring Singapore's neighbours (Indonesia in particular) that Singapore was not a China outpost.

Engaging China, 1990–2000

The story of Singapore's rapprochement with China, beginning with Deng Xiaoping's 1978 visit, is well-known and need not be rehearsed here. Suffice it to mention that Deng was impressed with Singapore's economic achievements and he also took to heart Lee Kuan Yew's advice about the need for China to cease supporting communist insurgents in ASEAN if China wanted cordial relations with the region. China acted on Lee's advice, paving the way for Indonesia's establishment of diplomatic relations with China in 1990. Singapore followed swiftly a few months later, and Singapore–China relations have been on an upward trajectory since.

To be sure, Singapore was "engaging" China before the formal establishment of diplomatic relations. Even during the Cultural Revolution years (1966–1976), when China was perceived as an ideological and political threat, total trade between the two countries averaged S$570 million a year.[15] Singapore voted in favour of the "one China" principle in the United Nations (UN) in 1971, helping unseat Taiwan from the UN. In 1985, the late Dr Goh Keng Swee was appointed as an economic adviser to China's coastal and special economic zones. Bilateral visits between top Singaporean and Chinese officials became more frequent in the 1980s. Total trade between the two countries rose from S$2.9 billion in 1990 to S$75 billion in 2010.[16] Bilateral ventures such as the Suzhou Industrial Park (since 1994) and the Tianjin Eco-city (since 2008) have reaped enough mutual gains that a third joint venture in China's west is being planned. Singapore has emerged as among the top inves-tors in China in recent years, while China became Singapore's number one trading partner in 2013.

Singapore's agility in adapting to China's rise can be seen in its "engaging China" discourse in the 1990s. The context of Singapore's argument in favour of engagement was the existence of a counter-discourse — especially in the US — about the need to contain China.[17] Through its words and deeds, Singapore demonstrated what was entailed in engaging China. In an earlier essay discussing Singapore's approach to engaging China, I argued that Singapore was pursuing a three-pronged approach. The first prong was eco-nomic; the second, political; and the third, a fallback military option. The goal of economic and political engagement was to help China develop a stake in regional stability/order, or to play by the "rules of the international [political and economic] game". The fallback option was a hedging strategy — in case China chooses to turn the tables on those rules and asserts itself militarily, Singapore, acting in tandem with others in the region, could move in the direction of augmenting the US alliance systems in Asia to deter China.[18]

Does the three-prong thesis still apply today? How has each of the prongs changed in the intervening years? And what do these changes reveal about Singapore's China policy and the regional environment? The economic and political engagement practiced by Singapore, ASEAN and the US in the 1990s have had their anticipated effects: China is a welcome and indispensable player in the region and it has developed a stake in regional stability. As successive Chinese leaders have reiterated, China desires a peaceful and stable environ-ment so that it can continue to focus on growing its economy. In fact, China has become so central to the region that "engagement" is no longer an adequate description of Singapore's or the US' approach to China. We are in the post-engagement phase. China has become a senior partner of the region, it is call-ing some of the shots, and the question now is what kind of a senior partner it is likely to be.

Engagement, in other words, has helped pave the way for China to be what it is today: an economic juggernaut, politically influential in Asia and beyond, and in possession of an increasingly powerful military. Accordingly, the dis-course has also shifted, from whether to engage or contain China, to the ques-tion of how one should respond to China's growing might.[19] What is Singapore's take on this development, usually discussed in terms of the shifting balance of power in Asia? A good place to start would be the views of former Minister

Mentor Lee Kuan Yew. Asked by two Harvard academic-practitioners whether China aspires to displace the US "as the number one power in Asia" or "the world", Lee opined:

> Of course. Why not? They have transformed a poor society by an economic miracle to become now the second largest economy in the world… The Chinese will want to share this century as co-equals with the US… It is China's intention to be the greatest power in the world. The policies of all governments toward China, especially neighbouring countries, have already taken this into account.[20]

Assume Lee is right and that Prime Minister Lee Hsien Loong and his colleagues share the same understanding of China's aspirations. Note that for the senior Lee, the path to being number one is a two-stage process: the first stage consists in sharing this century "as co-equals with the US". It is only in the second stage — in the 22nd century? — that China will seek to displace the US to assume the number one position. Lee is thinking in terms of centuries, in other words.

In what follows, we shall focus on the first stage, where China strives to be "co-equal" with the US. We will also touch on the second stage, where China might want to displace the US, but that will not be the main focus. The key question to be addressed is what is Singapore's position — judging from its actions and its words — on the desirability of China's quest for "co-equality" with the US? To answer this question, I shall revert to the three domains I used in the earlier essay — military, economic and political — to examine Singapore's position vis-à-vis the US and China.

The Military Dimension

Singapore, like many in ASEAN, has increased its military spending in the last 15 years. As most analysts agree, military prowess is aimed more at persuading neighbouring countries to respect Singapore's political sovereignty, and treat it with the respect and decorum it deserves. It is not very useful to view Singapore's military build-up as a response to a rising and more assertive China. Unlike the military acquisitions of countries — such as the Philippines and Vietnam — involved in territorial spats with China, the action-reaction armament logic is absent in Singapore's military acquisitions.

There is more to the military dimension than arms spending and specific acquisitions. The extent and depth of military cooperation — as in formal alliances and informal partnerships — also needs to be examined. Here, Singapore–US military cooperation in the 2000s has deepened substantially.

Some observers have argued that the Changi Naval Base, which became operational in 2000, was meant primarily as a "place" for US vessels — including aircraft carriers — to anchor. It is in effect a substitute for Subic Bay Naval base in the Philippines that the US lost in 1994. As one of the most ardent advocates of a strong US military presence in Southeast Asia, Singapore was putting its money where its mouth is, in building Changi Naval Base and in welcoming American warships there.

Further evidence of the strengthening of Singapore–US military ties can be seen from the signing of the Singapore–US Strategic Framework Agreement (SFA) in 2005; the inclusion of Singapore in US–Thailand (COBRA) and US–India (Malabar-2007) military exercises; and the training of RSAF (Republic of Singapore Air Force) pilots in Arizona and Iowa, where Singapore F-15 planes are also "based" for training purposes. Singapore's response to the Obama administration's 2011 pivot to Asia reinforces the view about Singapore's comfort with American military preponderance. The pivot to Asia attempts to shift the US' strategic focus back to Asia, with a major element being the reapportioning of US naval power from a 50–50% to 40–60% focus on Europe–Asia. For its part, Singapore agreed to host, on a rotating basis, up to four US littoral warships a year. The first of these visited in 2013, with both Singapore and the US making the point that "the deployment stops short of a basing agreement".[21]

Singapore–China military cooperation, in contrast, is more nascent and superficial. This is not surprising, given the mutual suspicions prevalent before the 1980s. For much of the 1990s, the upturn in Singapore–China relations was based on mutual economic and political, rather than military, engagement. However, there are indications of some ratcheting up of military cooperation between the two nations. Reciprocal visits by the Defence Ministers are becoming more frequent (Singapore's Minister Dr Ng Heng Yen visited Beijing in 2012 and 2014); Singapore and China also held their largest bilateral military exercise in Nanjing in 2014. On the multilateral front, Singapore has also been proactive in encouraging Chinese participation in the ASEAN Regional Forum (ARF), the Shangri-La Dialogue and the ASEAN Defence Ministers Meeting-Plus (ADMM-Plus).[22]

Despite the above signs of deepening Singapore–China military relations, the overall picture at least for the time being, is one where Singapore's military engagement with the US and China remains lopsided, in favour of the US.[23] In 2012, Chinese Defence Minister General Liang Guanglie, while visiting Washington, DC, raised the issue of co-equality between the People's Liberation Army and the US military. He proposed "that the two militaries build a new relationship based on equality, mutual benefit and cooperation".[24] Those familiar with US history and strategy will retort that it is most unlikely that the US will deal with any other military as a co-equal until it has been decisively overtaken by the latter. Even when the Soviets had more (though less accurate) nuclear missiles than the US, it did not feel that it was being treated as an equal. China remains far behind the US in military strength. Perhaps even more pertinent, America's national identity is tied to the idea that it is the greatest military power on earth. Singapore is at ease with that for it feels that the US has, by and large, used that power for good. Its strong leaning towards the US has historical and contemporary roots, the historical having to do with America's willingness to fight land wars in Asia (Korea and Vietnam) to prevent the spread of communism and to uphold its reputation as the guarantor of allies' security, while the contemporary is linked to the idea that US military preponderance has been a major factor in the keeping the peace in Asia for the last 50 years.[25]

The Economic Dimension

If China lags behind the US on the military front, it seems to be doing better on the economic front. Based on Purchasing Power Parity (PPP) measures, its GDP overtook America's in 2014, making it the world's largest economy. In absolute terms, the US economy remains far larger and richer, so no one in Asia is writing off the US as an economic giant upon whom the prosperity of the region also depends. Yet Asians have pointed to fact that in the last decade, China has gradually replaced the US as the number one trading partner of Japan, South Korea, Australia and virtually all the ASEAN countries, including Singapore. China is therefore the region's emerging economic hegemon, whose economy exerts an "inexorable pull" for all those interested in "growing with it". As Lee Kuan Yew put it: "None of the economies on its periphery can resist the attraction of China's market. Slowly, but inexorably, we are being drawn into China's economic orbit."[26]

As was suggested earlier, China is in the enviable economic position it finds itself today in part because the US and Asia chose to engage it economically and politically in the 1980s and 1990s. Those who worried about how an economically strong China might pose a threat to the existing (US-led) order cautioned against the blind engagement of China; they raised the prospect of "containing" China, although they failed to make much headway in persuading the Bill Clinton and George W. Bush administrations to go down that path. The US opened its markets to China, the Clinton administration supported China's ascension to the World Trade Organization, and President George W. Bush's

Secretary of State Colin Powell was fond of telling critics that US–China relations were never better than during his watch.

Singapore was an influential voice in arguing for the wisdom of engaging China. Singapore was especially effective in articulating the rationale behind engaging China: it was about integrating China into the international economic system and how that would incentivise it to play by the rules of the game. By the late 2000s, China was comfortably ensconced in the international economic system. Its rapid and sustained growth have catapulted it to becoming one of the main growth engines of the world economy, with expectations of its playing a helpful role in preventing a global recession stemming from the financial crisis of 2008. If the task in the 1990s was to facilitate China's integration into the world (capitalist) economy, the challenge of the next two decades seems to be to persuade China to adhere to, instead of attempting to rewrite, the rules of the international economic game. When Obama administration officials repeatedly inveigh China to accept the "rules of the road" — which have allowed China to prosper — they seem to be asking China to play by the (US-inspired) existing rules instead of trying to change them.

What is Singapore's take on co-equality for China vis-à-vis the US on the economic front? On the global front, Singapore is in favour of greater influence for China, for example, increasing China's voting rights in the international financial institutions to commensurate with its contributions and influence. On the Asian front, Singapore is only too aware that the issue is no longer co-equality, since China has replaced the US as the number one trading partner for most in the region. Its Asian trading partners have accorded it co-equality and more: they are the ones solicitous of growing with China and they are the ones who will have to accommodate China's *quid pro quo* requests.[27]

Singapore and other Asian nations anxious to avoid being cocooned in a single economic orbit (China's) seem to be counting on the US to provide a second orbit, to balance China economically, and to give them the manoeuvre space they feel they need. Like the engagement-containment debate of the 1990s, Singapore has again been at the forefront in articulating why the US should maintain a robust economic presence in the region. Singapore's narrative may be summed up in three words that its Prime Minister has used to warn his American friends about the dangers of retreating from the economic game: "Trade is strategy."[28]

Trade is strategy in Singapore's view because economics play a crucial role in shaping the political-strategic contours of the region. When the US was the most important trading and investment partner for most in East Asia, it reaped concomitant political-strategic advantages. The lure of the US market and desire for inward US investments made East Asians reliable partners who tended to be solicitous of US goodwill and aid. Insofar as strong economic growth provided the political legitimacy for many East Asian governments, and insofar as the US was their most important economic partner, non-communist East Asia was happy to play by the existing rules of the economic game.

Fast forward to 20 years later. China has replaced the US as the top trading partner for most in Asia; if this trend continues, it is likely that the majority will, in the first instance, be more solicitous of Chinese goodwill and aid. That implies a greater sensitivity to China's interests in the region and a willingness to accommodate them, so as to ensure that one has the opportunity to "grow with China". Witness the constraints on the Indochinese countries — with the exception of Vietnam — whose economies are closely intertwined with China's. When Cambodia was ASEAN Chair in 2012, it accommodated China's interests by refusing to include mention of the disputes in the South China Sea, resulting in the ASEAN's failure to issue a post-Annual Ministerial Meeting communiqué for the first time in its 45-year history.

China also signalled its displeasure with Philippines President Benigno Aquino for taking his country's maritime disputes with China to the Hague for arbitration by disinviting him from attending the 10th ASEAN–China Expo in Nanning in 2013. In leveraging on its economic strength to send signals to, or get its way with, its neighbours, China is no different from other great powers. Hugh White captures the dilemma faced by countries from Australia to Singapore to Vietnam well:

> National power has many manifestations… but history suggests it has only one fundamental source, and that is sheer economic scale… The openness of its economy means that for many countries, both in Asia and beyond, China has become their most important economic partner, and growing trade with China, or aid from China, is central to their future. This makes a lot of countries sensitive to China's interests… Canberra, like so many other capitals, knows that to protect its immense trading interests, China's key concerns must be respected.[29]

Singapore has always been careful in respecting the key concerns of China and the US, although it has not hesitated to stand its ground when the occasion demands. To be able to stand one's ground diplomatically, it helps to have room for economic manoeuvre. Diversification is therefore a mainstay of Singapore's economic strategy: it feels more secure if its economic well-being is not held hostage to one major economy. Hence Singapore's "multinational" economic strategy of trading with, and investing in, as many vibrant economies as possible: the US, China, India, ASEAN and increasingly the Middle East. The same rationale underlies Singapore's promiscuity in concluding free trade agreements (FTAs) with ASEAN, China, the US, Japan, India and many others. In all, Singapore has concluded 20 bilateral or regional FTAs with 31 countries, with another seven FTAs in the process of being negotiated.[30]

Singapore's interest in balancing Chinese economic influence with a robust US economic presence in Asia, therefore, must be seen in the context of its overall "multinational" strategy. Singapore's active promotion of the Trans-Pacific Partnership (TPP), however, does furnish clues about the kind of balance (of economic power) it would like to see in Asia. Like its position on the Obama administration's pivot to Asia, Singapore's take is that anything that helps strengthen America's economic presence is to be welcome. It gives the region the balance that, in Singapore's view, will allow it and other regional states "economic space" so that they are not held hostage to only one engine of growth.

The TPP had its origins as a "mini FTA" among Singapore, New Zealand, Chile and Brunei. From those humble beginnings, it has burgeoned into a "mega" region-transcending FTA, albeit one that (so far) excludes China, India and Indonesia.[31] Unusually, the US has seen fit to take a leading role in negotiating the TPP. It is possible to view the TPP — termed as a "high standard" FTA by the US — as the pact that would facilitate America's comeback to Asia by reinforcing economic rules that play to US strengths such as those pertaining to intellectual property rights, financial services and e-commerce. Others have argued it may be a belated attempt to contain China economically.[32] Singapore's view is more nuanced. Arguing for the importance of concluding the TPP in front of a Washington, DC, audience, Singapore Foreign Minister K. Shanmugam argued that the US pivot or "rebalance cannot only be military, it has to be economic as well" and that the TPP was "a critical part of the US economic strategy in Asia".[33] Failure to secure the TPP, Shanmugam implied, would put the US at a political-strategic disadvantage vis-à-vis other great powers in Asia. The Obama administration seems to agree. In his 2015 State of the Union address, President Barack Obama justified his request for fast-track authority from Congress to complete the TPP negotiations in terms of not ceding "critical ground to China" on free trade. Inaction on the part of the US would be risky because "China wants to write the rules for the world's fastest-growing region. That would put our workers and businesses at a disadvantage".[34] It is the US who should be writing those rules.

As the world's poster boy for free trade, Singapore already adheres to most of those rules; consequently, it does not have a problem with the proposed TPP rules in ways that others, such as China and Japan, might have. Given economic trends, the US probably cannot dethrone China from its pole economic position in Asia, but Singapore believes that it is vital for the US not to give up the game. Like many in the region, Singapore remains unsure how China will use its economic hegemony for strategic purposes, and that partly explains its activism on the TPP. To be sure, Singapore is also participating in discussions to create two China-inspired FTAs, the Regional Comprehensive Economic Partnership (RCEP, which excludes the US) and the Free Trade Area of the Asia-Pacific (FTAAP, which includes the US, but which appears to be an attempt to subsume the TPP); its enthusiasm for these, however, have yet to match that for the TPP.[35]

Singapore's approach to the changed distribution of economic power in Asia is to reach out farther afield to forge economic links with India and more recently, the Middle East, while working to ensure that the US remains one of the top trading partners of the region. The contrast with its approach on the military front is instructive: Singapore seems content with US military preponderance, but it is more anxious about Chinese economic preponderance. There could be two main reasons for this. First, having "chosen" the US as its main strategic interlocutor since the 1970s, and having done exceptionally well, Singapore has developed a level of strategic trust vis-à-vis the US that remains absent in its relations with China. The Cold War legacy, where China supported communist insurgents in Southeast Asia, is also probably relevant here. Perhaps, as China matures into the role of a benign (economic) hegemon, Singapore might feel more at ease with its economic dominance. Second, as a Chinese majority state, Singapore is always cautious about not being perceived as being too close to China, either by its Muslim neighbours, or for that matter, by the US. To dispel those perceptions, it helps to argue for the continuation of a strong US economic presence, and to diversify its trading partners.

The Political Dimension

It is in the political-diplomatic sphere that Singapore's even-handedness in dealing with the US and China is most evident. For all its ability to punch above its weight, Singapore does not expect to be treated as a military or economic equal by the US or China. It is on the political-diplomatic front that it expects co-equality vis-à-vis each of the great powers. Operationally, what that means is that Singapore expects the great powers to respect its political independence and sovereignty. Singapore's favourable stance on the co-equality issue is based on principle, interest, as well as pragmatism. As a small state, it is not surprising that it would insist on the equality of states in the international system. Although enshrined in the UN Charter, the sovereign equality of states exists more in theory than practice: small and/or weak states simply do not have the clout or get the attention that big and/strong states do. Yet the principle of equality is something that is worth insisting on because the small can point to the inconsistencies of the great powers — and thereby raise questions about the moral legitimacy — of the great powers when they ride roughshod over the small.

Singapore can be prickly when it feels these core principles have not been respected. Former Foreign Minister S. Jayakumar recounts two separate instances in the 1990s when Singapore chose to stand its ground vis-à-vis the great powers, and where it also sought to be consistent and even-handed in responding to their demands. The first involved China's putting pressure on Singapore to remove discussion of the South China Sea from the ARF agenda in 1999, when Singapore was the Chair. China was against "internationalising" the issue and accused Singapore of being "biased against them" and "favoring the United States by raising the issue".[36] S. Jayakumar's response was that as one of the flashpoints in the region, the South China Sea disputes were "a natural topic for discussion under ARF auspices… if the ARF was to be a credible forum, it was not really tenable to omit the South China Sea from its agenda".[37] In the event, Singapore refused to cave in to Chinese pressure despite the latter's "veiled threat" of retaliation, and the South China Sea issue was discussed at the ARF.

The second incident involved US unhappiness over the Chairman's Statement at the conclusion of the same ARF (1999). US Secretary of State Magdeleine Albright took exception to a sentence expressing "deep regret over the bombing of the Chinese Embassy in Yugoslavia… which had caused the loss of innocent lives and many casualties". Albright's "hectoring and bully approach" and her insistence that the wording was "unacceptable to the US" cut no ice with Singapore: the sentence stayed.[38] S. Jayakumar's point in recounting the two instances was to show that Singapore was consistent and even-handed in dealing with the two great powers, and that in so doing, Singapore protected "the reputation we have carefully built up as a credible and independent country".[39]

What Singapore expects from its interlocutors — co-equality in political relations — it is happy to wish upon China as the latter struggles to achieve co-equality with the power that matters most: America. Ex-Minister Mentor Lee Kuan Yew could not have been more explicit in his analysis of what contemporary China wants: "to share this century as co-equals with the US."[40] Yet it is always a struggle to ask for, much less achieve, "co-equality" with the US because it grants it sparingly and grudgingly, and usually only to states with the same political complexion, i.e., liberal democracies. Non-liberal democracies have a hard time getting the US to recognise it as a political equal. Autocracies are viewed as going against the tide of history and humanity, and there is always a degree of "pariah state" appellation attached to such non-democracies.[41] Political equality, in other words, can only be bestowed by the US upon other liberal democracies.

Singapore believes that is a mistake, in part because of its own spats with the US on the issue. But Singapore's position is also based on a hard-headed analysis of the ways of the world. Its position is Kissingerian in that it prefers the US to deal with China as it is, i.e., an autocracy.[42] The authoritarian nature of the Chinese government remains a key sticking point and source of strategic distrust among US policy-makers (and Americans in general). As Newt Gingrich put it while on a 1998 Congressional trip to China, if the Chinese refused to talk about human rights, then he had nothing to talk to them about. Gingrich's outburst verges on hyperbole, but it is representative of a major — if not dominant — strand of US thinking: democracies share fundamental values — such as the consent of the governed and the rule of law — and these values impact on their foreign policies positively and predictably; relations among democracies are peaceful in ways that are impossible to replicate in relations among democracies and non-democracies. Similarly, for Aaron Friedberg, an influential scholar and a former member of US Vice-President Dick Cheney's national security team, it is only when China becomes a democracy that the US can withdraw its legions from Asia. A democratic Chinese hegemon, in Friedberg's view, would be acceptable to the US in ways that an authoritarian hegemon would not.[43]

Singapore rejects such an ideological approach to China.[44] The issue here is political-moral equality vis-à-vis the US, and with that, the attendant rights to participate in shaping of the contours and outcomes of regional (Asian) affairs/issues. For Singapore, and most in Asia, these rights inhere in those with the requisite power and domestic legitimacy, regardless of political regime type or complexion, to shape events in the region. Hugh White makes the case that China's claim to equality is based on its economic achievements and clout. China's government, having lifted hundreds of millions of its citizens out of poverty, is considered legitimate by most of its citizens; it is also impacting on the economic fortunes of Asia — if not the world — in ways it did not in the 1990s. The US, in White's view, should deal with China as "an equal great power".[45] It is a view shared by Singapore's leaders.

There is thus a case for formalising China's clout by giving it a spot and proportionate sway in the top economic tables. Antics like denying China greater voting rights in the International Monetary Fund (IMF) are likely to be counter-productive: witness China's interest in setting up alternative financial institutions — such as the Asian Infrastructure Investment Bank (AIIB to rival the Asian Development Bank) and the New Development Bank (NDB or

BRICS Development Bank to rival the World Bank) — where its views and interests are better reflected. As the lead economy and the one that Asians want to grow with, when China sets up such institutions, the rest of Asia are very likely to jump on the bandwagon.

Finally, it is also in Singapore's interest to favour China–US co-equality because it demonstrates to the Chinese a sense of even-handedness that is less apparent on the military front and somewhat ambiguous on the economic front. In the final analysis, of course, Singapore can only counsel; the preroga-tive of whether to treat China as an equal rests solely in US hands. The assump-tion of Singapore and its Asian neighbours is that a China seen and treated as a co-equal by the US will be less psychologically fraught; with its international status assured, it will have less need to prove itself, and therefore see less need to overturn the existing order in Asia.

Conclusion

The international community's decision to engage, instead of contain, China in the 1980s and 1990s, facilitated its emergence as a strong and confident great power. Singapore was a strong voice for and supporter of engagement. Its chief spokesperson for engagement, Lee Kuan Yew, was prescient about how China would develop and the choices it would have to make as it becomes strong. Today, China has reached that crossroad and its Asian neighbours, as well as the US, are waiting to examine how China will choose to exercise its power.

Lee's counsel on engaging China in the 1990s was not devoid of a backup option: if China chose unwisely or acted aggressively when it was strong, he expected the US to have a fallback option ready, one that involved putting in place "set pieces" capable of deterring China or responding to its more asser-tive policies. Moreover, if "countries [in the region] are forced to take sides… [the US] would arrange to win over to America's side of the chessboard, Japan, Korea, Asean, Australia, New Zealand and the Russian Federation".[46]

What Lee might not have anticipated is how challenging it might prove to "win over" these countries today. Those favourably disposed toward the US for their military security will also feel the pull of China when it comes to their economic security. China has not been averse to reminding its Asian neighbours that it is a permanent resident in the region; the US, on the other hand, is in Asia by choice, the implication being that the US can choose to retrench from the region when its domestic politics or other exigencies demand it.

Singapore's thinkers and practitioners have been mulling over this issue, usually in terms of how much Chinese influence Singapore can or should accept and the implications for its relations with its neighbours and the US. In a recent opinion piece, Han Fook Kwang, managing editor of the Singapore *Straits Times*, suggested, with some discomfort, that China does not need to "conquer territory or use brute force" to spread its influence in Southeast Asia. China could spread its influence in three waves: economic, cultural, and then, in the final stage, language. As Han puts it, "After the economic and cultural domination, language will be the final conquest".[47]

Although it is difficult to say whether Han believes Singapore will succumb to this "conquest", the suggestion seems to be that "for Singapore in particular, the changes will come more quickly than in other countries because of its majority Chinese population".[48] But, for our purposes, the more interesting issue is what is absent in Han's account: there is no political-strategic wave. Would not the economic and cultural domination be followed by the political-strategic? That is, given the imperative of "growing with China" (with the US being eased out in terms of economic centrality) and the appreciation of Chinese culture (made more likely by the ability of many Singaporeans to read and speak Chinese), would it not follow that there would a greater willingness to accommodate China's political-strategic interests?

Here, veteran diplomat Bilahari Kausikan is more forthcoming. He points to how market forces can transform interstate relations, especially between China and Southeast Asia, with "political and strategic consequences". Traditional Westphalian notions of the state and interstate realtions are being redefined by market forces, and these forces are "stressing ASEAN as powerful centrifugal forces" pulling "members in different directions." What he seems to be saying is that market forces — in particular the attraction of the Chinese market and the need to "grow with China" — are making it more difficult for ASEAN to act as a united whole: those most reliant on trade with and investment in China will perforce adjust their political-strategic orientations in line with that of China. For Kausikan, this is worrisome:

> As the only Chinese majority country in Southeast Asia, it could pose special challenges for Singapore. Already Chinese diplomats and officials often refer to Singapore as a "Chinese country". We politely but firmly tell them that they are mistaken. And we will continue to do so. But the implications are worth pondering.[49]

The reason why Singapore needs to tell China that it is not a "Chinese country" is because it believes it is not, but perhaps even more importantly, it does not want to be perceived by its neighbours (Indonesia and Malaysia in particular) and the US (I would argue) as a Chinese country. A well-known fact of Singaporean diplomacy during the Cold War years was its policy of not establishing formal diplomatic relations with China until Indonesia had done so. The ostensible reason for pursuing such a policy is to reassure its Muslim neighbours — Indonesia in the main, and Malaysia to a lesser extent — who distrusted China that it would not be China's "fifth column" in Asia. It would not serve Singapore's interests for its neighbours and others to assume — mistakenly in Singapore's view — that as ethnic-cultural brethrens of China, it would share China's political-strategic imperatives. Singapore's leaders like to emphasise that its foreign policy is informed by pragmatic calculations aimed at protecting its autonomy and sovereignty. This factor, it seems to me, will be a central consideration and constraint on how far Singapore can gravitate in the direction of China.

To be sure, Singapore's policies toward the great powers are only partially dependent on its assessment of the evolving distribution of military and economic power and influence, and how its interests are best protected in such a fluid strategic context. Chinese and US actions (or lack thereof) will also be crucial in shaping Singapore's policies in the coming years. If China were to use military force, unprovoked, in its maritime disputes with the Philippines and Vietnam, Singapore and many (though not all) others in Asia are likely to read that as a signal of an aggressive rising power. In that case, Singapore may move even closer to the US orbit along all the three dimensions — military, economic and political — discussed in this chapter. On the other hand, a US that fails to bring to fruition the TPP, that is unable to cobble together a bipartisan approach to Asia, and that is repeatedly forced to prioritise meeting challenges in the Middle East over Asia, is likely to be perceived as unreliable by Singapore's leaders.[50] Over time, such a perception may persuade the latter to move closer to China. It is a choice that Singapore will not make lightly. For this author, it is what Singapore means when it says it does not want to be put in a position of choosing between the US and China.

Notes

[1] "Territorial Disputes Can Be Set Aside: PM Lee," *The Straits Times*, 6 February, 2015. Retrieved 26 May 2015, from http://www.straitstimes.com/st/print/3415647. On ASEAN's not wanting to choose, see "China-ASEAN Ties: Seeking a Balance," *The Straits Times*, 26 October 2013. Retrieved 26 May 2015, from http://www.straitstimes.com/the-big-story/asia-report/china/story/china-asean-ties-seeking-balance-20131026. Robert G. Sutter *et al.*, *Balancing Acts: The U.S. Rebalance and Asia-Pacific Stability* (Washington, DC: The George Washington University, 2013), provides a perceptive analysis of how the different Asian countries have navigated their "not wanting to choose" dilemma in the context of the US pivot to Asia.

2   See "Speech by Prime Minister Lee Hsien Loong at Central Party School," especially para-graphs 10–12, 6 September 2012. Retrieved 7 February 2015, from http://www.pmo.sg.

3   For the circumstances under which Australia might have to choose between the US and China, see Hugh White, "America or China: One Day, We Will Have to Choose," *The Sydney Morning Herald*, 28 May 2013. Retrieved 7 February 2015, from http://www.smh.com.au.

4   Kenneth G. Lieberthal and Wang Jisi, *Addressing U.S.–China Strategic Distrust*, John L. Thornton China Center Monograph Series no. 4 (Washington, DC: Brookings Institution, 2012). See also Graham Allison, "Thucydides' Trap Has Been Sprung in the Pacific," *Financial Times*, 21 August 2012. Retrieved 26 May 2015, from http://www.ft.com/cms/s/0/5d695b5a-ead3-11e1-984b-00144feab49a.html#axzz32c8nwPAH.

5   "Speech by Prime Minister Lee Hsien Loong at Central Party School," *op. cit.*, para-graph 12, 6 September 2012.

6   Graham Allison and Robert D. Blackwill (eds.), *Lee Kuan Yew: The Grand Master's Insights on China, the United States, and the World* (Cambridge, MA: MIT Press, 2013), p. 20.

7   Michael Leifer, *Singapore's Foreign Policy: Coping with Vulnerability* (Routledge: London, 2000), p. 27. For a more reserved view of Singapore and the US in the 1960s, see Ang Cheng Guan, *Lee Kuan Yew's Strategic Thought* (Routledge: London, 2013), pp. 28–29.

8   For a recent description of the US as "the dominant global power" and "a benign and constructive power" see Lee Hsien Loong's speech at the Nikkei Conference in 2014, "Scenarios for Asia, 20 Years on," *The Straits Times*, 23 May 2014. Retrieved 26 May 2015, from http://www.mfa.gov.sg/content/mfa/media_centre/singapore_headlines/2014/201405/headlines_20140523_01.html.

9   Lee Kuan Yew, *From Third World to First: The Singapore Story: 1965–2000* (Times Media: Singapore, 2000), p. 503.

10 *Ibid.*, p. 69.

11 *Ibid.*

12 *Ibid.*, p. 82.

13 Lee Hsien Loong (2014), *op. cit.*, paragraph 20.

14 Ang Cheng Guan, *Southeast Asia and the Vietnam War* (London: Routledge, 2010), pp. 55–56, 120–121.

15 Figure calculated from Poon Kim Shee, "Singapore–China Special Economic Relations: In Search of Business Opportunities," *Ritsumeikan International Affairs*, 3, 2005, p. 176 (Table 1: Singapore's Trade with China: 1965–2003).

16 John Wong and Catherine Chong, "The Political Economy of Singapore's Unique Relations with China," in Saw Swee-Hock and John Wong (eds.), *Advancing Singapore–China Economic Relations* (Singapore: Institute of Southeast Asian Studies, 2014), p. 32.

17 See Yuen Foong Khong, "Singapore: A Time for Economic and Political Engagement," in Alastair Iain Johnston and Robert S. Ross (eds.), *Engaging China: The Management of an Emerging Power* (London: Routledge, 1999), pp. 109, 115–116.

18 Khong (1999), *op. cit.*, pp. 109–128.

19 For an analysis of two different answers to the question, see Yuen Foong Khong, "Primacy or World Order: The United States and China's Rise — A Review Essay," *International Security*, 38(3), Winter 2013/2014, pp. 153–175.

20 Allison and Blackwill (2013), *op. cit.*, pp. 2–3. Since Lee spoke, China has become the world's largest economy in the world (2014), based on GDP measured in PPP terms.

21 "S'pore to Host US Warship for 10 Months," *The Straits Times*, 11 May 2012. Retrieved 11 June 2015, from http://www.straitstimes.com/print/World/Story/STIStory_797591. html. Robert Sutter *et al.* (2013), *op. cit.*, p. 2, observe that Singapore has been more forthcoming than some US allies in extending military-strategic cooperation to the US.

22 See Seng Tan, "Faced with the Dragon: Perils and Prospects in Singapore's Ambivalent Relationship with China," *The Chinese Journal of International Politics*, 5(3), Autumn 2012, p. 249.

23 Cf. Tan (2012), *op. cit.*, p. 254, which describes Singapore's behaviour as "hedging" vis-à-vis China. We agree however that the behaviour is best explained by a certain "wariness [on Singapore's part] of Chinese intentions".

24 "China to US: Equal Footing for Militaries," *The Straits Times*, 9 May 2012. Retrieved 11 June 2015, from http://www.straitstimes.com/print/Asia/China/Story/ STIStory_796723.html.

25 Lee Hsien Loong (2014), *op. cit.*

26 Lee Kuan Yew, "Inexorable Pull of China's Economy," *The Straits Times*, 9 December 2010. Retrieved 11 June 2015, from http://www.straitstimes.com/print/Review/Others/ STIStory_611844.html.

27 Lee Kuan Yew provides a fascinating take on China's "come grow with me" strategy and its implications for Southeast Asia in Allison and Blackwill (2013), *op. cit.*, pp. 6–7.

28 "S'pore Remains Pro-Business: PM Lee," *The Straits Times*, 4 April 2013. Retrieved 26 May 2015, from http://www.straitstimes.com/the-big-story/asia-report/singapore/ story/spore-remains-pro-business-pm-lee-20130404.

29 Hugh White, *The China Choice: Why We Should Share Power* (Oxford: Oxford University Press, 2012), pp. 41–42.

30 See http://www.fta.gov.sg for the complete list of FTAs as well as those under negotiation. The collapse of the Doha round was a major push factor in Singapore's pursuit of many of these bilateral and multilateral FTAs.

31 The 12 states involved in negotiating the TPP as of December 2013 are: Australia, Brunei, Canada, Chile, Japan, Malaysia, Mexico, New Zealand, Peru, Singapore, the US and Vietnam.

32 Zaki Laidi, "Trade Deals Show Power Politics Is Back," *Financial Times*, 31 March 2013. Retrieved 26 May 2015, from http://www.ft.com/intl/cms/s/0/e2aae9f4-9254-11e2-851f-00144feabdc0.html#axzz3bEF6NvW7.

33 "US Cannot Get Distracted from Asia: Shanmugam," *The Straits Times*, 24 September 2014. Retrieved 26 May 2015, from http://www.mfa.gov.sg/content/mfa/media_centre/ singapore_headlines/2014/201409/headline_20140924.html.

34 "Obama Seeks Trade Leap with Eye on China," *The Straits Times*, 22 January 2015. Retrieved 26 May 2015, from http://www.straitstimes.com/the-big-story/asia-report/china/story/obama-seeks-trade-leap-eye-china-20150122.

35 On the TPP, FCEP and FTAAP as rival trade pacts, see Fiona Chan, "Mega Trade Pacts and the Fight for Asia's Trade Future," *The Straits Times*, 16 December 2014 . Retrieved 26 May 2015, from http://www.straitstimes.com/the-big-story/asia-report/opinion/story/mega-trade-pacts-and-the-fight-asias-trade-future-20141216. On Singapore's enthusiasm for the TPP, see "PM Lee Urges US Business Community to Back TPP," *The Straits Times*, 26 June 2014. Retrieved 26 May 2015, from http://www.mfa.gov.sg/content/mfa/media_centre/singapore_headlines/2014/201406/headlines_20140626_01.html.

36 S. Jayakumar, *Diplomacy: A Singapore Experience* (Singapore: Straits Times Press, 2011), p. 117.

37 *Ibid.*

38 *Ibid.*, pp. 120–121.

39 *Ibid.*, p. 123.

40 Allison and Blackwill (2014), *op. cit.*, p. 3.

41 See "Remarks by President Obama to the Australian Parliament," 17 November 2011 (http://www.whitehouse.gov) for the strengths of democracies and the deficiencies of non-democracies. Cf. Bilahari Kausikan, "The Western Myth of Universality and China's Moment in History," *The Straits Times*, 9 January 2015, which provides a critique of the universality of democratic values. Retrieved 26 May 2015, from http://www.straitstimes.com/news/opinion/more-opinion-stories/story/the-western-myth-universality-and-chinas-moment-history-2015. White (2012), *op. cit.*, pp. 143–146, also engages with this issue in terms of democracy and political legitimacy.

42 See Henry Kissinger, *On China* (London: Allen Lane, 2011), pp. 520–526.

43 Aaron L. Friedberg, *A Contest for Supremacy: China, America, and the Struggle for Mastery in Asia* (New York: W.W. Norton, 2011), p. 252.

44 Kausikan (2015), *op. cit.*

45 White (2012), *op. cit.*, pp. 143–146.

46 Khong (1999), *op. cit.*, p. 121.

47 "Get Ready for a Formidable, Rising China," *The Straits Times*, 3 November 2013. Retrieved 26 May 2015, from http://www.straitstimes.com/the-big-story/asia-report/china/story/get-ready-formidable-rising-china-20131103.

48 *Ibid.*

49 Bilahari Kausikan, "Small? Become Extraordinary," *The Straits Times*, 28 January 2015. Retrieved 26 May 2015, from http://www.straitstimes.com/news/opinion/more-opinion-stories/story/small-become-extraordinary-20150128.

50 Both the US and Singapore see a relationship between the TPP and the US pivot to Asia. See "TPP Delay a Blow to US' Asia Pivot," *The Straits Times*, 12 December 2013. Retrieved 11 June 2015, from http://www.straitstimes.com/st/print/1842134.

Chapter 13

The Changing Terrorist Threat Landscape in Singapore

Rohan Gunaratna

Introduction

The terrorist threat to Singapore changed dramatically in the last 25 years. Enhanced communication, travel and migration to Singapore in the 1990s and 2000s enhanced the threat to Singapore. Increased globalisation created opportunities for insurgent, terrorist and extremist groups to recruit from and infiltrate into Singapore for fundraising and procurement. The developments in South Asia (Afghanistan and Pakistan), the Middle East (Syria and Iraq) and Southeast Asia (Philippines, Indonesia and Malaysia) impacted on Singapore's environment. The highly charged international and regional security environment challenged Singapore's security.

The government of Singapore comprehended the changing threat landscape. The government, working with industry and community partners, built a security architecture to protect Singapore from internal and external threats. Due to increased investment in security and by creating a dynamic system, Singapore has not suffered from terrorism. Nonetheless, the threat to Singapore both from operational terrorism and ideological extremism has not subdued. Singapore's geopolitical position and geostrategic orientations make her a target. In Southeast Asia, Singapore is the most prized target. The complexity of security in the region, including Singapore, changed with the rise of the Islamic State (IS) and the declaration of an Islamic Caliphate. With threats from both Al-Qaeda and IS families of groups, Singapore is threatened by groups from overseas, home-grown cells and individuals from within Singapore. Influenced by virulent Al-Qaeda and IS threat-centric ideologies, organised groups from abroad and a tiny segment of self-radicalised Singaporeans and residents threaten Singapore.

The Context

With the declaration of an Islamic State in the Levant, a new global and an Asian threat landscape is emerging. The Al-Qaeda-centric threat landscape is struggling to survive and an Al-Qaeda–IS hybrid threat landscape is struggling to be born. With the spread of IS ideology in Asia, the operational threat to the region is changing dramatically. IS associates and supporters are seeking to attack both coalition and host targets. With over a thousand Asians travelling to Syria and Iraq to fight, Asian governments are seeking to criminalise advocacy, support and participation in fighting in conflict zones. Despite governmental and societal efforts, every week Central, South, Southeast and Northeast Asians travel to fight in Syria and Iraq. With Asians returning home from the conflict theatre with motivation, skills and networks, they threaten domestic, regional and global security. The same way the Afghan trained veterans formed the nuclei of the current generation of threat groups, the IS-indoctrinated and -financed entities are likely to form the next wave of global terrorism and extremism.

With the emergence of a new Asian threat landscape, the region faces a growing threat. The threat to Asia is no longer from the resurgence of Al-Qaeda and its host Taliban in the Pakistan–Afghanistan theatre but the growing appeal of IS. Lured by the end of times prophecy, Asian nationals travel with their families to Syria forming a bridgehead that threatens a rising Asia. A number of Pakistani and Afghan groups have pledged allegiance to IS leader Abu Bakr al-Baghdadi. Similarly, IS is expanding its global footprint with groups in the rest of South, Central, Southeast and Northeast Asia expressing support to IS. As the threat grows, governmental and societal strategies are vital to mitigating the looming threat.

Singapore's national security agencies, law enforcement authorities and military forces rapidly oriented themselves to the changing threat. Singapore's foreward-looking approach has given her a good understanding of the changing threat and its implications for Singapore. To mitigate the extant and emerging threat, Singapore deployed its military forces in Afghanistan and Iraq. Its law enforcement agencies built capacities in its immediate neighbourhood, and its national security agencies developed a threat driven response to disrupt plots to strike Singapore both from overseas and from within. Singapore is proactive in its approach to detecting and neutralising threats to Singapore both from within and overseas. Singapore built a counter-terrorism infrastructure both to fight threats within her borders and built capacities overseas empowering its neighbours to tackle their threats. By building partnerships with industry, community, religious, educational and media organisations, the government of Singapore has already put in place a full-spectrum response. Nonetheless, the scale of threat requires a shift from cooperation to collaboration with domestic, regional and international partners and greater investment to counter the growing on line threat.

Background

Historically, Singapore witnessed the operation of four categories of terrorist groups on its soil. As a regional and global hub for communication, finance, procurement and shipping, Singapore suffered from left wing, ethnopolitical, politico-religious and state-sponsored terrorism. Singapore suffered from left wing terrorism starting with the Malayan Communist Party since the late 1950s. While the threat of violence by the communists continued, Singapore also suffered from the Indonesian *Konfrontasi* in the mid-1960s. While Singapore did not suffer from ethnopolitical terrorism, several foreign ethnopolitical groups exploited Singapore starting in the 1970s. Since the 1980s, politico-religious groups, both domestic and foreign operated in Singapore.

The left wing groups that attempted to operate in Singapore included the Communist Party of Malaya (CPM), the Japanese Red Army (JRA) and the Popular Front for the Liberation of Palestine (PFLP); the ethnopolitical groups included the Free Aceh Movement, Babbar Khalsa International and Liberation Tigers of Tamil Eelam (LTTE); the politico-religious groups included the Lebanese Hezbollah, Moro Islamic Liberation Front, Rajah Solaiman Revolutionary Movement, Abu Sayyaf Group (ASG), Jemaah Islamiyah (JI), Kumpulan Militan Malaysia and Al-Qaeda.

The terrorist threat to Singapore from domestic, regional and international terrorism fused with globalisation in the late 20th and early 21st centuries. The distinction between international and national terrorism blurred. While the bulk of Singaporeans rejected political violence and extremism, a tiny minority of the Singaporeans became vulnerable to their ideas and methods. Driven by extremist ideologies, a handful supported, participated and advocated agendas by the Moro Islamic Liberation Front, Abu Sayyaf Group, JI, Al-Qaeda and now IS. Singaporeans travelled to fight in conflict zones in South Asia, the Middle East and in Southeast Asia. Within these groups, when it came to targeting Singapore, there was no differentiation. Threat groups built long-standing relationships — Al-Qaeda and JI, MILF and JI, and ASG and JI worked together. They all regard the West and Singapore as an enemy! Those motivated, skilled and networked also wanted to carry out terrorist attacks in Singapore both against foreign and domestic targets. Furthermore, threat groups in the international and regional arenas established support and operational cells in Singapore to advance their aims and objectives. The differentiation between the international, regional and domestic threat narrowed.

There were a few terrorist groups that attempted to conduct terrorist acts against Singapore. However, their attacks were primarily directed against US, Israeli, British, Australian and other foreign targets, and not Singapore. Nonetheless, if the attacks were successful, both Singaporeans and its other residents would have suffered fatalities and injuries. The threat to Singapore grew significantly only in the late 1990s and 2000s. With the operation of Al-Qaeda and its associated groups, notably JI and the Lebanese Hezbollah, the threat spiked. Although JI operated in Singapore since its formation in 1 January 1993, the group came to the attention of the government in September 2001 and was identified as a threat only in October 2001. JI was disrupted in two waves of arrests beginning in December 2001.[1] The timely intervention led to the dismantling of a joint Al-Qaeda–JI infrastructure taking out its operational capability.

Al-Qaeda-Centric Threat — Phase One

The Al-Qaeda-centric threat to Singapore was manifested from JI, a regional and a domestic group, working together with Al-Qaeda. The contemporary threat to Singapore originated with Singaporeans joining Southeast Asians to train and fight in conflict zones. They left to Pakistan and Afghanistan to train and fight against the Soviets; Malaysia and Indonesia to train and fight against the Christians; and the Philippines to fight against government forces and Christians. It started in Pakistan, with training provided by Al-Ittihad al-Islami led by Abdul Rasool Sayyaf in Sada, Khuram Agency. After the Soviets withdrew, JI built their dedicated camp in Afghanistan. Even before the official formation of JI in 1993, Singaporeans joined eight batches of Darul Islam (DI) fighters sent to Afghanistan starting in early 1985 until 1993.

The genesis of Singaporean foreign fighters can be traced back to DI, an Indonesian group operating from Johor in southern Malaysia since 1988. Abdullah Sungkar and Abu Bakar Bashir split from mainstream DI led by Adnan Maszudi, alias Ajengan Masduki, and created JI. Contrary to popular belief, it was the DI leader Sungkar and not his assistant Bashir who travelled to Pakistan and met Osama bin Laden. JI was formed on 1 January 1993 by Sungkar and Bashir, both of Hadhrami Arab and Javanese descent. After forging ties with Al-Qaeda, JI embraced its ideology and established secret cells throughout Southeast Asia including in Singapore. At an operational level, JI member, and later leader, Riduan Isamuddin, alias Nurjaman/Hambali, maintained the Al-Qaeda–JI link by working with Khalid Sheikh Mohomed, alias KSM, the 9/11 mastermind. KSM and Hambali knew each other since the mid-1990s. A Singaporean self-thought cleric and a condominium manager, Haji Ibrahim bin Haji Maidin, the DI leader in Singapore, joined JI and grew the Singapore branch. The JI operational leader Hambali, who worked with KSM, had previously operated in Southeast Asia. Hambali built relationships with Ibrahim Maidin's deputy Mas Selamat Kastari and other eager Singaporeans to plan and prepare attacks both against Western and Singaporean targets.

Functionally and regionally organised, JI was influenced by Middle Eastern terrorist groups, notably from Egypt but was controlled by Al-Qaeda. The functional divisions were military, political, financial, intelligence, information and religious. The four regional divisions of the JI were Mantiqi 1 — Western Malaysia, southern Thailand and Singapore; Mantiqi 2 — Western Indonesia and Java; Mantiqi 3 — Eastern Indonesia, Eastern Malaysia, Brunei and southern Philippines; and Mantiqi 4 — Australia. As most wealthy members of JI lived in Mantiqi 1, it was called the JI bank and was known for raising funds. Most of the terrorist planners and operators lived in Malaysia and in Singapore. Mantiqi I can also be called the "killer mantiqi". A vast area, Mantiqi 2 was the recruitment mantiqi. After disruption of JI in Mantiqi 1, many second-tier leaders moved to Mantiqi 2 and operated mounting attacks. With the establishment of Hudaibiyah, a dedicated JI training camp in the southern Philippines, Mantiqi 3 was known as the "training mantiqi".

The conflict zones in Poso in Sulawesi and Ambon in Maluku — all part of Mantiqi 3 — provided motivated recruits. The latest mantiqi to be established, Mantiqi 4, was in Australia. Managed from Malaysia, Mantiqi 4 was also called the "other mantiqi". Until Hambali bypassed the Mantiqi 4 leaders and planned attacks on Australian soil, Mantiqi 4 provided funds and engaged in politico-religious activities. In Singapore, JI conducted surveillance on 70 to 80 targets at the behest of Al-Qaeda and to keep the operation simple, Al-Qaeda narrowed it down to four. With Al-Qaeda, JI planned to simultaneously hit four diplomatic targets in Singapore using truck bombs, rigged with ammonium nitrate and TNT. In addition to the US and Israeli embassies and the Australian and British high commissions, JI also conducted surveillance at Sembawang Wharf and Changi Naval Base, used by the US military, the American school, commercial buildings housing American companies, Changi Airport, the Ministry of Education building at North Buona Vista Drive, the Ministry of Defence headquarters at Bukit Gombak, and the water pipelines between Singapore and Malaysia. As Singaporeans were unwilling to be suicide bombers, Khalid Sheikh Mohommed (KSM) organised Arabs to carry out the attacks. Working with Hambali, KSM tasked Mohammed Mansour Jabarah alias Sammy, a Canadian-Kuwaiti surveillance expert, to fly from Pakistan via Hong Kong to the Philippines and Singapore. He was joined by an explosives expert Fathur Rohman Al-Ghozi alias Mike, an Indonesian who mostly operated from the Philippines. Together they surveilled the targets in the Philippines. The ammonium nitrate to be dispatched to Singapore was recovered in Malaysia and the TNT was recovered in the Philippines. Mike had ordered six tonnes of TNT and taken delivery of 1.2 tonnes, detonators and detonator cord. Based on Singapore intelligence, Sammy was arrested in Oman, and Mike was arrested when he attempted to escape. He was shot dead in the Philippines. Working through JI's operational leader Hambali, Khalid Sheikh Mohamed, the 9/11 mastermind, had financed and planned the joint Al-Qaeda–JI operation. Had the four trucks carrying five tonnes of ammonium nitrate/TNT exploded, it would have killed a few thousand civilians, an attack comparable in scale to the death toll caused by 9/11.

When Singapore's Ministry of Home Affairs (MHA) announced the JI plot, Singaporeans were shocked. Even prior to 1993, JI operated as DI. Both DI and JI had come to the attention of the government but as a religious group and not as a terrorist group. The belief that religion is associated with good deeds did not evoke suspicion in DI and JI. As its operatives functioned in secrecy using code words concealing JI's true intentions, the terrorist nature of the group was not apparent. No one within the group thought it was right to inform the authorities. They were convinced that the stated aim of JI, the establishment of an Islamic state (*Daulah Islamiyah*) in Indonesia, Malaysia, the southern Philippines, Singapore and Brunei, was right. JI followed Al-Qaeda's trajectory of targeting Western and Christian targets — that too did not appear wrong. Influenced and supported by Al-Qaeda, JI spearheaded most of the significant terrorist attacks in the region from August 2000. A few JI members and leaders believed it was wrong to attack non-Muslims, but because they had taken a pledge of allegiance they did not inform the authorities. Nonetheless, Singapore was protected from terrorism because Singaporean Muslims came forward from time to time to protect their country, people and faith.

Singapore dealt with the threat very responsibly. Singapore did not isolate the Muslim community but embraced it and countered the threat from within. In December 2001, after mounting surveillance on the JI network for nearly three months, the Internal Security Department (ISD) arrested 15 persons, of whom 13 were members of JI. The 13 JI members were detained whilst the remaining two were released in January 2002 on restriction orders. In August

2002, the ISD arrested another 21 persons, all of whom, except two, were members of JI. These two were members of the Moro Islamic Liberation Front (MILF), a group with close training and operational links with JI. Of the 18 detained, two JI members and one MILF member were released in September 2002 on restriction orders. Although preventive detention by Singapore was criticised by the West, with the rise of terrorism, the US, Europe and Australia adopted practices in preventive detention. Except the hardcore of JI who did not recant and renounce violence, the others were released after rehabilitation. Those who remain in detention include Ibrahim Maidin, the spiritual leader of JI, Mas Selamat bin Kastari, the operational leader of JI and Mohammed Aslam bin Yar Ali Khan, who travelled to Afghanistan to fight against Western forces. Except for the escape and rearrests of Mas Selamat in Malaysia, the JI threat was exceptionally well-managed by Singapore.

Singapore's JI had 80 members with a third engaged in operational activity. The security authorities shared intelligence on JI with their Malaysian counterparts before they crippled Singapore's JI.[2] Although the Malaysian security authorities disrupted the JI leadership in Malaysia, many JI Malaysian members fled to Thailand, Indonesia, Cambodia and Bangladesh.[3] As JI Singapore was subordinate to the Johor JI leadership, JI Singapore members including Mas Selamat, the JI Singapore leader, fled to Malaysia. Although intelligence agencies were alerted about JI cells, they survived for nearly a decade overseas. Mas Selamat who fled Malaysia and travelled to Thailand was linked with four JI Singapore members. In revenge for the disruption of their group, they planned to hijack and crash an Aeroflot plane to Singapore's Changi Airport. An exposure in the press deterred them from staging the operation. They had even purchased airline tickets. In addition to Mas Selamat, his associates Mohamed Rashid Zainal Abidin and Ishak Mohamed Noohu were arrested in Indonesia and were deported to Singapore in November 2006. In addition to Muhammad Hasan Saynuddin currently serving 18 years of imprisonment in Indonesia, Husaini Ismail was arrested by the Indonesian Police in Central Java on June 2009.[4] The JI terrorists also planned to attack the Singapore embassy in Thailand. Working with their Thai counterparts, Singapore disrupted the operation. Despite the disruption of the JI network in Singapore, JI reconstituted itself overseas and posed a sustained threat to Singapore.

With the disruption of the plot to attack Western targets in Singapore and its base of operations in Malaysia, JI shifted its operational activities to Thailand, the Philippines and Indonesia. The law enforcement, security and intelligence agencies of Malaysia and the Philippines collaborated with Singapore starting in December 2001 to dismantle JI, but Indonesia and

Australia did not believe in the scale of the threat. Al-Qaeda funded JI to attack the region's best-known tourist resort, Bali, in October 2002, killing 202 people including 88 Australians. Had Singapore not taken decisive steps to dismantle JI starting in December 2001, the attack that was carried out in Bali would have been staged in Singapore by JI. Although the Indonesian authorities targeted JI, the group survived and revived in Indonesia, conducting intermittent attacks. After the bombings in Bali in October 2002, JI's infrastructure was disrupted but not dismantled. JI used Al-Qaeda funding for the 2002 Bali bombings that killed 202 people including 88 Australians. The funding that remained from Al-Qaeda was used to bomb Jakarta's JW Marriott in 2003. After the arrest and interrogation of KSM in February and March 2003, the CIA worked with their counterparts in Southeast Asia to capture Hambali who was planning to hijack a plane and crash it into the Bank of America building in the West Coast. Thai Special Branch General Tritot Ronrittiwichai arrested Hambali and his wife Noralwizah Lee Abdullah in Ayutthaya on 11 August 2003. After Muklas and Hambali were arrested in Indonesia and Thailand respectively, Noordin M. Top and Dr Azahari Hussein, two Malaysians took over JI's operational leadership. They formed the Al-Qaeda organisation in the Malay Archipelago and created an infrastructure that mounted several attacks from the Australian embassy in September 2004 to Bali — two in 2005, and on JW Marriott and Ritz Carlton in July 2009. When the safe house of Noordin was raided, the authorities recovered a handwritten letter where he identified Singapore with the target countries — the UK, Australia and the US. The letter said, "Singapore was drinking the blood of the Muslims". Indonesia's elite counter-terrorism unit, Detachment 88 (D88), killed both Noordin, the operational leader, and the bomb maker Azahari in Batu Malang. It was in Malang that JI Singapore leader Mas Selamat was hiding. Although Mas Selamat was arrested by the Indonesian authorities in Bintan in early 2003, he escaped from Singapore on 27 February 2008.[5] When operating in Johor, a southern state of Malaysia bordering Singapore, he was rearrested by the Malaysian Special Branch (MSB) in Malaysia on 1 April 2009. Demonstrating the priority Singapore attached to intelligence; Mas Selamat was arrested in Indonesia and Malaysia based on intelligence provided by Singapore.

Al-Qaeda-Centric Threat — Phase Two

The disruption of JI in Indonesia, Thailand and the Philippines led to its transformation. To survive, JI's key figures created a new group, Jama'ah Ansharut Tauhid (JAT). Led by Bashir, the spiritual leader of JI, JAT was formed on 27 July

2008. JAT emerged in Solo, the nerve centre of Muslim radicalism in Indonesia with bases in Central Sulawesi. Both JI and JAT leadership came from Pondok Pesantren Islam Al Mukmin, the Islam boarding school in the village of Ngruki in Solo.[6] The Ngruki network of schools has produced most of the leadership and membership of JI, JAT and several other threat groups. To date, the central figure in JAT, Bashir, held the position of *amir* (spiritual leader) from 17 September 2008 until 10 August 2010.[7] Formed as an umbrella organisation, Bashir brought together a dozen radical and political groups and funded a training camp in Aceh. Under Bashir's instructions, Thoib, JAT's treasurer, funded Ubaid for Aceh military training. A new platform with multiple groups, *Tandzim Al-Qoidah Indonesia Serambi Makkah* (Al-Qaeda in Indonesia, the Gateway to Mecca), conducted training for multiple groups to mount Mumbai-style armed assaults and suicide bombings. Until then, Singapore had prepared for responding to the suicide bombings threat. After the Aceh camp was disrupted, Singapore responded to the threat by raising a new capability to meet the challenge of a hybrid threat, reminiscent of the Mumbai attacks.

Like JI, JAT too presented a threat to Singapore. However, the Indonesian counter-terrorism leaders such as General Tito Karnavian and Ansyad Mbai working with their Malaysian, Singaporean, and Filipino counterparts did not allow JAT to grow beyond Indonesia. Despite the challenge of criminalising JAT which operated a media office in Jakarta, its operational cells were targeted by D88. The members of the JAT executive council (*majlis shura*) include Ustaz Wahyudin, the principal of the school at Ngruki, and Bashir's son, Ustaz Rasyid Ridho Bashir. Although Bashir was succeeded by Achwan as the interim Amir since May 2010, Bashir ran the group from prison.[8] A member of JAT's executive council, Muhammad Achwan, was a Majelis Mujahideen Indonesia (MMI or Mujahedeen Council of Indonesia) leader in East Java. Like Bashir, Achwan had been involved in terrorism for decades. Achwan was implicated in the bombing of a Catholic church in Malang, East Java on 24 December 1984; the bombing of the Borobudur Buddhist temple complex in Magelang, Central Java on 21 January 1985; and a failed attempt to bomb Kuta beach in Bali in March of the same year.[9] Others associated with JAT have violent histories. Mustaqim Muzayyin, an Afghan veteran, is one of the members of the JAT executive council. Also known as Abu Hawari alias Muslih Ahmad/Kamarudin, he was a former JI military instructor and Head of JI's Hudaybiyah military camp in the Philippines.[10] Likewise, Syaifuddin Umar alias Abu Fida, a Ngruki alumni and Surabaya-based JI member, previously involved in the 2003 JW Marriott bombing, and Umar Burhanuddin, involved in the 2004 Australian embassy bombing, were also members of the executive council. An Afghan veteran, Imron Baihaqi also held a position in the executive council of JAT. Also known as Mustofa alias Panatayuda, Abu Tholut was investigated for the Medan CIMB Bank robbery and the militant training camp in Aceh. The former Head of JI's Mantiqi 3 and JI's military instructor in the Philippines, Abu Tholut was also involved in the Poso conflict. Arrested in Semarang on 11 July 2003, he was charged and sentenced to eight years of imprisonment on 11 May 2004 but was released for good conduct on 13 August 2007.[11] Afif Abdul Majid, the Head of JAT's administrative office, was MMI's Head of the Solo branch and also the first Chairman of the MMI administrative office. He resigned from MMI in 2005 because he saw MMI's organisational management being no longer in accordance with his interpretation of "Islamic principles".[12] JAT's secretary for the East Java chapter and the group's spokesman, Sonhadi Bin Muhadjir, was investigated for his role in the Australian embassy bombing. He was sentenced to four years in jail in 2005 for harbouring the new JI–Al-Qaeda operational leadership Noordin M. Top and Azahari Hussein.[13]

Both Singapore and Singapore's interests overseas remained a key target of the terrorists. In Indonesia, Singapore's diplomatic missions, Singaporean tourists in Batam and Singaporean troops conducting training came under threat. When Indonesian authorities uncovered Abdullah Sunata's network in February 2010, they discovered plans to launch a Mumbai-style terrorist assault, kill President Susilo Bambang Yudhoyono and other high-profile targets during Independence Day celebrations in August, and to attack the Orchard MRT in Singapore.[14] To hit Singapore, Sonata, the leader of Mujahedeen Kompak in Indonesia worked with another Indonesian, Maulana, a member of DI in Indonesia. After completing his training in the Philippines, Maulana was based in Sabah with DI Malaysia facilitating the travel of recruits for terrorist training in the Philippines. He fought in the Poso conflict in the early 2000s, and was implicated in the assassination attempt of deputy leader of the Indonesian parliament, Matori Abdul Jalil, in 2000. The perpetrators of the assassination attempt deemed Matori Abdul Jalil to have had betrayed the Islamic cause as he had turned to the left, becoming a communist.[15] At the time of Maulana's arrest and imprisonment in Malaysia from 2003–2008, he was planning to attack the police headquarters in Jakarta. After his release, Maulana expanded his network of operatives in the region including Singaporeans and Malaysians. By transporting weapons from the Philippines, Maulana facilitated the training in Aceh in 2010. A fugitive since February 2010, the police shot dead Maulana and his two accomplices as they tried to resist arrest in Cawang, East Jakarta on 12 May 2010.[16] Ammunition for automatic weapons, a revolver and an AK-47 were recovered from the scene.[17] Maps showing Singapore's

Orchard MRT station and the zoom in map of the area in the vicinity of Orchard Road were found in a backpack in the house of Maulana.[18] The attackers planned to enter Singapore through Malaysia.

In retaliation, another DI leader, Abu Umar planned to strike Singapore targets overseas. A DI faction known as DI-Akram planned to attack the Singaporean embassy and Kebun Jeruk and Cengkareng police precints in West Jakarta in June 2011.[19] To pre-empt the attacks, police arrested 11 terrorists and raided their houses in Bogor and Jakarta from 4–11 July 2011.[20] During the arrests, ammunition and weapons including pistols, rifles, silencers and at least one sub-machine gun were seized. In addition to attacking Indonesian police officers, Abu Umar said they would pick Singaporeans coming out of the compound and would not attack Indonesians.[21] He claimed his anger against Singapore was driven by its close ties to Israel. Abu Umar's roles included organising military trainings in Mindanao, Philippines and Sulawesi, Indonesia. Like Maulana, he also coordinated the smuggling of arms and ammunitions from the Philippines into Indonesia. In retaliation, the remnants of Abu Umar's group, Farhan Zamroni alias Farhan Mujahid (Abu Umar's stepson), Mukhsin and Bayu attacked police posts in Gemblegan, Solo on 17 August 2012 and Gladag, Solo on 18 August 2012. They also shot dead a police officer in Singosaren police post in Solo on 30 August 2012.[22] On the following day, 31 August 2012, the police killed Farhan and Mukhsin in Solo and arrested Bayu in Karaganyar, Central Java.[23] Abu Umar in Pasir Putih penitentiary in Nusa Kambangan island has not rejected his violent ideology and remains a threat in the event of release.

The threat to Singapore did not only come from threat groups operating in its southern neighbourhood of Indonesia but from its northern neighbourhood of Malaysia. In addition to JI and Kumpulan Militan Malaysia, Al-Qaeda maintained a robust infrastructure in Malaysia. The key Al-Qaeda facilitator was former Captain Yazid Sufaat, formerly a biochemist of the Malaysian Army. After joining JI, he conducted bombing of churches in Indonesia. He hosted in his apartment the first two 9/11 hijackers Khalid al Midhar and Nawaz al Hazmi in January 2000 before they entered the US. Yazid was also engaged in the procurement of explosives prior to the attempt of striking Singapore. In addition to Al-Qaeda's administrative Head of operations, Tawfiq bin Attash alias Khallad, the significant Al-Qaeda personalities that visited Malaysia included Zaccaria Moussoui, the so-called 20th hijacker. Yazif facilitated his entry to the US by providing him a letter. While attempting to enrol in a flying school in Malaysia, Moussoui said to a JI Singapore member that he had visions of crashing a plane into the White House. After Moussaoui was arrested on US soil, as the terrorist was uncooperative, the US had no idea of his role and target. The US appreciated Singapore's timely assistance.

Before the JI leadership relocated to Indonesia, it was based in Malaysia from 1985–1998. Even afterwards, the JI infrastructure remained intact. In Johor, JI leaders Wan Min Wan Mat and Noordin ran the Lukmanul Hakim Islamic Boarding School, the JI school in Ulu Tiram, Malaysia. Started by Abdussalam bin Abu Thalaibi, JI Malaysia was headed by Abu Hanafiah and Abu Bakar Bafana. JI Malaysia recruited and trained Singaporeans, Indonesians and Malaysians and had an estimated 200 members. Although the Malaysian Special Branch effectively dismantled KMM, JI and Al-Qaeda, the groups revived after the repeal of the Internal Security Act (ISA). Many operators and facilitators of KMM, JI and Al-Qaeda joined Ajnad al-Sham, IS and Jabat al-Nusra. Yazid Sufaat, who headed Al-Qaeda's anthrax programme was rear-rested for creating Al-Qaeda in Malaysia and sending Malaysian militants to Syria. Despite insurmountable legal challenges by the repeal of the ISA, the Malaysian Special Branch Counter Terrorism Division led by Datuk Ayub Khan was effective.

IS-Centric Threat — Phase One

With the rise of the Islamic State of Iraq and Syria (ISIS) in 2013–2014, the Al-Qaeda-centric threat reoriented to an IS-centric threat in Malaysia, Singapore, Indonesia and the Philippines. The ideology of IS was propagated by Aman Abdurrachman alias Oman Rochman/Abu Sulaiman, the Indonesian ideologue and leader of Jamaah Tauhid wal Jihad who translated the writings of Abu Muhammed al Maqdisi. Abu Muhammed al Maqdisi was the mentor of Abu Musab al Zarqawi, the founding father of IS. Amam was briefly Head of JAT's executive council and worked together with Bashir in prison.[24] A legally elusive group for the government to handle, JAT operated both politically and militarily. Although the group was not designated as a terrorist group by the Indonesian government, both JI and JAT were designated "Foreign Terrorist Organisations" by Western governments. Indonesia was reluctant to criminalise its terrorist groups and permitted their support activity — propaganda, fund raising, training and procurement. Like JI, starting from Solo, JAT influence spread throughout Indonesia. JAT established a modest presence in the Philippines for training, Thailand for procuring weapons and Malaysia for transit, but could not seed a presence in Singapore. Although Singapore's tight security created a hostile environment for such groups, Singaporeans accessed Anwar al Awlaki's and Abu Muhammed al Maqdisi's writings on the Web.

Until the spread of ISIS/IS ideology, JAT conducted terrorist attacks in Indonesia including suicide attacks. With the emergence of ISIS, the *jihad* arena shifted to Syria and Iraq. Although Southeast Asians were willing to kill and die in the region, they preferred to do so in the Levant. The turning point was when under the leadership of Bashir, 22 prisoners pledged their allegiance to IS in July 2014. Although JI remained with Al-Qaeda, JAT embraced IS ideology. Starting from late 2013, two dozen groups in the region, most notably in Indonesia, support ISIS and its successor IS.

(1) Ring Banten (a DI faction)

Supporting ISIS: November 2013.

Pledging allegiance to IS: probably April 2014.

(2) Mujahidin Indonesia Timur (MIT)

Pledging allegiance to IS: July 2014.

(3) Jamaah Tauhid wal Jihad (used to be the name of Aman Abdurrahman's followers)

Pledging allegiance to IS: April 2014.

(4) Forum Aktivis Syariah Islam (FAKSI) (since December 2014 became Forum Komunikasi Dunia Islam [FKDI]/Forum Kajian Dunia Islam [FKDI])

Pledging allegiance to IS: April 2014–present.

(5) Pendukung dan Pembela Daulah (PPD)/Forum Pendukung Daulah Islamiyah/Anshorud Daulah/Panitia Bersama Pendukung dan Pembela Daulah/Lajnah Anshoru Daulah

Pledging allegiance to IS: July 2014.

After the government's ban on support for IS, it withdrew its support for IS.

Since October 2014, the group metamorphosed into The Amir Institute.

(6) Gerakan Reformasi Islam (GARIS)

Pledging allegiance to IS: March 2014.

Since the government's ban on support for IS, GARIS no longer supports IS.

(7) Asybal Tauhid Indonesia

Pledging allegiance to IS: March 2014.

It is likely that the group also pledges allegiance to IS until now.

(8) Kongres Umat Islam Bekasi (KUIB)

Pledging allegiance to IS: February 2014–present.

(9) Umat Islam Nusantara (UIN)

Pledging allegiance to IS: February 2014.

It is likely that the group also pledges allegiance to IS until now.

(10) Ikhwan Muwahid Indunisy fie Jazirah al-Muluk (Ambon)

Pledging allegiance to IS: July 2014.

(11) IS Aceh (led by Abu Jundullah)

Pledging allegiance to IS: July 2014.

The group's current activity is unknown.

(12) Ansharul Khilafah Jawa Timur

Pledging allegiance to IS: July 2014–present.

(13) Halawi Makmun Group

Pledging allegiance to IS: February 2014–November 2014 (Halawi Makmun passed away on 20 November 2014).

(14) Gerakan Tauhid Lamongan

The leader (Zainal Anshori) pledged allegiance to IS on February 2014.

Currently the group does not support IS.

(15) Khilafatul Muslimin

Supports IS: July 2014–present.

(16) Jamaah Ansharut Tauhid (JAT)

Pledging allegiance to IS: July 2014–present.

(17) Laskar Jundullah

Pledging allegiance to IS: (likely from) July 2014–present.

(18) Mujahidin Indonesia Barat

Pledging allegiance to IS: July 2014–present.

(19) DKM Masjid Al Fataa (Al Fataa Mosque Administration, Central Jakarta)

Supports IS (organising pro-IS events): December 2014–present.

On 4 August 2014, the Indonesian government announced a ban on support for ISIS. Indonesia warned its citizens not to join the group's fight in Syria and Iraq. In an attempt to curtail its growth, the government rejected and banned the teachings of ISIS. However, there is no full-fledged law banning assistance to or involvement in foreign terrorist organisations including ISIS.

Many groups supporting ISIS/IS went underground and a few dismantled their structures. Indonesian groups supporting IS as of February 2015 are:

(1) Ring Banten
(2) Mujahidin Indonesia Timur (MIT)
(3) Jamaah Tauhid wal Jihad (Aman Abdurrahman's followers)
(4) Forum Aktivis Syariah Islam (FAKSI)/Forum Komunikasi Dunia Islam (FKDI)/Forum Kajian Dunia Islam (FKDI)
(5) Asybal Tauhid Indonesia
(6) Kongres Umat Islam Bekasi (KUIB)
(7) Umat Islam Nusantara (UIN)
(8) Ikhwan Muwahid Indunisy fie Jazirah al-Muluk (Ambon)
(9) Ansharul Khilafah Jawa Timur
(10) Jamaah Ansharut Tauhid (JAT)
(11) Laskar Jundullah
(12) Mujahidin Indonesia Barat
(13) DKM Masjid Al Fataa (Al Fataa Mosque Administration) (Central Jakarta)

With the creation of this ecosystem of groups in 2013, several thousands of Southeast Asians were influenced by ISIS/IS ideology. A few hundred Southeast Asians travelled to Syria and Iraq starting in 2014. To manage the growing Southeast Asian presence in Syria, IS supported the creation of a dedicated group — Katibah Nusantara Lid Daulah Islamiyah. The group communicated with like-minded Southeast Asians with the goal of recruiting and facilitating Southeast Asians to travel to Syria to defend the Islamic caliphate, and also to attack against governments that repressed caliphate supporters. Katibah Nusantara is the first Southeast Asian group that has direct operational links to IS. Although a few Singaporeans travelled to Syria to join IS, Katibah Nusantara is led by Indonesians and Malaysians operating in Iraq and Syria. Another group in Indonesia, Ansharul Khilafah, recruits Indonesians by disseminating propaganda. A network of cells of Ansharul Khilafah is active in Malang in the East Java province of Indonesia, and used a village mosque in Sempu as their headquarters.

In the Philippines and Malaysia, both existing and new groups support IS. ASG and Bangsamoro Islamic Freedom Fighters (BIFF) pledged allegiance to IS in August 2014. Abu Sayyaf leader, Isnilon Hapilon, and other masked men swore their allegiance or *bay'ah* to the Islamic State caliph Abu Bakr al-Baghdadi in late 2014. Abu Sayyaf declared in a message: "...stop supporting America in its killing of our Muslim brothers in Iraq and Syria, especially the mujahideen of the Islamic State." Abu Sayyaf kidnapped two Germans in exchange for ransom and demanded the cessation of coalition airstrikes against IS in October 2014. In Malaysia, Revolusi Islam and Jamaat ISIS Malaysia were created by IS supporters. The leadership of these groups were arrested by the Malaysian authorities. In addition to these two groups, there are other extremist groups and cells either affiliated or seeking affiliation to IS operating in Malaysia. Unlike Singapore, which was able to preventively detain suspects after it repealed the ISA, Malaysia could not because the requirement to provide counter-terrorism evidence in an open court compared to intelligence in an ISA hearing of introducing challenged the Malaysian authorities. Malaysia is in the process of introducing a new anti-terrorism act and it will include provisions that allow for detention without trial and the implementation of the Electronic Monitoring Device (EMD). As the security of Singapore and Malaysia are closely interlinked, the deterioration of security in Malaysia could adversely affect Singapore's security.

IS-Centric Threat — Phase Two

A new threat landscape emerged in Southeast Asia with the rise of ISIS and declaration of an Islamic caliphate. With the West supporting regime change in Syria and Western media highlighting the atrocities by the Bashar al-Assad regime, Muslims from worldwide including Southeast Asians began travelling to Syria. Western intelligence services realised in 2012 that foreign fighters in the ranks of Al-Qaeda's al-Nusra Front in Syria and Islamic State of Iraq (the forerunner of ISIS) and a few other groups radicalised their own Muslim communities and planned attacks in their countries. Their governments became more circumspect of supporting foreign fighters and their respective groups. To most, the Syrian regime was a bigger threat than the foreign fighters and the radicalisation of their own communities. By 2013, the West realised that Al-Qaeda, IS and other Salafist groups eclipsed the threat posed by nationalist groups fighting in Syria. By that time, ISIS had grown and captured parts of Syria and Iraq. In 2014, ISIS captured Mosul and declared a caliphate, and the influx of Muslim foreign fighters to Syria and Iraq including from Southeast Asia grew exponentially. The IS caliphate appealed to a vulnerable segment of Muslim communities worldwide. IS online propaganda indoctrinated and its tradecraft provided the skills to a tiny segment of Muslim communities to advocate, support and conduct attacks on their soil. Although social media emerged in 2005, it was not until the advent of ISIS that social media platforms were fully harnessed. After IS radicalised

Muslims, it urged the latter to attack governments participating in the coalition instead of travelling to the caliphate. From Canada to the US, France to Belgium, Copenhagen to Australia, radicalised Muslims mounted attacks on their soil or in neighbouring countries.

Singapore had twin concerns: foreign fighters returning to attack Singapore and radicalised Singaporeans and residents attacking Singapore. Singapore too experienced the transit of both recruits and a few trained foreign fighters. A French national, Mehdi Nemmouche, travelled to Malaysia and then flew to Thailand before visiting Singapore in early 2014. He travelled in Asia to disguise his travel to Turkey, the gateway to Syria. By travelling to Asia, he wanted to show that he was a tourist and not a terrorist. Had the French, or other services who knew of Nemmouch, alerted the Asian services, they would have watched him if not apprehended him. There were gaps in cooperation, especially sharing of intelligence. Upon his return to Europe, Nemmouche attacked a Jewish museum in May 2014, killing three and injuring one.

The international intelligence community perceived foreign fighters posing a greater threat than the IS external wing. As the IS external wing was in a nascent phase, to the guardians of security, the principal threat to their countries originated from foreign fighters. Although they realised that the developments in Iraq and Syria galvanised segments of their own Muslim communities, to them the threat stemming from foreign fighters was imminent. In the West, especially in Canada, Europe and Australia, their own Muslim migrant and diaspora communities became a concern. Despite living in the West, they had failed to integrate and assimilate with the mainstream communities. They became a threat not only to their countries of domicile but to countries of their origin and others, especially those who joined the coalition. In Singapore, the Muslim leaders led the fight against terrorism and extremism. The Muslim community identified with the government. The government working with their Muslim community partners engaged the tiny minority of Muslims vulnerable to radicalisation.

The idea of an Islamic caliphate and the imposition of Islamic law resonate with a larger community of Southeast Asians. Nonetheless, while the brutality of IS repels mainstream Southeast Asians, it appeals to radical Southeast Asians. Those attracted by IS ideology join the ecosystem of groups, cells and individuals that have emerged in Southeast Asia. Those who have the means to travel to the Levant, take flight. As there is no structured IS group operating in Singapore, those who cannot travel may support IS aims and objectives in other ways including by conducting attacks. Today, the dominant threat to Singapore is from home-grown terrorism. A handful of Singaporeans are influenced by extremist sites.

Extremist sites seek to legitimise the use of violence to uphold a political agenda. Southeast Asians visit several hundred extremist sites worldwide. Of about 300 extremist sites in Southeast Asia, more sites are posting IS propaganda. At least 100 are websites and blogs and most are in Bahasa Indonesia. The remaining 200 are Facebook accounts. The increase in number of media platforms over the years allows any individual to be a disseminator of extremist materials. Terrorist and extremist propaganda proliferated in the region with the creation of dedicated media wings of terrorist groups or the paring of media groups with terrorist groups in Indonesia.

The Southeast Asian governments and their partners are in the initial stages of addressing the online threat. Although Singapore has made progress monitoring 700 key sites, considering the magnitude of the online threat, counter-measures are insufficient. It is a complex threat that requires several partner inputs. To counter this growing threat, continuous efforts to counter the pernicious ideology through digital engagement campaigns are necessary. Furthermore, the online effort will have to be coupled with offline community engagement initiatives. Singapore's community leaders and teachers should lead the fight, and friends and families should stay vigilant and alert the government to ensure their loved ones are not misled by the misguided.

State and Societal Response

In the backdrop of increased globalisation, mitigating the extant and emerging terrorist threat to Singapore is complex. It requires preventive, protective and pre-emptive measures by a range of agencies working together. In the event these counter-measures fail to work, the government should also have a consequence management plan to deal with a successful terrorist attack. The essential first step to protect Singapore should be to understand the changing threat landscape. Of the spectrum of Asian threat groups, the two groups that presented the greatest threat to Singapore were Al-Qaeda and JI. When a Muslim Singaporean informed the government of suspicious individuals travelling to Afghanistan, Singapore became the first country to develop and share intelligence with the region about the Al-Qaeda-linked terrorist network in Southeast Asia. Singapore's success was its outreach to the community after 11 September 2001. Community engagement led to the discovery of other personalities engaged in extremist and terrorist activity. The government of Singapore constantly reaching out to the community made Singaporeans become the state's precious eyes and ears. Singapore leaders personally became involved in engaging the communities. With the discovery of the JI threat, then-Prime Minister Goh Chok Tong held dialogues with the leaders of the Muslim community, a practice that continues to date. Singapore's Deputy Prime Ministers, Wong Kan Seng and Teo Chee Hean engaged the communities too.

Based on the interviews of JI leaders and members by the case officers, psychologists and religious clerics, Singaporean leaders understood quite early on the threat of ideological extremism. They knew that segments of Singapore's Muslim community were vulnerable to the threat of radicalisation by the vicious ideology disseminated by violent extremist groups. As these threat groups were active outside Singapore and were not within the reach of Singapore, the government created programmes to reach out to vulnerable segments of the Muslim population. After the Al-Qaeda–JI threat was dismantled, a number of Singaporean Muslims that had either joined terrorist groups or planned terrorist attacks were detained. They could be held indefinitely. Singapore had to develop strategies to meet the contemporary challenge of ideological extremism that was radicalising and had radicalised a segment of its community. To continuously reach out to the community, Singapore's MHA has revitalised its robust Community Engagement Programme (CEP). To rehabilitate the JI's unrepentant hardcore and home-grown terrorists in custody, the Religious Rehabilitation Group (RRG) continues to search for new ways to engage and rehabilitate. These initiatives started as programmes unique to Singapore's context of terrorist threat management. RRG, a group of Muslim clerics in Singapore, works with the International Centre for Political Violence and Terrorism Research (ICPVTR) to innovate multifaceted rehabilitation to digital rehabilitation. Such programmes which aim to reduce the regional and global threat resulted in a series of conferences including the inaugural International Conference on Terrorist Rehabilitation in 2009 to the East Asia Summit Symposium on Religious Rehabilitation and Social Reintegration in 2015. Singapore's counter- and de-radicalisation initiatives offered insight into existing and aspiring programmes worldwide. The ICPVTR builds the capacity of domestic and foreign partners to better understand and respond to the threat of terrorism and extremism.

To secure Singapore from harm, the government adopted a threat-driven response. Then-Deputy Prime Minister and Coordinating Minister for Security and Defence S. Jayakumar announced on 26 October 2005 that Singapore was developing an early warning system, Risk Assessment and Horizon Scanning (RAHS), to identify and assess new emerging threats to national security. The system, developed by the National Security Coordination Secretariat (NSCS), became operational in 2007. To ensure all agencies of the ministries of defence and home affairs provided their inputs, NSCS was located at the Prime Minister's Office.

In addition to its Immigration and Checkpoints Authority, the Singapore Police Force (SPF), one of the finest in Asia, works closely with ISD to understand and respond to the threat. The intelligence-led approach made Singapore create new structures and strengthen existing structures to meet the threat. For instance, the SPF established a Police Mass Rapid Transit (MRT) Unit on 15 August 2005. To meet the rising threat to land transportation, the MRT Unit began operational patrols on the MRT network to protect the public transportation system. Personnel from the Special Operations Command (SOC) and the Gurkha Contingent (GC), two elite units, were deployed to complement other police officers on patrol. In addition, the Police Coast Guard (PCG) stepped up its effort to inspect ferries and other vessels in Singapore territorial waters. After the SuperFerry 14 was bombed by JI–ASG–RSM in the Philippines killing 118 passengers, Singapore invested significantly to improve its ferry security. With several threat groups developing both surface and underwater capabilities, Singapore enhanced its maritime security by adopting a coordinated and multilayered security regime. With the threat to land and maritime domains, Singapore created Singapore Maritime Crisis Centre (SMCC) and other capabilities.

Singapore believed in the need to strengthen existing and create new specialist units to fight terrorism. Specialised military, law enforcement and civil defence units of Singapore are the Singapore Special Operations Force, the Special Operations Command, and the Chemical, Biological, Radiological, and Explosive Defence Group. The Singapore Armed Forces (SAF) received additional powers with the parliament passing an amendment to the SAF Act in May 2007. In their new role, a few thousand SAF personnel support police and perform security operations in designated areas. They are empowered in a military security role to search, detain and use force against terror suspects.

Singapore learnt from all the major attacks — 9/11 (11 September 2001), Bali (12 October 2002), Madrid (11 March 2004), London (7 July 2005), Mumbai (26 November 2008), etc. The terrorist attacks in London against the underground tubes and a bus led Singapore to conduct Exercise Northstar V in January 2006. The entire government-and-society approach adopted by Singapore was evident when it invited 22 agencies, 2,000 emergency personnel and 3,400 commuters. They responded to simulated terrorist bomb attacks on four MRT stations and one bus interchange resulting in 500 mock casualties. In addition to raising awareness and preparedness, the exercise tested Singapore's readiness, effectiveness and coordination of government agencies to respond to a terrorist attack.

Robust counter-terrorism structures put in place to fight the threat of Al-Qaeda and JI immediately after 2001 forms the foundation to fight the threat of IS today. Singapore's global profile, its relations with the West, especially the US, and joining the coalition of countries fighting IS has made it a legitimate target among extremists and terrorists in the region. Despite regional efforts to bring down IS networks, the threat of ideological extremism and operational terrorism to Singapore persists and may grow.

Conclusion

Today, the world faces an unprecedented threat. With the insurgencies in Afghanistan and Iraq checkmating the Western armies, insurgency, terrorism and extremism is on the ascent. Lack of visionary leadership, political will, and international neglect of conflict zones is threatening the safety and security of the community of nations. Although Singapore is one of the safest countries today, the global threat environment is testing the resolve of Singapore's government, its citizens and residents to secure the Lion City from harm.

With Singapore joining the coalition to dismantle IS, will the threat to Singapore grow? Although Indonesia and Malaysia oppose IS, Singapore is identified by the Southeast Asian terrorists as the region's closest ally of the US. Furthermore, Singapore is considered the region's hub for counter-terrorism intelligence, education and training. Although Singapore's relations with the West and its hub status are its strengths, they also make Singapore a prized terrorist target.

The security landscape of Singapore is linked to the regional and global threat landscape. The security of Singapore cannot any longer be separated from the developments in the region. The developments in Iraq and Syria have· a profound impact on the stability and security of Southeast Asia including Singapore. The manifestation of the threat can be characterised in five areas:

(1) Home-grown terrorism from self-radicalised cells and individuals.
(2) IS sharing expertise with or funding pro-IS groups to mount attacks.
(3) Foreign fighter returnees with the expertise of mounting attacks.
(4) Creating the nuclei of new threat groups.
(5) IS fledgling external wing conducting attacks.

Singapore should continue to work with the international community to address the reality of global conflicts. Much of the conflicts in the world from Iraq to Libya and now Syria are man-made and they could have been avoided.

The pockets of protests in Syria for democracy during the Arab Spring received Western support. With the West harnessing NGOs, especially human rights groups, to promote democracy, the protests grew. The highly popular Bashar al-Assad and his regime in Syria responded with a heavy hand. The initial appeal of Muslims travelling to Syria was the brutality of the Syrian regime. In addition to motivated and experienced fighters in Iraq, Muslim youth from the Muslim world and the West travelled to Syria. The eagerness with which the US and Europe subscribed to supporting the anti-Syrian drama transformed Syria into a terrorist Disneyland. Such conflicts are the primary generators of extremist ideologies and terrorist groups. Although Singapore is a small state, it is a mini-superpower. With its reputation for good governance and fortitude, Singapore exercises disproportionate influence in the region and beyond. Singapore's approach can influence other powers to think and act strategically. The contemporary wave of terrorism was shaped by10,000 foreign fighters in Afghanistan's 10-year war. Considering the presence of over 30,000 Sunni and Shia foreign fighters in Syria within five years, the blow back of the Syrian conflict is likely to endure for many years.[*]

Notes

1. Ministry of Home Affairs, "White Paper: The Jemaah Islamiyah Arrests and the Threat of Terrorism." Retrieved 17 April 2015, from https://www.mha.gov.sg/get_blob.aspx?file_id=252_complete.pdf.
2. Rohan Gunaratna, "Sustaining the War on Terrorism: Singapore's International Counterterrorism Cooperation," *RSIS Commentaries* no. 139, 2013. Retrieved 20 April 2015, from http://www.rsis.edu.sg/wp-content/uploads/2014/07/CO13139.pdf.
3. Bilveer Singh, *ASEAN, Australia and the Management of the Jemaah Islamiyah Threat* (Australia: Strategic and Defence Studies Centre, Australian National University, 2003).
4. "All in Changi Plot Nabbed," *The Straits Times*, 2009. Retrieved 20 April 2015, from http://www.straitstimes.com/Breaking%2BNews/Singapore/Story/STIStory_395651.html.
5. MAJ Alan Foo Chai Kwan, "Countering Radical Islamic Terrorism in Southeast Asia — A Case Study on Jemaah Islamiyah (JI) Network," *Pointer*, 35(2), 2009. Retrieved 20 April 2015, from http://www.mindef.gov.sg/imindef/publications/pointer/journals/2009/v35n2/feature4.html.
6. Al Mukmin Islamic Boarding School website. Retrieved 20 April 2015, from http://www.al-mukmin.com/.

[*]Acknowledgements: I wish to thank Vidia Arianti and Jasminder Singh of the International Centre for Political Violence and Terrorism Research (ICPVTR) for reviewing this article.

7 "Ustad Achwan Gantikan Posisi Ba'asyir di JAT (Ustad Achwan Replaced Ba'asyir's Position in JAT)," *VIVAnews,* 2010. Retrieved 20 April 2015, from http://nasional. vivanews.com/news/read/170145-ustad-achwan-gantikan-posisi-ba-asyir-di-jat.

8 "Shoemaker Stoking the Flames of Sharia State," *The Jakarta Post*, 2010. Retrieved 20 April 2015, from http://www.thejakartapost.com/news/2010/08/27/shoemaker-stoking-flames-sharia-state.html-0.

9 "Itu Ledakan Dan Bom Bikinan Malang (That Explosion and the Bomb Was Made in Malang)," *Tempo Online*. Retrieved 1 November 2010, from http://majalah. tempointeraktif.com/id/arsip/1986/01/25/NAS/mbm.19860125.NAS36481.id.html.

10 Nasir Abbas, *Membongkar Jamaah Islamiyah* [Dismantling of Jamaah Islamiyah] (Jakarta: Grafindo Khazanah Ilmu, 2005), p. 22.

11 "Misteri Sosok Abu Tholut (The Mysterious Figure Abu Tholut)," *eramuslim*, 4 November 2010. Retrieved 5 November 2015, from http://www.eramuslim.com/ berita/analisa/kontroversi-sosok-abu-tholut.htm.

12 Muh Taufiq's interview with a contact close to MMI leadership in Bandung, 8 January 2006.

13 Rendi A. Witular and Hasyim Widhiarto, "Next in Line: Potential Leaders of Underground Jihadist Movement," *The Jakarta Post*, 11 August 2010, Retrieved 7 November 2010, from http://www.thejakartapost.com/news/2010/08/11/next-line-potential-leaders-underground-jihadist-movement.html.

14 Wahyudi Soeriaatmadja and Lynn Lee, "Orchard MRT Station Targeted by Terrorists," *The Straits Times*, 19 May 2010. Retrieved 20 May 2015, from http://news.asianone. com/News/the+Straits+Times/Story/A1Story/20100519-216992.html.

15 "Recycling Militants in Indonesia: Darul Islam and the Australian Embassy Bombing," ICG Asia Report no. 92, 22 February 2005. Retrieved 20 May 2015, from http://www. crisisgroup.org/en/regions/asia/south-east-asia/indonesia/092-recycling-militants-in-indonesia-darul-islam-and-the-australian-embassy-bombings.aspx.

16 "Indonesian Terror Suspects Killed in Raids," *The Straits Times*, 13 May 2010.

17 "Update 2: Police Confirm Five Terrorists Killed in Two Dramatic Jakarta Raids," *The Jakarta Globe*. Retrieved 12 May 2010, from http://www.thejakartaglobe.com/home/ update-2-police-confirm-five-terrorists-killed-in-two-dramatic-jakarta-raids/374631.

18 "Indonesia Gathering Evidence to See If Orchard MRT Was Potential Target," *Channel NewsAsia*. Retrieved 24 June 2010, from http://www.channelnewsasia.com/stories/ southeastasia/view/1060847/1/.html.

19 "How Indonesian Extremists Regroup," *Crisis Group Asia Report N°228*, 16 July 2012, pp. 10–11.

20 Mega Putra Ratya, "Kelompok Abu Omar Berencana Serang 2 Polsek di Jakarta Barat (Abu Omar's Group Was Planning to Attack Two Police Stations in West Jakarta)," *DetikNews*, 14 November 2011. Retrieved 3 September 2012, from http://news.detik. com/read/2011/11/14/172435/1767190/10/kelompok-abu-omar-berencana-serang-2-polsek-di-jakarta-barat.

21 "Singapore Embassy 'Targeted by Terrorists'," *The Jakarta Globe*, 21 July 2011. Retrieved 3 September 2012, from http://www.thejakartaglobe.com/news/singapore-embassy-targeted-by-terrorists/454269.

22 Ferdinan, "Pelaku Penembakan Pospam Gemblegan 2 Orang (There Were 2 Gunmen in the Pospam Gemblegan Shooting)," *DetikNews*, 17 August 2012. Retrieved 3 September 2012, from http://news.detik.com/read/2012/08/17/051828/1993813/10/pelaku-penembakan-pospam-gemblegan-2-orang. Also see "Pospam Gladag Dilempar Benda Yang Meledak, Tak Ada Korban (An Explosive Object Was Hurled at the Gladag Pospan, There Were No Casualties)," *Bandar Lampung News*, 19 August 2012. Retrieved 3 September 2012, from http://bandarlampungnews.com/cetak/index.php?k=hukum&i=12696-Pospam%20Gladag%20Dilempar%20Benda%20Yang%20Meledak,%20Tak%20Ada%20Korban.

23 Ade Rizal, "2 Teroris Solo Yang Tewas Masih ABG (The 2 Terrorists in Solo Who Were Killed Were Teenagers)," *Tribun News*, 1 September 2012. Retrieved 3 September 2012, from http://m.tribunnews.com/2012/09/01/2-teroris-solo-yang-tewas-masih-abg.

24 "Polisi Kembali Tangkap Tiga Teroris (The Police Re-Arrested Three Terrorists)," *Tempo Interaktif*, 2010. Retrieved 25 March 2010, from http://www.tempointeraktif.com/hg/hukum/2010/03/24/brk,20100324-235275,id.html.

Chapter 14

Managing Religious Diversity in Singapore: Context and Challenges

Mohammad Alami Musa and Mohamed Imran Mohamed Taib

Introduction

Singapore will celebrate her 50th year of independence in 2015. In spite of its small size and lack of natural resources, Singapore has achieved success to become one of the world's leading economies. Besides sustained economic prosperity, a high level of social cohesion has characterised much of Singapore's development over a span of 50 years, despite being the most religiously diverse nation.[1] The absence of social upheaval since independence can be attributed to religious leaders who readily embraced the ethos of peaceful coexistence and cooperated with the state that played an effective custodial role through a strong legal framework, and strict enforcement of policies to manage religious diversity. It was evident that there is strong political resolve and social commitment in safeguarding the foundational principle of secularism without curtailing the freedom to practice one's own religion. This tripartite state–community–religious sector relationship has been successful in keeping religious and racial discord at bay.

From its beginnings, Singapore can be considered as a "multicultural society". Here, multiculturalism is not defined simply by the presence and experience of diversity within a society; it is also a political process that "describes a set of policies, the aim of which is to manage and institutionalize diversity by putting people into ethnic and cultural boxes, defining individual needs and rights by virtue of the boxes to shape public policy".[2] Much has been written to discuss the management of ethnic and religious diversity in Singapore.[3] The "management of religious diversity" therefore, forms an integral part of governance in Singapore. This is even so, given that Singapore gained independence in 1965 amidst a tumultous period. A momentary merger with Malaysia had exposed the deep tensions that run along ethnic lines, particularly between the Chinese and Malay populations. Coupled with this was an irreconciliable ideological difference over the concepts of "Malaysia for Malaysians" and "Malay Malaysia". When a series of racial riots broke out in 1964, leading to an eventual separation between Malaysia and Singapore an year later, the PAP leadership then knew that diversity can tear society apart if not managed wisely. Traumatic events such as the racial riots proved crucial in shaping the political thinking of the early years of independence. A new national identity based on racial and religious harmony had to be forged.

It is therefore the aim of this paper to discuss the context and challenges that generate policy responses in post-independent Singapore. The task of documenting this process should help to ensure that good practices in governance are preserved for the memory of the next generation as Singapore enters her next phase of development.

The Early Years, 1965–1980: Religion as a Partner in Building Social Cohesion

By the end of the 19th century, Singapore had become a highly diverse society. The turn of the century saw the Chinese make up 74% of the population; the "natives of the Malay Archipelago" stood at 14%; "natives of India" stood at 8%; Eurasians at 2%; Europeans at 1%; and "other nationalities" at 1% (principally made up of the Arabs, Jews, Sinhalese and Japanese).[4] Under colonial rule, Singapore thus became what is known as a "plural society", which signified a situation where "different sections of the community live side by side, but separately, within the same political unit" and they meet "only in the market place" while the division of labour was divided "along racial lines".[5]

At the point of independence, the racial composition did not differ much from the immediate post-war period as shown in Table 1. This composition remains consistent throughout Singapore's developmental years till the present, despite changes in total population.

Table 1.   Racial Composition in Singapore.

	Percent			
	1931	1947	1957	1970
Total	100.0	100.0	100.0	100.0
Malays	11.6	12.1	13.6	15.0
Chinese	75.1	77.8	75.4	76.2
Indians	9.4	7.7	9.0	7.0
Others	3.9	2.4	2.0	1.8

Source: Department of Statistics Singapore, "Report of the Census of Population 1970 Singapore," Vol. 1.

To a large extent, post-1965 Singapore adopted a neat categorisation of ethnicity.[6] Each race was considered distinct and separate, or what is to be known as the CMIO model.[7] But unlike Malaysia's emphasis on the *bumiputera* (indigenous Malays), Singapore adopted "multi-racialism" as a founding principle of the state.[8] This was expressed by then-Minister of Law and Development, as "one of the cornerstones of the policy of the Government" where "[w]e are a nation comprising people of various races who constitute her citizens, and our citizens are equal regardless of differences of race, language, culture and religion".[9]

Race, Not Religion as Primary Focus

Significantly, "religion" was not a major component in the classification system emerging from colonial administrative rule: communal race was the lens through which society was classified and managed. Thus, it was only in 1980 that the item "religion" was canvassed in the population census.[10]

The primary focus on "race" and not religion was crucial in understanding the early years of independence. Singapore's independence was grounded in racial tensions and traumas of communal riots.[11] Three major riots had occurred in early Singapore history: the Maria Hertogh riots of 1950, the Hock Lee Bus riot of 1955 and the Prophet Muhammad's Birthday procession riot of 1964.[12] While the riot of 1955 was primarily based on industrial grievances and the 1964 riot was a clash between segments of the Chinese and Malay populations, it was probably the Maria Hertogh riot of 1950 that had a direct connection to religion.

Yet, the riot was not an interreligious conflict but rather, an outpour of rage over what the ethnic Malays considered as insensitive and unjust rulings of the colonial court over custody issues of a Dutch girl who had converted to Islam, raised by a Muslim family and married to a Muslim man. The outrage was then targeted towards the European and Eurasian communities who were seen as collaborators of the colonial government. If religion was the motivation in the outrage, it was primarily because it was intertwined in the identity of the ethnic Malays who were largely Muslims, and not as an expression of one religion against another.[13] Therefore, it can be argued that the manifestations of tensions in Singapore's early existence prior to independence were largely communal and not religious in nature.[14] This is consistent with many analyses that highlighted intercommunal issues as a primary consequence of colonial Britain's policies which seek to legitimise and strengthen colonial rule over the highly diverse population — thereby, leading to segregated communities with intense competition over resources filtered through colonial administrators.[15]

Race was the source of the traumatic experience leading up to the independence and early independence period. However, religion was viewed favourably as a positive force and a vehicle to maintain unity in a nascent city-state of Singapore. This view could be due to the role that the Inter-Religious Organisation (IRO) had played in the immediate aftermath of the Maria Hertogh riots. The IRO had been proactive in mobilising faith leaders to put forth the peaceful nature of religion and played a significant role in the reconciliation process within the population.[16] Religion, thus, was seen by the first generation of political leaders as a potential partner in the process of nation-building.

Religion as "Cultural Ballast": Religious Knowledge in Schools

In tracing the the role of religion, Tamney (1996)[17] noted that the "government sees [the] utilitarian benefit of religion to provide values conducive to productive economy and moral ballast for society to protect itself from the ills of westernisation". This early attitude can be seen from the Goh Keng Swee Report (1978),[18] which highlighted "the dangers of secular education in a foreign tongue" and "the risk of losing the traditional values of one's own people and the acquisition of the more spurious fashions of the west". By the mid-1970s, Singapore had gone full swing on her path of rapid economic development. Along with modernisation, there was fear that the current traditional values of society might be eroded by a more "hippy and decadent culture of the West". The anxiety on the part of the state towards the weakening of social ethos was noted by Hui (1984),[19] related particularly to the youths' "lack of a sense of purpose, community spirit and citizenship" emerging from importation of "individual-centred life-style" of "western culture".

Religion was thus seen as a "cultural ballast" to stem social decadence. In other words, morality was tied to religion and religious instruction was therefore needed to bolster the morals of a young nation that embarked on the path of modernisation. Mr Ong Teng Cheong pushed for this idea, a year after the Goh Keng Swee Report, through another Report titled "Report on Moral Education". This 1979 document reaffirmed that "religious studies help to reinforce the teaching of moral values".[20] It became the basis for subsequent introduction of compulsory Religious Knowledge (RK) in national schools in 1982.

Nonetheless, the road to implementation of RK was not without concerns. They were particularly related to the secular basis of the state. Calling it a "daunting task", a *Straits Times* editorial on 2 October 1979, cautioned that "the Education Ministry will do well to examine most thoroughly its intention to include religious instruction in the moral education programme for schools" and to "tread carefully...especially in multi-religious Singapore".[21] The Chairman of the Moral Education Committee, Mr Ong Teng Cheong did acknowledge that introducing religion in national schools would be a challenge, but rejected the idea that this would undermine the secular basis of the state. He noted that the MEC's recommendation emphasised the "ethical rather than the religious in content and stresses universal values such as honesty and integrity. But insofar as religion reinforces ethics, the MEC encourages a modification of the Education Ministry's policy of not allowing religious teaching in schools".[22]

The Period of Religious Resurgence, 1980–1990: Religion as Potential Conflict

The 1980s were markedly different in mood. Prior to the '80s, there was an academic consensus that as society modernises, religion will lose its significance and becomes a matter of private choice or conscience.[23] This was known as the "secularisation" thesis that was in vogue in the 1960s. However, what emerged thereafter was a new form of religiosity that "do[es] not recognise a division between the 'public' and 'private'; God is everywhere and thus everything is under scrutiny, nothing is 'private'".[24] Such a religiosity insists that God and faith should be at the heart of society and embedded within all society's structures and institutions, paving the way for a conflation of religion and politics in a new unprecedented scale.[25]

It became clear then that this new form of religiosity can have an impact on the social compact of Singapore. While the roots of religious resurgence remain at the global front of a volatile geopolitical situation, there was a corresponding fervour among sections of the religious communities in Singapore. Yet, it can be argued that the primary face of the resurgence period was an increasingly exclusivist expression of faith. This posed a new set of challenges to the state. In a Report of a national survey on "Religion in Singapore", religion was ranked high in importance in life, particularly within the Christian community (71.6%) and the Muslim community (79.6%) — two communities that had experienced a phenomenal revivalist phase.[26] A new context had thus emerged.

Impact of Religious Resurgence/Revivalism

While increasing religiosity in itself is not the cause of tension, the proselytising tendency underlying this new form of religiosity and the intrusion of religion into public space posed problems. Intra- and inter-religious tensions were more markedly seen. Such tensions were serious enough that the Ministry of Community Development commissioned a team from the National University of Singapore (NUS) in 1987, to conduct a research on religion and religious revivalism in Singapore. The Report highlighted "the shifting trends in recent years, both in the size of membership and in changing attitudes and activities, [that] may threaten to disrupt the subtle and delicate equilibrium which has characterized the religious scene in Singapore for decades".[27]

The state's concern was threefold. Firstly, there was a serious possibility of conflict, intra- and inter-community, as a result of exclusivist expressions of religion that characterised religious revivalist groups. Secondly, there was a real threat of religious movements becoming "activist" in questioning state policies and undermining the government's legitimacy in the eyes of the electorate. The second factor relates to a broader third concern of the incursion of religion into politics, which may pull interreligious relations apart through making narrow political demands, couched in religious terms, for each exclusive group. Such religious politics were already ocurring globally elsewhere.[28] Policy changes were thus necessary. Primary among them was the introduction of a new legislation — the Maintenance of Religious Harmony Act (MRHA) — which came into force in 1992.

Maintenance of Religious Harmony Act, 1990

Prior to the introduction of MRHA, several laws were in place to deal with varying degree of threats to social order and harmony. This includes the Sedition Act (Cap. 290), Internal Security Act (Cap. 143), Societies Act (Cap. 311) and Chapter 15 of the Penal Code (Cap. 224). However, these laws were deemed inadequate. In the White Paper detailing the need for MRHA, the government acknowledged the need for religions to proselytise and that this was guaranteed as a fundamental right accorded by Article 15 of the constitution. Nonetheless, the government cautioned against an unrestrained preacher who may cause dissention through denigrating other faiths, leading to loss of tolerance and mutual trust between religious communities.[29] Aggressive and insensitive proselytisation as well as the intrusion of religion into public space, thus, became major concerns in the preservation of religious harmony in Singapore.

A key target for the MRHA was religious leaders who overstepped their boundaries and engaged in activities that can disrupt social harmony or undermine the government of the day. Through MRHA, a separation of religion and politics was thus reinforced.[30] From the White Paper submitted to parliament, it was clear that the state considered religion and politics as two mutually exclusive domains and that any attempt to combine them will only bring strife and conflict. Thus, "mutual abstention from competitive political influence is an important aspect of religious tolerance and harmony".[31]

The Maintenance of Religious Harmony Bill was passed on 9 November 1990, and came into effect on 31 March 1992.[32] It allows for a renewable restraining order against individuals for up to two years. Through the MRHA, "the working rules by which many faiths can accept fundamental differences between them, and coexist peacefully in Singapore" were established.[33]

The Presidential Council for Religious Harmony

As noted earlier, the experiences in managing issues of racial diversity were relevant and applied in managing religious diversity. Singapore already has the Presidential Council for Minority Rights (PCMR) as a means to protect the interests of ethnic minorities by ensuring that Bills passed by the parliament do not discriminate against racial or religious minorities. The White Paper on MRHA proposed that a Presidential Council for Religious Harmony (PCRH) be set up, and its members be appointed by the President of the Republic, upon the advice of the PCMR. The roles of this council, as outlined in the MRHA, are:

(1) To consider and report to the Minister on matters affecting the maintenance of religious harmony in Singapore which are referred to the council by the Minister or by parliament; and
(2) To consider and make recommendations on restraining orders referred to the council by the Minister.

The PCRH came into effect in August 1992, with representatives from the main religious bodies: Buddhist, Muslim, Roman Catholic, Christian Protestant, Hindu and Sikh. It is now functional in forging a closer rapport between the government and key religious leaders in the interest of peace and harmony.

Reconfiguring the Religious Model

Yet, legal recourse alone such as the MRHA is not sufficient. The growth and expansion of religious groups throughout the 1980s meant that religion would continue to be a significant feature in public life. Since the early years, religious communities had, in fact, been involved in providing social welfare services in their public involvement. This energy was then harnessed and assumed greater focus from the 1990s onward. Interreligious conflicts can be minimised when religious communities engage themselves more in humanitarian work rather than focus on competing with each other. This expanded humanitarian role played by the religious communities fitted well with societal need to help those who could not cope with demands of the new economy from the 1990s onward.

The government would then work in partnership with religious organisations in identifying areas of needs and administering of social welfare benefits. This corresponds closely with Singapore's transition into a neo-liberal economy as the state retreats as a direct provider of welfare needs.[34]

For example, Eng (2009) noted that since the 1990s, many Buddhist organisations have formalised their role as providers of various types of welfare facilities and services to the general public.[35] At the same time, Mansor and Ibrahim (2008) noted that Muslim organisations began expanding their social services and programmes from the 1990s and started to work closely with various government bodies.[36] Thus, the role of religious groups in public life became more focused on humanitarian concerns and social welfare services as part of the "many helping hands approach". These were in line with the coming era of greater integration of Singapore into the global economic system informed by neo-liberal market capitalism where governments were expected to increase revenues and efficiency through privatising essential services and reducing public spending and dependency.

Discontinuation of Religious Knowledge in Schools

As a result of the attention paid to the negative effects of religious resurgence, a major area that was reviewed was the Religious Knowledge (RK) programme in public schools. Introduced in 1984, it was slated to be discontinued by 1989. The RK programme was replaced by Civics and Moral Education, which by the start of the 1990s, took a shift from "religion as an instruction for moral values" to "a good person is a good citizen" message.

The discontinuation of the RK programme was, in part, based on the Report on "Religion and Religious Revivalism in Singapore" cited earlier, which noted how schools became a site of proselytisation that can disrupt interreligious harmony.[37] It was clear that "contrary to the government's intent, the RK program did not so much provide an antidote to Western individualism as bring religious difference back into the public square".[38] A re-evaluation of policy was thus needed, and changes made.

Shared Values as National Ideology

With the discontinuation of RK, there was a need for a suitable set of core values that can be commonly embraced by all regardless of affiliations and which can bind the different communities together. Aptly called Shared Values, they were introduced in 1991.

The main concern was the rise of individualism that may erode the sense of community pivotal for the cohesion of the nation. Then-President Wee Kim Wee raised four core values in his address at the opening of parliament on 9 January 1989, which include "placing society above self, upholding the family as the basic block of society, resolving major issues through consensus instead of contention, and stressing racial and religious tolerance and harmony". He called for "a formal statement [that] will bond us together as Singaporeans, with our own distinct identity and destiny".[39]

On 2 January 1991, a White Paper on Shared Values was submitted to parliament.[40] It took into account a study commissioned to the Institute of Policy Studies (IPS) to identify national values which would help to unite all Singaporeans.[41] It was passed by parliament on 15 January 1991. Subsequently, the Shared Values were encapsulated as part of the National Education curriculum in schools.[42]

Rapid Globalising Phase, 1990s Onwards: Economic Imperatives as a Driving Force

With Singapore's economy maturing into the post-industrial phase, Singapore embarked on the shift towards a knowledge-based economy in the 1990s.[43] The build-up of capital and labour was beginning to decline and assume a lesser role in economic growth. It was thus crucial for Singapore's economy to build her capabilities to create, acquire, disseminate and apply knowledge in this new era. Key to this was enhancing the nation's innovative systems, entrepreneurship and education. It was also time to open up Singapore's economy through bringing in a new "creative class" that was located in some of the top cosmopolitan cities of the world. Tan (2007) observed that globalisation has produced a class of cosmopolitans who are geographically mobile; thus, the government needed "to turn Singapore into a stimulating and more tolerant place for a greater variety of lifestyle options" in order to attract the creative class while anchoring the Singapore cosmopolitans to the nation.[44]

One of the steps in this transition period was to reshape Singapore into a dynamic and vibrant city that would be attractive to the world's top talents. In

1992, the Ministry of Information and the Arts (MITA) released a Report on the Advisory Council for the Arts and Culture to "review the current state of the arts and culture in Singapore" and "to recommend measures that will make Singapore a culturally vibrant society by the turn of the century". Among others, the Report proposed relaxation of censorship, through new movie ratings and other measures. It was also during this period, in the year 2000, that MITA released the "Renaissance City Report".[45] This was followed by the green paper on "Investing in Singapore's Cultural Capital" and the Economic Review Committee Services Subcommittee Report on "Creative Industries Development Strategy" by the Ministry of Trade and Industry;[46] both in 2002. These signalled a new direction of Singapore's economy, that of moving into non-traditional activities. This also had an impact on society and the net result was undoubtedly increasing diversity driven by capital, migration and formation of new identities.[47] The new wave of migration that came along with an open economy did impact the religious landscape. New forms of religiosity emerged eventually, crafting social spaces that might change the dynamics of local forms and understandings in religiosity. Thus, new tensions did emerge as a result.[48]

Social Media Blurs Divide between Private–Public Domains

Throughout the 1990s, the secular space expanded considerably. Along with this, there has been a steady growth in the number of "non-religionists" who did not identify themselves with any religious category or regarded themselves as atheists or agnostics. Census reports showed the increase from 13.0% in 1980 to 17% in 2010.[49] Their value system may differ from the traditional and faith-based conservative values generally embraced by religionists. This coincided with the growing number of immigrants who brought along with them alternative beliefs, practices and lifestyles. Thus, conservative values upheld by society are being challenged. This phenomenon pushes the religious leaders to continue to reinforce their flocks with traditionally conservative teachings in the comfort of their own private sphere and away from the public gaze.

In 2010, a controversy emerged when video clips were uploaded onto YouTube and circulated widely via social media, that showed an interview with former Buddhists who had become church members and where Buddhism and Taoism were denigrated. The authorities did not take the issue lightly and had censured the party involved who admitted that the remarks were insulting and issued an apology to the Buddhist and Taoist communities.[50] Two years later, another controversy emerged when a Christian group in NUS issued a poster, calling for evangelical work to be done amongst Buddhists in Thailand — "a place of little true joy…and only one hundred Thais accept Christ each year", and among Muslims in Turkey where "much prayer and work is needed". The poster was uploaded on social media and was circulating widely through Facebook. Soon, a complaint was lodged and the poster was taken down and an apology issued.[51]

What can be observed from the above two incidents is the blurring of boundaries of private–public spheres, particularly with the rise of new technology and social media sites such as blogs, YouTube, Facebook and Twitter. The accelerated use of social media had certainly impacted the terrain of interreligious relations. In particular, exclusivist religious teachings which were imparted to the faithful remained within the confines of the congregation and did not enter the public sphere. Hence, much of the existing prejudices, stereotypes and misinformation of the religious other had survived, despite the widening of the common space in public life. However, the advent of social media has blurred the private–public boundaries as what are normally said within the confines of the congregation can now enter public discourse.

The second consequence of the proliferation of social media sites lies in the fact that it accentuates diversity through providing a platform and means towards the formation of new social groupings and identities. One of the most obvious was the mobilisation of previously marginalised voices of the lesbian, gay, bisexual and transgender (LGBT) people.[52] In 2007, amidst the controversy over the call by activists to repeal Section 377A of the Penal Code that criminalises homosexual acts, Prime Minister Lee Hsien Loong noted in his parliament speech that on matters concerning moral values, "we will let others take the lead, we will stay one step behind the front line of change; watch how things work out elsewhere before we make any irrevocable moves".[53]

One of the most prominent incidents signifying a new social fault line occurred in 2009, when a group of Christian conservatives took over the leadership of a secular women's organisation, the Association of Women for Action and Research (AWARE), for what the former perceived as being a conduit for lesbianism and advocacy platform for gay rights. Coincidentally, the "AWARE saga", as the incident came to be known, occurred in the year that the Pink Dot SG — a campaign for acceptance of the LGBT community in Singapore — started.[54] The AWARE saga, vis-à-vis the emergence of openly gay advocacy groups, must be understood within the context of Singapore being a morally conservative society. What has thus emerged now is a new set of dynamics between different communities which are not defined along race or religion, but along affiliations and orientations within a highly diversified society. This has been described as the new "contestation of ideas" that will pose an emerging challenge to the landscape of social harmony in Singapore.[55]

Post-9/11: Global Conflicts and Security Issues

Even as Singapore's economy underwent a major transformation in the 1990s, a global event that occurred on 11 September 2001 provided yet another challenge to social cohesion. In January 2002, the Internal Security Department detained 13 persons for suspected links and involvement with the Jemaah Islamiyah (JI). Further arrests were made in August 2002, with 19 members of JI and two members of the Moro Islamic Liberation Front being detained. These arrests marked the beginning of rigorous counter-terrorism work embarked by the government, which coincided with the "global war on terror" launched by American forces in response to the attacks on the US World Trade Center. To coordinate efforts at counter-terrorism effectively, the government established the National Security Coordination Centre in 2004 under the Prime Minister's Office.

One of the lessons emerging from 9/11 was that religious communities must interact more frequently and openly to foster trust and understanding. The Muslim community, in particular, cannot afford to allow negative perceptions to persist, given that there were greater attention and suspicion towards them as a result of the discovery of the JI cells within the community. The government too, saw a need to foster greater interaction among the races and religious believers in order to forge greater intercultural understanding and positive exchanges. These would have the effect of breaking down stereotypes and prejudices. In the government's "White Paper: The Jemaah Islamiyah Arrests and the Threat of Terrorism" (2003),[56] it proposed for further strengthening of social cohesion and religious harmony, apart from other enhanced security measures and surveillance. It acknowledged that "[t]he vast majority of Singaporean Muslims are moderate, tolerant and law-abiding, and do not support the actions of the Muslim militants" and that "it would be tragic if the terrorist attacks and the JI case caused distrust and suspicion between Singaporeans".

It was clear that the government's worry was that a terrorist attack may be inevitable, and hoped that should it occur, "good sense will prevail" and "reactions will be calm, considered and based on facts" to avoid "a major confrontation between the races and religions".[57] Thus, greater engagement and stronger networks must be forged to strengthen social relations and minimise suspicions and stereotypes. This was eventually done through a series of initiatives: (1) the formation of the Inter-Racial and Religious Confidence Circle; (2) the Declaration of Religious Harmony; and (3) the institutionalisation of the Community Engagement Programme. These constitute what Tan (2009) calls "soft law mechanisms" that aim to win the "hearts and minds" of people by "persuading the relevant stakeholders that violence and conflict are not the solution".[58] Within this framework, a collective and holistic approach towards tackling the terrorist threat was adopted by the Singapore government through involving a cross section of the ethnic and religious communities beyond the Malay/Muslim community.

Nonetheless, the Muslim community had been most proactive in dealing with the terrorist threat. The Muslim community cannot slide back on the present harmony, given that there were increasing distrust and suspicion towards the community in the immediate fall out from the focus on Al-Qaeda and JI. There was also a need to ensure that extremist ideologies do not take root within the Muslim population. To deal with this challenge, the Islamic Religious Council of Singapore (also known as Majlis Ugama Islam Singapore/MUIS) embarked on several inititives, which included the launch of an interfaith initiative and institution, the Harmony Centre in 2007. The Harmony Centre is the Muslim community's most extensive effort to date, to foster goodwill and positive interreligious relations among people of different faiths. In addition, the Religious Rehabilitation Group was also formed in 2003 to assist the Ministry of Home Affairs (MHA) to counsel JI detainees as well as embark on counter-ideology work among Muslims prone to misinterpreting Islam to justify violence and conflict.

Inter-Racial and Religious Confidence Circle

Soon after the tumultuous events of 9/11 and the discovery of the local JI cell, the government formed the Inter-Racial Confidence Circle (IRCC). It serves as a bridge between religious, ethnic and other community organisations with the aim of building trust and friendship. As mentioned by the Prime Minister when tasking the People's Association to set up the IRCC at the grassroots level, the network was meant "to provide a platform for confidence-building among the different communities, as a basis for developing, in time, deeper friendships and trust. Regular interactions will build up inter-racial and inter-religious rapport. They will also provide opportunities for all parties to address immediately racial and religious problems on the ground".[59]

After the devastating London bombing of 7 July 2005, the work of the IRCC was expanded to go beyond the focus of building positive race relations;

religion was included as a core component in facilitating the network of cooperation, harmony, respect and trust — four core values of the IRCC. It was thus renamed as the Inter-Racial and *Religious* Confidence Circle (IRCC).

Today, under the coordination of the Ministry of Culture, Community and Youth (MCCY), there are 87 IRCCs formed across the Republic. It continues to build trust and deepen ties between communities and deepen people's understanding of various faiths, beliefs and practices. The resulting bonds within the community will ensure that Singapore society will stay united and recover quickly from any crisis that has an impact on inter-racial and -religious relations.

Declaration of Religious Harmony

Following the second round of arrests of JI members, the Prime Minister met community leaders in a dialogue session on 14 October 2002, and proposed a Code on Religious Harmony to be adopted. It was hoped that such a code "can be a framework to guide all religious groups, and will help to crystallise the consensus of Singaporeans of all races and religions about the way we should conduct ourselves as we pursue our respective religious beliefs in multi-racial Singapore".[60] The code was to serve as a moral persuasion for a moderate and non-threatening multireligious existence in secular space. Key to this is the acceptance of the secular basis of the state — a key foundational principle that will ensure Singapore will not disintegrate amidst racial and religious diversity. As seen from the rise of religious fervour in the 1980s to the 1990s, ensuring the common space is not encroached by religious-based action, has been a central concern. The JI arrests highlighted the importance of acknowledging the secular basis of the state — given that one of the JI's expressed goals is to create an "Islamic State" or the *Daulah Islamiyah Nusantara* — a conception rooted in the history and myth of a pan-Islamic superstate or a caliphate comprising much of Southeast Asia.[61]

In finalising the Code of Religious Harmony, the buy-in from religious leaders became crucial. This was to ensure that the code was not seen as another attempt by the government to regulate and impose its will on religious matters that religious communities should have autonomy in. After a series of consultation with religious leaders, the code was reworked with several crucial changes, and accepted as a Declaration of Religious Harmony (DRH).[62]

The DRH was eventually adopted in 2003. Following that, the representatives involved in the drafting of the DHR were inducted into a new network called the Inter-Religious Harmony Circle. The representation from all the major faiths involved in the drafting of the DRH would ensure the document is owned by the respective groups to shape the norms and values of religious moderation in a diverse setting of Singapore society. Following the DRH's acceptance by religious leaders, the government has also urged national institutions and religious bodies to recite the DRH annually on Racial Harmony Day, which is on 21 July each year.

Community Engagement Programme

Following the suicide bombing in central London on 7 July 2005, a new alarm was raised and efforts to foster interreligious relations took centre stage once again. In February 2006, Prime Minister Lee Hsien Loong raised the need to "widen and deepen linkages among our people, to involve more people, build up the networks which have been developed by the IRCCs, the Harmony Circles, to cover more groups, the grassroots, the religious and community organisations, schools, businesses, unions, media — all the key institutions and organisations in our society". This comprehensive strategy is now known as the Community Engagement Programme (CEP). The CEP's rationale is that "the objective of a successful terrorist attack in Singapore would be not only to kill people and destroy property but also to create suspicion, tension and strife between different racial and religious groups in the country". Thus, "Singaporeans must therefore face such a crisis united as one nation and one people…The crucial challenge is to ensure that society stays strong and united during and after such a crisis so that Singapore can recover quickly and Singaporeans can continue to work, study and live together in peace and harmony".[63]

To achieve this, a Ministerial Committee on Community Engagement was formed to steer the CEP, involving six government agencies. These six agencies were tasked to look into the implementation of CEP in various corresponding clusters of (1) religious groups, ethnic-based organisations and voluntary welfare organisations; (2) educational institutions; (3) media and the arts; (4) businesses and unions; and (5) grassroots organisations. Three strategic thrusts were outlined: (1) to build networks of trust among communities; (2) to build capability for a resilient community; and (3) to build an operationally ready community prepared for crises. The vision for CEP is "A Singapore united and resilient in times of adversity". A grant of up to S$100,000, called the "Harmony Fund", was also set up and administered by MCCY to assist non-governmental organisations with creative projects that promote racial and religious harmony in Singapore.

The net result of the shift towards greater community engagement and fostering of interracial and religious interactions in Singapore is the burgeoning of new interfaith initiatives from the grassroots level. These initiatives are typically small and organic, with participation from lay religious people, rather than the community's elites or leaders that usually form the more established groups such as the IRO. An example is the Explorations-into-Faith programme supported by the Southeast Community Development Council.

While the effectiveness of the CEP cannot be measured fully without a major crisis happening to put it to test, a survey conducted in 2009 may give indicators on the level of consciousness within society with regard to the objectives of the CEP. According to the survey that was commissioned by MHA, 74.4% of respondents trusted fellow Singaporeans to help them if a terrorist attack were to occur in the Republic; 78.2% agreed that Singaporeans of all races and communities would stand united after a terrorist attack; and 86.7% thought that Singaporeans in general respected other religions.[64] These indicators showed the initial success that CEP had generated, while highlighting gaps that are still work in progress.

Conclusion

What has been notably clear is that religion is an area that has received a fair bit of attention with regard to public governance. In discussing Singapore's public policy in general, Leong (2000) has noted that "The uniqueness and variations in Singapore's public policy and the interactions of policy actors can be best explained when they are allocated in the proper strategic, political, historical, economic and social contexts of the city-state".[65] The preceding discussion has located the changing context of interreligious relations as it informs as well as reacts to state policies in changing circumstances. Much of this can be attributed to the state's desire to see that every community leads its religious life and at the same time preserves religious harmony and social cohesion.

According to Tong (2007), the state adopts a threefold strategy: (1) ensuring religious tolerance among various religious groups, and equality of treatment for all religions; (2) religions and religious groups must not pose any security threat to the nation; and (3) religions should not enter the political realm.[66] The secular basis of the state has always been safeguarded as policies are worked out in response to changing social context and religious developments. Within the context of Singapore's society, secularism is the pillar of harmony because of the religious reality and the diversity in faiths while the constitution guarantees the freedom to practice religion.

While managing religious diversity is always work in progress, there have been results that point to the effectiveness of ongoing efforts. Surveys serve as a good starting point of capturing a snapshot on the state of interreligious relations in society. Among the Christian community, Chong's survey revealed that an average of 91% church respondents believe that Christians should interact more with non-Christians. More than 70% also indicated that they have friends from different religions.[67] In May 2011, MUIS released its internal Report on Religious Outlook Survey. The Report indicated that there was a healthy level of inclusiveness among Muslims: 94.6% did not have a problem with having close non-Muslim friends and neighbours; more than half of the respondents would be willing to visit their neighbours' homes during special occasions; and more than four-fifths were willing to help others regardless of their religious affiliations.

A more comprehensive study on race relations was done by the Centre of Excellence for National Security at the S. Rajaratnam School of International Studies. A key finding of this 2007 survey was that "inter-racial and inter-religious ties were sturdy in the public sphere" and that "race and religion did not play an important role in the choices Singaporeans made".[68] A similar study was replicated in 2011 and found that racial and religious harmony remain resilient, with the Inclusive Index for Singaporeans increasing by between 45–50% in 2007, to 65–69% in 2011.[69]

A more recent study was done by IPS, in collaboration with the Lee Kuan Yew School of Public Policy and OnePeople.sg. Broadly, the study found that there was an absence of discrimination in using of public services, an absence of inter-racial and -religious tensions, and an absence of minority discrimination in the workplace. However, there were areas where intercommunity relations could be further improved.[70]

This is to be expected as race and religious relations in Singapore will continue to evolve. While much has been achieved over the past 50 years, several challenges still linger in the coming shape of Singapore's multicultural society. Firstly, conflicts in other places will continue to have a global impact. Secondly, the proliferation of new technology and new media will mean that the spread of hate, sedition, rumour and misinformation can occur in a more rapid and widespread manner. Thirdly, with globalisation, Singaporeans will continue to live with an increasing number of immigrants and have to manage diversity in their lives. All these will form part of the new challenges that the multicultural state of Singapore will have to respond in the coming future.

Notes

[1] Pew Research Center, "Global Religious Diversity: Half of the Most Religiously Diverse Countries Are in Asia-Pacific Region," April 2014. Retrieved 27 April 2015, from http://www.pewforum.org/2014/04/04/global-religious-diversity/.

[2] Kenan Malik, *Multiculturalism and Its Discontents* (Calcutta, India: Seagull Books, 2013), p. 8.

[3] Khun Eng Kuah, "Maintaining Ethno-Religious Harmony in Singapore," *Journal of Contemporary Asia*, 28(1), 1998, pp. 103–121; Michael Hill, "The Rehabilitation and Regulation of Religion in Singapore," in James T. Richardson (ed.), *Regulating Religion: Case Studies from Around the Globe* (New York: Kluwer Academic/ Plenum Publishers, 2004, Chapter 24, pp. 343–358; Eugene K. B. Tan, "Norming 'Moderation' in an 'Iconic Target': Public Policy and the Regulation of Religious Anxieties in Singapore," *Terrorism and Political Violence*, 19(4), 2007, pp. 443–462.

[4] Brenda S. A. Yeoh, *Contesting Space: Power Relations and the Urban Built Environment in Colonial Singapore* (Kuala Lumpur: Oxford University Press, 1996), p. 38.

[5] J. S. Furnivall, *Colonial Policy and Practice: A Comparative Study of Burma and the Netherlands Indies* (UK: University Press, 1948), pp. 304–305.

[6] Nirmala Srirekam Purushotam, "Disciplining Differences: Race in Singapore," Working Paper Series no. 126, Department of Sociology, National University of Singapore, Singapore, 1995.

[7] Sharon Siddique, "Singaporean Identity," in K. S. Sandhu and P. Wheatley (eds.), *Management of Success: The Moulding of Modern Singapore* (Singapore: Institute of Southeast Asian Studies, 1989), Chapter 26, pp. 563–577.

[8] Geoffrey Benjamin, "The Cultural Logic of Singapore's Multiculturalism," in Riaz Hassan (ed.), *Singapore: Society in Transition* (Kuala Lumpur: Oxford University Press, 1976), Chapter 6.

[9] Cited, Raj K. Vasil, *Governing Singapore* (Singapore: Eastern University Press, 1984), p. 99.

[10] See, Khoo Chian Kim, "Census of Population 1980, Singapore: Administrative Report," Department of Statistics, Singapore, 1983, p. 8. The only census on religion available prior to 1980 was in 1931. See, Tong Chee Kiong, "Religious Trends and Issues in Singapore," in Lai Ah Eng (ed.), *Religious Diversity in Singapore* (Singapore: Institute of Southeast Asian Studies, 2008), Chapter 2, p. 35.

[11] Stanley Sanders Bedlington, *Malaysia and Singapore: The Building of New States* (Ithaca: Cornell University Press, 1978).

[12] Richard Clutterbuck, *Riot and Revolution in Singapore and Malaya, 1945–1963* (London: Faber, 1973).

[13] See, Tom Eames Hughes, *Tangled Worlds: The Story of Maria Hertogh* (Singapore: Institute of Southeast Asian Studies, 1980). Hughes cites the findings of the Commission of Inquiry into the riots, which stated that although the Malays were mainly involved in the riot, it took a religious turn when Muslim Indians and Pakistanis joined in the agitations.

14 A case in point too was the emergence of a small group of Malay extremists who went by the name of *Angkatan Revolusi Tentara Islam Singapura*, who planned to overthrow the government. Their modus operandi was again to stoke racial tensions by inciting Malays against the Chinese, as the latter was seen as dominating what was considered to be the rightful land of the Malays.

15 Collin Abraham, *The Naked Social Order: The Roots of Racial Polarisation in Malaysia* (Malaysia: Pelanduk Publications, 2004); Hua Wu Yin, *Class and Communalism in Malaysia: Politics in a Dependent Capitalist State* (London: Zed Books, 1983), Chapter 4, pp. 69–87.

16 Syed Muhd Khairudin Aljunied, "Beyond the Rhetoric of Communalism: Violence and the Process of Reconciliation in 1950s Singapore," in Derek Heng and Syed Muhd Khairudin Aljunied (ed.), *Reframing Singapore: Memory — Identity — Trans-Regionalism* (Amsterdam: Amsterdam University Press, 2009), Chapter 4, pp. 69–87.

17 Joseph B. Tamney, *The Struggle over Singapore's Soul: Western Modernization and Asian Culture* (Berlin: Walter de Gruyter, 1996).

18 Goh Keng Swee and the Education Study Team, "Report on the Ministry of Education, 1978," National Printers, Singapore, 1998.

19 Ong Jin Hui, "Future of Religion and Education in the Asia-Pacific Age: A Report from a Modern Multi-Cultural Industrial Nation." Paper presented at the Conference on the Asia-Pacific Culture: Its History and Prospects, Tenri, Japan, 1984.

20 Ong Teng Cheong and Moral Education Committee, "Report on Moral Education," Singapore National Printers, Singapore, 1979, p. 12.

21 "Moral Duty," *The Straits Times*, 2 October 1979, p. 12.

22 "Duty of Every Teacher — Show by Example," *The Straits Times*, 17 September 1979, p. 14.

23 Bryan R. Wilson, *Religion in Secular Society* (London: C. A. Walker, 1966).

24 Julie Scott Jones, *Being the Chosen: Exploring a Christian Fundamentalist Worldview* (Surrey, England: Ashgate, 2010), p. 2.

25 Steve Bruce, *Fundamentalism* (Cambridge: Polity Press, 2008); Jose Casanova, *Public Religions in the Modern World* (Chicago: The University of Chicago Press, 1994).

26 Eddie C. Y. Kuo and Jon S. T. Quah, "Religion in Singapore: Report of a National Survey." Prepared for Ministry of Community Development, 1988, Table 43; Chandra Muzaffar, *Islamic Resurgence in Malaysia* (Petaling Jaya: Fajar Bakti, 1987); and Tan Chow May Ling, *Pentecostal Theology for the Twenty-First Century: Engaging with Multi-Faith* (Aldershot: Ashgate, 2007).

27 Eddie C. Y. Kuo, Jon S. T. Quah and Tong Chee Kiong, "Religion and Religious Revivalism in Singapore." Report prepared for Ministry of Community Development, 1988, p. 2.

28 Mark Jurgensmeyer, *Global Rebellion: Religious Challenges to the Secular State, from Christian Militias to Al Qaeda* (California: University of California Press, 2008).

29 Government of Singapore, "Maintenance of Religious Harmony." Presented to parliament by Command of the President of the Republic of Singapore; ordered by parliament to lie upon the table, 26 December 1989, p. 5.

[30] *Ibid.*, p. 1.

[31] *Ibid.*, p. 7.

[32] Select Committee on the Maintainence of Religious Harmony Bill, "Report of the Select Committee on the Maintainence of Religious Harmony," Bill no. 14/90, Singapore National Printers, Singapore, 1990.

[33] *Ibid.*

[34] Chua Beng Huat and Kwok Kian-Woon, "Social Pluralism in Singapore," in Robert W. Hefner (ed.), *The Politics of Multiculturalism: Pluralism and Citizenship in Malaysia, Singapore, and Indonesia* (Honolulu: University of Hawaii Press, 2001), p. 96.

[35] Kuah-Pearce Khun Eng, *State, Society and Religious Engineering: Towards a Reformist Buddhism in Singapore* (Singapore: Institute of Southeast Asian Studies, 2009), p. 188.

[36] Enon Mansor and Nur Amali Ibrahim, "Muslim Organizations and Mosques as Social Service Providers," in Lai Ah Eng (ed.), *Religious Diversity in Singapore* (Singapore: Institute of Southeast Asian Studies and Institute of Policy Studies, 2008), pp. 459–488.

[37] Kuo, Quah and Kiong (1988), *op. cit.*, p. 2.

[38] Hefner (ed.) (2011), *op. cit.*, p. 39.

[39] "Government's Aim to Create a Better Life for All Singaporeans," *The Straits Times*, 10 January 1989, p. 12.

[40] Government of Singapore, "Shared Values," Singapore National Printers, Singapore, 1991.

[41] Jon S. T. Quah (ed.), *In Search of Singapore's National Values* (Singapore: IPS, 1990).

[42] Lana Khong, Joy Chew and Jonathan Goh, "How Now, NE? An Exploratory Study of Ethnic Relations in Three Singapore Schools," in Lai Ah Eng (ed.), *Beyond Rituals and Riots: Ethnic Pluralism and Social Cohesion in Singapore* (Singapore: Marshall Cavendish International, 2004), Chapter 7, p. 172.

[43] Linda Low, "The Singapore Developmental State in the New Economy and Polity," *The Pacific Review*, 14(3), 2001.

[44] Kenneth Paul Tan, "New Politics for a Renaissance City?," in Kenneth Paul Tan (ed.), *Renaissance Singapore? Economy, Culture, and Politics* (Singapore: NUS Press, 2007).

[45] Ministry of Information and the Arts (MITA), "Renaissance City Report: Culture and the Arts in Renaissance Singapore," MITA, Singapore, 2000.

[46] Creative Industries Working Group, "Creative Industries Developmental Strategy: Propelling Singapore's Creative Economy," Report of the Economic Restructuring Committee Services Subcommittee, Singapore, 2002.

[47] Selvaraj Velayutham, *Responding to Globalization: Nation, Culture and Identity in Singapore* (Singapore: Institute of Southeast Asian Studies, 2007).

[48] For example, new Indian migrants who are Hindus came with a socio-religious context that differs from local Hinduism. One aspect is the intertwining of the caste

system with religious understanding that is still prevalent in certain parts of India. This caused tensions with local Hindus, who were largely of South Indian descent, with no caste practices in Singapore. Within the Muslim community, MUIS has acknowledged the need to deal with diversity in Islamic practices and understanding that may not be familiar to the local largely Sunni Malays of the Shafi'e *mazhab* (school of thought).

49 Singapore Department of Statistics, "Census of Population 2010: Statistical Release 1 on Demographic Characteristics, Education, Language and Religion," 2010. Retrieved 27 April 2015, from http://www.singstat.gov.sg/publications/publications_and_papers/cop2010/cop2010_sr1.html.

50 "Leaders of Buddhist, Taoist Groups Urge Restraint," *The Straits Times*, 9 February 2010, p. A4.

51 "Christian Group Says Sorry for Remarks," *The Straits Times*, 17 February 2012, p. A3.

52 Lynette J. Chua, *Mobilizing Gay Singapore: Rights and Resistance in an Authoritarian State* (Singapore: NUS Press, 2014).

53 Terence Chong, "Filling the Moral Void: The Christian Right in Singapore," *International Journal of Contemporary Asia*, 41(4), November 2011, pp. 566–583.

54 Terence Chong (ed.), *The AWARE Saga: Civil Society and Public Morality in Singapore* (Singapore: NUS Press, 2011).

55 This may bear semblance to the notion of a "culture war" in American society; a phenomenon that was first identified the 1980s as a struggle between the "orthodox" (conservative or traditional) and the "progressive" (liberal or modern) camps along moral issues and religious politics. See, James Davison Hunter, *Culture Wars: The Struggle to Define America* (New York: Basic Books, 1991). For the notion of "culture war" surrounding the debates on 377A, see Jianlin Chen, "Singapore's Culture War over Section 377A: Through the Lens of Public Choice and Multi-Lingual Research," *Law & Social Inquiry*, 38(1), 2013, pp. 106–137.

56 Ministry of Home Affairs (MHA), "White Paper: The Jemaah Islamiyah Arrests and the Threat of Terrorism," MHA, Singapore, 2003.

57 *Ibid.*

58 Eugene K. B. Tan, "From Clampdown to Limited Empowerment: Soft Law in the Calibration and Regulation of Religious Conduct in Singapore," *Law & Policy*, 31(3), July 2009.

59 MHA (2003), *op. cit.*; Ministry of Information and the Arts (MITA), "Censorship Review Committee Report," MITA, Singapore, 1992.

60 *Ibid.*

61 National Security Coordination Centre NSCC, "The Fight against Terror: Singapore's National Security Strategy," NSCC, Singapore, 2004.

62 Tan (2009), *op. cit.*

63 Asad-ul Iqbal Latif, *Hearts of Resilience: Singapore's Community Engagement Programme* (Singapore: Institute of Southeast Asian Studies, 2011), p. 23.

64 Latif (2011), *op. cit.*, p. 28.

[65] Ho Khai Leong, *The Politics of Policy-Making in Singapore* (Oxford: Oxford University Press, 2000), p. 12.

[66] Chee Kiong Tong, *Rationalizing Religion: Religious Conversion, Revivalism and Competition in Singapore Society* (Leiden: Brill, 2007).

[67] Terence Chong and Hui Yew-Foong, *Different under God: A Survey of Church-Going Protestants in Singapore* (Singapore: Institute of Southheast Asian Studies, 2013).

[68] Yolanda Chin and Norman Vasu, *Ties That Bind and Blind: A Report on Inter-Racial and Inter-Religious Relations in Singapore* (Singapore: Centre of Excellence for National Security, RSIS, NTU, 2007).

[69] Yolanda Chin and Norman Vasu, "Ties That Bind and Blind: Scorecard of Singapore's Multicultural Bonds," *RSIS Commentaries* no. 55, 30 March 2012.

[70] "Concerns Raised at Forum on Racial Relations," *Today*, 12 September 2013.

References

Asian Conference on Religion and Peace, "A Brief Report of the Asian Conference on Religion and Peace: Singapore, 1976," Asian Conference on Religion and Peace, Tokyo, 1977.

Bobby E. K. Sng and You Poh Seng, *Religious Trends in Singapore, with Special Reference to Christianity* (Singapore: Graduates' Christian Fellowship and Fellowship of Evangelical Students, 1982).

Bryan S. Turner, Adam Possamai and Jack Barbalet, "Introduction: States, Consumption and Managing Religions," in J. M. Barbalet, Adam Possamai and Bryan S. Turner (ed.), *Religion and the State: A Comparative Sociology* (London: Anthem Press, 2011), pp. 1–22.

Chua Beng Huat, *Communitarian Ideology and Democracy in Singapore* (London: Routledge, 1995).

Curriculum Development Institute of Singapore (CDIM), *Confucian Ethics Textbook Secondary Four* (Singapore: Educational Publications Bureau, 1986).

Eddie C. Y. Kuo, "Confucianism as Political Discourse in Singapore: The Case of an Incomplete Revitalization Movement," Working Paper no. 113, Department of Sociology, National University of Singapore, 1992.

Eugene K. B. "Keeping God in Place: The Management of Religion in Singapore," in Lai Ah Eng (ed.), *Religious Diversity in Singapore* (Singapore: Institute of Southeast Asian Studies and IPS, 2008), pp. 55–82.

Government of Singapore, *Singapore: The Next Lap* (Singapore: Times Editions, 1991).

Inter-Religious Organisation (IRO), *Harmony among Religions* (Singapore: IRO, 1987).

Inter-Religious Organisation (IRO), *IRO-40: Inter-Religious Organisation Singapore 40th Anniversary Commemorative Book* (Singapore: IRO, 1990).

Kay Gillis K. *Singapore Civil Society and British Power* (Singapore: Talisman, 2005).

Lai Ah Eng, "Religious Diversity in Singapore," in Terence Chong (ed.), *Management of Success: Singapore Revisited* (Singapore: Institute of Southeast Asian Studies, 2010), pp. 309–334.

Lai Ah Eng (ed.), *Religious Diversity in Singapore* (Singapore: Institute of Southeast Asian Studies, 2008).

Mariam Mohamed Ali, "Uniformity and Diversity among Muslims in Singapore," Unpublished MSocSc thesis, Department of Sociology, National Uuniversity of Singapore, 1989.

Martin E. Marty and R. Scott Appleby (eds.), *Fundamentalisms Observed* (Chicago: University of Chicago Press, 2001).

Mathew Mathews, "Saving the City through Good Works: Christian Involvement in Social Services," in Lai (ed.) (2008), *op. cit.*, pp. 524–556.

Matthew Matthews, "Indicators of Racial and Religious Harmony: An IPS–OnePeople.sg Study," 2013. Retrieved 27 April 2015, from http://lkyspp.nus.edu.sg/ips/wp-content/uploads/sites/2/2013/08/Forum_-Indicators-of-Racial-and-Religious_110913_slides.pdf.

Michael D. Barr, *Cultural Politics and Asian Values: The Tepid War* (London: Routledge, 2002).

Michael D. Barr, "Singapore's Catholic Social Activists: Alleged Marxist Conspirators," in Michael D. Barr and Carl A. Trocki (eds.), *Paths Not Taken: Political Pluralism in Post-War Singapore* (Singapore: NUS Press, 2008), Chapter 12, pp. 228–247.

Michael Hill and Lian Kwen Fee, *The Politics of Nation Building and Citizenship in Singapore* (London: Routledge, 1995).

Ministry of Information and the Arts (MITA), "Censorship Review Committee Report," MITA, Singapore, 1992.

Ong Teng Cheong, "Report of the Advisory Council on Culture and the Arts," Advisory Council on Culture and the Arts, Singapore, 1989.

Pergas, *Moderation in Islam* (Singapore: Pergas, 2004).

Raj K. Vasil, *Asianising Singapore: The PAP's Management of Ethnicity* (Singapore: Heinemann Asia, 1995).

Religion Must Never Be Source of Friction, Says Lee "*The Straits Times*, 18 November 1972, p. 8.

Richard L. Florida, *The Rise of the Creative Class: … And How It's Transforming Work, Leisure, Community and Everyday Life* (New York: Basic Books, 2002).

Richard L. Florida, *The Flight of the Creative Class: The New Global Competition for Talent* (New York: Harper Business, 2005).

Saat A. Rahman, *Winning Hearts and Minds, Promoting Harmony: A Decade of Providing Care and Support* (Singapore: Khadijah Mosque, 2013).

Singapore Department of Statistics, "Population in Brief 2013," September 2013. Retrieved 27 April 2015, from http://population.sg/population-in-brief/2013/#.U9IJab-k2P8.

Suzaina Kadir, "Muslim Politics, the State, and Society," in Kenneth Paul Tan (ed.), *Renaissance Singapore? Economy, Culture, and Politics* (Singapore: NUS Press, 2007), Chapter 8, pp. 131–157.

Tan Chwee Huat, "Confucianism and Nation Building in Singapore," *International Journal of Social Economics*, 16(8), 1989, pp. 5–16.

Thio Li-Ann, "The Secular Trumps the Sacred: Constitutional Issues Arising from *Colin Chan v Public Prosecutor*," in Garry Rodan (ed.), *Singapore* (Aldershot: Ashgate, 2001), Chapter 7, pp. 135–212.

Trevor Ling, "Religion," in K. S. Sandhu and P. Wheatley (eds.), *Management of Success: The Moulding of Modern Singapore* (Singapore: Institute of Southeast Asian Studies, 1989), Chapter 31, pp. 692–709.

Tu Wei-Ming, *Confucian Ethics Today: The Singapore Challenge* (Singapore: Curriculum Development Institute of Singapore and Federal Publications, 1984).

Vineetha Sinha, "Theorising 'Talk' about 'Religious Pluralism' and 'Religious Harmony' in Singapore," *Journal of Contemporary Religion*, 20(1), 2005, pp. 25–40.

Vivienne Wee, "Secular State, Multi-Religious Society: The Patterning of Religion in Singapore." Paper presented at the Conference on Communities in Question: Religion and Authority in East and Southeast Asia; 2–10 May 1989, Hua Hin, Thailand.

Part 2
Personal Reminiscences

Chapter 15

Safeguarding Singapore's Security: Defence and Diplomacy

S. R. Nathan

Singapore has enjoyed peace and security the past 50 years of its independence. From being virtually defenceless when we separated from Malaysia on 9 August 1965, Singapore has been able to build its armed forces comprising a full-fledged Army, seagoing Navy and modern air force, comprising 45,000 to 50,000 well-trained and equipped soldiers, sailors and airmen, with over 250,000 reservists who can be mobilised in short order. Looking back at the growth and development of our small island nation from a third world entrepot port to a first world global trading hub and financial centre, I believe we succeeded in doing so because we had been able to build up our defence capability in tandem with our economic development, while pursuing a foreign policy that sought a maximum number of friends and maintaining the freedom to be ourselves as an independent nation.

I was among the pioneers who manned the new Ministry of Foreign Affairs and engaged in carrying out the first part of the equation, i.e., making the maximum number of friends. After five years I was posted to the Ministry of Defence (MINDEF) (Security and Intelligence Division) in 1971 where I watched the development of the Singapore Armed Forces. I saw the way resources were put in and built up and the way people themselves grew in the job. I have seen the changes in leadership, the gradual development, training, exposure to other armies and acquisition of equipment — all leading to the development of a sort of self-reliance. I have seen all those grow, right up to the time I became President of Singapore (in 1999). I knew that we had a fully capable army, air force and navy, meeting the needs of the situation in the region.

Ours is not a counter-insurgency army; we are fully-equipped. We have bite. We have realistic exercises abroad, e.g., jungle warfare. When I was in MINDEF, one of the roles I played outside my core function was to develop contacts, whereby we could get overseas training facilities, support and guidance for the armed forces. So we made a lot of contacts in that sense and facilitated the development of the armed forces. I was involved in arranging access to overseas training facilities, e.g., in Taiwan at a time when nobody wanted to give us space, but they did. Subsequent to that we had facilities in the Philippines, Australia, New Zealand, Thailand, and even India and Indonesia. We sent our bright cadets to Japan and Britain. In recent years we have had access to training facilities in Germany, France as well as the United States. All these training missions and exercises overseas carry human resource and financial costs, but they give our troops real-time exposure. In a way they are ambassadors for Singapore; the way they perform abroad, in staff colleges, exercises and training are performance indicators of what we are as a nation.

Defence Diplomacy

In the early 1970s there was some tension between Singapore and Indonesia, a consequence of which was the adoption of "defence diplomacy" by MINDEF. It was decided that we had to forge links with the Indonesian defence and intelligence establishment, which had a significant role in maintaining peace and security in the region and determining Indonesia's foreign policy. We therefore initiated a framework of intelligence exchanges with Indonesia with a view to improving understanding of each other's security concerns, promoting regional resilience in the face of the communist threat, strengthening political and defence ties, and opening up a communications channel. The outcome was the setting up of regular annual intelligence meetings between the two countries, with benefits which reached into the defence spheres and enhanced understanding at the highest political levels.

Singapore has established military-to-military relations with other ASEAN members, as well as with partners from beyond the region, such as with India, the US and China. The SAF also builds strong relations by training with the armed forces of many countries in bilateral and multilateral exercises. Singapore has been a member of the Five Power Defence Arrangement since its inception in 1971 involving the United Kingdom, Australia, New Zealand and Malaysia. Singapore is also involved in transregional security cooperation networks such as the ASEAN Defence Ministers' Meeting and ADMM-Plus with partners in the East Asia Summit: the US, Russia, China, India, Japan, South Korea, Australia and New Zealand. Thus, in 50 years Singapore has transformed itself from being a vulnerable outpost in a fraught region divided between two contending spheres of influence, to a self-reliant and secure hub playing a pivotal role in the transregional security network that straddles the Indo-Pacific oceanic littoral.

The British Withdrawal

The British military withdrawal from East of Suez was announced in 1967 and by 1971 most of their troops had gone. As the same time, the Vietnam War was also intensifying and it was not clear at that stage whether the south would capitulate. It was a time of uncertainty, and the question arose whether Singapore would be forced closer to the American camp. But we were able to move away from total dependence on the British to some kind of relationship with the US.

In the early years when we had not developed our capabilities, the term "poisoned shrimp" was applied to Singapore's military capability. We were terribly vulnerable. We had to think in terms of "if you swallow me I'll poison you and you'll regret it; there'll be a price to pay". Now people are thinking along more conventional lines, but I think the idea of the shrimp is still relevant. As for identifying the SAF's potential enemy, it is very difficult to be specific because defence strategies are always hypothetical. But when we separated from Malaysia we were really exposed; we were independent but not in a position to defend ourselves. We had just one company of troops fighting Confrontation up in Borneo: the Singapore infantry regiment under the British. We had Malaysian troops based in Singapore. Fortunately for us, at that time Indonesia's Confrontation policy ensured that we still had Australian, New Zealand and British troops around.

We did not have a counter-insurgency role because the communist insurgency was mainly up the peninsula around the Thai border although there were constant forays down south, sometimes getting close to Kuala Lumpur. Communist activity in Singapore was really related to an insurgency that was going on further north. Awareness of our vulnerability drove us. At the time of separation in 1965 the communists were attempting a comeback. So we were motivated to build up our capability in a fairly untoward situation.

National Service (NS) was introduced as a way of upgrading Singapore's military capability as well as primarily as a nation-building educational exercise. It was a mixture of both. There was a need to inculcate in the young the idea that they have a defence role to play regardless of their position in society. Even disabled people were given some kind of work in the armed forces, and a music and drama company started for our artistic types who could not fit into a conventional army role. One of the purposes of our leaders must have been to bring about a levelling up of society. Both rich and poor had to do their NS. NS helped break down barriers between racial communities, having Indians,

Chinese and Malays in the same camps. Today, NS has become second nature; everybody accepts it. Reservists convey the message that your mission does not end after two years. Defence is an ongoing obligation.

In the Forefront of Changing World Order

Now, having built and developed our own defence capability by mastering the new technologies and transformations in military affairs, we have to keep developing our human resources and capacities to compensate for Singapore's limited size and population in facing the uncertainties of the future. Whatever changes and challenges the 21st century brings, Singapore's geopolitical situation will be constant, defined by its location at the fulcrum of the East-West sea routes between the Indian and Pacific oceans, and situated between two larger archipelagic entities which are not its hinterland but locking its sea, shelf and airspace. Singapore has and must continue to turn this acute vulnerability to its advantage by making itself a bridge between its neighbours.

Singapore has to maintain its position as a key node in the transregional connectivity by road, rail, sea, air and telecommunications. Singapore has to continue being in the forefront of the rapid technological changes and tectonic shifts in the global economy and new security order. While no one is sure what new security architecture will emerge in the next 50 years, with the emergence of two giants in Asia, i.e., China and India, and the waning interest of European powers and the US, Singapore has to maintain a pivotal role regionally with ASEAN and internationally as a strategic partner of all the major powers on the Pacific littoral and across the Indian and Atlantic oceans. Maritime security is another challenge where Singapore has to be engaged in both defence and diplomacy. Singapore plays a key role in the region, especially in the key Malacca and Singapore straits, where there are practical arrangements such as coordinated sea patrols and surveillance by Malaysia, Singapore, Indonesia and Thailand. Singapore has also contributed to maritime security beyond the region by deploying ships and surveillance aircraft to the western Indian Ocean where the Gulf of Aden sits on one of the major sea lanes of the world connecting Europe to East Asia and America via Singapore.

An emerging strand in global security is cyber-security involving cyberattacks, cyber-espionage and cyber-crime. Civilian as well as defence agencies in many countries are being tasked to take on this scourge. While not every country can have the capacity to ensure its own cyber-security, Singapore seeks to play a catalytic role through the new INTERPOL Global Complex for Innovation which has opened in Singapore. In the new global order and given the interrelated challenges that the world faces, there is an imperative and the opportunity to build a cooperative and collaborative world. However, that does not mean that defence and armed forces have become irrelevant. Countries still need armed forces so that they are able to defend themselves and avoid tempting others. The use of military force extends to non-traditional roles such as humanitarian assistance and disaster relief and creating conditions for capacity and institution building. It also extends to peacekeeping and peace-making, where acting under an international mandate or sanction should be the norm. Over the past three decades, Singapore has taken part in or contributed to peacekeeping or international operations, in keeping with our small size and capacity.

It has been our good fortune that Singapore's defence capability has not been put to the test at any time in the past 50 years. But the SAF has not taken any chances or been complacent — with the size and strength of the various services, both in quantity and quality and the lethality of their weaponry, with the most advanced army, air force and navy, equipped with long-range artillery and missiles, fighter aircraft, stealth frigates and corvettes and submarines. Our defence forces are geared to protect the security of Singapore, to deter and repel any attack by hostile forces of any external power. The SAF has to keep upgrading its capability to meet the challenges of warfare in the years ahead even as it has to increase the quality of its manpower to sustain its high-technology, knowledge-based economy to maintain its position as a key node in the global economic order.

Three Principles for Security

To conclude, let me cite three principles which have served Singapore well. From the start we sought to make friends with all who would be friends with us. We built up ASEAN as the core of regional solidarity. We also looked beyond the region to make friends in the wider world. We have to make ourselves relevant to countries in the developed and developing world so that they have an interest in cooperating with us. Second, we work for a multilateral system that is fair and equitable to countries big and small. As a small state we seek out like-minded partners to magnify our collective voice so that smaller countries have a greater role in shaping the global agenda. And finally, we must always maintain the ability to protect our sovereignty and defend what is critical for our survival. The primary role of the SAF remains to defend Singapore and to be the final guarantor of our sovereignty. We cannot just depend on others for our survival and must be able to take our fate and future in our own hands.

Chapter 16

Organising for National Security — The Singapore Experience

Peter Ho

Introduction

National security covers a wide spectrum ranging from internal security to external defence. Because it usually absorbs a significant part of the government budget, organising for national security is an important aspect of good governance.

Pre-Independence Focus on Internal Security

On separation, newly independent Singapore inherited from Malaysia national security legislation that focused on internal security, reflecting the concerns of the day. Laws like the Preservation of Public Security Ordnance (PPSO) of 1955, the Internal Security Act (ISA) of 1960 and the Public Order (Preservation) Act (POPA) of 1963 had been enacted to deal with the turbulent post-war period of communist-instigated labour unrest, student demonstrations and riots culminating in the Malayan Emergency.

Post-Independence Focus on External Defence

But even before independence, with the end of the communist insurgency, the centre of gravity of national security had already begun to shift to external defence. In 1963, Indonesia launched an armed Confrontation — *Konfrontasi* — against the "neo-colonialist" creation of Malaysia, including Singapore. Following the Gulf of Tonkin Incident, the Vietnam War started to escalate. Even after separation, Malaysian Armed Forces still maintained a presence in Singapore. Its commander, BG Alsagoff, insisted on providing a military escort for Prime Minister Lee Kuan Yew when he went to the opening of the first parliament in

December 1965. This was a less than subtle message to Mr Lee and his cabinet that the defence of Singapore was not in the hands of Singaporeans.

In these circumstances, it was natural that external defence should exercise the minds of the Singapore leadership. Furthermore, although the British maintained a large military presence in Singapore and Malaysia, political pressure was growing back in London to cut its military presence East of the Suez.

The Early Phase — The Ministry of Interior and Defence

Given the strength of our national security system today, most Singaporeans will not remember that our beginnings were very modest. At independence, Singapore had only two understrength infantry battalions, an ageing wooden gunboat and not a single aircraft. Dr Goh Keng Swee hastily assembled a small team to form a new Ministry of Interior and Defence (MID). MID would be responsible for both internal security as well as external defence, combining the functions of internal security and external defence into a single ministry. The license plates of military vehicles prefaced with the letters "MID" remind us of this legacy.

The British Military Withdrawal

Reflecting the priority of the day, one of Dr Goh's first acts was to move a Bill in parliament to establish the Singapore Armed Forces — the SAF. Then, in February 1967, Prime Minister Lee Kuan Yew announced the government's intention to introduce National Service (NS).

When NS was introduced, it looked as if the British would maintain their military presence in the region until at least 1975. This would buy Singapore a bit of time. But then in January 1968, the new British Labour government under Harold Wilson dropped a bombshell. It announced the complete pull out of British forces East of the Suez by the end of 1971. Singapore would lose its security umbrella much earlier than expected. So the build-up of the SAF had to shift into high gear.

MID No Longer Fit for Purpose

In these new circumstances, MID was clearly no longer fit for purpose. It would not have the bandwidth to deal with the competing needs of internal security, and law and order, on the one hand, and the pressing needs of building up the SAF and implementing NS, on the other.

As a result, in 1973, the government split MID into two ministries — the Ministry of Defence (MINDEF) and the Ministry of Home Affairs (MHA). This reorganisation has remained in place to the present. It has enabled the systematic development of each of the two main complementary components of national security — internal security and external defence — in a way that arguably could not have been achieved if both had remained under the responsibility of a single ministry.

Beyond Military Defence — Total Defence

But as Singapore steadily built up its external defence capability, planners and policy-makers in MINDEF began to realise that in the event of conflict or war, it was not enough to depend on the SAF alone to defend Singapore. Instead, the mobilisation of the entire nation, its people and its resources, would be as vital to the defence of the country, as much as a strong SAF.

Inspired by the experience of Sweden and Switzerland, both small countries that also operate a national service system, under the leadership of its then-Permanent Secretary of Defence, Lim Siong Guan, MINDEF developed the concept of Total Defence.

The premise of Total Defence, launched in 1984, is that the defence of Singapore stands not just on the military pillar of the SAF, but also on four other pillars, namely, civil defence, economic defence, social defence and psychological defence. It could be argued that Total Defence is a modern expression of the Clausewitzian view that war is only part of a broader spectrum of political and national activity, and therefore a more holistic approach is necessary to manage it.

Total Defence had to be backed up by an organisation to ensure its implementation, in order to translate concepts into real plans and policies. For example, the Ministry of Trade and Industry would be responsible for building a national stockpile of food and fuel. The Ministry of National Development had to oversee a shelter programme under legislation that mandated not only the construction of bomb shelters in MRT stations, but also in public housing and other residential buildings. The then-Ministry of Communications had to incorporate emergency runways into Singapore's road network. The government enacted the powerful Requisition of Resources Act to enable the mobilisation of civilian resources (including property, ships, aircraft, vehicles, cranes, low-loaders and so on) in times of emergency, to meet the needs not just of the SAF, but also of the other Total Defence organisations. The mobilisation of civilian resources had to be exercised in order to familiarise their owners with the procedures.

The Whole-of-Government Approach in National Security

The implementation of Total Defence was centred on MINDEF because of its orientation to external defence. But given its massive scale and scope, it required a lot of coordination at the policy and planning level, as well as at the operational level. As a result, many coordinating committees had to be set up, driven from the top by one overall Total Defence Steering Committee chaired by the Head of the Civil Service. The centralised-decentralised approach would not only ensure speedy and effective execution of plans, but also provide top-level oversight of the sprawl of government agencies involved in Total Defence.

Total Defence is an early example of a "whole-of-government" approach to national security. Indeed, because it tapped into the resources of the entire nation, and because it depended on the support of the whole citizenry, it could be argued that it is even a "whole-of-nation" approach.

Beyond Total Defence — Total Security

Some years later, I recall tinkering with the concept of Total Security, in an attempt to conceptualise national security as a larger idea within Total Defence. The following equation encapsulated the concept of Total Security:

Total Security = Total Defence + Internal Security + Diplomacy

This never left the drawing board, but it acknowledges that even Total Defence might not be sufficient a concept to cover the needs of national security when the operating environment is inherently complex, changeable and uncertain. Effective diplomacy plays a complementary role by helping to create a stable and peaceful external environment. Internal security ensures that there are no weak links in the chain domestically.

In my mind, Total Security as a concept reminded policy-makers never to see defence in isolation but as part of a larger strategic effort to ensure that Singapore would be strong on all fronts. Instead of looking at national security as zero-sum, in which resources allocated for diplomacy or domestic security would be at the expense of military defence, taken together, the whole would be more than the some of its parts. Carrying this argument to its logical conclusion, perhaps the government should allocate a single budget to national security, instead of separate budgets to defence, home affairs and foreign affairs. But maybe this is a bridge too far.

Challenges of the Whole-of-Government Approach

The whole-of-government approach is about getting people from different agencies — from *within* (and even from *outside*) government — to come together, to pool their knowledge, in order to discover solutions to wicked problems, and then to coordinate the implementation of these solutions. This approach harnesses the capabilities of the many to overcome the limitations of the few.

But while the whole-of-government approach may be an imperative, it is not easily achieved. Governments, like any large hierarchical organisation, tend to optimise at the departmental level rather than at the whole-of-government level. Vertical silos need to be broken down and cooperative mechanisms need to be set up, to enable the sharing of information and to strengthen collective and coordinated action. This is the approach taken in Total Defence. Breaking down these silos is a *Sisyphean* effort, requiring strong leadership and constant attention.

The Rise of Transnational Terrorism

I was in Washington, DC, when the 9/11 Al-Qaeda attacks in the United States (US) took place. I saw the American Airlines jet moments before it crashed into the Pentagon. It is hard to describe the shock of being a witness to that event.

Then, a couple of months after the 9/11 Al-Qaeda terrorist attacks in the US, on 7 December 2001, the security authorities in Singapore announced that they had uncovered the Jemaah Islamiyah (JI) terrorist network that aimed to build a pan-Southeast Asian Islamic Caliphate. The JI's methods were extremely violent and its ambitions huge. Its plans to attack targets in Singapore involved the construction of seven truck bombs, each packed with three tonnes of ammonium nitrate. If the JI had succeeded, many would have been killed.

The uncovering of JI was a *black swan* event for Singapore, as the 9/11 attacks were for the US. I was then Permanent Secretary of Defence, and I concluded that Al-Qaeda and JI presented a new type of threat. While the dangers they posed were not existential, neither were they episodic. We would have to spend years, if not decades, confronting the threat of transnational terrorism based on religious extremism. A lot of resources would have to be expended in the process, and in a way, life as we knew it was going to change.

Organising to Confront Transnational Terrorism

For me, this threw into sharp focus two important questions about national security. *First*, if it was a threat that required a sustained response over many years, was Singapore appropriately organised to deal with it? But if the threat was not about external defence, was it just a problem of internal security?

This was clearly an asymmetric threat, demanding the deployment of an inordinately large deployment of resources against it. It reminded me of the Irish Republican Army (IRA) taunt to the British government after the infamous 1984 bombing of the Brighton hotel where Prime Minister Margaret Thatcher was staying during the Conservative Party Conference — "We (the IRA) only have to be lucky once. You have to be lucky always."

No single agency within government has the wherewithal to deal with all aspects of this threat, which includes the protection of critical infrastructure and key installations, and the guarding of borders. Public areas need to be secured and security beefed up all around. The local community, including its religious and community leaders, have to be engaged to deal with the many-faceted societal issues arising from religious extremism.

It clearly could not be just an internal security response. The early experience of Total Defence suggested the way forward. It clearly had to be a whole-of-government — and even a whole-of-nation — response, because the resources and expertise needed to confront the threat of transnational terrorism resided in many agencies, and even in the broader community.

But the organisation would have to differ from Total Defence in one significant respect. Unlike Total Defence, countering transnational terrorism was not just about making plans in anticipation of a future and perhaps unknown threat. It was about dealing with a clear and present danger that needed a sustained operational organisational capability.

Organisation for National Security with the Rise of Transnational Terrorism

I knew Ashton Carter, then a Professor in the Kennedy School of Government, and respected his views. I came across a paper that he had written after the 9/11 attacks. It shaped our thinking in Singapore.

In "The Architecture of Government in the Face of Terrorism", Carter argued that to respond to the complex and multifaceted threat of terrorism, it was not enough to depend on a single agency to deal with it.[1] Instead, a matrix organisation with coordination from the centre was needed, drawing on the resources, experience and expertise of many agencies, without diluting their primary functions. Singapore took this approach, in contrast to the US which formed the Department of Homeland Security by extracting a couple of dozen departments from a host of government agencies to form the Department of Homeland Security.

Organising for Black Swans

The reason for adopting Carter's approach is not just that it demands far less resources, but also that it indirectly addresses the *second* question on national security raised by the emergence of the JI threat. The JI threat was clearly a black swan for Singapore. But the growing complexity of our operating environment caused in part by globalisation on the one hand, and the impact of technology on the other, means that it would not be the last. We can expect to be surprised in future by more black swans or Donald Rumsfeld's unknown unknowns. Just in the last decade or so, we encountered a couple of black swans after JI: the SARS crisis in 2003, and the global economic and financial crisis of 2008–2009.

So the *second* question is: can we afford a major reorganisation each time a new black swan event occurs? The practical response to this question is that it is not possible to create a new agency each time we are surprised by a black swan or unknown unknown. A small country like Singapore cannot afford the resources to take this route.

Instead, the real question is how to develop a resilient organisation that can absorb strategic surprises without causing undue turbulence in the organisation, or imposing huge and unsustainable demands on resources of money and people. The approach of a matrix organisation is a large part of the answer, because it draws mostly on existing resources, overlaid by a small coordinating centre.

Establishing the National Security Coordination Secretariat

So in reponse to the threat of transnational terrorism, the government established the National Security Coordination Secretariat (NSCS) under the Prime

Minister's Office, charged with coordinating the whole-of-government — and indeed the whole-of-nation — efforts in counter-terrorism. The role of NSCS is not operations. It is coordination of policy at the strategic level. Each government agency remains responsible at the operational level for its duties in counter-terrorism.

But the reality is that a whole-of-government approach does not come naturally. Agencies will resist it because they are most comfortable operating within their respective silos. Because I was appointed the first Permanent Secretary of National Security and Intelligence Coordination, I recall that the establishment of NSCS and gaining acceptance for its role as a coordinator was hardly a walk in the park. Some agencies felt that national security was none of their business. Instead it was best left to MINDEF and MHA, to the SAF and the police, and to the Security and Intelligence Division (SID) and the Internal Security Department (ISD) that, they felt, were set up to deal with such issues. Turf issues also frequently arose among the security agencies. Many agencies wanted additional government funding as they viewed national security as a function outside their scope of responsibility.

These observations are not meant as a criticism, because as a student of organisational behaviour, I have come to the conclusion that getting agencies to cooperate across vertical silos is in practice very difficult to achieve, even in high-performing organisations. It is human nature. Matrix organisations may make a lot of sense on paper, but to make them work in practice is a huge challenge. Strong leadership and constant oversight is required; otherwise the agencies will lapse into normal patterns. The *holy grail* of whole-of-government approach must be ministries and agencies, even individuals, working together in a strategic and coordinated way, spontaneously, without the need for compulsion or a crisis.

Resilience and Strategic Surprise

While black swans and unknown unknowns cannot be eliminated, steps can be taken to reduce the frequency of their occurrence, and when they happen, to mitigate their impact through anticipatory or contingency planning and policies.

Setting aside some resources in foresight, and thinking systematically about the future is an important part of building resilience in national security. Resilience is strengthened if the government is able to achieve the capacity to anticipate emergent threats, and then organise itself in a whole-of-government approach to develop and roll out policies and plans to minimise their impact, even if they cannot be altogether avoided.

In this regard, 20 years ago, the Singapore government set up a National Infocomm Security Committee (NISC) to develop the strategic policies and plans for cyber-security from a whole-of-government perspective, in anticipation of the challenges emerging from the rise of the Internet. I chaired the NISC for 15 years.

The NISC was organised to include all the major stakeholders. I soon discovered the wisdom of taking such a whole-of-government approach for wicked problems such as cyber-security. Otherwise, the debate on policy direction would either be dominated by security considerations, or distorted by economic priorities, without seeing the larger strategic picture. In my experience, in making policy in areas of national security such as cyber-security, firstly, try to make things as anticipatory as possible, and secondly, try to find a reasonable balance between security needs and other considerations.

Today, with at least two major Disturbed Denial of Service (DDoS) attacks against nations — Estonia in 2007 and Georgia in 2008 — the deployment of sophisticated digital weapons like the Stuxnet worm, and the recent hack of Sony Corporation, the NISC looks prescient. But it may not be enough in today's reality. The establishment of the Cyber Security Agency under the Prime Minister's Office reflects another principle of organising for national security. There is no end point, but constant adaptation to changing circumstances. But the principles of whole-of-government and anticipating future threats should drive any upgrade.

The Use of Technology to Enhance Organisation

Foresight and futures thinking is not about predicting the future. But some of the challenges (and opportunities) lurking just over the horizon can be anticipated. In 2004, aware that more tools would be needed to help security agencies look over the horizon, NSCS started work on what became the Risk Assessment and Horizon Scanning (RAHS) programme. Today, RAHS is a computer-based suite of big data tools designed to help analysts detect, investigate and better anticipate emerging strategic threats and opportunities. Designed as an open shared platform, the RAHS system also helps to break down silos and in so doing, encourages greater collaboration between agencies on perspective-sharing, horizon scanning and modelling. This reflects the ideal of whole-of-government approach.

Conclusion

In summary, the Singapore experience in national security is driven by optimising the use of limited resources through the whole-of-government approach, and by building resilience against strategic shock by anticipating future threats.

Note

[1] Ashton B. Carter, "The Architecture of Goverment in the Face of Terrorism," *International Security*, 26(3), 2002, pp. 5–23.

Chapter 17

Pragmatic Adaptation, Not Grand Strategy, Shaped Singapore Foreign Policy

Bilahari Kausikan

Seeking Security through Diplomacy

What is this protean thing we call "security"? The common meaning is freedom from fear or danger. Can one seek security in the abstract or in absolute terms? I doubt it. Unless contextualised by specific circumstances and given focus by reference to specific threats or challenges, such a quixotic quest is more likely to lead to perpetual insecurity. If one does not know what one fears then everything may seem fearful. But even when a specific threat can be identified, no two countries, even the closest of allies, will ever have exactly the same assessment of any particular situation or define their interests in exactly the same way.

Assessments and interests change over time as circumstances change or sometimes even when they do not. And since fear is a subjective psychological phenomenon, even within a single country, security will not mean exactly the same thing to a diplomat, to an intelligence officer, to a soldier or a policemen, let alone the trade official or the bean counter in the Finance Ministry. Or even the man in the street.

Reflecting back on my career in the Foreign Ministry — a career that spanned more than three decades — what strikes me most now is incoherence. Although we may fondly believe otherwise, every country's policy in every domain is always a series of messy improvisations in response to unpredictable events. Consistency is only possible at such a high level of generality as to be practically useless. A foolish consistency can in fact be harmful. I have never understood the obsession of some academics with the so-called "grand strat-egy"; a meaningless term. One must set goals. But having done so, all one can do is keep a distant star in sight even as one tacks hither and thither to avoid treacherous reefs and shoals or to scoop up opportunities that might drift within reach. Nor are the stars that we steer by necessarily constant. The first third or so of my career coincided with the last decade of the Cold War, not that anyone then knew that the Cold War was ending. The remaining two thirds were in the post-Cold War, an era that we are still experiencing and whose meaning is still subject to debate, so much so that we cannot even describe it except by reference to its past. Each era had its own complexities and contradictions.

Cold War Conflict and Diplomacy

Whatever its dangers, the Cold War had at least the virtue of clarity. There was never much doubt about where to position ourselves, although that still left a lot of room for argument about how to get there and what to do once we got there. The most immediate Cold War issue when I joined the Ministry of Foreign Affairs in the early 1980s was the 1979 Vietnamese invasion and occupation of Cambodia. Hanoi's ostensible reason for doing so was to save the country from the genocidal Khmer Rouge regime, an explanation that many in the West, tired and demoralised after defeat in the long Vietnam War, were inclined to take at face value. That the Khmer Rouge were murderous was beyond doubt. But Singapore, together with other ASEAN members, was concerned about the broader consequences for Southeast Asia should the Vietnamese get away with a blatant act of aggression.

Still flushed with victory over the United States (US), Hanoi supported by the Soviet Union was then boasting loudly about bringing "genuine independence" to all of Southeast Asia. So ASEAN set out to prevent a *fait accompli* and make the Vietnamese occupation as painful as possible by isolating Vietnam and the puppet regime it had installed in Phnom Penh. To this end, ASEAN waged a decade-long global diplomatic campaign to deny occupied Kampuchea, as it was then called, even the slightest hint of legitimacy or diplomatic recognition. There was no arena too minor to be ignored. We did not always succeed. But we did keep the issue in play until the constellation of great power politics shifted and compelled the Vietnamese to withdraw, enabling the Cambodians to determine their own future under United Nations (UN) supervision.

For my generation of Foreign Service Officers, this was the definitive experience of our careers. It taught us our trade and valuable real life lessons about diplomacy. I cannot deal with every twist and turn of this 10-year long struggle, but some episodes may serve to illustrate the general observations with which this essay began. In late September 1981, barely four months after I joined the Foreign Ministry, our then-Permanent Secretary, Mr S. R. Nathan, summoned a senior colleague, Ambassador Michael Cheok, who was then in charge of international organisations, and myself to his office. The Red Cross, he told us, was going to hold its 24th International Conference in Manila early in November. We had learnt that Cambodia was to be represented by someone from the Heng Samrin regime installed by Vietnam. This was against ASEAN's policy, so go stop it, Mr Nathan instructed, adding almost as an after-thought, that this was supported by Imelda Marcos, the First Lady of the Philippines. I was a green Foreign Service Officer still wet behind the ears. To say I was flabbergasted and flummoxed would be an understatement! How? That my senior colleague was equally at a loss, was scant consolation. But refusal was not an option. So we hastily joined the Red Cross and off to Manila we flew. It was my first overseas diplomatic assignment. I cannot speak for Michael, but my mood was elegiac. I thought my career was over before it really began.

We arrived in Manila to find that the situation was even worse than we thought. The Red Cross is a complicated organisation and its decision-making process was unclear, at least to us. The Filipino Foreign Service was hamstrung because the decision to invite the Heng Samrin regime was at least tacitly endorsed by their President's wife. For much the same reason we could not involve our embassy too directly; they had to preserve relations with the host government. No other ASEAN member had sent diplomats. Apart from us, the conference was populated only by *real* Red Cross members, intent on good works, shunning any hint of politics lest it defile their purity. We were lepers. Even the Singapore Red Cross delegation wanted nothing to do with us.

Desperate situations called for desperate measures. We decided to split up. Michael went to see the President of the ICRC while I went to see the President of the Assembly of Red Cross and Red Crescent Societies. He was a venerable and very distinguished gentleman; I was a somewhat disreputable looking very junior diplomat. To this day I do not know why he agreed to receive me. I repaid his kindness by threatening him. Brushing aside his explanation that the Red Cross was apolitical and purely humanitarian, if the Heng Samrin representative was allowed to attend, we would have to wreck the conference, I said as menacingly as I could. I later learnt that Michael had told the ICRC much the same thing, albeit infinitely more elegantly. It worked. The Heng Samrin representative never turned up. In retrospect, it was probably our very incongruity among the great and the good that lent credibility to threats that we had no idea how to carry out, isolated as we were. It sometimes pays to be a thug in a seminary.

There was undoubtedly some damage to our relations with the International Red Cross. But it passed and today Singapore enjoys a good reputation in the International Red Cross movement. The lesson I took away is that diplomacy is not just about making oneself agreeable; one does what one must, someone else will if necessary clean up the damage. It is all very well to talk abstractly about the long term, but one has to survive the short term in order to get to the long term. At any rate it was a lesson that stood us in good stead at a time when the Soviet Union and its bloc of satellites and fellow travellers seemed permanent features of the international system with some even arguing that they were the "natural allies" of the Non-Aligned Movement (NAM). Diplomacy under such circumstances cannot be a reasoned and civilised discourse, if it ever is. One incident stands out in my memory. In 1983 the NAM held its Seventh Summit in New Delhi. Cambodia was naturally a hot topic. It could not be ignored. But how was the situation to be reflected in the communiqué?

A preliminary meeting of the Coordinating Committee was scheduled to discuss the text. But the Chair, India, then closely aligned with the Soviet bloc, had conveniently neglected to mention the time and venue to anyone except Vietnam and its allies. ASEAN delegations fanned out throughout the cavernous conference centre. I stumbled upon the meeting room. The only ones there were Vietnam, Laos, Cuba and others of that ilk. I barged in and sat down only to be told it was a closed meeting. All non-aligned meetings are open-ended, I replied. Whereupon two heavily muscled goondas appeared and bodily put me out of the room. Nothing deterred, I went in again. The goondas put me out again, this time somewhat less gently. I took the hint and decided that honour being satisfied, discretion was the better part of valour and retired with *amour-propre* more or less intact and my skin wholly so.

The end of this story holds another lesson. Later that same evening, the Political Committee convened to formally consider the Cambodia text. It was customary in the NAM for the Soviet bloc to schedule meetings on controversial issues as late as possible in the expectation — alas, not unwarranted — that their supporters being more disciplined would turn up in force whatever the hour, whereas the good guys — our side — being fonder of the good things in life like parties, alcohol and sleep, would be thin on the ground at night, at least in conference rooms, and so easily overwhelmed by what we then dubbed "the NAM steam-roller".

And that is what transpired. Speaker after speaker from ASEAN — there were then only five ASEAN members — and our friends argued our case only to be drowned out by wave upon wave upon wave from the pro-Vietnam side. Gradually out of exhaustion, our friends slowly disappeared and even ASEAN voices became muted. Kiasu Singapore persevered, determined to extract our pound of flesh even if we could not get our way. So the debate raged on, increasingly one-sided. At about four in the morning the Chair, an African, I forget from which country, called a halt and said he would present his own text. We protested but he gravelled it through. We morosely retired muttering maledictions against a biased Chair, thinking we had lost. It was only a year or two later that we realised that the Vietnamese were also upset with the Chairman's text and felt that he had been biased in our favour. Then of course we began to defend that same text with our lives.

Absurd Diplomacy

The point is not merely that diplomacy can be absurd; it often is, particularly multilateral diplomacy. The more important point is that it is not always obvious who your friends are or even what is in your own interests. This was brought starkly home to me a few years later when I was posted to Washington, DC. Among our tasks was to secure US$5 million in non-lethal American aid to the non-communist Cambodian resistance, a paltry sum compared to the huge amounts of arms and other kinds of assistance China was supplying to the Khmer Rouge but of great political significance as a supplement to the lethal aid that some ASEAN countries were supplying to the non-communist Cambodians. It would have demonstrated in a concrete way that the US was as committed to the non-communists as the Chinese were to the Khmer Rouge.

A no-brainer, you would have thought? Alas, no. The stiffest opposition came from the State Department, still traumatised by the defeat in Vietnam, who convinced themselves that a few ponchos, boots and radio sets would lead them down a slippery slope into another quagmire. The State Department cynically hid behind the slogan of "following ASEAN's lead", fully aware that some ASEAN members were ambivalent about supplying the resistance and harboured the illusion that the Vietnamese could be brought to the negotiating table without pressure on the ground. It was disappointing but not entirely surprising. At the 1981 International Conference on Kampuchea, the US had taken China's side against ASEAN and in effect supported a return to the *status quo ante*, that is to say the return of the Khmer Rouge, as the goal for Cambodia after a Vietnamese withdrawal. The then-Assistant Secretary of State for our region, John Holdridge, even threatened our Foreign Minister with "blood on the floor" if we did not relent in our opposition to what China wanted. We held firm and the floor remained clean. And by using Congress to force the State Department's hand, we eventually got the US$5 million in non-lethal assistance.

But the most complex and delicate negotiations during the 1980s were not between ASEAN and the major powers. It was not even between ASEAN and Vietnam and its Soviet bloc allies. We knew where they stood and countering them called for tactical ingenuity, nothing more. As the decade grew to a close, the Soviet Union under Gorbachev adjusted its policies and it became possible to envisage a solution to the Cambodian issue within a reasonable timeframe; what took up the most time and resources was diplomacy *within* ASEAN to keep a united position. After some initial hesitation, all ASEAN members had long agreed that the invasion and occupation of a sovereign state was unacceptable.

But what was an acceptable solution? How best to get there? This was not so obvious and there were important differences in the positions of ASEAN members. Indonesia, in particular, regarded itself as a privileged interlocutor with Vietnam and opened direct negotiations with Hanoi, while barely adhering to the common ASEAN position. The notion that Indonesia alone could negotiate an acceptable solution was an illusion. It was never within Indonesia's or even ASEAN's capacity to resolve what was essentially a Sino–Soviet proxy conflict. The crucial decisions were always going to be made by the major powers, especially the five permanent members of the UN Security Council. But it was an illusion that boosted Indonesia's perception of its role in the region and the world and Jakarta clung to it tenaciously. This is not the place to go into the details of intra-ASEAN diplomacy over Cambodia. That would take a book and not just a chapter. What is important is that underlying the differences over details were fundamentally opposed concepts of regional security.

Regional Security Approaches

As the largest Southeast Asian country, Indonesia's preferred approach was "regional solutions to regional problems" which should be understood as Indonesian solutions or Indonesian dominance. This was not surprisingly anathema to a small country like Singapore, whose preferred approach to regional security is to promote a balance of major powers in Southeast Asia that would keep our larger neighbours honest and give us room for manoeuvre. So crucial a point was this that Singapore's first Foreign Minister, S. Rajaratnam, almost walked out of the 1967 Bangkok meeting that established ASEAN until an eleventh hour compromise was found around the fiction that foreign bases in Southeast Asia were "temporary". As every other ASEAN member was smaller than Indonesia, one would have thought that a balance of major powers was in their interests too. Yet, since 1971, ASEAN has been formally committed to promoting a Zone of Peace, Freedom and Neutrality (ZOPFAN) in Southeast Asia. ZOPFAN was based on the superficially attractive but entirely delusionary notion that regional security could best be secured by excluding the major powers from the affairs of Southeast Asia. Inconvenient questions such as how the major powers could be persuaded to show such forbearance and what to do if they refused were ignored. Even more curiously, ZOPFAN enthusiasts apparently failed to notice that at least one major power, China, was geographically contiguous to Southeast Asia, could not therefore be excluded from the region, and in 1971 was still supporting communist insurgencies or subversive movements in several ASEAN member states. Self-delusion, if not irrationality, plays a larger role in security matters than commonly believed.

ZOPFAN was never a practical proposition and we went along with the ASEAN consensus without ever really believing in it. But it was nevertheless a political inconvenience to Singapore, which was and remains unequivocal in its support for the US presence in Southeast Asia. It was a handy stick for our neighbours to beat us with whenever the opportunity arose. The pressures were manageable but dealing with them was a distraction and an unnecessary irritant in already complicated bilateral relationships. When Singapore concluded an MOU in 1990 with the US for very limited use of our facilities by a small logistics unit of the Seventh Fleet, there was a storm of protests from Malaysia and Indonesia. That the outrage was hypocritical — both these countries have their own defence ties with the US — did not make it any less of a nuisance. So when the Cold War ended and the opportunity arose to change the ASEAN concept of regional security, we grabbed it.

Significance of ARF

This is the real significance of the ASEAN Regional Forum (ARF) established in 1994 in accordance with the decision of the Fourth ASEAN Summit held in Singapore two years earlier. The ARF has been derided, not unjustly, as a mere talk shop. But that is beside the point. The ARF is a forum devoted to discussions on regional security created by consensus of the sovereign decisions of ASEAN member states to which, again by consensus of their sovereign decisions, the ASEAN member states have invited all the major powers to participate. Who then can credibly argue that the major powers have no legitimate role in the security of Southeast Asia? ZOPFAN remains on the books, but in effect, ASEAN has now quietly adopted balance as the *de facto* organising concept for regional security; not necessarily "balance" in the Cold War sense of being directed against one power or another, but balance conceived of as an omnidirectional state of equilibrium that would enable ASEAN to benefit from close relationships with every major power without having to make invidious choices. At any rate, in 2005, the US and Singapore concluded a Strategic Framework Agreement that was far wider in scope than the 1990 MOU. There was nary a whimper from our neighbours.

I do not want to overstate the case. The ARF also illustrates a key point that is often overlooked by academics. Regional institutions can have an important role in ensuring regional security. But no international institution can play such a role without the support or at least tact acquiescence of the major powers, and no major power is ever going to allow any international institution to curb its freedom of decision, particularly in matters of security. The paradox of all international institutions, from the UN to the ARF, is that they work best when they do not work too well. The major powers then find them useful as tools to advance their interests, while being assured that they cannot frustrate their most vital designs. This is true too of the other concept around which ASEAN builds its notions of regional security: the notion of its "centrality". If ASEAN has had some success in establishing regional norms through the accession of all major powers to the Treaty of Amity and Cooperation, and if these powers have used ASEAN-led platforms like the East Asia Summit as a secondary means of ordering their relationships with each other and other countries in the region, it is not because of ASEAN's strategic weight but because ASEAN lacks strategic weight. ASEAN is "central" because it is occasionally useful without ever becoming harmful. And if ASEAN ever seems to threaten major power interests, they will not hesitate to divide and weaken ASEAN as China has already done over the South China Sea. These are realities that the *de facto* change of concept cata-lysed by the ARF cannot alter.

SEANWFZ and Right of Reservation

And I do not mean to imply that *de facto* acceptance of balance as a security concept has changed fundamental attitudes. In 1995, ASEAN signed a Treaty establishing a Southeast Asia Nuclear Weapon Free Zone (SEANWFZ) which was conceived of as a component of ZOPFAN. The SEANWFZ Treaty came into force in 1997. During the decade-long negotiations over SEANWFZ, Singapore fought hard, and on occasion alone, to ensure that nothing in the Treaty would compromise the right of the US to deploy its military assets to and through Southeast Asia. It was only when this right was enshrined in Article 7 of the SEANWFZ Treaty that negotiations were concluded. Whereupon began another round of negotiations with the Nuclear Weapon States (NWS) on a Protocol for their accession to the SEANWFZ Treaty. These were concluded in November 2011 with the signing intended to take place at the 45th ASEAN Ministerial Meeting in Phnom Penh the following July. It never occurred. At the eleventh hour, the UK, France and Russia submitted reservations to the SEANWFZ Treaty. All three sets of reservations were fundamental. But one Russian reservation in particular struck at the very heart of the SEANWFZ Treaty with Moscow asserting the right to retract from the Protocol if it should unilaterally determine that an ASEAN member had allowed foreign vessels or aircraft with nuclear weapons to enter or transit their waters and airspace. It thus effectively undercut Article 7 of the SEANWFZ Treaty.

It was not at all surprising that the NWS should have submitted reservations. It was always a pipe dream to think that they would accede to the Protocol without reservations. What provided food for thought was Indonesia insisting that ASEAN should accept the reservations. Singapore refused and other ASEAN members were happy to hide behind us. But why did Indonesia take such a position? Jakarta has always had a penchant for form over substance and their Ministry of Foreign Affairs in particular sometimes seems to regard diplomacy as a form of therapy to massage its own notions about its place in the world. But more importantly, if ASEAN had accepted the reservation, it would in effect abrogate what is to Singapore the most important part of the SEANWFZ Treaty and establish a precedent to unilaterally object to American naval vessels or aircraft deployed to or through our region. Indonesia has improved its own military ties with the US and it would still have to deal with China. But Indonesia has always overrated its strategic weight and importance to the major powers, an attitude that the US and China have for their own reasons encouraged, and Jakarta may well believe that such a situation would place it in a privileged position as the preferred partner for Washington and Beijing in Southeast Asia: "regional solutions to regional problems" redux. Am I thinking too tortuously? More prudent to assume the worst.

In any case, what was more shocking than Indonesia's position was that the Obama administration too was prepared to go along and encouraged ASEAN not to object to the reservations. The Obama administration stated that it had submitted the Russian reservation to its legal experts who concluded that it posed no legal impediment to America's ability to deploy its forces into or through Southeast Asia. This was completely beside the point. All nuclear weapon free zones are primarily political and the core issue is political and not legal. If another NWS, possibly China, should in future object to the US military presence citing the Russian precedent, it would have to be dealt with politically and not legally. At the very least, it could confuse public opinion in states hosting US military assets. Why did the Obama administration take such an irresponsible position? It was perhaps because officials were loath to contradict their President who had received the Nobel Peace Prize at least in part for his advocacy of a world free of nuclear weapons. They would not want to be seen to stand in the way of SEANWFZ as a step in that direction. It is notable that American officials of the previous administration did not hesitate to express concern that the 2006 Central Asian Nuclear Weapon Free Zone should not disrupt "existing security arrangements" in that region. Or perhaps American officials were merely eager to ingratiate themselves with the President and his staff? At any rate, the Obama administration's attitude towards the SEANWFZ Treaty seems to have been driven more by bureaucratic and careerist imperatives than strategic calculations.

Post-Cold War Security Challenge

I highlight ZOPFAN and SEANWFZ not merely to underscore the fecklessness of some officials in the US or within the ranks of our ASEAN brothers. The crucial point about these episodes is that the definition of security interests is never the result of a clinical application of reason but more often than not is the consequence of a political process whose outcome is not necessarily rational. This is a reality that could prove more than an inconvenience under conditions of post-Cold War ambiguity because it is precisely this ambiguity that poses the most complex post-Cold War security challenge. How do we understand China's re-emergence as a major East Asian power and in particular, how do we understand the search for a new *modus vivendi* between China and the US? Clearly, simplistic and deterministic dichotomies popularised by the media and some academic works on the dynamic between a "rising power" and "declining power" or a "revisionist power" and "status quo power" are misleading. Chinese leaders have made contradictory statements and Chinese practice has not been consistent. Nor have US statements and practice been consistent. Relationships between major powers now defy simple characterisation. The US, China and Japan are profoundly interdependent in a way that the US and the Soviet Union never were, but simultaneously profoundly mistrustful of each other. How we position ourselves vis-à-vis the US and China, and position ourselves across a variety of policy domains and not just foreign policy, is the central strategic issue not just for Singapore, but is a question that will preoccupy all of East Asia for many decades to come. Wrong assessments could have very serious consequences. The late Malcom

Fraser, former Prime Minister of Australia, has argued that Australia's alliance with the US has now become a liability. He has identified the problem in an exaggerated albeit not incorrect manner, but has completely misunderstood the policy issue that arises. It is true that all countries in East Asia, whether or not formal US allies, now face some degree of divergence between their economic calculations, where China will loom ever larger, and their security calculations, where for the foreseeable future the US will be an irreplaceable factor. But the point about such a situation is not that it forces choices but that it defines the entire purpose of diplomacy as avoiding choices. If we place ourselves in a position where we have to choose, we would have failed. So far the situation has been manageable. But this is not to be taken for granted, particularly in Southeast Asia.

A Symmetrical Naval Equation

Having carefully studied the mistakes of the Soviet Union, China is not going to bankrupt itself in a futile attempt to surpass America's military pre-eminence. But China does not need to match the US everywhere. China is steadily acquiring sufficient naval capability to give the US pause in waters along the continental periphery of East Asia and must eventually acquire the capability to project naval power to protect its energy supply routes to the Persian Gulf. These routes are currently secured by the Fifth and Seventh Fleets. It is unnatural for any major power to indefinitely rely on its principal rival to secure supplies of a vital commodity and the current situation cannot hold. These sea routes pass through Southeast Asia where burgeoning trade and infrastructure investments are blurring state boundaries and binding southwestern China and mainland Southeast Asia into one economic space.

This trend can be attenuated but not deflected. It creates mutually beneficial economic opportunities but will certainly also have political and strategic consequences. The US is not declining and will not disappear from our region. But a more symmetrical naval equation must eventually develop in the South China Sea which is already becoming something of a proxy for US–China and Sino–Japanese strategic competition. Will greater parity between Chinese and American naval capabilities promote greater convergence of interests and concepts between the US and China? There are some faint signs that this is not entirely a pipe dream: in 2014, China justified its deployment of a surveillance vessel to observe the RIMPAC Exercise in terms almost identical to those that the Seventh Fleet uses to justify similar activities in the South China Sea; activities to which China currently objects. Or will mainland and archipelagic

Southeast Asia be pulled in different directions, rendering ASEAN's aspiration of fostering a balanced and open regional architecture hollow? Too early to tell.

Singapore like all other members of ASEAN will certainly be affected one way or another. But unlike all other Southeast Asian states, Singapore has a majority ethnic Chinese origin population in a region where the Chinese have generally not been an entirely welcome minority. At the same time, Singapore defines itself as a multiracial meritocracy and this is what makes Singapore unique in this region. These two facts very largely drive the dynamics of Singapore's relations with countries near and far.

Impact of China's Re-Emergence

How will China's re-emergence as a major power affect these factors? I think in at least three ways. First, through its impact on the internal political dynamics of other members of ASEAN. Up to now, the primary influence on the position of the overseas Chinese of Southeast Asia has been the internal politics of the countries in which they live and of which they are citizens. This is true whether the space available to them has broadened as in post-Suharto Indonesia, or whether it has narrowed as it seems to have of late in Malaysia. Will this hold? How will China's rise, and the redefinition of Westphalian notions of state and boundary that the development of more intimate ties between Southeast Asia and China seems to have set in motion, affect the domestic politics of Southeast Asian states? It will not necessarily be positive for every overseas Chinese community. But whether positive or otherwise, it will certainly have an impact on how their governments view Singapore.

Secondly, through its impact on ASEAN–China relations. In 1998, in the final months before Suharto fell from power, anti-Chinese riots broke out in Jakarta. Beijing, breaking with its own practice of many decades towards overseas Chinese and its general aversion to commenting on the domestic politics of other countries, felt obliged to administer a mild admonition. Seventeen years ago social media was in its infancy. Today, China has some 600 million or more netizens whose opinions, as far as can be discerned, seem generally highly nationalistic if not chauvinistic. The days are long gone when even the most powerful Chinese leader can ignore a public opinion that the Chinese Communist Party today both uses and fears. If a major anti-Chinese event should again occur in Southeast Asia — which unfortunately cannot be entirely ruled out — we should not assume that Beijing will necessarily have the luxury of responding in a calm and calibrated manner as in 1998. How then will China respond? What will be the implications for ASEAN–China relations and consequently on the attitudes of other ASEAN members on Singapore?

Thirdly, China already seems to have great difficulty in accepting Singapore as a multiracial meritocracy; it seems that this is to the Chinese an alien mode of conceptualising an ethnic Chinese majority country. At any rate, Chinese officials, sometimes at very senior levels, constantly refer to Singapore as "a Chinese country" and ask for our "understanding" — by which there is reason to suspect they mean "agreement" — of their policies on that basis. Of course, we politely, but clearly and firmly, point out that we are not "a Chinese country" and that we have our own national interests that we cannot compromise without grievous and probably irreversible internal and international damage. But they persist. Can we change such attitudes? How will China respond if we continue to, as they probably think, "stubbornly" deny what they consider to be self-evident? The Chinese Communist Party still has a United Front Work Department under its Central Committee.

As Singapore's domestic political space becomes more complex, the opportunities for external influences multiplies. China is not the only possible actor. If other major powers believe that Chinese influence is being enhanced, they will not stand idly by. In the late 1980s, Singapore was compelled to expel a US diplomat who, with the support and encouragement of his State Department superiors, was promoting certain opposition figures in Singapore. Of course, all diplomats can legitimately meet all shades of political opinion in their country of posting. Indeed they must in order to understand the political dynamics of the country. But the line between understanding and promotion of one current or another of political opinion is fine and not always clear, particularly when the instinct to whip the heathen along the path of righteousness still infuses the DNA of Western diplomacy. Experienced observers will have no difficulty in identifying some Western diplomats in Singapore — not necessarily American — already treading perilously close to the line.

Chapter 18

Dr Goh Keng Swee and the Building of Singapore's Defence Industrial Capability:
A First-Person Account of the Early Challenges in Building the Republic's Defence Industry

Philip Yeo

I have largely been associated with the Economic Development Board (EDB). Few people, however, know that I actually began my career with the Ministry of Defence (MINDEF). In this, I am very fortunate to have worked with Dr Goh Keng Swee, the man who built the economy and the defence capability of Singapore. Indeed, it all started with Dr Goh. A tribute by the Defence Science Organisation (DSO) in 2002 describes him accurately as the architect, engineer and hand-craftsman of modern Singapore. He transformed Singapore of the 1960s into today's gleaming, ultra-modern capital of industry, finance, commerce and communications. But Dr Goh also felt that economic confidence and progress were built on a nation's ability to provide security and defence for its people. He projected that future outcomes would depend on the capability of a national service (NS) force, well-trained and equipped with the most advanced technology of the day. Starting from scratch, Dr Goh built an army, navy and air force capable of achieving national security and deterring a wide range of threats. This was the Singapore Armed Forces (SAF).

I joined MINDEF in 1970, as a young administrative service officer working on logistics systems. I was a fresh University of Toronto Industrial Engineer posted to MINDEF to set up the Systems and Research Branch of MINDEF's Logistics Division. By the time I left MINDEF on 31 December 1985 as Second Permanent Secretary I had served under three Defence Ministers — Dr Goh Keng Swee (who had left for the Ministry of Education in February 1979), Howe Yoon Chong (1979–1982) and Goh Chok Tong. I was on MINDEF's payroll on loan to EDB as Executive Chairman. I was not an EDB staff member until I left the administrative service and crossed over on 1 April 1999. I was a Board Member of EDB from January 1982 but in addition to my work in EDB, I was mainly in MINDEF handling logistics, technology and research, and founder Chairman of the National Computer Board (1981–1987).

MINDEF began as the Ministry of Interior and Defence (MID) under Dr Goh Keng Swee as first Minister, followed by Lim Kim San. This was later split to form the Ministry of Home Affairs (MHA) and MINDEF. Dr Goh returned to MINDEF in August 1970 from the Ministry of Finance (switching places with Lim Kim San). I joined MINDEF in July 1970 when it was still MID. The key MINDEF leader was Minister of Defence Dr Goh Keng Swee. Then there were Permanent Secretary Pang Tee Pow, Director of Security and Intelligence Division S. R. Nathan, Director of Manpower Division Chia Choong Fook and Director of General Staff Division Brigadier Kirpa Ram Vij.

The Logistics Division was headed by Director of Logistics Ong Kah Kok. When you have soldiers, you have to feed them, clothe them, house them, equip them with weapons, everything. Soldiers fight on their stomachs, their reliable weapons and ammunition. From 1971 to 1972, I was Head of the Organisation and Control Department in the Logistics Division. From 1972 to 1974, I was Director of the Finance Division and I built up the defence budgeting and programming system. In 1972, I was only 26 years old, the youngest of the five Directors under Dr Goh.

At that time, the British were pulling out from East of Suez. The SAF ramped up. We were building battalions almost every day. My job was to equip and build up the SAF. Under logistics, I was also responsible for all equipment, weapons and camps. The building of army camps was under my responsibility. After four hectic years in MINDEF, I needed a break. I applied for and won a two-year Fulbright Scholarship to Harvard Business School (HBS) in August 1974. In early 1975, South Vietnam fell. Dr Goh wanted to recall me from HBS. He wanted me to "drop out and come home". I asked him to let me finish my MBA. In January 1976, Permanent Secretary Pang Tee Pow wrote a letter telling me that Dr Goh had directed him to advise me not to take any vacation after my MBA but to return home immediately. My plan for a European 1976 summer vacation evaporated into thin air! When I returned in late May 1976 to be Director of Logistics, Dr Goh took out a bundle of files and handed them to me, saying: "Kept these files for you for the past two years!".

The fall of South Vietnam in early 1975 was scaring Singapore. We had to really build up the SAF!

Defence, Technology and Research: Building the Defence Industrial Complex

My responsibility was in three areas. I was in charge of logistics, which was a huge area. The army, air force and navy — I was responsible for equipping them. Dr Goh established the Chartered Industries of Singapore (CIS) in 1967. He was not just building the SAF; he was building the defence industrial base. Dr Goh created a slew of defence industrial companies. In early 1974, as Director of Finance, MINDEF, I co-registered an "umbrella" holding company with ex-Director of Logistics Ong Kah Kok for these nascent companies, with a range of activities from repairing military trucks and AMX tanks for the SAF to building missile gunboats for the Republic of Singapore Navy (RSN) and refurbishing second-hand US Navy Skyhawk aircraft for the Republic of Singapore Air Force (RSAF). Dr Goh personally chose the name for the umbrella company Sheng Li (Victory) Holdings Pte Ltd. Today it is called Singapore Technologies. In 1987, although I was no longer physically in MINDEF, I helped set up Singapore Technologies for the myriad family of 87 small and large defence industrial companies.

I was also in charge of defence research. Dr Goh had always believed that for a small country, the most important capability was advanced technology. Dr Tay Eng Soon was the founder Director of the DSO in 1972. When I returned to MINDEF in mid-1976, Dr Goh asked me to support and supervise DSO. I was Chairman of the DSO Executive Committee. In 1980 Dr Tay Eng Soon went into politics. Working together with me then were Tham Choon Tat, Su Guaning and Ho Ching. From 1976 until I left for EDB in 1986, DSO reported directly to me. I was Permanent Secretary for logistics, defence research and industry. No such appointment exists today. When I left in 1986, there was a vacuum in the defence industry portfolio. Although I was at EDB, I was still on MINDEF's payroll till 1999. I wore many hats, but had only one salary.

Our Key Challenges

When I joined MINDEF, the SAF had scarce equipment. That was our first big challenge. So I went around like a *karung-guni* man[1] amassing surplus equipment left behind by the British as they rapidly withdrew from Singapore from

1969/1970 — the British Army ordnance supply bases and repair workshops, Royal Navy workshops, and Changi, Seletar and Tengah Airbases. The SAF was being built up very fast — 100 battalions in a few years. But where were all the much needed military trucks and land rovers? What I did was I went to the British bases where they were pulling out from, took over all their equipment, brought the surplus military trucks and land rovers to different locations in Bedok and Jurong, got them repacked, and then issued them out to the army until we purchased new equipment.

Our second biggest challenge was the lack of experience. We had no experience! So what I did was to ask Dr Goh to allow me to recruit thousands of civilian storekeepers and mechanics retrenched by the British. I did a direct recruitment of all the retrenched Singaporeans. I took them all in and placed them in our supply, maintenance and repair bases. Thus, our defence logistics capability was built up from scratch.

The MINDEF unit I created in 1970 was called the Systems and Research (S&R) Branch, which later became the home of the "famous" Systems Engineers. All the graduate NSmen who were medically unfit, and all the returned Colombo Plan scholars and engineers, were recruited. In less than one year, I had 250 engineers working for me. All at S$90 a month! No need for a uniform, no guard duty. We solved the problem. So MINDEF logistics was built by young raw engineers.

Equipping the SAF was the biggest challenge. In those days, not only had I to equip them but I also had to build up the defence industry. Dr Goh asked us to build because we believed that we should be self-sufficient. We are the only young country in our region to this day that has a strong defence industry. All because of Dr Goh. One way we built up our own weapons systems to become self-sufficient was through *reverse-engineering*. When I came back from Harvard in June 1976, there was an urgent demand for 1,000 GPMGs (7.62 mm general purpose machine guns). The army wanted them urgently. I called up my engineers and told them, let us reverse-engineer it. My engineers said "we can do it". So we reverse-engineered — copied — and manufactured the GPMGs, saving the licence fee of 14 million Belgium Francs. Dr Goh gave us the go ahead.

Eventually the army bought more than 4,000 GPMGs. We are probably the only country to produce GPMGs without a licence. So how did we do this? All fresh graduate engineers from universities all over the world bonded. We just reverse-engineered. Even the mortar system and artillery guns. Sure we made many mistakes. But we learned and improved. From 1976 onwards, we saw the biggest defence industrial capability build-up. So we reproduced and reverse-engineered. Reverse-engineering means to copy — take everything apart — and reverse-produce. We did the same for our new 54 Super Skyhawks from 110 surplus Skyhawks A4C bought from a US Air Force base in Arizona.

The Challenge of Corruption in the SAF

Another reason why equipping and providing logistics to the army was most challenging was the problem of corruption. When the army camps were being built up, all the food contractors delivered directly to the camps. So what happened? Corruption! Every battalion had a quartermaster. It is a very tempting job. The ministry experienced rampant short-changes. Suppliers and contractors would bring the eggs, pork, etc., and then between the quartermaster and the contractor, they would *pakat* (strike a deal under the table). Egg delivery was short-changed. Food contractors would bribe the quartermasters with gifts sent to their homes with such things as new fridges and other things. It was a big problem! So every other day we had court martials of quartermasters. The Corrupt Practices Investigation Bureau (CPIB) was called in to help. I advised Permanent Secretary Pang Tee Pow that we create a company called Singapore Food Industries (SFI). All the food supply from the contractors would be delivered to one central place. CPIB officers were placed there and reported to me directly. No more corruption! SFI had its beginning in the battle to fight corruption!

Regional Instability and Singapore's Defence Industry

Another challenge was regional instability. When I came back from Harvard in 1976, Thailand was under threat following the fall of South Vietnam. In late 1976, Dr Goh directed me to go up to Bangkok, Thailand to meet General Kriangsak, the Supreme Commander of the Thai Armed Forces. In December, I flew to Thailand with a team of three other officers. I was only 29 years old then. We were given full permission to visit all their defence industries — their H&K rifle plant, ammunition and artillery plants. From there, we took 1,000 Thai technicians to be trained in our defence industry. We trained them to produce mortar bombs and 500-pound aerial bombs. We helped them to design the bombs and bought our RSAF to test-drop the bombs in air ranges in Thailand.

Why did Dr Goh want to help Thailand? The reason is very simple. During World War II, the invading Japanese passed through Thailand to Malaya and on to British Singapore. Dr Goh said in the event of an aggressive Vietnamese communist expansion, Thailand, Malaysia and Singapore would be threatened.

In 1976, the Vietnamese had 10 divisions bordering Thailand. Dr Goh was very worried. The common joke there was that we should not be too worried. They said if the 10 divisions from Vietnam entered Thailand, two-thirds would be wiped out by the traffic jam in Bangkok!

Dr Goh, Churchill and the Technological Edge

Singapore was built not only by young NS men, but also by engineers. The greatest support for engineers was from Dr Goh and Howe Yoon Chong. So the history of MINDEF is defence technology. Dr Goh was a great admirer of Churchill, the Prime Minister of Britain, for fighting the Germans during World War II. Churchill had a group based in an area called Bletchley Park. That was where all the brilliant scientists were helping Churchill to break the codes of the Germans; they also developed new weapons. So DSO was Dr Goh's Bletchley Park. It was classified. People worked in DSO but nobody knew where and who they were. The only way for Singapore to survive was not by numbers but by superior people and technology. I had to see Dr Goh regularly to report what was happening. Tay Eng Soon was recruited because he was a scientist from the National University of Singapore (NUS).

But we had no war experience. We were a bunch of fresh engineers who had the courage to reverse-engineer. But the Minister was important. When I told Dr Goh we would reverse-engineer, he asked how long it would take and at what price. If the international price was one dollar, he would give S$1.05 — a 5% advantage. As I had no funds to buy production equipment, I would ask him for down payment. He would ask how much. So MINDEF would pay down payment, which we used to buy the equipment. Our mission was to produce. So again the key person was the Minister. MINDEF was created by Dr Goh. By 1985, the economy was going down. Lee Hsien Loong, then-Minister of State, Tony Tan, then-Minister of Trade and Industry, and Lee Kuan Yew, then-Prime Minister, asked me to come over to help the EDB. I decided to go work full-time in EDB in January 1986.

The Rise of DSO

When we were trying to help the Thai military officers to prepare for the logistics of war, we were serious about producing for our own defence industry. Without equipment, food, boots, clothes and ammunition, you do not have a defence force. Singapore's strength lies in logistics and technology. A lot of things we bought we would customise for ourselves. All of this was done by defence engineers and DSO. People do not understand but this is the strongest group. How did we build this up?

When I was Permanent Secretary, I visited NUS and met the Dean of Engineering. His faculty's intake was 300 engineering students a year. I needed to recruit about 150–200 engineers a year. When I was in MINDEF, I had 2,500 engineers working for me and 1,000 people in DSO. When I came to EDB, I thought how could we build an industrial Singapore economy with 300 engineers a year? So when the Dean asked how many engineers we really needed, I said 3,000 per year.

When the Head of DSO Tay Eng Soon went into politics in 1980, I assumed the helm of DSO as Chairman Exco. As narrated in the DSO's tribute to Dr Goh, MINDEF embarked on a drive towards technical excellence in the SAF; thus DSO grew rapidly in capability and numbers. MINDEF formed the Defence Technology Group (DTG). This unified the technology and logistics groups in MINDEF and established DSO as the centre of R&D for the SAF. It was during this time that the SAF began to display an appreciation for technology to bring SAF into the technological age. DSO eventually turned to its next mission — to become "the best environment for applied R&D".

It has been some 40 years since Dr Goh embarked on this drive to acquire the technological edge for Singapore's defence and security. You look at Singapore today: We produce our own ammunition, our own tanks and our own naval ships. A nation with no military experience, a nation created out of people who were brought from everywhere, which Sir Stamford Raffles did as the first internationalist. My challenge was how to build up and equip as quickly as I could — with no experience. But I was lucky because I had a good minister who supported me. Yes, some call me a maverick. That is because Dr Goh was the key maverick. Today there is nobody doing things that we did in those early SAF days. If you have another Dr Goh, there might be another Philip Yeo, hopefully. When Dr Goh retired from politics in 1984, his monthly pension was S$4,000. When he passed away in May 2010, his pension then was S$8,000 per month. Dr Goh had done more than anyone for the defence capability of Singapore. Had there not been Dr Goh I would not have stayed long in MINDEF. The key person was Dr Goh. MINDEF was my first job. I did not stay because I was bonded. I could have left to become personally wealthy. I stayed because of Dr Goh; to instead provide wealth and security for Singapore.[2]

Notes

[1] Refers colloquially to the "rags and bones" man who goes arround estates collecting mostly unwanted items to re-sell for a small profit.

[2] This article is based on an interview by Yang Razali Kassim, Senior Fellow, and assisted by Christabelle He Shimin, Research Analyst, of the S. Rajaratnam School of International Studies (RSIS), Nanyang Technological University (NTU).

Conclusion

Strategic Certainties Facing Singapore in 2065

Barry Desker

This article attempts to look at Singapore in 2065, after 100 years of independence.[1] Crystal ball gazing is a testing task. Our projections of trends even five or 10 years into the future involve weighing the influence of different alternative courses of action and an assessment of the most likely developments. The further down the road we go, the more we move away from describing the world as we know it today. What is striking is how much our imaginations are prisoners of the present. Even though we want to look beyond today and aim to conceive of a world which will unfold in the years ahead, we are shaped by our memories and experiences. Linear projections are common. We struggle to grapple with the possibility of discontinuities, of changes which break existing moulds. At the same time, our natural optimism leads us to plot a future which highlights Singapore's role at the forefront of nation-states, a beacon of economic growth, social development and political stability. When we discuss the possibility of changes, the tendency is to think in terms of incremental shifts. Few consider the possibility of paradigm shifts, which should not be ignored.

Geographical Location as the Key

It is essential that we look beyond a narrow view of security and recognise the importance of economic, social and political factors in shaping Singapore's evolution and the security challenges facing Singapore in the years ahead. This article argues that Singapore's future will be shaped by its geographical location. Even as we consider the possibility of incremental changes, discontinuities and paradigm shifts, there will be constants which will shape our responses to events as well as mould the perspectives taken by Singapore and Singaporeans. One key constant is geography, which influences the opportunities, risks and challenges facing Singapore. Singapore is not an island in the middle of the Pacific Ocean and this reality shapes the future security environment which policy-makers and citizens alike will have to grapple with.

While older Singaporeans recall the trauma of separation from Malaysia in 1965 and the difficult task of nation-building and economic development in an insecure environment, younger Singaporeans feel that today's Singapore faces different challenges. They feel secure in Singapore and conclude that the world and the region is safe and not threatening, especially as Singaporeans tend to visit countries where personal security is not an issue. A frequently heard view in Singapore, especially among younger Singaporeans, is that we are part of a globalising world and that our economy today depends on trade and invest-ment relationships with developed regions such as the United States (US) and Europe as well as rising powers such as China and India. Proponents of this view would argue that unlike 1965, our role as an entrepot has diminished and that Singapore has succeeded in overcoming the constraints of its regional environment. Such perceptions are reinforced by the ease of travel and com-munications, which leads Singaporeans to leapfrog the region. Singaporeans go abroad to study in the developed countries and now China, more learn French and German or even Spanish than Indonesian or Vietnamese, and many Singaporeans spend their vacations in distant lands, travelling to the region mainly on short visits for business or weekend breaks.

However, as then-Minister Mentor Lee Kuan Yew observed in the 2009 S. Rajaratnam Lecture, "we must never delude ourselves that we are a part of the First World in Southeast Asia, a second and third world group of countries. Our region has its own special features. Singapore's destiny would be very dif-ferent if we were sited in Europe or North America. We cannot transplant our island elsewhere. Therefore, a recurrent issue for Singapore is how to differenti-ate ourselves from our neighbours in order to compete and survive, and also get along with them. This is a perennial foreign policy challenge".[2]

Singapore is situated on a critical node of global trade at the strategic intersection of the Pacific and Indian Oceans. The narrowness of the Strait of Malacca and Strait of Singapore in the waters around Singapore created a choke point for international maritime navigation, a critical factor in Singapore's successful emergence during the colonial era as an entrepot and major British naval base. But location is not enough. Singapore's rapid growth after its founding in 1819 occurred because Singapore's status as a free port under British rule contrasted with the mercantilist protectionist policies of the Dutch who were the dominant colonial power in the archipelago. Singapore's success led to the emergence of an informal economic zone centred on Singapore. Proximity to Singapore facilitated Johor's development of an export economy centred on rubber, relying on imported Chinese labour and capital from Singapore, even though political control and administrative authority remained in ethnic Malay hands. A symbiotic relationship developed between Johor sultans and British colonial governors in Singapore, symbolised by the magnificent residence of the Sultan of Johor on Tyersall Road in Singapore before the Second World War.

Singapore's Informal Influence

Freedom of movement occurred not just between Singapore and Malaya, which were seen as one entity under British rule, but also between Singapore and Riau. Although the Johor–Riau Sultanate had been divided by the Anglo–Dutch Treaty of 1824, Singapore emerged as the economic heart of the Riau archipelago. The Straits dollar was the currency in Riau from its incorporation into the Dutch East Indies in 1913 until President Sukarno banned trade with Singapore in 1963. When I was on a visit to Riau with the Indonesian Coordinating Minister for the Economy Radius Prawiro in 1989, he recalled how as a young Indonesian finance ministry official in 1955, he was sent to audit the accounts of the local government in Riau and had to convert his subsistence allowance paid in Indonesian rupiah to the Straits (Malayan) dollar. This pattern continues today. In September 2014, the local regional administration reminded hotels in Bintan that they were not allowed to use the Singapore dollar for transactions. These linkages with Singapore go beyond the tourism sector. Singapore television and radio broadcasts, for example, have a significant following in Riau. Even in the late 1970s, when I visited outlying areas in Sumatra, I was surprised that the owners of rubber plantations listened to short wave broadcasts from Singapore which carried the daily price of rubber traded on the Singapore Rubber Exchange. The prevailing Singapore rubber price determined the price at which they sold their rubber to dealers. I was told that tin miners and rubber traders relied on these broadcasts even before World War II. Today, regular access to television and radio broadcasts, the use of Singapore as a business, educational, and medical hub, as well as the increase in business and tourist traffic between Riau and Singapore have resulted in Riau residents having an excellent idea of current developments in Singapore.

Singapore's informal influence goes beyond its immediate surroundings to the wider region. Because of its role as a regional hub, ideas flow from Singapore to the region. As East Asia rises in global importance, our links with the region will be a major asset for Singapore. Our location will have a critical impact on how Singapore is perceived globally as well. It will shape the diplomatic, political, and security opportunities and challenges faced by Singapore in the future, just as it has influenced the past and present. Our geographical location also has a continuing economic relevance, especially as the sub-regions around Singapore become increasingly integrated into the Singapore economy and Asia's economic development acts as a locomotive for Singapore's growth. This combination of opportunities as well as vulnerabilities and risks arising from our geographical location will remain a critical factor for Singapore over the next 50 years.

Managing Security Relationships with Malaysia and Indonesia and the Development of Global Linkages

Indonesia and Malaysia share maritime boundaries with Singapore. Historical memories of Singapore's relationship with these states influence its attitudes towards these states and mutual perceptions. The sharp exchanges between Malaysian and Singapore leaders in the aftermath of Singapore's departure from Malaysia in 1965 and the memories of Indonesian Confrontation in the early 1960s created an acute sense of vulnerability, which shaped independent Singapore's foreign and defence policies. Over the past 50 years, bilateral relations with both Malaysia and Indonesia have improved significantly. Nevertheless, during periods of stress in the domestic politics and economies of Singapore's neighbours, criticisms of Singapore come to the fore, including allegations of Singapore benefitting from the outward flow of funds from ethnic Chinese Indonesian conglomerates during the Asian Financial Crisis in 1997–1998, threats by Malaysian politicians to cut off Singapore's water supply, and attempts to undercut Singapore's role as an aviation, maritime, and logistics hub for the region. Despite the considerable improvement in bilateral relations with both Malaysia and Indonesia, Singapore's geographical proximity to both these neighbours and memories of threats posed in the past will ensure that Malaysia and Indonesia will remain as Singapore's principal security concerns. This consistent perspective was conveyed in Singapore's first Prime Minister Lee Kuan Yew's warning in 1966 that "your neighbours are never your best friends wherever you are".[3] Managing Singapore's bilateral relationships with Indonesia and Malaysia will therefore remain a critical priority of any leadership governing Singapore over the next 50 years.

Such concerns have led to Singapore's continuing interest in strong external linkages beyond the region. By developing global connections, promoting the use of its facilities by Singapore's partners and creating an environment which welcomed transnational corporations, Singapore used its strategic location to build an outward looking global city-state. In turn, Singapore's support for freedom of navigation through the Straits of Malacca and Singapore, which are used for international shipping, as well as freedom of overflight highlighted Singapore's role as a nexus of international trade, finance and communications. Singapore has welcomed the presence of major powers in the region as a reassurance that there will not be domination by a regional hegemon. This has reflected Singapore's consistent policy favouring the access of major powers to its naval facilities, willingness to participate in bilateral and multilateral military training exercises, support for the inclusion of major powers in Asia-Pacific institutions, and the promotion of bilateral and multilateral political and economic agreements which enmesh the major powers in the region.

Re-Imagining Singapore

While Singapore's location has facilitated its emergence as a global telecommunications network hub, major international airport and global seaport, alternatives and competitors will emerge over the next 50 years as our neighbours build up their capabilities and benefit from cheap, plentiful land. How Singapore responds to these challenges will provide a critical test for a new generation of Singaporeans. A visionary approach not rooted in the recent past would see such facilities as complementary to Singapore and would work towards integrating the use of these key transportation and communications infrastructures around Singapore.

Re-imagining Singapore in 2065 should lead us to think beyond the boundaries of present day Singapore. There is no reason why the region surrounding Singapore cannot be integrated into a larger economic space providing scope for work, play and travel for Singapore as well as our neighbours. Movement towards this freer two-way flow of people and ideas will require a mindset change in Singapore as well as Malaysia and Indonesia. Policy-makers will have to welcome the freedom of movement, not just of tourists but also of workers and professionals. The opening of borders will be a sharp discontinuity from the practices of the last 50 years. As Singaporeans become accustomed to commuting, we should not be surprised that more will live in Johor or in Bintan, Batam and Karimun, enjoying the space that will not be available in Singapore, just as skilled workers, managers and professionals may live in Singapore and commute to factories, shipyards and state-of-the-art offices in the surrounding region. The creation of an integrated economic zone around Singapore will be a reversion to a mode of relationships which resulted in

Singapore's emergence as the pre-eminent trading, financial and communications centre in Southeast Asia a century ago. Successful implementation of such an approach will require the development of a group of policy-makers familiar with the languages, culture and environment of our nearest neighbours — a significant challenge as trends in our educational system have resulted in greater awareness of developed countries rather than the region around us!

On the other hand, we should not presume that Singapore's future is foretold in the heavens. The focus of security challenges will continue to be the region around Singapore. Many were filled with foreboding when we became independent in 1965, as Southeast Asia was seen as a cockpit of conflict and the Balkans of Asia in the 1950s and 1960s. Some felt that the Malaysian leadership agreed to separation and independence for Singapore because the challenges facing a resource-poor, conflict-riven small state would overwhelm its political leadership, which would be forced to seek re-merger with Malaysia at a future date on terms much less favourable. Singapore would then be offered terms similar to other states in peninsular Malaysia. There was even a minority in Indonesia and Peninsula Malaya who felt that there should be one unified Indonesia Raya. Nationalists holding such views would not have countenanced the existence of an independent and sovereign Singapore. A larger group, especially in Indonesia, worried that an independent Singapore would be a third China and would act as a vanguard for China's interests in the region. This resulted in the Singapore government taking the position soon after diplomatic relations were established with Indonesia in September 1967 that it would be the last country in the Association of Southeast Asian Nations (ASEAN) to establish diplomatic relations with the People's Republic of China, so as to reassure the new Indonesian government under acting President Suharto (who took over as President in March 1968) that it wanted to build an independent Singapore acting in its own interests and not as a proxy for external parties.

Compared to the gloomy predictions of many when Singapore became independent in 1965, the contrast is telling. Today, Singapore is seen as a safe haven. Southeast Asia is regarded as a zone of opportunity and a rising region benefitting from the strong growth of China and an emerging India. Singapore has prospered from these developments, emerging as the largest foreign investor in China and India in 2014 and attracting interest from investors around the world as a springboard into these dynamic economies, even as we are increasingly integrated with the robust economies of the member states of ASEAN. A critical factor in the development of a more positive assessment of the geopolitical environment around Singapore was the establishment of a close, cooperative bilateral relationship with Indonesia during Suharto's tenure as President of Indonesia from 1968 to 1998. While Suharto did not throw his weight around within ASEAN, he was the most influential leader within ASEAN. He earned respect because he was consistent and provided space for each ASEAN state to develop in its own way. In this, he practised the Javanese dictum, *mikul dhuwur, mendhem jero* (to look for the best in others and to forgive the trespasses of those whom we respect). This has led some security analysts to argue that since the end of Confrontation, Singapore has not had a "predatory neighbour" and is located in "one of the most benign regional environments", resulting in the evolution of its foreign policy into a "post-survival" phase.[4] But a reversion to tension and conflict in the region should not be ruled out and should be considered in evaluating likely developments over the next 50 years.

Future Security Challenges

The possibility of domestic instability in neighbouring states spilling over into Singapore needs to be factored into assessments, just as external threats (including the view that Singapore poses a threat to them) could be highlighted by Singapore's neighbours to paper over domestic divisions. This occurred in the early 1960s when Sukarno's Indonesia embarked on the policy of Confrontation with the newly established Federation of Malaysia. As a constituent state of Malaysia, Singapore experienced more than 50 bomb attacks from 1963 to 1965. Another possibility is that great power conflict in the Asia-Pacific could extend into our region, as was seen during the American involvement in the Vietnam War from 1963 to 1973 and in the conflict in Cambodia, which resulted from Vietnam's invasion and occupation of Cambodia from 1978 to 1991. Nevertheless, such negative scenarios could have positive outcomes. Singapore benefitted from the Vietnam War as a source of supply for petroleum products, a major logistics hub and a tourist destination for American servicemen on "rest and recreation" leave spells. Similarly, Singapore played a major role in marshalling opposition to the Vietnamese invasion and occupation of Cambodia, leading to greater awareness of Singapore's capabilities, and recognition of its role as a diplomatic player to be consulted on important developments in regional and international affairs. Future security challenges facing Singapore include major power conflicts in the region, conflicts over maritime territorial claims in the South China Sea, the threat of irredentism affecting states in Southeast Asia and direct security threats to Singapore with the emergence of powers hostile to Singapore. In the next 50 years, a key test of a future leadership of Singapore will be its capacity to turn adversity into opportunity.

At the same time, a series of new domestic challenges will shape the future Singapore security environment. Managing these challenges will require a willingness to look beyond straight linear projections. The problem lies in deciding which weak signal to zoom in on and amplify as a possible major force for change. The difficulty is one of avoiding assessments being undermined by "black swans", to use Nassim Nicholas Taleb's term — rare, large impact, hard-to-predict and discontinuous events beyond the realm of normal expectations.[5] Similarly, the futurologist John Petersen has discussed the impact of "wild cards".[6] These are high impact events occurring out of the blue, creating major strategic surprises. Wild cards develop fast but governments and societies react slowly. Even as we are focusing on strategic certainties, we should be aware that the unexpected can occur and may have a dramatic impact on future outcomes.

Such unexpected challenges in anticipating future trends can be seen in the current debate in Singapore over the domestic population challenge. Singapore is an ageing society with a total fertility rate of 1.25 in 2014 and 1.19 in 2013, well below the replacement level of 2.1.[7] In retrospect, high levels of economic growth over the past two decades resulted from increases in capital and foreign labour deployed, not from significant productivity increases. However, the unsustainable sharp influx of foreigners granted permanent residence as well as employment permits in recent years have resulted in a backlash, which has made the issue of immigration politically toxic. Immigration suddenly appeared as a major domestic political issue. It is not just younger Singaporeans concerned about competition for university places or preferred jobs. Older Singaporeans worry about the changing environment around them as they have neighbours with alien languages and different lifestyles. There is a sense of insecurity in areas like Little India and Geylang as foreigners dominate these areas on public holidays and engage in anti-social behaviour. While some welcome the influx of new ideas, different cuisines, and fresh faces, others are concerned by the disappearance of comfort foods and familiar styles of behaviour. Even SAF commanders have had to adjust to the growing numbers of first generation Singaporeans born overseas in intakes of National Servicemen. Although ethnic ghettos in HDB estates have disappeared as legislation has ensured an ethnic balance, condominiums are beginning to see such ghettos as new immigrants and expatriates congregate in preferred locations.

The past two years have seen rising anti-immigration sentiment in Singapore. The strong domestic reactions were not anticipated. The views of the general public have been influenced by the pressure placed on Singapore's infrastructure because of the sharp increase in the number of people residing in Singapore. MRT trains are crowded, hospitals are always full, traffic jams occur frequently, and once quiet parks are filled with foreign workers on weekends. The rapid pace of the foreign influx resulted in growing criticism and an undercurrent of resentment reflected in postings on social media sites. Particularly unexpected was the sharp criticism of China-born Chinese by Singaporean Chinese. One area of resentment has been that new citizens have benefitted from Singapore's secure environment while adult male Singaporeans sacrificed two years in National Service (NS) to provide this benefit to them. The opposition to immigration has led to the tightening of government policy on foreign workers in recent months. Now that restaurants, offices and department stores, for example, cannot rely on cheap foreign labour, we see Singaporeans employed for such jobs. One wonders where these people were employed before the restrictions were imposed. The ease with which foreign labour was recruited has resulted in depressed wages for a segment of our population with minimal educational qualifications, unskilled and often in their 50s and 60s. This has led to calls for the introduction of a minimum wage, a move resisted by the government over the years.

The reality, however, is that immigration will continue and there will be more foreign labour employed, if low birth rates continue. This creates the risk of conflicts with migrant-sending states, which may be protective of the interests of their nationals. Issues such as the integration of new citizens, the expansion of NS obligations to cover new citizens and women, the desirability of adopting laws permitting dual citizenship, the rights of migrant workers and preferences for Singapore nationals will feature in the domestic political debate. Over the longer term, the question of the ethnic composition of Singapore's population and whether the classification of the population into CMIO (Chinese, Malays, Indians, Others) is still relevant will arise as interethnic marriages as well as Singapore–foreigner marriages become more common. The management of these issues will test governments in the years ahead. By 2065, the long-term viability of Singapore as a nation-state could be reflected in the percentage of Singaporeans who identify themselves as Singaporeans rather than as CMIO. Just as this debate over the population challenge has suddenly attracted public attention and has wider security implications, other issues will also arise. There is a need to think of the unexpected and to develop flexible mindsets capable of adjusting to changing environments.

Enduring Security Problems

But there are also enduring security problems, issues which will bedevil policy-making in Singapore a generation from now, just as such issues feature today and were a concern a hundred years ago. For example, the Special Branch of the Straits Settlements from its establishment in 1916 had the mandate to undertake "…security work against political movements and suspects…[It] concentrated on all racial, religious and social activities, and kept an eye on the trend in neighbouring countries".[8] The Special Branch was formed after the Indian Mutiny of February 1915 when Indian Muslim soldiers based in Singapore rebelled against the British authorities because they were unhappy at the prospect of fighting against their co-religionist Turkey. They were also influenced by anti-colonial Indian Muslim activists and by German efforts at subversion. The mutiny was the most serious challenge to colonial authority in Singapore which was faced in the early years of the 20th century and was only overcome through the deployment of police and military forces from neighbouring colonies and friendly navies.

Today, the Internal Security Department's (ISD) Mission Statement highlights that "Singapore, like every sovereign country in the world today, faces security threats from international terrorism, foreign subversion and espionage. In addition, however, Singapore being a multi-ethnic society, faces a major potential threat from communalism or racial and religious extremism. This reflects the sense of vulnerability inherent and fundamental in our makeup as a society".[9] In handling security issues, the ISD's focus is on the threats of terrorism or politically-motivated violence, foreign subversion, espionage and communal extremism. These constant factors in Singapore's domestic and regional environment render it likely that the agency responsible for internal security will have a similar mission in 2065.

The existence of enduring problems is exemplified by the threat of terrorism faced by Singapore since the exposure of the Jemaah Islamiyah (JI) network in Singapore and the region, in the wake of the 11 September 2001 terrorist attacks in the US and the Bali bombings on 12 October 2002. Effective ISD action in late 2001 prevented an Al-Qaeda plan to mount truck bomb attacks in Singapore with the assistance of the local JI network. The targets were the American, British, Australian and Israeli embassies, the Singapore Ministry of Defence, and Western multinational corporations operating in Singapore. They also surveyed potential targets in Singapore including ministry buildings, water pipelines, Changi Naval Base, Changi International Airport and several MRT train stations. The JI operatives were influenced and trained by Al-Qaeda. This highlights the increasing influence of developments in the Middle East on Muslim radicals in Southeast Asia. More recently, a rise in jihadi activity has been noticeable because of the rise of the Islamic State of Iraq and greater Syria (ISIS). The competition between an Al-Qaeda offshoot, the al-Nusra Front, and ISIS has been replicated in the region and there have been Singaporeans who have gone to Iraq and Syria to participate in the ongoing conflict there. The proclamation of a caliphate by ISIS with Abu Bakr al-Baghdadi as caliph and the establishment of the Islamic State on Ramadan (29 June 2014) is particularly significant. It marks a claim to oversight of Muslims around the world and will resonate with some members of Muslim communities even in Southeast Asia, just as the Ottoman Caliphate enjoyed the support of many Muslims in the region 100 years ago. While the number of Singapore Muslims supporting such groups is small, Singapore will be influenced by developments in the surrounding region. When JI built a network to establish an Islamic state (Darul Islamiyah Nusantara) linking Malaysia, Indonesia, southern Thailand and southern Philippines, Singapore was included as it is located in the heart of the archipelago, even though Muslims are a minority in Singapore.[10]

With the rise of ISIS and its claims to have established a caliphate, a more potent threat will exist in the decades ahead. The challenge to the Muslim religious leaders in the region arising from more radical interpretations of Islam has been a recurrent pattern in Southeast Asia since Salafi-inspired returned Minangkabau pilgrims from West Sumatra launched the Padri revolt against the traditional elite (*uleebalang*) and Sufi-influenced religious teachers in 1803. In the 19th and 20th centuries, modernist Muslim teachings were spread by books and periodicals published in Singapore by scholars who had returned from the Middle East, who questioned the more traditional Sufi religious practices of Muslims in the archipelago, and urged a purification of the religion and a return to the practices of Islam in the golden age of the seventh century. The issue in the years ahead will not be the extent of influence of Salafi doctrines but whether adherents accept the existence of the nation-states in the region. As turmoil and conflict rages in the Middle East and easy access facilitates contacts between Southeast Asia and the Middle East, this issue will be a source of continuing concern for Singapore.

Shaping Singapore's Destiny

These strategic certainties have defined the approach taken by successive generations of leaders and policy-makers in Singapore. While a present-centred view would emphasise the risks and opportunities arising from the rise of

Singapore's neighbours, the lessons of the past are that Singapore has also benefitted from the strength and prosperity of its neighbours. Recessions in Singapore have usually occurred because of sharp economic downturns among its neighbours. Political risks have also increased in periods of political instability, social conflict and economic stress in the region. By strengthening regional relationships and promoting greater regional integration, Singapore policy-makers believe that its security could be enhanced while creating economic and political space. An optimistic analysis would draw attention to the increasing integration of the region through ASEAN and the emergence of multiple forums in the East Asian region. Pessimists, however, would focus on the relatively shallow level of such integration as regionalism remains an elite exercise creating a diplomatic community while attracting minimal support at the level of the man in the street. Whether the current fashion for greater regional integration continues or not over the next 50 years, the fundamental continuities underpinning Singapore's security outlook remain. Singapore's security challenges will be shaped by its geographical location and the changing environment around it. Unexpected challenges will occur and the task of future governments and future generations of Singaporeans will be to anticipate and respond to these challenges.

Notes

[1] An earlier and shorter version of this article which focused on socio-economic aspects was published as "Singapore in 2065: Geo-Political Certainties in a Changing Global and Regional Environment," in Euston Quah (ed.), *Singapore 2065: Leading Insights on Economy and Environment by Singapore's 50 Icons and beyond* (Singapore: World Scientific, forthcoming, 2015).

[2] Lee Kuan Yew, *The Fundamentals of Singapore's Foreign Policy: Then & Now* (MFA Diplomatic Academy, Singapore, 2009), p. 7.

[3] Transcript of a speech by the Prime Minister, Mr Lee Kuan Yew, at a seminar on International Relations held at the University of Singapore on 9 October 1966.

[4] See Amitav Acharya, *Singapore's Foreign Policy: The Search for Regional Order* (Singapore: World Scientific, 2008).

[5] See Nassim Nicholas Taleb, *The Black Swan: The Impact of the Highly Improbable* (New York: Random House, 2007).

[6] See John Petersen, *Out of the Blue: How to Anticipate Wild Cards and Big Future Surprises* (Arlington, VA: Arlington Institute, 1997).

[7] Statement by the National Population and Talent Division (NPTD), Government of Singapore, 16 February 2015.

8 René Onraet, *Singapore — A Police Background* (London: Dorothy Crisp and Company, n.d.) cited in Ban Kah Choon, *Absent History: The Untold Story of Special Branch Operations in Singapore 1915–1942* (Singapore: SNP Media Asia, 2001), p. 75.

9 "About ISD," Ministry of Home Affairs. Retrieved 13 February 2014, from https://www.mha.gov.sg/isd/pages/about-isd.aspx.

10 Barry Desker "Islam and Society in South-East Asia after 11 September," *Australian Journal of International Affairs*, 56(3), 2002, pp. 383–394.

World Scientific Series on Singapore's 50 Years of Nation-Building

Forthcoming (continued from page ii)

50 Years of Eurasian Community
  edited by Timothy James De Souza (The Eurasian Association, Singapore)

50 Years of Indian Community
  edited by Gopinath Pillai (Ministry of Foreign Affairs, Singapore)

50 Years of Malay-Muslim Community
  edited by Zainul Abidin Rasheed (Former President, Singapore Islamic Religious Council, Singapore)

50 Years of Materials Science
  edited by Freddy Boey (Nanyang Technological University, Singapore), Subramanian Lakshmi Venkatraman (Nanyang Technological University, Singapore) and B.V.R. Chowdari (National University of Singapore, Singapore)

50 Years of Real Estate in Singapore
  edited by Deng Yongheng, Seek Ngee Huat, Sing Tien Foo and Yu Shi-Ming (National University of Singapore, Singapore)

The Singapore Research Story
  *edited by Hang Chang Chieh (National University of Singapore, Singapore), Low Teck Seng (National Research Foundation, Singapore) and Raj Thampuran (A*Star, Singapore)*

50 Years of Science
  edited by Lim Hock (National University of Singapore, Singapore), Bernard Tan (National University of Singapore, Singapore) and K.K. Phua (World Scientific Publishing Company, Singapore, and Imperial College Press, London)

Singapore–China Relations: 50 Years
  edited by Zheng Yongnian and Lye Liang Fook (East Asian Institute, National University of Singapore, Singapore)

Singapore's Economic Development: Retrospection and Reflections
  edited by Linda Y C Lim (University of Michigan, USA)

50 Years of Technical Education in Singapore: How to Build a World Class Education System from Scratch
  by N. Varaprasad (Partner and Principal Consultant, Singapore Education Consulting Group, and founding Principal and CEO, Temasek Polytechnic)

50 Years of Transportation in Singapore: Achievements and Challenges
  edited by Fwa Tien Fang (National University of Singapore, Singapore)

50 Years of Urban Planning in Singapore
  edited by Heng Chye Kiang (National University of Singapore, Singapore)

www.ingramcontent.com/pod-product-compliance
Lightning Source LLC
Chambersburg PA
CBHW080548270326
41929CB00019B/3237